W9-BCY-707

First Nights

First Nights

FIVE MUSICAL PREMIERES

Thomas Forrest Kelly

YALE UNIVERSITY PRESS   NEW HAVEN AND LONDON

Published with assistance from the Louis Stern Memorial Fund.

Designed by Sonia Scanlon.
Set in Bulmer type by Running Feet Books.
Printed in the United States of America by Sheridan Books, Chelsea, Michigan.

Library of Congress Cataloging-in-Publication Data
Kelly, Thomas Forrest.
First nights : five musical premieres / Thomas Forrest Kelly.
p. cm.
Includes bibliographical references and index.
ISBN 0–300–07774–2 (alk. paper)
1. Music—First performances.   I. Title.
ML63.K44 2000
780'.78'09—dc21   99–050265

A catalogue record for this book is available from
the British Library.

The paper in this book meets the guidelines for permanence
and durability of the Committee on Production Guidelines for
Book Longevity of the Council on Library Resources.

10   9   8   7   6   5   4   3   2

to Sarah Danforth French

Contents

1.

2.

3.

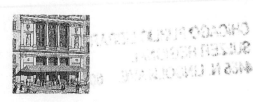

Preface

This book, which recounts the first performances of five famous pieces, is a mosaic in more than one sense. Each chapter focuses on one piece and presents a narrative about the preparation and execution of a single performance on a single day. To present the fullest account possible, I have also included a selection of illustrations that help situate the look of the times, the people, the place, and the performance; a variety of original texts that help set the scene by allowing us to hear words thought, written, or spoken at the time; and a section of original documents—reviews, letters, memoirs, newspaper articles—related to the performance. These substantial collections of texts, all translated into English and gathered in one place, will, I hope, be of interest to those who like to put together for themselves a picture of what was going on at the time and what it was like to be present at the performance.

For those wishing to know more, I have included a brief section of bibliographical references for each chapter. The discography, prepared by Jen-yen Chen, will guide readers to interesting recordings.

My friends advise me not to mention that the materials in this book come from years of teaching in a university setting. They fear that it will reveal a dry academic trying to make boring material interesting (or worse, that it will result in ruining interesting material).

So be it. I acknowledge with pride and pleasure that over several years many hundreds of people have thought with me about these five pieces of music, about their first performances, and about the societies that brought them into existence. What I present here, then, is more a mosaic than a painting, more a digest than a single work.

I am particularly grateful to many friends and colleagues who read portions of this book in its early stages, made suggestions, and provided advice that has made the result a much better book: Peggy Badenhausen, Renato Berzaghi, Peter Bloom, Carlo Caballero, Paolo Carpeggiani, Sarah French, Kern Holoman, Christina Huemer, Lowell Lindgren, Lewis Lockwood, Alexander Parker, William Prizer, Mark Risinger, Rodolfo Signorini, Roberto Soggia, Richard Taruskin, Christopher Thorpe, Dmitri Tymoczko, and Craig Wright. Thanks to Peter and Cynthia Rockwell for personal and technical support. I am particularly grateful to Harry Haskell, Karen Gangel, and the staff of Yale University Press for shepherding this complicated book into its very attractive fold.

Introduction

Making music is exciting for everyone involved. The visceral experience of participating in a performance—as composer, performer, or listener—gives music a freshness, a novelty, a sense of *now,* that we often lose in the world of recorded music.

This book is about the first performances of five famous pieces of music: Monteverdi's *Orfeo* (1607), Handel's *Messiah* (1742), Beethoven's Ninth Symphony (1824), Berlioz's *Symphonie fantastique* (1830), and Stravinsky's *Rite of Spring* (1913). Thousands of pages have been written about each of these, and each has been performed and recorded innumerable times. They are part of our musical heritage, and our taste is formed in part by our experience of them.

These five pieces, selected from an enormous smorgasbord of choices, have become part of a modern, hybrid musical culture. They are masterpieces that have stood the test of time and that come highly recommended and accompanied by a great deal of historical and critical baggage. If we experience these pieces in the concert hall, they are presented by an organization of high cultural standing, like a symphony orchestra, which has a regular roster of personnel, a fixed season, an ample rehearsal schedule, and a concert series of familiar, well-performed music.

None of the pieces discussed here, however, originated in such a context. Handel was a visitor to Dublin and had to recruit musicians he didn't know to perform his *Messiah* in a newly constructed and unfamiliar hall. Beethoven's Ninth Symphony was presented in an opera house by a mixture of professional and amateur musicians recruited for this one occasion—and after only two rehearsals. Hector Berlioz had to hire an orchestra for the *Symphonie fantastique,* and on the day of the concert he was still buying strings for the violas and mutes for the violins. Stravinsky's *Sacre du printemps* was conducted by a superb musician and played by a pickup orchestra of professional musicians. Although the Théâtre des Champs-Elysées was brand-new, there were serious problems fitting the enormous ballet orchestra in the pit, and the uproar in the hall at the premiere made it impossible to hear most of the music. Such situations are rare in modern musical life.

Sometimes we think of these pieces in relation to a family tree, with a lineage of stylistic predecessors and artistic descendants. Some of us listening to Berlioz may be aware of his position as the first of a long line of composers to use the orchestra as an instrument of color. Perhaps we are tempted to hear in Monteverdi's *Orfeo* a precursor of certain operatic marvels that we know followed. And we may know that Wagner greatly admired the Ninth Symphony. But in this book we want to imagine hearing a familiar piece as though it were contemporary, as though what came later had not yet happened. We want to see how others heard music we know. This approach gives any composition, any artifact, added luster, for it unites the rich cultural meaning of the piece in its time with the ageless value it may have acquired afterward. Furthermore, re-experiencing an original musical setting may give us new ideas about the perception of music and the meanings attached to it.

Why choose premieres? Why not examine, say, the last performance of a piece during the composer's lifetime or a performance of exceptional importance, either with the composer present or at some later time? After all, music is not painting; a first performance is not the "original," and the ones that follow mere copies. Later performances of a given piece, when audiences and performers have had time to reflect on its novelty and assimilate its difficulties, might in some ways be better.

Premieres are exciting: they are visceral and new. Our own experience of premieres (usually a new production of an old piece) is frequently full of anticipation and doubt. How will it go? Will the double basses manage the big solo? Will the sopranos sing flat? Will the audience like it? We now use the word *premiere* as a verb: premiering is the act of bringing something into existence by performing it. This is not an operation limited to musicians, however: it is society in action, bringing into being a new cultural object. The premieres in this book required the participation of a great many people beyond musicians and listeners: writers, censors, instrument makers, floor sweepers, police, chair bearers, prostitutes, milliners, and others who were part of the scene.

Composers—even great composers writing great works—create for people. Aware of a given society's values and behaviors, they calculate the place of their new composition in its world. How do those involved—the composers, performers, listeners—expect it to sound? *Does* it sound that way when it's played? And why or why not?

Each great work has its infancy, when it is new and fresh, when tradition, admiration, and history have not yet affected its shape, when its audience is unencumbered by previous expectations. Its birth is a moment of importance and excitement; its creation is in performance. This is not to belittle the work of the composer, who, well before the performance, "creates" the work, or the directions for it, on paper. But surely it becomes music only when it is heard.

There is no particular reason that we should privilege these premieres, except perhaps to indulge our own time-travel fantasies. After all, it is our own appreciation that we want to deepen, not that of some long-dead Mantuan. The modern revival of older music, with its attempt to re-create antique performing styles and techniques—a phenomenon often associated with the terms "Early Music," "authenticity," or "historical performance"—is unique to our century. Some would call it a reflection of our own fin-de-siècle nostalgia or restlessness. But even though our interest in a wide range of music makes a book like this a reflection of our culture, this volume is not meant as a rallying cry for historical purity.

It's unlikely, in fact, that we would get much musical enjoyment from one of these first performances—excitement, yes, because of our historical interest, but not deep musical pleasure. Some were probably dreadful: underrehearsed, poorly understood, and distracting because of an unruly audience; they may not have represented the composer's last, or best, versions of the piece; and the performance style may have been different enough from what we are used to, or what we prefer, to make them grotesque to modern ears. Our interest here is in how they were heard at the time.

I am not suggesting that *we* ought to reconstruct first performances. Even if we could recover enough information to feel confident about details, the idea itself is problematic. First of all, the performances would probably not be considered "good"—that is, mature, well digested, well rehearsed, precise, and fully expressive. But even if they were, the act of trying to reproduce them would instantly betray us: rather than performing, we would simply be going through somebody else's motions.

I do believe, however, that some of the best and most exciting musical performances being given today are by performers using old techniques and period instruments. Musicians must somehow make the music and the performance their own—they must add to, not subtract from, a musical text.

I offer some history of performance in this book—background on the performers' technical abilities, their behavior, their instruments, their training, their place in society, their attitude toward music. Is it possible that the amazing C-flat major scale played by the fourth horn near the end of the slow movement of the Ninth Symphony was actually intended to be played on a hand horn with no valves? The curious dark color of the many notes that must be stopped with the hand in the bell of the instrument would certainly increase the sense of tonal distance. Is it possible that in the double fugue of "Seid umschlungen, Millionen" Beethoven was not just bowing to necessity when he had the trumpets double the voice but skip certain notes—notes that the trumpet cannot play? Just possibly, the cross-rhythms this produced were helpful in the larger rhythmic profile of a complicated passage. After all, it would have been possible to leave the trumpets out entirely. These may be small details, but they just might make us think that performers and composers have often made beauty out of the materials and techniques at hand.

Although this is not a book about performance practice as such, I do reassess the ideas of unchanging performance standards. I treat every piece of music as an element of its culture, providing classic case studies. This, I hope, will help demonstrate how changing traditions of performance are important to the sound and the effect of music and possibly make an argument for the ultimate impossibility of "authentic performance."

As important as the study of historical performing techniques is the understanding of historical listening. Instrumental and vocal practices vary with time and place, but so do performance situations, the values placed on music and musicians, the relative importance of novelty and tradition, and the experience that a listener brings to a new piece of music. The listeners who experienced these five pieces did so with ears accustomed to music of their own time. A courtier in Mantua in 1607, familiar with madrigals, solo songs, and instrumental dances, might feel a special joy in seeing how a play cast in the well-known shape of a Greek theater piece uses familiar and unfamiliar musical styles to heighten and color the drama and bring the humanistic poetry to life in a spectacularly modern fashion. That listener would be struck by the novelty of melding classical mythology, modern poetry, and the sometimes daring music of Monteverdi. Those attributes, however, may not be what strikes the modern listener first.

Each place and time has its particular fashions and conventions, and a listener hearing a new piece fits it into a matrix of existing traditions, experiences, and repertories. Our own traditions, backlogs, and repertories are vastly different from those of the people who heard these pieces when they were new. An attempt to hear them as they were heard then provides each piece with a new and fresh look and sound.

Successive performances add to the history, the understanding, and the baggage of a piece. The later history of a piece, the *Rezeptionsgeschichte,* as some musicologists like to call it, is a study of its own: it involves a retrospective look at the reciprocal effect of a work of art on its surroundings and the progress (or lack of it) with which the work is received, understood, transmitted, described, admired, or ridiculed over time. This is essential to cultural history, to the understanding of works of art as essential and formative parts of the web of human achievement.

It becomes ever more clear, through the study of reception history, that the work changes: not only the perception of the work—what successive generations, or nations, think about it—but in a sense the work itself. This is especially evident, of course, for an artwork that requires performance in order to exist. In the case of an enduring musical work, like those in this book, the piece has had every opportunity to change as it travels, through modifications in instruments, patterns of rehearsal, orchestral seating, buildings and their arrangements, and ideas about how music ought to be performed to be beautiful. Only the modern recording media have frozen some of the dynamics of performance, though our varying perceptions of the same recording prove that not even the record has killed performance: perhaps it has only stunned it.

But here we are concerned not with the growth, only with the birth. When these pieces were new, there were no canonical standards for the pieces, no customary tempos, no famous conductor who took the slow movement a little too fast. This is the only performance the piece has ever had, and it is happening *now.*

The five pieces included here, which represent music making from the Renaissance to the twentieth century, are talismans, tokens, symbols. It's hard to imagine many other premieres that would evoke as much recognition and fondness in the minds and hearts of modern listeners. These are the benchmarks against which much other music is measured. They are all seen as breaking ground, as planting the seeds of musical ideas that have borne much fruit. That we already have some sense of where these pieces fit into a continuum makes the material presented here particularly vivid, because the music is about to come to life.

Each of the five pieces has words, either sung (*Orfeo, Messiah,* Ninth Symphony) or narrated (*Symphonie fantastique, Le sacre*). And each in its way tells a story. Is this why they rise to the top of our consciousness? We remember the words when we think of the music, and the music makes us think of the words. Who can say "Every valley shall be exalted" without thinking of Handel's rhythms? Who can hear the guillotine stroke in the *Symphonie fantastique* without knowing something of the story?

The premieres of these pieces were particularly interesting events, and they are relatively well documented. There is enough variety in their details to give us a panorama of performance conditions and to raise many questions about understanding and interpretation. The circumstances of their performance range from a privately commissioned aristocratic program (*Orfeo*) to a speculative commercial concert (the Ninth Symphony); and the personalities, from a young upstart composer (Berlioz) to the most famous composer in the world (Beethoven).

These are big pieces requiring a massive group effort. Each premiere is a combination of the usual and the new: usual in that all the performers were used to the problems of making new music, though in a familiar style, and new in that they faced the challenges of combining chorus with orchestra, conjoining music and dance, confronting taxing new musical techniques, or simply working together in such large numbers. Performances with orchestras, dance companies, and choruses offer us a wide perspective on musical culture and society in a way that the first performance of a piano sonata might not.

Admittedly, I chose these pieces because they are favorites of mine, but they are also excellent candidates for a study of this kind in that the information available about each of them has enabled me to reconstruct a picture of the premiere. There are many works of comparable interest for which this would simply be impossible. The materials are valuable and varied: Beethoven's conversation books, with priceless daily trivia; Berlioz's memoirs, literary and revised though they are, combined with the strength of the French press; the uniqueness of Monteverdi's score for *Orfeo* and the fortuitous survival of a few letters. Because it is impossible to see a picture in all its details, a certain amount of retouching and infilling of the image is needed. The habits and assumptions of particular times and places therefore provide the background against which the details of an individual piece can be seen.

Each piece presents problems and challenges and yields information in different ways. One would think that *Le sacre du printemps,* the most famous musical premiere of them all, would have so much information available as to make its reconstruction simply a matter of assembling the details in a coherent fashion; or that so much had been written about the Ninth Symphony that there could be nothing further to say. But in the first case, the loss of materials from the Théâtre des Champs-Elysées, the evanescence of Nijinsky's choreography, and the cacophony of conflicting memoirs make it difficult to sort out fact from fanciful recollection; and in the case of Beethoven, it is surprising how little interest there seems to have been in the details of performance.

In making the effort to understand what went on, who was there, how the music was rehearsed, who the musicians were, and how much like other performances of its time this particular one was, we are trying to clear our ears, to hear a piece we believe to be important from the perspective of contemporaries. We are visiting another place and time. We may not intend to stay there, but we want to make the journey.

First Nights

For this century, like the golden age, has restored to light the liberal arts, which were almost extinct: grammar, poetry, rhetoric, painting, sculpture, architecture, and music, the ancient singing of songs to the Orphic lyre.

—Marsilio Ficino, 1492

When Claudio Monteverdi was asked by the elder son of Duke Vincenzo Gonzaga to provide a "fable in music" for the local learned academy, he could hardly refuse. Collaborating with the young poet and court secretary Alessandro Striggio as librettist, Monteverdi created the fable of *Orfeo*. Its two performances were small local events, but the power of *Orfeo*'s drama and the charm of its music have turned it into a timeless classic whose success would have astounded the few dozen Mantuan aristocrats present at the first performance.

In 1607 the forty-year-old Monteverdi was living in the northern city of Mantua with his wife, Claudia, and his two surviving children (Francesco, five years old, and Massimiliano, three; an infant daughter had died). He had served the duke as chief musician for seventeen years, beginning as a string player and singer at court.

Monteverdi's duties weighed heavily on him at this time. He complained in 1608 that "the fortune I have known in Mantua for nineteen consecutive years has given me more occasion to call it misfortune, and inimical to me, and not friendly." He went on to lament the out-of-pocket expenses that made the duke's glorious service more burdensome than rewarding.

But although Monteverdi may have been a servant at home, his reputation as a producer of contemporary music extended beyond Mantua. He had published eight collections of vocal music; his recent books of madrigals had enjoyed five reprintings; and more reprints, and more music, were in the works. He was, as he called himself on the title page of his fourth book of madrigals, "Maestro della musica del Sereniss. Sig. Duca di Mantova" (Master of the music of the Most Serene Lord Duke of Mantua). He was in charge of music for the entire ducal establishment, and as such responsible not only for organizing the day-to-day concerts and musical recreations but also for providing music for important court events. He was enormously busy, reported his brother, Giulio Cesare Monteverdi, in the preface to Claudio's *Scherzi musicali* of 1607, "because of his responsibility for both church and chamber music, but also because of other extraordinary services, for, serving a great prince, he finds the greater part of his time taken up, now with tournaments, now with ballets, now with comedies and various concerts, and lastly with the playing of the two *viole bastarde*."

Orfeo, together with the opera *Arianna,* produced the following year, was a turning point for Monteverdi. As his fame grew, he spent much time away from Mantua and within a few years was appointed maestro di cappella of Saint Mark's Basilica in Venice, a job he was to hold from 1613 until his death, in 1643.

Claudio Monteverdi

This engraving of Monteverdi, showing him in his later years, appears on the title page of Giovanni Battista Marinoni, *Fiori poetici raccolti nel funerale del . . . signor Clavdio Monteverde* (Venice, 1644), printed after Monteverdi's death. It is apparently based on the only known painting of Monteverdi, now in Innsbruck.

Orpheus in Music

The myth of Orpheus tells universal human truths about duty and desire, passion and persuasion, life and death—natural and timeless subjects for meditation and representation. The story has various versions, but at the center are the singer Orpheus and the beautiful Euridice. When Euridice dies and is taken to the underworld, Orpheus follows where no mortal is allowed and through the power of his song convinces Pluto to allow Euridice to return to the upper world. There is only one condition: that as he leads Euridice upward, he must not look back to see whether she is following.

It is a story about the relationship of heart to mind, of emotion to reason: Orpheus leads Euridice out of the underworld, but his emotion gets the better of his reason, he does look back, and he loses Euridice forever. This moment speaks to us all and is retold in thousands of ways in song, story, fable, and theater. Children who shout at puppets to warn the downstage character about the upstage policeman with the club always know that the club will strike. We want to shout at Orpheus not to look back, yet we know he *will* look back. The story is always gripping, because we are Orpheus.

But this is also the tale of a singer and of the power of music, of the demigod Orpheus, whose music charms wild beasts and almost gets him into the realm of the dead. And, at least in this telling, it is a story of Orpheus's father, Apollo, god of the sun and of music (an art named for the muses who consort with Apollo on Mount Parnassus). Such a story, in which music is central to the plot, serves as a particularly suitable vehicle for sung drama, especially in the new recitative style of that time, which distinguished between speaking and singing.

It is often a problem in opera to get used to hearing people sing what we normally say ("Where is the soap?"), though once we get used to it, we understand the convention that someone singing on the stage is representing someone speaking in the nonoperatic world. But then it becomes difficult to represent singing onstage, for if

Andrea Mantegna, *Parnaso* (detail), 1497

Mantuans were familiar with the legend of Orpheus through this allegorical work by Mantegna, which shows the figure of Orpheus charming the beasts with his music and inspiring song and dance, as in act 1 of *Orfeo*.

singing represents speech in the world, what could represent a song in life? The recitative supports this distinction handsomely, for its declamatory style is really akin to speech in its speed, its rhythms, and its lack of the more unspeechlike traits of melody—exceptionally long notes, many notés per syllable, and so forth. And if this is used onstage for speech, as it is in *Orfeo* and other works of its kind, then *song* can be used for song, and the difference will be clear. Orfeo sings songs in the opera: in act 2; when he tries to cross the Styx; and when he rejoices at the prospect of seeing Euridice again. We immediately recognize these as songs from a great singer. So what better subject for an opera, particularly one in the new recitative style, than one about the most famous singer of legend?

Almost four centuries after its creation, *Orfeo* can still charm us, because it tells a universal story and does so with breathtakingly beautiful songs and speeches. Some will say that it stands at the threshold of the history of opera, that it foreshadows great things to come, that it is an early version of an art form that will later be more highly developed. But that is to look at a future that in 1607 did not yet exist. Nevertheless, we recognize today much of what the Mantuans heard. We hear individual performers delivering their lines in a rhythm not unlike that of speech and being accompanied by a changing combination of chord-playing instruments: harpsichords, lutes, harps, organs, and sometimes the snarling *regale* (a little organ with reed pipes). We also notice those parts oriented more toward musical form: beautiful songs, spirited dance rhythms, grand choruses, lively instrumental interludes. We hear a wide variety of instrumental colors: strings, recorders, trumpets, trombones, cornetti (a cornetto is a finger-hole wooden instrument with a trumpet mouthpiece that creates a clear and radiant sound). Our first impression, in short, is one of high drama combined with opulent variety. But it is not the opulence of nineteenth-century grand opera. *Orfeo* at its origin is intimate and exclusive, and it is extravagant only in the amount of care lavished on a small private entertainment.

Orfeo, unlike the other pieces in this book, was first performed not in public but in private, for a learned association, an academy of male nobles in the duke's palace in Mantua, at the end of the carnival season preceding Lent. *Orfeo* was a combination of learned experiment and courtly entertainment. The audience consisted of members of the academy, which held regular meetings in the palace, and some invited guests. Perhaps two hundred persons could have crowded in. After one further performance a few days later (to which women were invited), *Orfeo* was not heard again until the twentieth century.

      If *Orfeo* was an academic exercise designed to intrigue those few members of an elite who could be its critics, how did it come to occupy such an important position in our own time, as the first great opera, as a masterpiece of expression and drama, as a brilliant musical kaleidoscope of genres and forms? In short, because of Monteverdi's musical genius. Although the persons for whom the performance was intended were perhaps an academic and courtly elite, they were also like us, in that they were moved as much as we are and fully aware of the universality of the myth of Orpheus. But they were more attuned than most of us to many details in the performance. They knew the story and understood every nuance of the poetry. They knew something of the musical and dramatic experiments in Florence that had preceded this version. They would instantly have seen how closely *Orfeo* was linked with the traditions of classical drama as codified by Aristotle. They were at home with the conventions of the pastoral setting from the poetry and drama of their own time. Some of the music sounded to them like the music they were used to at court, and some of it was entirely new in style and concept. So their appreciation must have been different, and perhaps richer, than ours. When we consider the world in which these people lived, and the things they expected to see, we may come to a more varied view of *Orfeo* and a deeper appreciation of its originalities.

Mantua

      In the beginning of the seventeenth century the Italian peninsula, geographically so distinct, was divided into many small and not-so-small territories, each with different currencies and units of measure and their own capital cities, ambassadors, and governments. The lower peninsula, including Naples and Sicily, was governed by

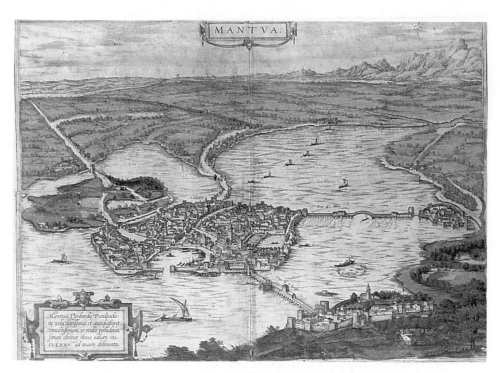

View of Mantua, 1575

This map of the city of Mantua was made thirty-two years before the performance of *Orfeo*. The Alps, in the background, are to the north, and the flat plain of the Po Valley stretches down to Mantua. The river Mincio has been dammed to turn the lakes that surround Mantua into a moat. The complex of the ducal palace stands between the two bridges.

viceroys appointed in Spain; the central portion, around Rome, was ruled by the pope; and the many smaller principalities to the north were ruled by princes and dukes. Piedmont, Savoy, Urbino, and Florence were all governed by hereditary rulers. Exceptional were the republics of Genoa and Venice, great seagoing powers whose dukes (or doges) were in principle elected and did not inherit their position. The balance of power among these dynasties—influenced by the pope's desire to possess Ferrara, the Spanish influence in Naples and Milan, the ambitions of the Austrian emperor, the duke of Savoy's long-standing desire to possess the principality of Monferrato (which belonged to the duke of Mantua)—led to wars, arranged marriages between princely families, and many spies and armies.

In Monteverdi's day the city of Mantua (Mantova in Italian) was the center of an important dukedom, the capital of a Renaissance city-state, and the residence of a great prince and his court. Situated in the flat land of the Po Valley, the city was, as it still is, surrounded by lakes formed from widenings of the Mincio River. Since the fourteenth century the city and its territory had been ruled by the Gonzaga family; their imposing ducal palace, a combination of residence and fortress that had achieved enormous dimensions, was in itself a history of a family's involvement with the arts.

The city was rich: the twenty thousand ducats from the mills are an indication of the strength of the woolen trade; commerce and trading—much of it undertaken by the large Jewish community—made Mantua a flourishing city.

Today the city center still retains its medieval and Renaissance layout and many of its old buildings. Grand palaces and private houses survive, along with piazzas suited for markets, public assembly, and evening strolls. The largest piazza fronts the largest building, the one that dominates the city in almost every way: the palace of the dukes. In the sixteenth century the palace was said to be the largest building in the world. It encloses many courtyards, hanging gardens, a large area for equestrian display

Domenico Morone, *The Expulsion of the Bonacolsi in 1328*, 1494

This painting of the Gonzaga family's seizure of power in 1328 seems to show
Mantua at the time Morone painted the picture. The Palazzo del Capitano,
part of the ducal palace, is to the right, and the cathedral, as Monteverdi knew
it, is in the center.

(the Gonzagas were famous for their love of horses), the large Palatine Basilica of Santa
Barbara, a miniature version of the shrine of the Scala Santa in Rome, a fortress surrounded by a moat, and innumerable apartments, salons, galleries, and other necessary
spaces, built and rebuilt from the fourteenth through the early seventeenth century.

A general economic decline around the turn of the seventeenth century
marked the beginning of a downturn in Mantuan fortunes; the Gonzaga line expired,
and the city, sacked by imperial troops in 1630, ultimately became a possession of Austria in 1708. But it is often on the protected farther slopes of the peaks that culture flowers most richly; and the early years of the seventeenth century were the culmination of
a long period of important artistic patronage.

Vincenzo Gongaza, the forty-four-year-old reigning duke of Mantua and Monferrato since 1587, had done much to cultivate the arts. He inherited great wealth and
power from his father, Guglielmo, and, like him, felt the desire, even the princely obli-
gation, to employ his wealth in splendor, in largesse, and in generosity.

Vincenzo's military enthusiasm had led to a number of expensive campaigns,
most recently against the Turks in 1601, though none brought much in the way of political gains. In recent years Vincenzo had retreated from active participation in government, relying for most decisions on his counselors and his duchess, Eleonora de'
Medici. In his youth Vincenzo had led a life of pleasure; hunting, gambling, travel,
amorous adventures, music, and theater had been his passions, and to these he re-

Piazza Sordello, Mantua, with Cathedral and Ducal Palace, 1990s

The ducal palace has not changed much since Domenico Morone painted it in
the fifteenth century. The Venetian-Gothic façade of the cathedral was altered
in the eighteenth century, and the piazza is now generally free of automobiles.

turned in his later years. He was a generous patron, an attentive listener, a compas-
sionate ruler, and his court was magnificent. He also succeeded in dissipating a substantial amount of the family wealth.

Mantua was in one sense a country, and in another a single household. The
operation of a great princely court was no small matter. An enormous number of func-
tionaries were needed to support the financial and administrative operations of the
duchy, and a great many servants to maintain the life of the ducal family, the supporting
nobles, and the court. Ducal accounts report the income from hundreds of properties,
rents, and taxes, and the array of officials needed to administer and keep track of them
all. No less important were the needs for a civil government to provide justice, peace-
keeping, and other social services and for a standing army to provide defense.

The ducal household—as distinguished from the public administration and
the management of private holdings elsewhere—was in itself an enormous operation.
Some eight hundred persons ("mouths," as they were called in court records) were on
the ducal payroll. Aristocratic courtiers furnished particular services to the duke, his
family, or his household; these included officers of the ducal chancery and secretariat,

The Venetian ambassador describes Duke Vincenzo:

I will only say that Vincenzo Gonzaga was the son of Duke Guglielmo, and he is the head of this family and is now duke of Mantua and Monferrato. Given that his exterior features are very well known to Your Most Excellent Lordships, I will speak only of his interior ones, among which shines forth principally his liberality and humanity, for which he has until now gained both the reputation of being the most splendid duke to have been in that city and the universal love as much of the nobles as of the people, having increased his bodyguard, made many gifts and eliminated many taxes, also behaving towards his subjects with much affability, but in a manner that he is honored, feared and revered by all. He listens with great patience to the requests and grievances of all, and to their supplications, which was not done by his father, and which therefore made him as disliked as the son is kind and pleasing. He delights greatly in hunting, in which he spends almost all his time, wishing to kill the wild animals with his own hands and not without personal danger, even though it is a matter of his own life. From this one can understand his own inclination towards the military, of which he is so enamored that he does not think or speak of anything else, and thus he seeks the occasion to fulfill this his keenest desire.

who had public functions but lived at the palace. Officials of the treasury included the *guardia camera* (chamber guards), five *camerieri* (stewards), two ushers, and an assistant, all overseen by a superintendent who in turn was assisted by a notary and a goldsmith. Various courtiers close to the duke were provided with income and housing; these might be friends, counselors, or they might be the artists, poets, musicians, philosophers, and scientists who add luster to the renown and the eminence of a great court. They might bear such titles as *gentiluomo* (gentleman), *scudiere* (squire), or *coppiere* (cupbearer). The duchess was surrounded by her ladies-in-waiting and any number of young pages. Alchemists were charged with producing poison gases for military strategy.

Other professional staff included *scalchi* (literally, carvers of meat) and *staffieri* (footmen), physicians, pharmacists, barbers, and medical assistants; tutors and *spendi-*

tori (stewards), who made all the court's purchases; clergy for the services in the ducal chapel; and waiters, chamberlains, assistants, cooks, drapers, wood gatherers, gardeners, guards, servants for the pages, farriers, blacksmiths, bell ringers, clock-winders, and falconers. Not to mention the horses. The Gonzagas were enormously proud of their thoroughbreds, which in 1581 numbered 520, requiring substantial stables, pasture, and personnel.

The Gonzagas were among the great ruling princely houses of Europe. Vincenzo's maternal grandfather had been the emperor Ferdinand; his forebears included Cardinal Ercole Gonzaga, who had presided over the Council of Trent in 1561. It was incumbent on a great prince to have a great court, which meant surrounding himself with the finest thinkers and artists and showing his grandeur in works of beauty and his nobility in acts of generosity. The dukes of Mantua amassed an enormous collection of valuable paintings and classical statuary.

The arts were important to society and in particular represented the taste, the wealth, and the status of princes, ruling houses, aristocrats, and wealthy bourgeoisie. The commissioning and decoration of churches, chapels, and palaces provided work for architects, painters, and sculptors and reflected glory at least as much on the patron as on the artist. Artists themselves held a kind of ambiguous status; they were respected for their talent, but their social standing as artisans prevented their full acceptance in a society where status was determined more by birth than by ability. In such a context, performing musicians played a role as servants, providing a pleasant background for courtly activities and occasionally giving performances that engaged the active attention of an audience. The status of composers—who usually were also performers—was sometimes a bit higher than that of other musicians, and the most respected composers sometimes found themselves in the company of intellectuals, scientists, and fellow artists engaged in discussions about the nature of beauty, the role of the arts in the good life, and the relationship of the arts as described by the ancients to the arts of today.

Since the fifteenth century the Gonzagas had been patrons of the finest artists and musicians in Italy and elsewhere. Isabella d'Este, wife of Marquis Francesco II and one of the greatest patrons of her time, died at Mantua in 1539; Leon Battista Alberti, the architect and theorist, served the Gonzagas, and his masterpiece, the Basilica of Sant'Andrea, stands in the center of Mantua; Andrea Mantegna, whose *Camera degli sposi* in the palace is one of the great monuments of Renaissance painting, was court painter from 1460 to 1506; Giulio Romano, painter and architect, died in 1546 after enriching Mantua with monumental works. Of musicians there were plenty, as we will see.

Duke Vincenzo had made considerable improvements in the grand ducal palace; with his architect and the Prefect of the Ducal Fabric, Antonio Maria Viani, he built the Galleria della Mostra (a splendid gallery to show off the most beautiful paintings and statues), the Loggia di Eleonora, and the outer portion of the Galleria degli Specchi and added a ducal theater (not yet built at the time of *Orfeo:* it opened the next

Peter Paul Rubens, *The Gonzaga Family Adoring the Holy Trinity*

The great Flemish master was recruited as court painter in Mantua around 1600
by Duke Vincenzo, who collected paintings of beautiful women. In its present
form, this religious work shows the duke and duchess of Mantua, Vincenzo
Gonzaga and Eleonora de' Medici, in the foreground; behind them are their
predecessors, Duke Guglielmo and his wife, Eleonora of Austria. The original
work contained portraits of the duke's children and other figures. Painted for the
Church of the Trinity in Mantua, it now hangs in the ducal palace.

year with the premiere of Monteverdi's *Arianna,* from which only the poignant lament
survives). In Vincenzo's time the palace numbered more than five hundred rooms and,
with the gardens, occupied some eight and a half acres.

Peter Paul Rubens went to Mantua in 1600 to serve Vincenzo and was based
there for several years, though he seems to have spent much of that time in Rome. He
painted three large canvases for the church of the Santissima Trinità, and in 1605 he finished the famous painting of the Gonzaga family adoring the Holy Trinity (the viewer
of which might spend more time contemplating the Gonzagas than the Trinity).

Duke Vincenzo had a particular taste for the stage. Long before the opening
of his new theater in 1608, he had arranged for regular visits of touring theatrical com-

panies, like the Gelosi, the Accessi, and the Uniti. Such visiting companies, often made
up of extended families of actors, provided all sorts of entertainment during their period of residence, from improvised low comedy to high rhetorical drama in verse.
Women were regularly members of such companies, and in at least one case a woman
was the head of the company, the chief actor, and a playwright. Plays were performed
sometimes in the palace, sometimes in the public theater (the *scena pubblica*) in the
town. The Jewish community of Mantua regularly performed plays for the duke, the
court, and the public, often to mark the carnival season.

The duke's fondness for the theater and his taste for the pastoral were combined when he brought to court the poet Battista Guarini and repeatedly planned to
stage his influential play *Il pastor fido* (*The Faithful Shepherd*) in the 1580s; this was finally performed, with musical interludes, in 1598. The spectacle was to include an
amorous game of blindman's buff, with dance and singing to music of Giangiacomo
Gastoldi—a moment that may have inspired the *balletto,* the dance-song, of shepherds
in the first act of *Orfeo.*

The poets of Italy engaged the duke's interest and dedicated works to him:
Torquato Tasso, whose great *Jerusalem Delivered* served Monteverdi for his dramatic
Combat of Tancred and Clorinda; Gabriello Chiabrera, source of many of Mon-
teverdi's musical texts, including the 1607 *Scherzi musicali;* Guarini, whose *Faithful
Shepherd* had a profound influence on Italian pastoral drama. In particular, Ottavio
Rinuccini, the leading poet at the Medici court at Florence, had many discussions with
the duke on musical and poetical subjects; and Rinuccini's own musical drama on the
subject of Orpheus was to have a strong effect on Monteverdi's *Orfeo.*

Grand entertainments of all sorts were staged whenever an occasion presented
itself: a wedding, a papal or imperial election, the birth of the son of the king of Spain

(for which in 1605 special constructions and triumphal arches containing fireworks were displayed throughout the city); artistic supervision for such celebrations, and for all dramatic events, was in the hands of the court official Federico Follino, who selected themes and texts, supervised the construction of sets, and arranged for musicians and singers.

During Vincenzo's reign, music took on a particular importance in Mantua. After the drama, the duke was particularly fond of singers, especially female singers (the duchess thought him entirely too indulgent in this regard). He established a trio modeled after a famous group in nearby Ferrara, and the skill of the Mantuan ladies was soon known throughout Italy.

The composers of Mantua were a source of considerable pride, and the dissemination of the works of the ducal composers through printed editions brought prestige to Mantua and its ruling family. Monteverdi continued the Mantuan tradition of madrigals established by Giaches Wert and Benedetto Pallavicini. Salomone Rossi, composer of dances, Jewish liturgical music, and much else, was director of instrumental music (only in 1606 had he been honored by being excused from wearing on his hat the yellow badge that identified Jews). Ludovico da Viadana, whose *Concerti ecclesiastici* were to have such wide currency, was chapel master at the cathedral from 1593 to 1597. Giangiacomo Gastoldi was director of music at the ducal basilica of Santa Barbara; his balletti were imitated by the Englishman Thomas Morley, Queen Elizabeth's favorite, and other composers around the European world.

Music at Court

Although the court at Mantua had a distinguished group of professionals, anyone well educated was a musician of some sort. Singing, playing the lute or some other instrument, learning to read music—these were all skills that a well-rounded member of a princely court was expected to acquire. Like dancing, fencing, and equestrian talents, musical skills were understood to contribute to the smooth and agreeable ordering of society and to create in the soul of the performer and the listener a pleasure that was one of the delights of social intercourse. Baldassare Castiglione, born of a noble family near Mantua, described what a courtier ought to acquire in the way of music in his treatise *The Book of the Courtier*, used as a model in many Italian courts: "I am not satisfied with our Courtier unless he be also a musician, and unless, besides understanding and being able to read music, he can play various instruments."

Most of the audience for *Orfeo* therefore had some musical ability and familiarity with songs, madrigals, instrumental music, and dance music. When they heard the songs and dances and choruses in *Orfeo,* they recognized a style of music in which they themselves participated and which they were able to judge and enjoy in a way that many of us are not. We are accustomed to a strong distinction between virtuosic performances by professionals and music made by amateurs, and we marvel at the skill of

> **It was Duke Vincenzo's custom to entertain his court with musical performances every Friday evening, as Monteverdi tells us in a letter of 1611:**
>
> Every Friday night music is performed in the Hall of Mirrors. Signora Adriana [Adriana Basile, a stunning soprano who arrived in 1610] comes to sing in concert, and lends the music such power and so special a grace bringing such delight to the senses that the place becomes almost like a new theatre.

the trained musician. And whereas this distinction was certainly true in Mantua—there was indeed professional virtuoso performance and difficult music—it is also true that *Orfeo* is generally of a level of difficulty that is readily accessible to a musically competent listener. It is lovely music, and much of it sounds like music that one might sing or play oneself.

But a few places in *Orfeo* are so dazzlingly virtuosic that they move from the realm of normal music making to the realm of the expert: for example, the solos by Orfeo, a few instrumental passages, and some highly impressive duets and trios by nymphs and shepherds. These moments would have been especially impressive and noteworthy to listeners, who would instantly have recognized the expertise required of composer and performer.

Although music was a popular pastime for many, there was still a need for professional musicians. The receptions, feasts, and entertainments of court life required vocal and instrumental music; the regular concerts, competent performers and composers; and church services, a large stock of masses and motets.

What we know of the music of the court is limited mostly to the music published by Monteverdi and other Mantuan musicians. This gives us a look at the *musica da camera* (chamber music), the madrigals, solos, trios, and the *scherzi musicali* (literally, "musical jokes" or light song), the music that people actually listened to and that showed off the skills of the court singers. What it does not do is give us much of a look at the dance music, the occasional music, the music played by instruments for ceremonial occasions, or the trumpet music that accompanied the duke in the streets.

Monteverdi's job was extraordinarily difficult and taxing. Not exactly a servant, neither was he a genius in residence. Although his letters show him to be regularly in contact with the duke and the highest court officials with regard to providing music for specific occasions, Monteverdi never felt that the compensation and respect given to him in Mantua came up to the standards of his music or of the quantity of his work. As noted, he was enormously busy, "now in tournaments, now in plays, now in *balletti*." A letter of 1611 from Monteverdi to Prince Francesco Gonzaga concerning some possible new musicians gives us an idea of the variety of jobs a musician had to perform: "His Highness the Prince . . . very much likes not only to hear a variety of wind instruments, he also likes to have the said musicians play in private, in church, in procession, and atop city walls; now madrigals, now French songs, now airs, and now dance-songs." Three *balli* (theatrical dance scenes) published in Monteverdi's madrigal books give us a look at court entertainments for special occasions. These begin with short dramatic scenes (the shepherd Tirsi and the shepherdess Clori flirt; or the Poet is crowned by the Nymphs; or Pluto, Venus, and Cupid discuss ingratitude in love), and the opening scene is followed by a long series of dances. Like ballets in France and masques in England, these balli were entertainments that mixed theater and ballroom, musician and courtier, since the entertainment that began as a performance ended as an evening of social dancing for everyone.

The virtuosity required of the singers in *Orfeo,* and the rich variety of its instrumental colors, are a tribute to the depth and the strength of Mantuan music making. The musical establishment of the court included about fifteen singers, eight string players, several keyboardists, lutists, and guitarists (Spanish music was much in fashion), and a small number of wind players. Their job was to provide all the music necessary for court ceremonies, entertainments, worship, and such special occasions as called for music. They were directed by Monteverdi and by his assistant maestro di cappella, Don Bassano Casola. What we know about these performers helps us reconstruct the sound and the spirit of the original *Orfeo,* for most of them were involved in its performance.

The court of Mantua was known for its virtuoso singers. Duke Vincenzo had spent much time at Ferrara in the 1580s, and his musical establishment reflected something of the taste of the Este court, both in its personalities and its makeup. At Ferrara the *concerto delle donne* (the consort of ladies), for which so much impressive music was written by Luzzascho Luzzaschi, set a standard for virtuosity, established a new style of singing, and created a sound for which Ferrara was widely famous. Vincenzo Gonzaga created a similar ensemble at Mantua, as noted, though his interest may not have been exclusively musical: he seems to have shown a possibly unsuitable extravagance toward these ladies.

The singers available in Mantua, however, fell short of the number needed to stage *Orfeo*. We will see shortly how outside help was sought, and how the casting was arranged.

Vincenzo Giustiniani, a Roman noble and a cultured music lover, describes the Mantuan singers along with those from Ferrara and gives us a view of an admired singing style that surely was part of the sound and look of *Orfeo*:

They moderated or increased their voices, loud or soft, heavy or light, according to the demands of the piece they were singing; now slow, breaking off with sometimes a gentle sigh, now singing long passages legato or detached, now groups, now leaps, now with long trills, now with short, and again with sweet running passages sung softly, to which sometimes one heard an echo answer unexpectedly. They accompanied the music and the sentiment with appropriate facial expressions, glances and gestures, and no awkward movements of the mouth or hands or body which might not express the feeling of the song. They made the words clear in such a way that one could hear even the last syllable of every word, which was never inter-rupted or suppressed by passages [*passagi*] and other embellishments.

The Culture of Orfeo

Given Duke Vincenzo's taste for the theater, the pastoral, and music, it seems entirely fitting that the three should come together, under the auspices of the local academy and through the guidance of his heir, in the performance of a musical pastoral for the theater on the subject of Orpheus. *Orfeo* is a courtly entertainment, the project of an intellectual academy, and as such reflects much of the intellectual activity of court life at that time.

The Accademia degli Invaghiti (the academy of the lovestruck, the fascinated, or those who have taken a fancy to something) was an association of gentlemen dedicated to the arts, poetry, rhetoric, and the courtly virtues. Academies like this, centered usually on noble courts, were common in Renaissance Italy. They had similar names (the Elevati, the Alterati, and so on), though each academy believed it had a special mission, an emphasis that set it apart from all the rest. Academies met to hear disputations, poems, rhetoric of various kinds (such as eloquent memorial minutes for deceased members) and to engage in elaborate ceremonies. Such academies, limited for the most part to aristocratic members, played a large part in the intellectual life of the time.

The Mantuan academy was founded in the 1560s by Cesare Gonzaga (duke of Guastalla, whose wife, Camilla Borromeo, was the pope's niece), and it originally met in Cesare's palazzo next to the church of Santa Maria del Popolo. It was reorganized under Cesare's son Ferrante in the 1570s and occasionally gave theatrical productions to which the public might be invited. By Monteverdi's time the academy held its meetings in the palace under the protection of the duke, and its members included Francesco and Ferdinando Gonzaga. The court poet and diplomat (and *Orfeo* librettist) Alessandro Striggio was a member, but Monteverdi apparently was not; evidently intellectual and artistic rank were not always sufficient to guarantee membership in such a group. Striggio was an aristocrat and an important official of the court, and though other intellectuals and artists (Galileo Galilei, Peter Paul Rubens, for example) might hold protected positions as ornaments of a courtly nature, Monteverdi was an employee—highly respected and of the first rank among the musicians, to be sure, but still not suitable for membership in the Invaghiti.

In 1607 the Invaghiti were treated to such creations as an "Oration in Praise of St. George, the Valorous Cavalier of Christ," by Giulio Cesare Facipecore, and a discourse by Count Scipione Agnelli, not yet eighteen years old ("but in wisdom most aged") in praise of Saint Barbara, patroness of the ducal church. And in the same year, of course, the academy produced, under the leadership of Prince Francesco Gonzaga, the fable of *Orfeo*, written by their fellow member Striggio and set to music by the court composer.

The spectators at the first performance of *Orfeo* were instantly aware that they were being shown a drama in the classical tradition of Greece and Rome. The revival and study of the learning of classical antiquity, the humanism of the Renaissance, brought with it an interest in the expressive power of ancient music as reported by Plato and others. In the course of much discussion among scholars and artists, it was agreed that the power of classical drama owed much to the fact that its actors sang their roles, and that they sang not in the learned polyphony of the sixteenth century but in a sort of simple recitation with only the plainest of accompaniment.

The moment the allegorical Musica appeared in the prologue, the Mantuan audience knew what to expect. A prologue in classical tragedy, as defined by Aristotle, is whatever comes before the first chorus. Normally the prologue involves one individual (an actual person, e.g., a watchman) who sets the scene and engages the sympathy of the spectator. In classical comedy, the prologue is a figure who stands in for the author and speaks to the audience to gain their sympathy and introduce the plot. In this sense, Musica ("I am Music, who with sweet accent can calm any troubled heart"), who addresses the audience ("Famous heroes, of the noble blood of kings"), tells the plot ("Now I'll tell you of Orfeo"), and sets the scene ("Let no bird move among these trees; let no wave sound on these banks"), is a combination: she stands outside the action (as in comedy) but performs the traditional and expected role of classical drama (as in tragedy). This is not a comedy, and not a tragedy: it is a *favola,* a fable.

The Theater at Sabbioneta

Built by Vespasiano Gonzaga for his ideal city near Mantua and inaugurated
during the carnival season of 1590, this theater served as the basis for the one
built at the ducal palace in Mantua itself. One of the few surviving
Renaissance theaters, it surely represents an ideal in court design and was
well known to those who planned the theater for *Orfeo*. The semicircular
risers surround an open area in front of the stage; the decorative colonnade
above provided standing room.

The spectators also knew the format of classical drama, made up of episodes
(or acts), in which characters generally deliver long poetical speeches. Scenes of dialogue, in which actors alternate speech quickly, are reserved for special moments. In
Orfeo these are the two highly dramatic moments when Orfeo loses Euridice: the first,
when death removes her from the world, and the second, when Orfeo himself chooses
passion over reason and looks back at her.

In classical theater the episodes, or acts as they are called in *Orfeo,* are separated by choral odes. Members of the chorus are part of the action (here, they are
nymphs and shepherds or infernal spirits), but they also stand outside it and comment
on it. In *Orfeo,* not only do they have individual speaking roles, but as a chorus they announce ("Ecco Orfeo!"—Here comes Orfeo!) and react ("Ahi! Caso acerbo!"—Ah, bitter event!). They also comment on the scene, especially between the acts, interpreting
it to the spectators. "Mortal man should not put his faith in transitory things," they sing
after Orfeo gets news of Euridice's death, "which suddenly flee away, and often a great
ascent precedes a fall." In fact they get a bit preachy; after Orfeo is ejected from the underworld, the chorus makes the point plain: "Orfeo conquered the Inferno, and was

then conquered by his passions; worthy of eternal glory should be only he who conquers himself." In yet another sense, they are ourselves, as they react to and reflect on what happens.

Orfeo is also a pastoral drama, as any good courtier would have immediately recognized. The pastoral tradition is a poetic and dramatic convention in which shepherds and shepherdesses, always young and free, live in a beautiful natural environment of mountain, vale, stream, and meadow. It is a mythical time and place, where nymphs and shepherds associate with gods, where politics, economics, social difference, warfare, physical suffering, and aging have no place. A land where the weather is always good and the sheep need no tending, allowing its inhabitants to explore the things that matter: love and its complexities. The elimination of external distractions makes the pastoral the locus par excellence for the study of emotional states and for the display of the changing passions that is the theme of poet and dramatist and the delight of the sensitive spectator.

The pastoral idyll, which has a tradition stretching back to classical Greece and Rome, was revived in fifteenth- and sixteenth-century Italian poetry and drama. At the end of the fifteenth century, Jacopo Sannazaro's *Arcadia* set the stage for the revival. "Back then the greatest gods did not disdain / to lead their sheep in wood and meadowland / and, as we do today, they used to sing" (*Arcadia,* published in 1502, sixth eclogue). Pastoral drama had included Torquato Tasso's *Aminta* (1573) and Guarini's *The Faithful Shepherd* (1589), a piece of enormous popularity and influence all over Europe. Everybody knew it. Musicians used texts from this play for madrigals and *canzonette* (lighter songs).

We are not much inclined to pastorals nowadays. But we too have conventional settings: the Western, the television sitcom, the detective novel. The value of such formats is their efficiency: we understand much in advance—for example, the setting and the general shape of the plot; and we know that this is a world especially constructed for our delight.

If gods and heroes occasionally invade Arcadia, they do so that the mythological setting, at once real and timeless, might contribute by its unreality to our focus on things internal. And it is entirely suitable that Orfeo should find himself in an Arcadian environment, for the pastoral setting is a place of recreation, of poetry and music.

Poetry and Music

Speech was almost poetry in Arcadia. Is it any wonder that the people in *Orfeo* speak in verse? Drama was usually in verse, of course, and we are aware of how much pleasure can be derived from listening to people speak in this unnatural yet delightful way.

Giovanni Battista Doni, the Florentine classicist who devoted himself to the rediscovery of Greek music, wrote what may have reflected Mantuans' understanding of the pastoral:

As far as the pastoral is concerned . . . one may concede that it has music in all of its parts; . . . in particular because the gods, nymphs, and shepherds there appear in that primeval age, when music was natural and speech was almost poetry.

The spectators at the first *Orfeo* were Italians; most readers of this book probably are not. This is an enormous and essential difference, since the Mantuan audience not only understood every word but were able to detect the subtleties of language, the versification, the imagery, and the elegant turns of phrase that their English contemporaries were admiring in Shakespeare's dramas. We must remember how important Italian is to the piece, not only in what it tells but also in how it tells it.

Many of us who do not understand Italian are unable to hear all that, though we may be aware of certain aspects. We may realize that different kinds of verse are used for different purposes. Perhaps we can hear the eleven-syllable line used by great poets for elevated sentiments—what Orfeo uses when he wishes to impress the boatman Caronte (elide vowels to count syllables): "Possente spirto e formidabil nume / Senza cui far passagio a l'altro riva" (Powerful spirit and formidable god / Without whom no one passes to the other shore). It is the meter of Dante, one of whose most famous lines is quoted by Speranza as she reads the gates of the infernal regions: "Lasciate ogni speranza, voi ch'entrate" (Abandon all hope, ye who enter).

We can hear the contrast between that and the eight-syllable line used for lighter sentiments, especially for songs. Orfeo uses this when he sings at the beginning of act 2: "Vi ricorda o boschi ombrosi / de miei lungh'aspri tormenti?" (Shady woods, do you remember my long and bitter torments?).

How might we react to the elegant creation of a courtly poet, telling a story that we know, in a way that is new and that moves and delights us? Monteverdi's friend Cherubino Ferrari had this to say: "The poetry is lovely in conception, lovelier still in form, and loveliest of all in diction; and indeed no less was to be expected of a man as richly talented as Signor Striggio."

The audience for *Orfeo* was interested in the ways poetry and music were related, in the ways music can heighten and express language and emotion. These were

Marsilio Ficino, the Florentine humanist, on song:

Remember that song is the most powerful imitator of all things. For it imitates the intentions and affections of the soul, and speech, and also reproduces bodily gestures, human movements and moral characters, and imitates and acts everything so powerfully that it immediately provokes both the singer and hearer to imitate and perform the same things.

in fact some of the most talked-about topics in the intellectual life of the time. Renaissance Italians knew that poetry and music had common functions and aims: recreation, relaxation, appreciation of beauty, moral instruction.

These humanistic ideas, based on an understanding of music in classical times, had been of great concern to musicians. Jacopo Peri, in the preface to his *Euridice* (1600), wrote, "Keeping in mind those modes and accents which serve us in our sorrow, in our joy, and the like, I made the bass move in time to these, now more, now less, according to the affections."

Attempts to re-create the ancient style of reciting in music had been undertaken here and there, but nowhere with such attention or such effective repercussions as among the learned musical artists of Florence around 1600. In particular, recent musical settings of a libretto by Ottavio Rinuccini, *L'Euridice,* by Jacopo Peri and Giulio Caccini, had aroused a great deal of musical interest—so much so that Rinuccini's setting became a powerful influence on Alessandro Striggio's libretto for *Orfeo,* and Monteverdi kept Peri's musical setting of the same subject constantly in view. *Orfeo* is Mantua's answer to the Florentine pieces based on the same story.

To someone familiar with Monteverdi's *Orfeo,* even a quick glance at Peri's *Euridice* shows many parallels. First, the librettos are remarkably similar, despite their different endings. Naturally we expect two tellings of the same legend to have many similarities, but the parallels here suggest that Monteverdi and Striggio were acutely aware of Peri and Rinuccini's accomplishment. Peri's opera has five scenes, each closing with a chorus; *Orfeo* has five acts, each also closing with a chorus. These choral scenes marked divisions, along the lines of the *intermedii* of music and dance, which were often used to separate the acts of spoken plays. In each version there is a tripartite division of settings, the fields of Thrace flanking a central infernal scene. The arrangement and deportment of nymphs, shepherds, and infernal spirits is also similar.

Orfeo is led to the brink of Hades by an allegorical figure, Peri's Venus becoming Monteverdi's Speranza (Hope). In both operas allegorical figures deliver the prologue. Rinuccini's Tragedia declaims seven strophes that begin, in Peri's setting (and also, for that matter, in Caccini's), with a rhythm echoed several times by the figure of Music, who introduces *Orfeo*.

Peri adorns his opening scene with a balletto, a dance chorus that begins imitatively and shifts from duple to triple rhythm; Monteverdi does the same with "Lasciate i monti." Each opera ends with a final strophic chorus followed by an instrumental dance. Peri's reiterated chorus of lamentation, "Sospirate," is paralleled and brilliantly transformed by Monteverdi in the "Ahi! Caso acerbo!" with which the chorus amplifies the Messenger's recitative. And it is difficult not to see in Peri's setting of Orfeo's lament a harmonic idea—the juxtaposition of E-major and G-minor harmonies—which serves Monteverdi not only as an expressive moment but as a significant structuring force.

Any one of these parallels might well seem fortuitous, but taken together they strongly suggest what is already suspected about the Florentine-Mantuan artistic rivalry: that Monteverdi was keenly aware of Peri's achievement and wanted to surpass it. He did.

The Mantuan *Orfeo* looks over his shoulder at the Florentine *Euridice,* and for once the result is not disastrous. The Mantuan fable was created to entertain a certain audience on a single day. But it was also rather like a scientific experiment. *Orfeo* was Monteverdi's solution to the problem already posed among musical humanists as to how to relate music and poetry in drama. Monteverdi certainly knew the previous solutions, and if they were used as models it was not because he lacked imagination but precisely because he wanted his—far superior—work to stand in that tradition. His printed score is designed for the learned to look at, and it is full of expert notational devices sure to impress any musical scholar who examines it.

That the music was published, like the settings of Peri and Caccini, underscores the intellectual and academic aspects of the work, for scores of occasional pieces, especially operas, were usually set aside immediately after they were performed, and often never seen again. Such publications were customarily financed by their dedicatee; in this case Monteverdi dedicated the score of *Orfeo* to Francesco Gonzaga (see page 53; document 1). The printed score of *Orfeo* is, among other things, a record of current activities at Mantua. That it also showed Monteverdi's genius, and preserved his opera for us where others have not survived, is a stroke of enormous luck. The second publication, of 1615, no longer bears the dedication to Francesco. Perhaps the publisher knew a market; but even if Monteverdi paid for it himself, such a second publication shows that the fable from Mantua was already known and admired in wider circles.

Orfeo is a chamber opera, designed to be performed for an intimate and select audience. This small-scale performance is right in the tradition (if so young a genre can

Title Page of the 1609 Edition of *L'Orfeo*

The printing of *Orfeo*, two years after the first performance, gives much valuable information about the event. This page reads: "The *Orfeo*, fable in music, by Claudio Monteverdi, performed in Mantua in the year 1607 and newly published. To the Most Serene Lord Don Francesco Gonzaga, Prince of Mantua, and of Monferrato, etc. In Venice, by Ricciardo Amadino. 1609."

be said to have one) of "fables represented in music." Jacopo Peri's *Euridice* was also a small-scale entertainment. As part of the festivities celebrating the wedding by proxy of Maria de' Medici to Henry IV of France, *Euridice* was performed in what one witness described as "a small room upstairs in the Pitti Palace"; its setting was simple, requiring no stage machinery. *Orfeo*, too, was performed in a room in a palace.

This is not the sort of opera we are used to. For us, opera implies a large, opulent theater designed for the purpose; an overdressed audience; a magnificent spectacle, both onstage and in the hall—in short, the grandest and most expensive entertainment possible. The elitism of opera persists to this day, but the grandeur of opera has nothing to do with *Orfeo*.

Of course, Mantua was the site of spectacular entertainments presented to enormous audiences at great expense. An opera performed in 1608 highlights the difference in scale between the pastoral fable and the grand entertainment. As part of the festivities celebrating the marriage of Francesco Gonzaga to Margaret of Savoy, Monteverdi's *Arianna* was produced in a small hall, using only a single set, and lasted about two and a half hours. Three days later a staged assault was acted out on a specially constructed fortress in the Lago di Mezzo, with an elaborate fireworks display; two days later Guarini's comedy *L'idropica* was performed, with grand intermezzi and elaborate stage machinery, entertaining some five thousand spectators for several hours.

It is therefore clear that resources were not the issue in presenting pastorals. Yet these small-scale works had a considerable attraction. The Florentine dramas and *Orfeo* were born of a combination of artistic and intellectual interest within a small group for an elite court, but they stirred considerably wider interest. *Euridice* and *Orfeo* both had scores published and circulated, and they gave rise to an operatic energy that continues to this day. It was Monteverdi's genius, however, that took *Orfeo* out of the local humanistic academy and made it a work of sublime and timeless beauty.

During 1608, with ducal support and financing, the rehearsals for Monteverdi's *Arianna* took five months. But preparation time for *Orfeo,* presented the previous year, was shorter, and the resources available were no doubt more limited. Carnival events such as this in Mantua generally included plays (by the Jewish community or by visiting companies), tournaments, and banquets.

The twenty-one-year-old Francesco Gonzaga, heir to the dukedom of Mantua, was the originating force behind the composition and performance of *Orfeo*. As a member of the Accademia degli Invaghiti, Prince Francesco had often been involved in planning theatrical and other entertainments (he had chosen the theme for the carnival tournament in 1606), though he was far more serious and reserved than his pleasure-loving father. In the dedicatory letter of the first printing of the score, Monteverdi writes that the *favola d'Orfeo* was performed "in the Accademia of the Invaghiti, under the auspices of Your Highness"; it should be signed with no other name, Monteverdi continues, "since it was born under Your Highness's propitious star: may those serene rays of your grace continue to favor the progress of its life."

Francesco Gonzaga was deeply involved in the planning and production of *Orfeo:* a series of letters between him and his younger brother, Ferdinando, gives most of the information we have about the preparations for the performance and reveal Francesco as the guiding spirit.

Already in early January, Francesco Gonzaga knew that he was going to produce a "fable in music" and that he would need performers from elsewhere. On Janu-

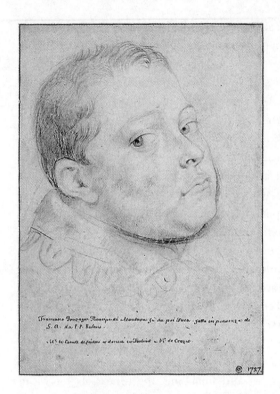

Peter Paul Rubens, *Francesco Gonzaga*

This chalk drawing of Prince Francesco Gonzaga, "made in the presence of His Highness by P. P. Rubens," according to legend, dates from a few years before Francesco became involved in the preparations for *Orfeo*. Francesco, the eldest son of Duke Vincenzo Gonzaga, was the patron and dedicatee of this opera. Francesco and his brother, Ferdinando, exchanged letters in which they discuss the production of *Orfeo* (see documents).

ary 5 he wrote to his brother in Pisa: "I have decided to have a play in music performed at Carnival this year, but as we have very few sopranos here, and those few not good, I should be grateful if Your Excellency [that is, Ferdinando] would be kind enough to tell me if those castrati I heard when I was in Tuscany are still there. I mean the ones in the Grand Duke's service, whom I so much enjoyed hearing during my visit. My intention is to borrow one of them (whichever Your Excellency thinks the best), as long as you agree that the Grand Duke will not refuse to lend him, if you yourself do the asking, for a fortnight at most." Francesco wants to "borrow" a singer, as though he was borrowing a book or a cup of sugar. The distance between prince and musician, even a talented musician of the Medici court, is enormous. Ferdinando acts quickly: he finds a castrato (a male singer emasculated before puberty to preserve the high range of his voice). This singer is not one of those Francesco had already heard, but he recommends him highly: he is a pupil of the famous Giulio Caccini (the Florentine connection again) and has performed successfully on the stage. Francesco is quick to accept his brother's advice; his reply encloses a request to the grand duke of Tuscany for the loan of the singer, and he also sends the part (evidently more than one role) the singer is to learn.

A flurry of letters between the two ensues in early February: Francesco expresses his impatience; Ferdinando writes to introduce the singer, who is on his way: "This is to introduce Giovanni Gualberto [Magli], a young castrato whom I am sending to your Highness to take part in the performance of your play. You will hear from his own lips of the difficulty he has had in learning the part which was given him; so far he has managed to commit only the prologue to memory, the rest proving impossible because it contains 'troppo voci' [too many notes? words? too wide a range?]."

Again in early February, increasingly anxious because he still has not heard from the singer, whom he needs even more desperately, Francesco writes: "I had expected that the castrato would have arrived by now, and indeed it is essential that he should be here as soon as possible. He will now have not only to play the part that was sent to him, but also to learn that of Proserpine, as the singer who was to take the role can no longer do so. So I am awaiting him from day to day with great eagerness, as without him the play would be a complete failure."

When the singer finally arrives, Francesco is not happy, because the castrato has not learned his part. There is only one week left before the performance, and Francesco, ducal heir or not, is worried, as any impresario would rightly be. He cannot delay the performance, because it is scheduled for the end of carnival, and once Lent begins, there can be no more theatrical performances until the Easter season. But the singer is a quick learner: "He knows only the Prologue, and seems to think that he will not have time to learn the other part before the Carnival; in which case I shall have no choice but to postpone the performance of the play until Easter. This morning, however, he began to study not only the music, but the words as well; and if he were able to learn the part (although it does contain 'troppo voci' as Your Excellency says), he would at least know the melody, the music could be altered to suit his needs, and we would not waste so much time ensuring that he knows it all by heart."

And on the eve of the performance Francesco is pleased and encouraged. The play will not only take place but will go well, at least the parts assigned to Magli. The "import" has evidently justified the effort of looking as far as Florence for singers, and Ferdinando's judgment is vindicated: "The musical play is to be performed in our Academy tomorrow, since Giovanni Gualberto has done very well in the short time he has been here. Not only has he thoroughly learned the whole of his part, he delivers it with much grace and a most pleasing effect; I am delighted with him. The play has been printed so that everyone in the audience can have a copy to follow while the performance is in progress."

The previous day, there had been some anticipation of the performance, to judge from a letter of the courtier Carlo Magno to his brother in Rome (document 12): "Tomorrow evening the Most Serene Lord the Prince is to sponsor [a play] in the main room in the apartments which the Most Serene Lady of Ferrara had the use of [nella sala del partimento che godeva Mad.ma Ser.ma di Ferrara]. It should be most unusual, as all the actors are to sing their parts; it is said on all sides that it will be a great success. No doubt I shall be driven to attend out of sheer curiosity, unless I am prevented from getting in by the lack of space [l'angustia del luogo]."

The letters just cited are essentially all the information we have on the first performance of *Orfeo,* except for one other important source: Monteverdi's published score. From a close reading of the score, we learn much about the singers, the instruments, and even the staging (none of which is mentioned in the letters).

The dedicatory letter, to Francesco Gonzaga, of the

first edition (1609) of the score of *Orfeo:*

Most serene lord my lord and most respected patron:

    The fable of Orpheus which was once musically staged in the Academy of the Invaghiti under the auspices of your highness on a narrow stage, and now being about to appear in the great Theatre of the universe to show itself to all men, is no reason for it to appear signed with any other name than the glorious and happy name of Your Highness. To you I therefore humbly consecrate it, so that you who were propitious at its birth in the guise of a lucky star, with the most serene rays of your grace, may deign to favor the progress of its life, which I dare to hope, thanks to Your Highness, may be equally as durable as humankind. I beg Your Highness to accept this token of my devotion, with that grandeur of spirit which is characteristic of you, and which links the souls of all those who happen to have dealings with you. And here, bowing with submissive reverence to Your Highness, I pray the Lord to grant your every desire. In Mantua, the 22nd of August, 1609.

        Your highness's

                Most humble and grateful servant,

                   Claudio Monteverdi.

There is no surviving music for *Orfeo* in Monteverdi's hand (or in anybody else's): no instrumental parts, no composer's score, no separate vocal parts (with or without "troppo voci"). Like all the other pieces considered in this book, the score was published well after the performance. But, unlike much printed music of later date, which has a prescriptive purpose—directions for how to make this music on a future occasion—the score of *Orfeo* has a descriptive purpose, at least in part: it describes how this music was performed on a specific occasion in the past. We can tell this from comments printed in the score, such as "Two organs, and two chitarroni, accompanied this song, one sounding from the left corner of the scene, and the other from the right." Not "should accompany," but *did* accompany.

    The score is therefore a memory book, a record of what was performed and how it was done. In this sense it is part of the tradition of advertising grand spectacles, such as the Florentine intermedii of 1589, through books that described the events, complete with engravings of the scenery and, sometimes, of the music.

Monteverdi was particularly anxious, of course, that a copy of the score be presented to the prince as soon as it was available. In a letter to Striggio, Monteverdi wrote in August 1609: "I have nothing else to tell your lordship about *Orfeo:* I hope that tomorrow, which is the 25th, my brother will receive the finished publication from the printer, who will send it to him by the courier from Venice which arrives tomorrow, as it happens. And as soon as he receives it he will have one copy bound and will give it to His Highness the Prince [Francesco], and when he does so I beg your lordship to put in a few words with the Prince." Monteverdi the employee is clearly concerned with the prince's continuing favor; perhaps he hopes that the prince will recognize the genius of a fellow human?

All the comments and labels printed in the score are presented in their original Italian and translated as document 15. It is easy to see that some of these describe what happened and that others are in the present tense, as they might be in a modern score: "Here a noise is made behind the curtain" (no. 22), "Here Orfeo turns" (no. 23). We can't be absolutely sure that a significant difference is intended between the descriptive (past tense) indications and the others—perhaps the latter are recommended but not necessarily part of the first performance?

The Performance

Where was *Orfeo* performed? In a small, narrow room, as we know: "nell'Accademia degli Invaghiti," says Monteverdi; "nella nostra Accademia," says Francesco Gonzaga; "in the main room of the apartments which the Most Serene Lady of Ferrara had the use of," says Magno.

It appears that the accademia did not have a regular place of meeting, so that "nell'Accademia" must mean something like "for the Academy" or "in the presence of the Academy," wherever they happened to have gathered. Margherita Gonzaga (the "Most Serene Lady of Ferrara," the ex-duchess of Ferrara and sister of Duke Vincenzo) had occupied the *camere lunghe* (the long rooms) on the ground floor of the palace, just inside the principal entrance. One of these rooms, relatively spacious but not as grand as the principal rooms on the main floor above, must have been the site of *Orfeo*.

As members of the academy arrived, they passed by the guards at the ground-floor entrance in the principal piazza, and found themselves in an ample interior courtyard. There, rather than take the large wooden exterior staircase that led to the principal apartments above, they turned left and passed into an antechamber; turning right, they entered the room in which the fable of Orpheus was to be performed.

This room, measuring about twenty-eight by thirty-nine feet, still exists, its

A Reconstruction of the Room in Which *Orfeo* Was Performed

This model was created by P. Guillou for the Musée de la Musique, Paris. The room now lacks decoration and has a vaulted ceiling. *Orfeo* lasts about ninety minutes, so standing through the performance may not have been overly tiring.

vaulted ceiling intact. For the production, three windows on the right were curtained to enhance the theatrical lighting created by candles and reflectors, which provided the proper atmosphere for *Orfeo*. At the far end of the room was an elaborate proscenium stage covered with a curtain, in front of which a large number of instrumentalists were seated and behind which, presumably, the costumed singers were preparing for the performance.

In this small room, on this temporary stage, several other performers joined Giovanni Gualberto in the first performance of *Orfeo*. Monteverdi's list of characters includes characters with names; choruses of nymphs and shepherds; choruses of infernal spirits; and a final chorus of shepherds who danced the moresca at the end. Elsewhere in the score there are individual nymphs, shepherds, and spirits who are not named in the cast list and who are presumably also members of the chorus.

With this information we can reconstruct a probable cast, guided also by the structure of the music. *Orfeo* is filled with characters who sing only a little music, or only in one act. The Prologue, Musica, sings five strophes and disappears; the nymph Sylvia delivers the bad news and leaves to hide herself forever; Speranza appears only briefly at the beginning of act 3; Caronte sings twice and falls asleep; Plutone and Proserpina are each heard only in act 4. Apollo's appearance in act 5 is impressive but brief. Except for that of Orfeo himself, the most taxing roles in the opera are those of the two shepherds who sing duets in the opening acts. And the disposition of choral voices in the score makes it clear that they also were sung by individual singers. For example, the final chorus of rejoicing in act 5 has only one tenor part, whereas most of the other choruses have two; this second tenor is unavailable for this chorus because he has just departed, as Apollo, flying Orfeo to heaven aboard his cloud.

Some of the solo singers who performed at Mantua in the early years of the century are known to us by name. Although we cannot say for sure that they performed in *Orfeo,* it seems unlikely that a professional on hand would not be employed if asked by the crown prince.

Among the regular singers employed at court, the names of Francesco Rasi, whom we know to have sung in *Orfeo,* and Caterina Martinelli, the famous Roman soprano who had been in Mantua for years, should be singled out.

Rasi, a Mantuan singer, poet, and composer with a wide reputation, must have taken the role of Orpheus. He had studied in Florence with Giulio Caccini, the most famous singing master of the day, he had traveled with Carlo Gesualdo, prince of Venosa and composer of avant-garde madrigals, and he had been attracted to Mantua in 1599. Rasi had a remarkably elevated position for a court musician and may in fact have lived in the palace. Rasi was described as a performer in *Orfeo* by Eugenio Cagnani, in his *Lettera cronologica* of 1612 (document 14): "that signor Francesco Rasio, so famous for his excellence in his profession that everyone agrees that there are few in the world who can excel him." According to Giustiniani, Rasi was one of those Caccini-trained artists who "sang, whether bass or tenor, with a range consisting of many notes, and with exquisite style and passage-work, and with extraordinary feeling and a particular talent to make the words clearly heard." This exactly describes what is needed for the role of Orfeo: a range between tenor and baritone, an ability to sing florid ornament, and a dramatic ability in expressing the words. Monteverdi surely had Rasi in mind when composing the role. Rasi was "a handsome man, jovial and with a strong and sweet voice," wrote Severo Bonini about 1650 in his counterpoint treatise, and "his animated face and dignity . . . made his singing seem angelic and divine."

The famous castrato Giovanni Battista Sacchi was also a Mantuan court singer and undoubtedly took part in *Orfeo*. Other court singers, some of them of great reputation, probably did not take part in the performance because they were women. Caterina Martinelli (called "La Romana" or "La Romanina") had lived in Monteverdi's house until 1606 and may well have studied singing with Monteverdi's wife, Claudia

Cattaneo; we know that she sang—at the age of nineteen—in Marco da Gagliano's *Dafne*, presented in Mantua in 1608. She was to have performed the title role in Monteverdi's *Arianna*, but she died of smallpox in March 1608. Martinelli is not mentioned at all in the correspondence concerning *Orfeo*, and indeed it is suggested that there is a lack of good sopranos. Her participation must not have been suitable, for she surely would have been talked about had she performed. Other female court singers included the sisters Lucia and Isabella Pellizzari and the Neapolitan singer Lucrezia Urbana (though we will see that Urbana may have been among the instruments). And yet there was a shortage of sopranos!

It looks as though all the parts were sung by men. We already know that female characters were sung by males, since we know that two of Giovanni Gualberto Magli's three roles were female: the personification of Music, in the Prologue, and Proserpina, in act 3. Most surprising of all, perhaps, is the fact that the role of Euridice was played by a *soprano castrato,* a priest named Girolamo Bacchini. A carmelite monk who had long served at Mantua, Bacchini had composed masses for the ducal church of Santa Barbara and also participated as a singer in concerts of chamber music. Why the role of Euridice, of all the roles in the opera, should be assigned to an emasculated soprano priest is something of a mystery. Euridice has a small role but has very beautiful music. Perhaps Bacchini's purity of voice, or his small stature (he was called "that little priest —*pretino*—who played Euridice in the *Orfeo* of the Most Serene Lord Prince") made him the right choice for the role.

In any event, though there were women singers at court, the choice roles for female characters in *Orfeo* were given to male sopranos. Because the Academy was an organization of men, the performance must have been thought inappropriate for women. We know, too, from a report of 1608 that the duke did not normally allow his female singers to appear in any sort of spectacle, public or private. If Euridice, Proserpina, and Musica were all sung by men, I think we can presume that the rest of the cast was also male.

Regrettably we do not know what arrangement of singers Monteverdi actually used. What we do know is that Monteverdi accepted the idea of a singer playing more than one role; Giovanni Gualberto Magli sang three, including the Prologue (Musica) and Proserpina; the third role might be the little part of the Ninfa in act 1 (who could come on late, giving time for Musica to put on Arcadian dress); or it might be Speranza, leading Orfeo to the underworld (there would be the whole duration of Orfeo's famous aria "Possente spirto," and more, to allow Speranza's change to Proserpina); or it might be the messenger who brings bad news to Orfeo. I suggest this last part, because we know from the introduction to Peri's *Euridice* that the analogous messenger there was played by Jacopo Giusti, "fanciuletto Lucchese" (the lad from Lucca), and because it gives Magli an opportunity to display the expressiveness for which he was praised by Francesco. The poignance of having a (presumably innocent-looking and -sounding) youth deliver such tragic news would have been as effective for Monteverdi as for Peri.

A Proposed Cast List for Orfeo:

Orfeo	Francesco Rasi
Euridice	Girolamo Bacchini, *soprano castrato*
Soprano 1	(Giovanni Gualberto Magli): La Musica; Messagiera; Speranza; chorus, act 5
Soprano 2	Ninfa; Proserpina; chorus, acts 1, 2, 5
Alto	Pastore, acts 1, 2; duet and trio, act 1; chorus, acts 1–4
Tenor 1	Pastore, acts 1, 2; duets, acts 1, 2; Spirito; Apollo; chorus, acts 1–4
Tenor 2:	Pastore, acts 1, 2; duets in acts 1, 2; Spirito; chorus, acts 1–5
Bass 1:	Plutone; Echo; chorus, acts 3, 4
Bass 2:	Pastore, act 1; Caronte; chorus, acts 1–5

Assuming that the chorus is sung by characters on stage and that time is available for changes of costume, an arrangement of seven singers, with the addition of Orfeo and Euridice, allows all roles and choral voices to be covered.

The performance of an opera by nine singers, rather than by two or three times that number, suggests a scale appropriate to a narrow room at a court with a limited number of suitable singers. So there are nine people waiting behind the curtain for the beginning of the performance.

What about the orchestra in front of the curtain? Monteverdi gives a long list of instruments at the beginning of the score: it includes strings, recorders, trumpets, trombones, cornetti, harp, and a host of instruments to accompany the singers—harpsichords, lutes, organ, and a regal. Monteverdi really intends this piece to be accompanied by a grand band of exquisite sounds. Some pieces are accompanied by "tutti gli stromenti," and that is a long list indeed.

The instruments are arranged in choirs of similar sound: two choirs of strings; a choir of trombones with the upper parts played on cornetti; a choir of trumpets. Such groupings were a tradition in sixteenth-century music and allowed Monteverdi to use characteristic instrumental sounds for places or persons: trombones for the infernal regions, strings for the upper world, trumpets for the duke of Mantua.

There are many wind instruments (besides the ducal trumpets): trombones, cornetti, recorders. Perhaps like the singers they played more than one role. The wind players, led by the cornettist Giulio Cesare Bianchi, had to be flexible. It is suggestive that, in a letter of 1609, Monteverdi agreed to help Prince Francesco negotiate with "that group of cornet and trombone players, as he commissioned me to do." How did Francesco know about these players? Had he perhaps heard them as guest artists in *Orfeo?* Three of them, says Monteverdi, "play all the wind instruments," and "they play together well and readily both dance and chamber music, since they practice every day." Eighteen months later, Monteverdi has one more candidate for Prince Francesco's wind band: he has found a musician who plays recorder, cornetto, trombone, flute, and bassoon. The ability to play many instruments would help in *Orfeo:* the cornetti might also play recorders; perhaps even a string player or two knew how to play trombone: the strings and the trombones, each representing a different part of the universe — Arcadia and Inferno — do not play at the same time.

One of the most remarkable musical parts in *Orfeo* is for the harp, the *arpa doppia,* one of the solo instruments in "Possente spirto." The double harp was considered very modern indeed; a number of instruments are in fact called arpa doppia: what they have in common is a second set of strings set at an angle so as to intersect the main strings at only one point, so that additional notes, usually sharps and flats, can be easily added without retuning the instrument.

The noble Roman amateur Vincenzo Giustiniani might almost be describing the *Orfeo* solo when he describes the "difficult trill," which is certainly a feature (along with the use of sharps and flats characteristic of parts for the double harp) of the Orfeo solo.

The name of Lucrezia Urbana, a singer and harpist from Naples (home of the double harp), appears in Mantuan payment records from 1603 to 1605 (those from the years immediately following have apparently not survived); it is easy to imagine her playing the solo (virtually the only surviving harp solo from the period) especially written for her and showing off the trill that she could play perhaps as well as any Horatio Mihi. One wonders whether the duke's reluctance with regard to female singers applied also to those in the orchestra.

Among the instrumentalists at Mantua were the Rubini brothers, Giovanni Battista and Orazio, who had been playing violin at the ducal court since 1597 (presumably in company with Monteverdi himself) and who perhaps also played the theorbo (an expanded lute); and Monteverdi's friend and pupil Giulio Cesare Bianchi, a virtuoso cornettist. Harp, violin, cornetto—these are the solo instruments Monteverdi uses in the "Possente spirto" of act 3.

But the chief instruments in *Orfeo* are those that accompany the singers, which together provide the continuous background harmonies that allow the actors to recite their parts in the classical tradition. These chord-playing instruments—lutes, harpsichords, organ, regal—are used in various combinations: organ and chittarrone (a large, long-necked, wire-strung lute), harpsichord and lute, solo regal (a buzzy reed organ used for underworld characters). One can tell from the places where Monteverdi specifies the accompanying instruments that his intention is not to identify a specific sound with specific characters (except for the infernal regal) but to vary the combination of accompanying instruments for color, especially for changes of mood and passion. These instruments play the *basso continuo,* the bass-line melody provided with all singing parts; they play appropriate chords using the bass line and the singer's part as guides. Although they are occasionally given further clues by figures and other signs in their parts, essentially they are improvising a flexible and expressive supporting part for the singers.

Some theaters of the time arranged musicians on both sides of the stage, not in front, so as not to block sight lines. Other theaters had a sort of musicians' gallery behind or to the side of the scene itself. In *Orfeo,* however, instrumental music is played from at least three locations: in front of the acting area (considered normal now, this position in relation to the players was unusual at the time); from the front corners of the stage (at one point in act 5); and behind the stage—what Shakespeare calls "within" and Monteverdi calls "dentro." At the beginning of act 2 Orfeo arrives from offstage, announcing himself by singing "Ecco pur ch'io voi ritorno." This is preceded by a ritornello played from within. Subsequent ritornelli also played from within reveal the presence of two harpsichords, three chitarroni, two recorders, and six of the twelve string players. There are two bands of strings, which is why Monteverdi specifies twelve players. He chooses this number not with the intent that the ensemble resemble a modern orchestra with many players but so that each part can be played by a single player and the spatial effects of sound coming from many places can be achieved without moving musicians around.

An Italian Archlute by Magnus
Tieffenbrucker, Venice, ca. 1600

In the score of *Orfeo,* Monteverdi calls
for "chittarroni," which, like archlutes,
are large lutes with extra bass strings and
an extended pegbox to accommodate
them. The instrument was perfect for
playing discreet and sensitive continuo
accompaniments for singers.

The performance began when the lights were lowered, the candles behind the stage were lit, and the audience was in place. The court trumpeter Giovanni Srofenaur led a threefold playing of a trumpet fanfare before the curtain went up. The first called the audience to attention: the second announced the arrival of the duke; and the third signaled the beginning of the play.

Trumpeters usually kept their music to themselves; if Monteverdi writes out this toccata (the English word *tucket* also means a flourish of trumpets), it is not for the trumpeters to read—they know the music by heart—but for the other musicians, who for once must play at the same time as the ducal trumpets. This toccata is surely the standard fanfare for the duke of Mantua: Monteverdi used the same music to open his Vespers of 1610, again writing out the music because it was to be played by someone other than trumpeters. As a result, we have a rare glimpse into the trumpeter's art. Not that he was so poor in invention that he needed to use the same music twice. It was simply that no other music would do for an event attended by the duke.

As a description of another entertainment indicates, trumpets were a normal starting signal: "When the candelabra were lit inside the theatre, the usual signal of the sounding of the trumpets was given from inside the stage, and when it started to sound the third time, the great curtain which covered the stage disappeared in the twinkling

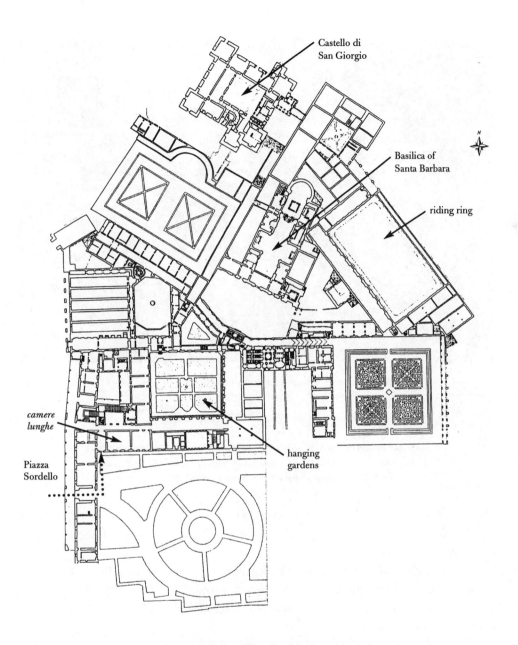

Castello di
San Giorgio

Basilica of
Santa Barbara

riding ring

*camere
lunghe*

Piazza
Sordello

hanging
gardens

Floor Plan of the Ducal Palace (detail)

This plan shows the location of the *camere lunghe,* where *Orfeo* was first
performed. From the Piazza Sordello, spectators came into the courtyard,
turned left, and entered the ground floor of the palace; just inside this
entrance was the room that had been fitted out as a temporary theater for
the performance of *Orfeo*. The palace included hanging gardens; the
medieval castello di San Giorgio; the basilica of Santa Barbara; and the
cortile della cavallerizza, or riding ring.

Theater Setting Similar to One Made for *The Triumph of Honor*
in Mantua, 1608

This engraving may give some idea of how a pastoral setting was arranged.
The rocks and trees painted on side panels and the mountains on a back
curtain probably required only a few modifications to become the rocks and
mountains of the underworld setting. The back curtain for *Orfeo* may have
included a temple, since act 1 includes a procession to a temple.

of an eye, with such speed that even as it was being raised there were few who perceived
how it disappeared. So it was that with the sight of the stage revealed to the audience,
one started to see . . ."

Just what *did* one start to see? In the theater one expects to *witness* something:
drama, illusion, another reality. An opera is not a concert, and although the performance of a fable in music was a new idea, the theatrical setting added to the excitement
of the Mantuan audience.

As for the look of the performance, the stage, and the setting, we can deduce
a surprising amount of information, even though we unfortunately have no pictures. We
know, both from the dedication in the 1609 score ("Sopra angusta scena") and from
Carlo Magni's remark ("unless I am prevented from getting in by lack of space") that
the hall was small and narrow. There was some sort of platform for a stage, at the corners of which the continuo players took their places for Orfeo's monologue and its echo
in act 5. There is a curtain at the back, behind which a noise is made just before Orfeo
turns around at the critical moment of act 4: this curtain is also what conceals those mu-

sicians who play from "within." There is also a curtain at the front, which is raised after the opening toccata.

The Prologue, Musica, appears and sets the scene for the acts to follow. After a charming ritornello, she sings the first of five strophes that alternate with versions of the instrumental ritornello. In these verses she greets the distinguished audience and introduces herself as the art that inflames noble hearts with passion and desire; requesting that we be silent for the story of Orpheus, she describes the setting. "While I sing of Orfeo," she says, "let no bird make any noise among these branches; nor any waves sound from these stream-banks." This is the same setting as that at the end of the fable; it is described further by Orfeo when he is unwillingly returned to it from the underworld: the fields, trees, and streams of Thrace, the scene of his former happiness, set amid mountains and rocks that had wept at the loss of Euridice.

Into this fairly normal arcadian setting comes a nymph, who invites her choral companions to join her in celebrating Orfeo's love for Euridice. On they come, singing and dancing. Monteverdi provides us with an engaging sequence of choruses, duets, trios, all interspersed with lively instrumental ritornelli. Orpheus himself appears, and his first words are a hymn of thanks to his father, Apollo, the sun ("Rose of the heaven, life of the world"). A beautiful, if short and public, exchange of loving words between Orpheus and Euridice precedes a solemn procession to the temple no doubt visible at a distance—perhaps to solemnize their marriage. A choral ode of beautiful ensembles and instrumental interludes concludes the first act.

Orfeo returns, now alone, and sings to the assembled company a lively song of five verses in praise of Euridice; just as he finishes and is invited to sing again, the nymph Silvia suddenly interrupts ("Ahi! Caso acerbo!"—Ah! Dreadful news!). She has come to report that Euridice is dead, poisoned by a serpent. Here Monteverdi makes a shocking change in the music. Whereas before all has been melody, song, and dance, the messenger now sings in the declamatory style called recitativo, delivering her awful news in a lurching, angular music that sounds like sobs and that makes her sound impulsive and horrified. This new declamatory musical element, used in places of heightened emotion, reaches a peak when the dumbstruck Orfeo finally speaks, delivering one of the most passionate, and musically expressive, laments ever created by Monteverdi, or anyone else. Full of rhetorical questions and poetical contrasts ("Tu se' morta, ed io respiro?"— You are dead, and I breathe?), the musical structure parallels that of the rhetoric, but the details of expressive intervals, changing speech rhythms, and bitter harmonies heighten Orfeo's grief and give it an unforgettable plangency. At the height of his misery and rage, he resolves to go where no human has gone, to rescue Euridice or die. A beautiful choral ode on the lament of Euridice closes the act and gives us the opportunity of hearing some of Monteverdi's most moving musical lamentations.

At this point the setting changes. Such alterations were easily accomplished with sliding panels, some painted with trees, others with rocks; the curtain at the back

Antonio Maria Viani, *Saint Ursula and Saint Margaret
in Glory with the Trinity*

Viani was the Prefect of the Ducal Fabric at the time of *Orfeo*'s production and
would likely have been involved in the construction of the theater and the set
decorations (perhaps in collaboration with the engineer Gabriele Bertazzoli?).
He is known to have constructed a theater at Mantua in 1608. Viani was also an
architect and painter, and many of the decorations of the ducal palace in this
period are attributed to him. This painting, executed for the Mantuan Church
of Saint Ursula in 1618, may suggest the style used for the sets of *Orfeo*.

might well have been a painted backdrop. (There is no mention of its changing, so perhaps it fit both settings—a distant background of rocks and caverns.) A means must be
found to simulate a boat crossing a river and a cavern from which Pluto, Proserpina,
and finally Euridice can emerge. All these are more or less standard settings—they
might have already existed at Mantua from other productions: plenty of people remembered the performance of the Arcadian *Faithful Shepherd*.

The set designer was probably Antonio Maria Viani, the painter and architect
who was noted for his stage designs; experts had come from Milan to study his ma-

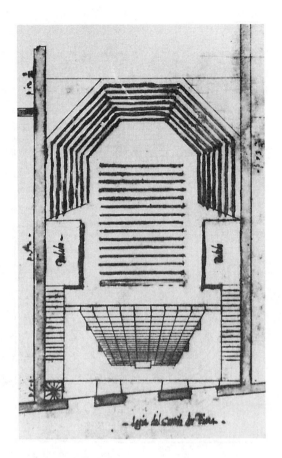

A Theater Arranged in a Palace in Ferrara, 1565

Designed by the Mantuan engineer Gabriele Bertazzoli, this temporary palace theater has risers in a polygonal arrangement, which was simpler to build than a semicircle, with seating in the center as well. At the side of the stage are what appear to be boxes for instrumentalists. In *Orfeo* the instrumentalists, or at least some of them, were probably in the middle, as in a modern theater.

chines for the 1598 production of *The Faithful Shepherd.* He was no doubt already at work on the theater that was to open the following year, and he was later the set designer for Monteverdi's *Arianna.* Although *Orfeo* was not strictly a ducal performance, the importance of Francesco Gonzaga as patron of the academy and the duke's interest in the theater would have assured Viani's participation: it certainly engaged Monteverdi's. A small set, in a small room, using more or less standard materials, ought not to have been too difficult.

We have no drawings of Viani's theatrical work (though we do have a good sample of his painting), but we can imagine the physical arrangement of the temporary theater for *Orfeo* from the shapes of other theaters set up in rooms: a temporary theater constructed in a room in Ferrara in 1565; and the theater built for the Accademia degli Intrepidi in Ferrara, designed in 1604–5 by Giovanni Battista Aleotti for a learned academy that wanted to do plays in imitation of the Mantuans! Monteverdi had actually dedicated his fourth book of madrigals to the Accademia degli Intrepidi; perhaps there is a stronger connection here than we know.

These designs give some idea of the possible layout for *Orfeo.* Both theaters feature a perspective stage, seating for the audience on semicircular or polygonal risers (we know that the Mantuan theater of 1549 also had semicircular risers), though this might require more effort than the purely temporary theater for *Orfeo* merited. One theater has room at the front to place a group of instruments; the other seems to have platforms at the sides. In both there seem to be some indications of *telai,* the sliding panels of painted scenery that allow instantaneous set changes.

Ground Plan of a Theater Designed by G. B. Aleotti for the Accademia degli Intrepidi in Ferrara, 1605

This theater, designed for a learned academy at a princely court, may give us an idea of what the theater in which *Orfeo* was performed looked like. Note the deep perspective of the stage (as indicated by the narrowing grid lines) and the semicircular auditorium with a central open space. A set was apparently composed of a series of panels at each side, which, together with a curtain at the back, presented the impression of a continuous background. The *Orfeo* theater was probably similar but not as elaborate.

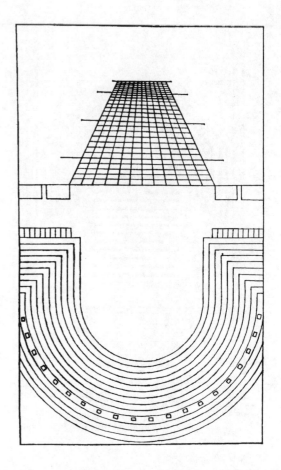

Act 3 opens to the sound of trombones, cornetti, and regals, and the scene changes to the realm of death. The new vista is described for us by Orfeo's guide, the personification of Hope. It is dark here (says Orfeo), but Speranza points out the black swamp, the river bank, and the oarsman Caronte, who carries departed spirits to the other shore, where Pluto reigns. The stone entrance bears the motto borrowed from Dante: "Abandon all hope, ye who enter," and so Speranza of course cannot enter. There is a boat in which Orfeo will ultimately cross; and since no change of setting is mentioned, it seems that the act of crossing the river gets Orfeo to Pluto's kingdom, which is already on stage. It consists of horrible caverns, which perhaps are revealed—by a revolving mountain?—during the chorus that separates acts 3 and 4.

Orfeo is stopped by Caronte who, accompanied by a regal, says that he is forbidden to carry living mortals over the river to the land of the dead. Orfeo prepares to use his unparalleled skill in singing to entreat the fearsome Caronte, and it is natural that he should first invoke Apollo, both as his father and as the power of music, before he launches his virtuoso appeal. This invocation takes the form of a little sinfonia, whose meaning can be understood only partly at that point—though it becomes gradually clearer.

Orfeo then sings the central piece of music in the play, "Possente spirto," the only one that is accompanied by melody instruments: solo violins played by the Rubini brothers; two cornetti, one played by Giulio Cesare Bianchi; the double harp played by Lucrezia Urbana; and then a quartet of strings. Each in turn provides dazzling

A Page from the 1609 Score of *Orfeo*

In this famous solo in 3 of *Orfeo*, Orfeo directs his virtuosity at
Caronte, the boatman who prevents the living from entering the realm of
the departed. The direction at the top reads: "Orfeo, to the sound
of the organ, and a chitarrone, sings one only of the two parts," the one
place in *Orfeo* where melody instruments are heard with solo voices.
Monteverdi provided two versions: one simple (so that it could be
interpreted with passion, or could serve as the basis for improvisation?)
and one highly ornate (conquering with virtuosity rather than with
passion, or representing what Francesco Rasi actually sang in 1607?).

Stage Setting by Francesco Guitti, Showing the Underworld, 1632

Although this engraving is not from *Orfeo*, it may give some idea of what the
stage was meant to look like. The chariot of Proserpina appears in the
foreground; in the background is the flaming entrance of a cave—the mouth of
the underworld. *Orfeo* may have had a similar set in acts 3 and 4, in which
Pluto and Proserpina (and later Euridice) appear after Orfeo crosses the river
Styx and approaches Pluto's realm. Clouds, rocks, and other effects at the
sides suggest a series of parallel painted panels.

interludes during and between the five strophes. It is a passionate and persuasive piece
of music, the centerpiece of the central act and therefore of the whole opera.

Curiously, we don't quite know what Rasi sang here. Monteverdi's score provides two parallel vocal versions for this famous song: one is extremely simple, the
other a marvel of florid virtuosity. The score provides this note: "Orfeo, to the sound
of the organ, and a chitarrone, sings one only of the two parts."

So this place in the score is not a record of a single performance. Many choose to
see the two parts as (1) the basic melodic structure or (2) one way of embellishing it (or
even as Francesco Rasi's way of embellishing it on a single occasion; or again, as Monteverdi's recommended way of embellishing it, for those who are able to sing such difficult music). Others, notably Nino Pirrotta, have suggested that the two versions might be
an expression of two powers of music, the two ways an Orpheus might use his talent: the
dazzlingly technical, designed to stun Caronte, and the intimately passionate, the simply
emotional, designed to strike to the heart. Only one version could have been sung at the

first performance (or any other performance), so the score is to some degree prescriptive as well as descriptive. I cannot imagine that Rasi did not sing a highly embellished version, given his ability to interpret challenging music. Monteverdi's elaboration is stunning in its difficulty and sets this important moment apart from anything else in the play.

Orfeo is a good singer, but not good enough. Although Caronte is moved by the music, he is still unwilling to let Orfeo pass. Only when Orfeo has failed does a higher power intervene: the (Apollo-)sinfonia, used earlier as an invocation, is heard again, played pianissimo by strings and organ. By the time it is over, Caronte has fallen asleep, and Orfeo slips past. Magic has happened, just as it did once before, during the same sinfonia. Even if we do not know precisely what or who caused the magic, at least we will recognize the tune and its supernatural power if it returns.

A chorus of infernal spirits praises the endurance of humankind. These are not the infernal spirits of the Christian hell, who torment lost souls: they are the chorus, the inhabitants of the world of the departed, who do Pluto's bidding but who nevertheless recognize a hero when they see one.

Proserpina and Pluto are revealed. Proserpina, admiring Orfeo's love, reminds Pluto of his passion for her and urges him to let Euridice go. Pluto, who with Proserpina represents a world in which passion overrules everything else, agrees to release her, on one condition—and we, the audience, know what it is. Orfeo is overjoyed: he sings his happiest song, to the accompaniment of violins of the upper world, and starts upward. But he has doubts, which he expresses in halting and nervous recitative; when a loud noise is made behind the curtain, he can no longer resist and turns around: there she is ("Eyes of my beloved, at last I see you!"). Euridice sings a brief and incredibly wrenching farewell ("Ah, vision too sweet, and too bitter") as she is drawn downward, while Orfeo is thrust upward to the "hateful light." The chorus makes its Neoplatonic point clear:

> Orfeo conquered the Inferno, and was then conquered
> by his passions;
> worthy of eternal glory
> should be only he who conquers himself.

The set changes back to the upper world, while the strings play the instrumental refrain with which the opera opened and which marked the end of the upper-world scene at the end of act 2. We are back where we began, but with a huge difference. Orfeo is alone: there are no nymphs and shepherds, no singing and dancing, above all no Euridice. Orfeo delivers a long dramatic monologue, which includes the musical and poetic trick of hearing and conversing with his own echo. He laments his bitter fate; he sings the praises of the beautiful lost Euridice; and he goes a little mad: compared to Euridice, all other women are nothing—full of charm but lying and deceitful. He will have nothing further to do with any woman.

Seventeenth-Century Stage Machinery

Nicola Sabbatini's highly influential *Pratica di fabricar scene, e machine ne' teatri* (1637) contains many illustrations on the construction of theatrical scenery and machines. Here he shows how to make a flying machine supported from the side for use in a theater with a low ceiling—perfect for the arrival of Apollo at the end of *Orfeo*.

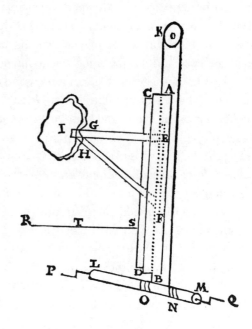

Here an amazing thing happens. If we are following along in the word-book provided to the audience, we have not only admired the beauty and structure of the poetry but have occasionally glanced ahead to see what happens next. And in our word-book we note that at this point a band of frenzied women, worshipers of Bacchus, send Orfeo fleeing off-stage; a final choral scene performed by them will end the spectacle.

But instead, just at the point when the women should appear, a miracle! The little sinfonia that we heard in act 3 is played, and Apollo himself descends from heaven in a cloud! (If we did not realize what that otherworldly sinfonia represented when we heard it twice before, it is plain now: this is Apollo, god of the sun, father of Orfeo, representative not only of music but of balance in all things. And if ever Orfeo was unbalanced, it is now.) Apollo calms him, tells him that he will be with Euridice forever among the perpetual and unchanging harmonies of the stars, where his unruly passions will no longer trouble him; the two of them are raised to heaven as they sing a splendid duet. Nymphs and shepherds arrive to sing a chorus and to perform a final dance to the tune of an instrumental moresca.

The reader should note that there is a serious problem here: how do we know which version of the ending was performed, the Bacchic finale of the original myth and of the libretto or the intervention of Apollo, the deus ex machina in the score? Many scholars have thought about this, and I have chosen what I think is the correct answer (see more on my solution in the bibliographic note).

About ninety minutes after it began, the fable of *Orfeo* concludes, the curtain is lowered, and we are left to applaud and to reflect on the piece we have seen and heard.

The performance came off handsomely, to judge from the only report we have from a spectator—that being the proud godfather, the lucky star (as Monteverdi describes him

Sketch of a Shepherd's Costume, by Baccio del Bianco

This drawing was done for a spectacular entertainment called "The Wedding of the Gods," presented in Florence in 1634. The costume is elaborate but perhaps gives an idea of how an Arcadian shepherd in *Orfeo* might have appeared.

in his dedication), Francesco Gonzaga, again writing to his brother: "The play was performed to the great satisfaction of all who heard it. The Lord Duke, not content to have been present at this performance, or to have heard it many times in rehearsal, has ordered it to be given again; and so it will be, today [March 1], in the presence of all the ladies resident in the city. For this reason Giovanni Gualberto is to remain here at present; he has done very well, and given immense pleasure to all who have heard him sing, especially to My Lady."

"To the great satisfaction of all who heard it": modern listeners may have difficulty imagining what the nature of that satisfaction was. Not that it was lacking in the satisfaction we feel today on hearing *Orfeo*. We are moved by the ageless story; we know how Orfeo feels. Even more, perhaps, we are "satisfied" with Monteverdi's music: the charming songs with their delightful instrumental interludes, each catchier than the preceding. We are moved by the expression he builds into the dramatic moments: the announcement of Euridice's death, the moment when Orfeo decides to look back only to hear Euridice's voice for the last time. We are impressed by the grand choruses that serve as pillars between the acts.

But we can't help wondering what a member of the Accademia degli Invaghiti or a noble of the Mantuan court or Duke Vincenzo himself thought and felt. Our unique experiences and values shape our appreciation; their experiences and values no doubt differed vastly from ours.

Here is a familiar tale, but with a particular slant. Although it is based on classical mythology, on pastoral convention, it is really a tale of letting the passions run away with the intellect. In a way Apollo, god of music but also of balance, is central to the plot. He twice intervenes for Orpheus: first when he gets him into the underworld, and again when he rescues him upon his return to earth. The lower world is that of the

A Performance of *Orfeo* at the Boston Early Music Festival, 1993

Caronte, the oarsman who ferries the dead to the underworld, refuses to carry
Orfeo. In his impassioned "Possente spirto," Orfeo pleads his case. His
costume here is not unlike the one sketched by Baccio del Bianco (p. 49).

passions; the celestial sphere of Apollo is that of reason and balance; the land between
the two—where *we* live—is the place where the two interact. Our job is to keep the two
in equilibrium. There is a clear moral for us, which is pointed out more than once in
the poetry of the chorus.

Given the Christian society of Mantua—an enormous basilica is part of the palace—it was difficult not to see parallels between Orpheus and Christ. Orfeo goes to the land of the dead and returns; he prays to his father and is ultimately taken up into heaven. Such a parallel goes unspoken, but it is part of the intellectual humanistic movement that seeks to reevaluate the learning and the philosophy of the ancients and to reconcile them with the Christian morality of the present.

But if our interest is chiefly musical, the moments of sheer pleasure, where nymphs and shepherds sing and play music, must have given as much delight in 1607 as they do now. The charming instrumental interludes between verses of songs, which make such delightful shapes in the second act, would have seemed to the audience very like Monteverdi's *Scherzi musicali* (published that very year); and when Orfeo sings just such a song, with just such an instrumental refrain, in hell, we are painfully aware of what he is not: that the musical joke, the scherzo, is on him.

The audience, noticing the musical effects in certain songs, was reminded of the madrigals with which Monteverdi and numerous other contemporaries and predecessors had entertained them. In such a piece, a composer might make a little picture in music from a particular word or idea: for example, when the chorus sings "a gran salita il precipizio è presso" (in a great ascent, the precipice is nearby), Monteverdi can't resist giving a leap upward to each voice as it sings "salita" and a precipitous drop at "precipizio." An effect, like so many others, not lost on its hearers.

Mostly, the listeners would have marveled at the richness of the musical setting. They heard madrigals, choruses, scherzi musicali, dances, a variety of instrumental colors, virtuoso singing, and passionate music in the new and highly expressive recitative style. *Orfeo* had everything, though it was not a hodge-podge.

As the performance was taking place, the audience probably watched one another and the duke. One can imagine that they listened with enjoyment to the poetry and the music. And perhaps they thought that this was the most effective and moving, if not the most lavish, carnival entertainment they had enjoyed in many a year.

Although *Orfeo* was intended by Prince Francesco and the Accademia degli Invaghiti as an occasional piece, Monteverdi put all his skill and genius into it. In later years, the composer himself remembered *Orfeo* with pleasure. In 1616, after he had left Mantua, he wrote to a correspondent about a proposed libretto featuring personifications of the winds that evidently did not please him at all: "Ariadne moved us because she was a woman, and similarly Orpheus because he was a man, not a wind. . . . I do not feel that [the proposed story] carries me in a natural manner to an end that moves me. *Arianna* led me to a great lament, and *Orfeo* to a righteous prayer, but this fable leads me to I don't know what end."

Monteverdi was moved in composing *Orfeo*. And his contemporaries thought it beautiful, not just clever. Cherubino Ferrari, the Carmelite father who was Monteverdi's friend and the Mantuan court's theologian, wrote to Duke Vincenzo (document 13) that "[Monteverdi] has shown me the words and let me hear the music of the play which Your Highness had performed, and certainly both poet and musician have depicted the inclinations of the heart so skilfully that it could not have been done better. The poetry is lovely in conception, lovelier still in form, and loveliest of all in diction; and indeed no less was to be expected of a man as richly talented as Signor Striggio. The music, moreover, observing due propriety, serves the poetry so well that nothing more beautiful is to be heard anywhere."

In 1612 Francesco Gonzaga became duke of Mantua. For personal and economic reasons, he had fired Claudio Monteverdi (who had in any case been seeking his release). Francesco ruled during ten months of political and economic crisis; he died in the smallpox epidemic that also took the life of his son and heir and was succeeded by his brother, Ferdinando. Monteverdi was named to the prestigious post of Maestro di Cappella of Saint Mark's Basilica in Venice, where he produced sacred music for the basilica and operatic music for the city's theaters.

Documents: Monteverdi, *Orfeo*

Monteverdi's Dedication of the Score

1. *The dedicatory letter of the first edition (1609) of the score of* Orfeo:

Most serene lord my lord and most respected patron:

The fable of Orpheus which was once musically staged in the Academy of the Invaghiti under the auspices of your highness on a narrow stage, and now being about to appear in the great Theatre of the universe to show itself to all men, is no reason for it to appear signed with any other name than the glorious and happy name of Your Highness. To you I therefore humbly consecrate it, so that you who were propitious at its birth in the guise of a lucky star, with the most serene rays of your grace, may deign to favor the progress of its life, which I dare to hope, thanks to Your Highness, may be equally as durable as humankind. I beg Your Highness to accept this token of my devotion, with that grandeur of spirit which is characteristic of you, and which links the souls of all those who happen to have dealings with you. And here, bowing with submissive reverence to Your Highness, I pray the Lord to grant your every desire. In Mantua, the 22nd of August, 1609.

> Your highness's
> Most humble and grateful servant,
> Claudio Monteverdi

[Claudio Monteverdi, *L'Orfeo* (Venice: Amadino, 1609; rpt., Florence: Studo per Edizioni Scelti, 1993), following title page; see p. 26]

Excerpts from Letters of Francesco and Ferdinando Gonzaga Relating to the Preparations for the Performance

[Documents 2–10 are printed in Iain Fenlon, "Correspondence Relating to the Early Mantuan Performances," trans. Stephen Botterill, in *Claudio Monteverdi, Orfeo,* ed. John Whenham, Cambridge Opera Handbooks (Cambridge: Cambridge University Press, 1986), 167–72.]

2. *Francesco Gonzaga, Mantua, January 5, 1607, to Ferdinando Gonzaga in Pisa:*

I have decided to have a play in music performed at Carnival this year, but as we have very few sopranos here, and those few not good, I should be grateful if Your Excellency would be kind enough to tell me if those castrati I heard when I was in Tuscany are still there. I mean the ones in the Grand Duke's service, whom I so much enjoyed hearing during my visit. My intention is to borrow one of them (whichever Your Excellency thinks the best), as long as you agree that the Grand Duke will not refuse to lend him, if you yourself do the asking, for a fortnight at most. Please will Your Excellency let me know about this, so that if I do decide to use one of these singers I can write to you asking for your support in my approach to the Grand Duke.

3. Ferdinando Gonzaga, Pisa, January 14, 1607,
to Francesco Gonzaga in Mantua:

In accordance with Your Highness's orders I have engaged a castrato, who is, in fact, not one of those whom Your Highness heard; but he has performed with great success in musical plays on two or three occasions. He is a pupil of Giulio Romano [Giulio Caccini] and receives a stipend from the Grand Duke.

4. Francesco Gonzaga, Mantua, January 17, 1607,
to Ferdinando Gonzaga in Pisa:

Enclosed with this you will find a letter for the Grand Duke, in which I ask him to be so kind as to lend me one of his castrati for the coming Carnival, so that I can use him in the performance of a musical play which is currently being composed in our Academy. I have already written to you about this. Because I hope that His Highness will be good enough not to refuse my request, and in order not to waste time waiting for your reply, I am sending you the said castrato's part, so that he can study it and learn it thoroughly, should the Grand Duke lend him to me. He should be able to set out at the beginning of next month; on this occasion I must ask Your Excellency to give him some money to cover the expenses of his journey, which I will repay by being of service to you here in any way that I can.

5. Francesco Gonzaga, Mantua, February 2, 1607,
to Ferdinando Gonzaga in Pisa:

By the time Your Excellency receives this, my much-needed castrato will have arrived here, or will at least be on his way. . . . Without this soprano it would be quite impossible to stage [the play] at all.

6. Ferdinando Gonzaga, Pisa, February 5, 1607,
to Francesco Gonzaga in Mantua:

This is to introduce Giovanni Gualberto, a young castrato whom I am sending to your Highness to take part in the performance of your play. You will hear from his own lips of the difficulty he has had in learning the part which was given him; so far he has managed to commit only the prologue to memory, the rest proving impossible because it contains too many notes [troppo voci].

7. Francesco Gonzaga, Mantua, February 9, 1607, to Ferdinando Gonzaga in Pisa:

I had expected that the castrato would have arrived by now, and indeed it is essential that he should be here as soon as possible. He will now have not only to play the part that was sent to him, but also to learn that of Proserpine, as the singer who was to take the role can no longer do so. So I am awaiting him from day to day with great eagerness, as without him the play would be a complete failure. Meanwhile, I must ask Your Excellency to thank the Grand Duke for the kindness he has shown me; I will thank him myself by letter when the castrato returns to you.

8. Francesco Gonzaga, Mantua, February 16, 1607, to Ferdinando Gonzaga in Pisa:

The castrato arrived yesterday. . . . He knows only the prologue, and seems to think that he will not have time to learn the other part before the Carnival; in which case I shall have no choice but to postpone the performance of the play until Easter. This morning, however, he began to study not only the music, but the words as well; and if he were able to learn the part (although it does contain too many notes [troppo voci], as Your Excellency says), he would at least know the melody, the music could be altered to suit his needs, and we would not waste so much time ensuring that he knows it all by heart.

9. Francesco Gonzaga, Mantua, February 23, 1607, to Ferdinando Gonzaga in Pisa:

The musical play is to be performed in our Academy tomorrow, since Giovanni Gualberto has done very well in the short time he has been here. Not only has he thoroughly learned the whole of his part, he delivers it with much grace and a most pleasing effect; I am delighted with him. The play has been printed so that everyone in the audience can have a copy to follow while the performance is in progress; I am sending Your Excellency a copy, and I shall let you have, by another messenger, some notices just published about a tournament which may take place on Carnival day.

10. Francesco Gonzaga, Mantua, March 1, 1607, to Ferdinando Gonzaga in Pisa:

The play was performed to the great satisfaction of all who heard it. The Lord Duke, not content to have been present at this performance, or to have heard it many times in rehearsal, has ordered it to be given again; and so it will be, today, in the presence of all the ladies resident in the city. For this reason Giovanni Gualberto is to remain here at present; he has done very well, and given immense pleasure to all who have heard him sing, especially to My Lady.

Other Letters

11. Giovanni Striggio to his brother Alessandro Striggio, February 17, 1607:

Having recounted as well as I know how the fable of Orfeo, your excellency's own work, to my wife, I have such a powerful desire to see it performed that I could not deny her such a just request to hear it, both because it is your honor's creation, and because it is a new thing, and never heard by her with this kind of singing. We have thus arranged a means of transport, since signor Vivaldino, so as not to toil without the presence of his wife, has found a boat for her and is taking her to Mantua, next Monday, and I have resolved to come myself, both for the company and on account of the small cost of the trip, with my wife to enjoy these few days of Carnival in the city.

[Mantova, STATE Archive, Gonzaga Archive 2706, transcribed in Susan Parisi, "Ducal Patronage of Music in Mantua, 1587–1627: An Archival Study," Ph.D. diss. 2 vols., University of Illinois at Urbana-Champaign, 1989, 1:189]

12. *Carlo Magno, Mantua, February 23, 1607, to his brother Giovanni in Rome:*

Tomorrow evening the Most Serene Lord the Prince is to sponsor a [play] in the main room in the apartments which the Most Serene Lady of Ferrara had the use of [nella sala del partimento che godeva Mad.ma Ser.ma di Ferrara]. It should be most unusual, as all the actors are to sing their parts; it is said on all sides that it will be a great success. No doubt I shall be driven to attend out of sheer curiosity, unless I am prevented from getting in by the lack of space [l'angustia del luogo].

[Fenlon, "Correspondence," in Whenham, *Orfeo,* 170]

13. *Cherubino Ferrari, Milan, August 22, 1607, to Duke Vincenzo Gonzaga in Mantua:*

Monteverdi is here in Milan, staying with me; and every day we talk about Your Highness and vie with one another in paying tribute to your virtues, your goodness and your royal manners. He has shown me the words and let me hear the music of the play which Your Highness had performed, and certainly both poet and musician have depicted the inclinations of the heart so skilfully that it could not have been done better. The poetry is lovely in conception, lovelier still in form, and loveliest of all in diction; and indeed no less was to be expected of a man as richly talented as Signor Striggio. The music, moreover, observing due propriety, serves the poetry so well that nothing more beautiful is to be heard anywhere.

[Fenlon, "Correspondence," in Whenham, *Orfeo,* 172]

14. *The Mantuan anthologist Eugenio Cagnani's 1612 printed collection included this mention in the chronology:*

However, it should not surprise anyone, since it is in the nature of the signori Academicians of the Invaghiti to do wondrous works at all times, as more recently did the most illustrious signor count Alessandro Striggio already mentioned, in defending the various conclusions of love, which can still be seen in print, with such facility and richness that everyone was full of amazement, he himself having published, under the name of the "Reserved Academician Invaghito," *l'Orfeo,* a fable to be acted, composed in the most graceful verses of Tuscan speech, which, set to music by the virtuous signor Claudio Monteverdi, was acted in a large theatre with the most noble apparatus, and singing in it that signor Francesco Rasio, so famous for his excellence in his profession that everyone agrees that there are few in the world who can excel him.

[Eugenio Cagnani, *Raccolta d'alcvne rime di scrittori mantovani fatta per Evgenio*

Cagnani. Con vna lettera cronologica & altre prose, & rime dello stesso ... (Mantua: Osanni, 1612); trans. in Warren Kirkendale, "Zur Biographie des ersten Orfeo, Francesco Rasi," in *Claudio Monteverdi: Festschrift Reinhold Hammerstein zum 70. Geburtstag*, ed. Ludwig Finscher, 305–6]

Instruments in the Score

15. Instrumental indications in the 1609 score of Monteverdi's Orfeo:

[Spellings and punctuation are as in the original; italics indicate vocal accompaniments; numbers have been added for reference.]

1. Toccata che si suona avanti il levar de la tela tre volte con tutti li stromenti, & si fa un tuono più alto volendo sonar le trombe con le sordine.

1. Toccata which is played before the raising of the curtain three times with all the instruments, and it is done a tone higher wishing to play the trumpets with mutes.

2. Questo canto fu concertato al suono de tutti gli stromenti.

2. This song was performed to the sound of all the instruments.

3. Questo Balletto fu cantato al suono di cinque Viole da braccio, tre Chittaroni, duoi Clavicembani, un'Arpa doppia, un contrabasso da Viola, & un flautino alla vigesima seconda.

3. This Balletto was sung to the sound of five *viole da braccio,* three chitarroni, two harpsichords, a double harp, a double bass, and a little flute [recorder] at the twenty-second.

4. Questo ritornello fu suonato di dentro da un Clavicembano, duoi Chitaroni, & duoi Violini piccioli alla Francese.

4. This ritornello was played from within by a harpsichord, two chitarroni, and two little French-style violins.

5. Questo Ritornello fu sonato da duoi Violini ordinarij da braccio, un Basso de Viola da braccio, un Clavicembano, & duoi Chittaroni.

5. This ritornello was played by two ordinary violins, a bass violin, a harpsichord, and two chitarroni.

6. *Due Pastori. Un Clavicembano & un Chittarone.*

6. *Two shepherds. A harpsichord and a chitarrone.*

7. Fu sonato di dentro da duoi Chitaroni un Clavicembano, & duoi flautini.

7. This was played from within by two chitarroni, a harpsichord, and two little recorders.

8. Fu sonato questo Ritornello di dentro da cinque Viole da braccio, Un contrabasso, duoi Clavicembani & tre chitarroni.

8. This ritornello was played from within by five *viole da braccio* [a choir of violin-style strings], a double bass, two harpsichords, and three chitarroni.

9. *Messagiera. Un organo di legno & un Chit.*

9. *Messenger. An organ and a chit[arrone].*

10. *[Pastore] Un clavic. Chitar. & Viola da bracio.*

10. *[Shepherd] A harpsichord, chitarrone and viola da braccio [cello].*

11. *Orfeo. Un organo di legno & un Chitarone.*

11. *Orfeo. An organ and a chittarone.*

12. *CHORO. Duoi Pastori cantano al suono del Organo di legno & un Chitarone.*

13. *Qui entrano li Tromb. Corn. & Regali, & taciono le Viole da bracio, & Organi di legno Clavacem. & si muta la Sena.*

14. *Caronte canta al suono del Regale.*

15. *Orfeo al suono dell'Organo di legno, & un Chitarone, canta una sola delle due parti.*

[labels in successive strophes of "Possente spirto":]

> Violino/Violino
> Duoi Cornetti
> Arpa dopia/Arpa dopia
> Violino/Violino/Basso da brazzo

16. Furno sonate le altre parti da tre Viole da Braccio, & un contrabasso de Viola tocchi pian piano.

17. Questo Sinfo. si sonò pian piano, con Viole da braccio, un Org. di leg. & un contrabasso de Viola da gamba.

18. *Orfeo canta al suono del Organo di legno solamente.*

19. *Qui entra nella barca e passa cantando al suono del Organo di legno.*

20. Coro de spirti, al suono di un Reg. Org. di legno, cinque Tromb. duoi Bassi da gamba, & un contrabasso de viola.

21. Ritornello. Violino/Violino.

22. *Qui si fa strepita dietro la tela. Segue Orfeo cantando nel Clavicembano Viola da bracio, & Chittarone*

23. *Qui si volta Orfeo, & canta al suono del Organo di legno.*

24. *Qui canta Orfeo al suono del Clavic.* Viola da braccio basso, & un Chitar.

12. *CHORUS. Two shepherds sing to the sound of the organ and a chitarrone.*

13. Here enter the trombones, cornetti, and regals, and the violins, organs, and harpsichords are silent, and the scene changes.

14. *Caronte sings to the sound of the regal.*

15. *Orfeo to the sound of the organ, and a chitarrone, sings one only of the two parts.*

> violin/violin
> two cornetti
> double harp/double harp
> violin/violin/bass violin

16. The other parts were sung by three *viole da braccio,* and a double bass, played very quietly.

17. This sinfonia was played very quietly, with *viole da braccio,* an organ, and a *contrabasso de Viola da gamba.*

18. *Orfeo sings to the sound of the organ only.*

19. *Here he enters into the boat and passes singing to the sound of the organ.*

20. Chorus of spirits, to the sound of the organ, five trombones, two bass gambas, and a *contrabasso de viola.*

21. Ritornello. Violin/Violin.

22. *Here a noise is made behind the curtain. Orfeo follows singing to the harpsichord, strings, and chitarrone.*

23. *Here Orfeo turns, and sings to the sound of the organ.*

24. *Here Orfeo sings to the sound of the harpsichord, bass viola da braccio [cello] and a chitarrone.*

25. Tacciono li Cornetti, Tromboni & Regali, & entrano a sonare il presente Ritornello, le viole da braccio, Organi, Clavicembani, contrabasso, & Arpe, & Chitaroni, & Ceteroni, & si muta la Sena.

26. Duoi Organi di legno, & duoi Chitaroni concertorno questo Canto, sonando l'uno del angolo sinistro de la Sena, l'altro nel destro.

25. The cornetti, trombones and regals fall silent, and there enter, to play this ritornello, the strings, organs, harpsichords, double bass, and harps, and chitarroni, and ceteroni, and the scene changes.

26. Two organs, and two chitarroni, performed this song, one playing at the left corner of the scene, and the other at the right.

George Frideric Handel, Messiah

"Han't you been at the Oratorio?" says one. "Oh, if you don't see the Oratorio you see nothing," says t'other; so away goes I to the Oratorio, where I saw indeed the finest assembly of People I ever beheld in my very Life, but to my great surprise, found this sacred Drama a mere Consort [i.e., concert], no scenery, Dress, or Action, so necessary to a Drama; but H-l was placed in a Pulpit (I suppose they call that their oratory). By him sat Senesino, Strada, Bertolli and Turner Robinson, in their own Habits. Before him stood sundry sweet singers of this our *Israel,* and Strada gave us a Hallelujah of Half an Hour long; Senesino and Bertolli made rare work with the *English* Tongue, you would have sworn it had been *Welsh.* I would have wished it had been *Italian* that they might have sung with more ease to themselves since, but for the name of *English* it might as well have been *Hebrew.*

—*See and Seem Blind: Or, a Critical Dissertation on the Publick D[i]versions,* 1732

By 1741 George Frideric Handel had been in London for almost thirty years. Like his earlier patron, the elector of Hanover, who became King George I, Handel never fully mastered the English language, though he was famous for his entertaining stories told in a mixture of German, French, Italian, and English. This linguistic diversity describes his cosmopolitan background: after spending his youth in Germany, studying composition in Italy, and learning the French of international communication, Handel settled in London and with the help of the fashionable elements of the nobility set himself up as a producer of opera. Italian serious opera was in style: opera sung in Italian by Italian singers and composed in Handel's best Italianate manner, but with a touch of that special extroverted genius that always sets his music apart. Opera is seldom a profitable business, and Handel's artistic successes did not always guarantee financial security. In recent years he had also turned his hand to the production of oratorios, grand dramatic pieces on religious subjects, which were cheaper to produce because one could use English singers and needed no scenery or costumes.

The opera season of 1740–41 had been disastrous for Handel, and he had growing doubts about his future as a producer of operas in London. He was therefore in a position to accept the invitation to Dublin offered by William Cavendish, third duke of Devonshire, lord lieutenant of Ireland, on behalf of three charitable organizations. Handel stayed nine months and produced a number of concerts, including his latest oratorio, *Messiah*, composed in the summer of 1741, which he brought with him.

The arrival of the "celebrated Dr. Handel" was announced in the Dublin papers: both the composer and his music were eagerly anticipated. Handel brought with him an organ, an enormous amount of music, and several musicians who were to work with him (Mr. and Mrs. Maclaine, organist and singer from Chester, and Signora Avolio, the Italian singer from Germany by way of London; the papers do not say that these collaborators arrived on the same boat). Handel lodged in a house in Abbey Street, near Liffey Street, and got to work as an impresario.

Handel announced a series of six concerts for December 1741 and another six for February 1742 (document 1; these did not include *Messiah*). The programs were essentially large-scale works for solo singers, chorus, and orchestra, with words in English. They included oratorios already tried out in London (*Esther, Saul*), settings of English poems (John Dryden's *Alexander's Feast,* Milton's *L'allegro ed il penseroso*), and the charming pastoral *Acis and Galatea;* at all his concerts Handel performed organ concertos of his own composition during the intermissions. The series was a success; not only were there crowds, making access to the music hall difficult, but tick-

George Frideric Handel, by Thomas Hudson

This portrait of Handel was done when he was sixty-four, six or seven years after the premiere of *Messiah*. Note the copy of *Messiah* under Handel's left arm. His white wig may be the one he used in oratorio: "Handel wore an enormous white wig, and, when things went well at the Oratorio, it had a certain nod, or vibration, which manifested his pleasure and satisfaction" (Charles Burney).

ets were impossible to get because the subscription had sold out. On January 30, Faulkner's *Dublin Journal* printed the following notice concerning the forthcoming performance of *Esther:* "It is humbly hoped that no Gentlemen or Ladies will take it ill, that none but subscribers can be admitted, and that no Single Tickets will be delivered, or Money taken at the Door."

The second series of concerts was announced (document 2) in terms that made clear this was an important occasion: "By the Desire of several Persons of Quality and Distinction there will be a new Subscription made for Mr. Handel's Musical Entertainments, for Six Nights more, on the same Footing as the last. No more than 150 Subscriptions will be taken in, and no Single Tickets sold, or any Money taken at the Door. Subscriptions will be taken in at Mr. Handel's House in Abby-street near Lyffee-street, on Monday next, being the 8th Day of February from 9 o'clock in the Morning till 3 in the Afternoon. The Performances are to continue once a Week, till the 6 Nights are over."

The second series was crowded as well: on February 13 the announcement of the upcoming performance of *Alexander's Feast* included the following: "N. B. For the conveniency of the ready emptying of the House, no Chairs will be admitted in waiting but hazard Chairs, at the new Passage in Copper Alley."

Dublin was aware of the exceptional quality of Handel's music, even though the city had a rich musical life of its own. But there had not yet been a piece performed especially for Dublin, a piece not yet presented in London. That would come in April, with Mr. Handel's New Sacred Oratorio, called *Messiah*.

Handel's House in London, by John Bucker, 1839

Handel's house, now 25 Brook Street, was his residence from 1723 until his
death in 1759. It was one of a group of four adjoining houses built in 1721–22.
It has been much altered and restored since Handel's day.

Handelian Oratorio

The great tradition of oratorio includes masterpieces by Elgar (1857–1934),
Mendelssohn (1809–47), Haydn (1732–1809), and other composers and stretches back
to Handel, though not much further. Compositions known as oratorio had existed
since the seventeenth century, but they were not much like those of Handel and his suc-
cessors. *Oratorio* is the Italian term for a place, an oratory, a place of prayer—and
specifically for a particular such place, the chapel of the Congregation of the Oratorio,
founded by Saint Philip Neri in Rome. The first large-scale musical-dramatic work performed in the oratorio at Rome was Emilio de' Cavalieri's *Rappresentazione di anima,*

e di corpo (*Representation of Soul and Body,* 1600), featuring the new recitative style familiar to us from Monteverdi's *Orfeo.* But the subsequent pieces called oratorio take place not in church but in the theater.

Generally speaking, an oratorio is a long piece of music both like an opera and unlike an opera. Oratorios are like operas in that they are entertainments intended for use in the theater and for a paying audience. They are dramatic and generally resemble operas of their time as to musical style. They tell their story in the same way that stories are told in the opera house: individual characters react to situations, provoke other situations, and act and react in a kind of music familiar to theatergoers. Like an opera, an oratorio traditionally begins with an overture and is divided into acts. Before performing *Messiah,* Handel had produced several oratorios on the London stage, including *Esther, Deborah, Athalia,* and *Saul,* which told in operatic style heroic stories of grand events from the Old Testament. Handel had devised his oratorios as a substitute for opera, to provide a familiar kind of musical entertainment—though on religious subjects—during the six-week Lenten season before Easter, when theaters were forbidden to produce operas and operagoers had no place to go for such music.

But oratorios, at least the sort with which Handel's Dublin audience was familiar, differ in many ways from operas. They are in English, not Italian. And they usually center on sacred subjects, like those just named. But oratorios are not for church: and they have no official place in the services of the Church of England (or any other church), and the words are not liturgical. The texts are often biblical stories, though usually in the narrative verse of opera librettos: for example, King Saul, jealous at David's triumph over Goliath, sings not a biblical text but an operatic one devised by Handel's librettist Charles Jennens:

> A serpent in my bosom warm'd
> would sting me to the heart;
> But of his venom soon disarm'd
> Himself shall feel the smart.
> Ambitious boy! Now learn what danger
> It is to rouse a monarch's anger!

Saul here throws his javelin at David, according to the wordbook, although no javelin actually moved in the performance. Oratorios were not acted out; they were performed by singers in street clothes in theaters without settings; the audience understood the action through the words of the singers, the effects of the music, and such hints as were printed in the spectator's helpful wordbook.

Handel's oratorios generally give a substantial role to the chorus. In opera, a chorus is a short song sung by a few characters on stage to bring the curtain down at the end of the act. In oratorio, however, the chorus often assumes a role like that of the chorus in classical tragedy (or like that in Monteverdi's *Orfeo*). Choral movements occur

William Hogarth, *The Oratorio Singer,* 1732

The satirist Hogarth here takes aim at an oratorio chorus. From the boys in
front to the elderly myopic gentlemen in the back, nobody seems to be paying
much attention to questions of ensemble. Note that two or three singers read
each part; a double-bass player is nearly swamped at the rear.

throughout the oratorio and are often the grandest pieces. The chorus may represent
characters in the plot (some of Handel's best choruses are sung by enemies: infidels,
Philistines, worshipers of Baal); most often they are the Israelites, the supporters of the
protagonist, who sing grand hymns of praise not only to God but also to the king and
the state. It was not difficult for Handel's audiences to see in the Old Testament stories
of triumphant kings an allegory of the glories of the Hanoverian monarchy and to understand a chorus like this one from *Athalia* in more than one sense:

> May God from whom all mercies spring
> Bless the true Church, and save the King!

Messiah is like Handel's other oratorios in many ways: it is divided into acts (or
parts), it has a variety of solo singers and chorus, and it uses the same musical style that

Handel used for his Italian operas. But in many ways it is not typical of Handelian oratorio, though we may know it so well that we measure the others by their deviation from *Messiah*.

Unlike most of Handel's other oratorios, *Messiah* does not have characters. Although in some sense it is the story of Christ, it is not at all like a Passion, in which an evangelist tells the story of Christ's crucifixion, and historical characters—Christ, Pilate, and so on—sing their parts. Indeed, this sort of characterization is carefully avoided in *Messiah*.

Its text is biblical and ecclesiastical, selected from the Old Testament—mostly prophetic texts—and from the Book of Common Prayer, the service book of the Church of England. This is unusual for Handel, whose other oratorios, even when on biblical subjects, tend to be set to versified texts like opera librettos. Whereas the biblical and liturgical texts are mellifluous, they are in prose and probably required a different sort of consideration on Handel's part when setting them to music: there are not necessarily balanced pairs of lines or rhyming couplets with which to make corresponding or contrasting phrases. Handel had used English biblical texts before—in the oratorio *Israel in Egypt,* in anthems, and elsewhere—so he already had some experience in these matters.

In addition to the internal features that set it apart, Handel seems to have had a special feeling for *Messiah*. From its inception, this composition may have been intended as a special work of charity. It was first performed at a charitable gathering in Dublin, which the newspapers noted was being given "for the relief of the prisoners in the several Gaols, and for the support of Mercer's Hospital in Stephen Street, and of the Charitable Infirmary on Inn's Quay." It was an extraordinary event: a special committee oversaw the financial arrangements, and the ticket selling was, for once, out of Handel's hands.

Handel was perhaps a bit worried about whether an audience would consider this appropriate subject matter for a paying entertainment. After his return from Dublin, Handel for a time avoided presenting *Messiah* in London, even though it had been a success in Dublin and even though he was now committed to oratorio. When he did present it, he avoided its name: he at first called it only "A New Sacred Oratorio" (1742) or "A Sacred Oratorio" (1745), and the name *Messiah* appeared in print in London only after 1749. Handel later produced annual charitable performances of *Messiah* at the Foundling Hospital in London, to which he also left a score and a set of parts, presumably so that the oratorio could continue its charitable benefits after his death. By the end of the century *Messiah* was seen as Handel's special humanitarian offering. As Charles Burney, the historian of music, wrote, "It has fed the hungry, clothed the naked, fostered the orphan, and enriched succeeding managers of Oratorios, more than any single musical production of this or any country."

Sir John Hawkins, another eminent eighteenth-century music historian, was

Charles Burney, the distinguished and indispensable eighteenth-century historian of music, tells an amusing but possibly apocryphal story about Handel's journey to Dublin:

When HANDEL went through Chester, in his way to Ireland, this year, 1741, I was at the Public-School in that city, and very well remember seeing him smoke a pipe, over a dish of coffee, at the Exchange-Coffee-house; for being extremely curious to see so extraordinary a man, I watched him narrowly as long as he remained in Chester; which, on account of the wind being unfavorable for his embarking at Parkgate, was several days. During this time, he applied to Mr. [Edmund] Baker, the Organist, my first music-master, to know whether there were any choirmen in the cathedral who could sing *at sight;* as he wished to prove some books that had been hastily transcribed, by trying the choruses which he intended to perform in Ireland. Mr. Baker mentioned some of the most likely singers then in Chester, and, among the rest, a printer of the name of Janson, who had a good base voice, and was one of the best musicians in the choir. . . . A time was fixed for this private rehearsal at the *Golden Falcon,* where Handel was quartered; but, alas! on trial of the chorus in the Messiah, *"And with his stripes we are healed,"*—poor Janson, after repeated attempts, failed so egregiously, that Handel let loose his great bear upon him; and after swearing in four or five languages, cried out in broken English: "You shcauntrel! tit not you dell me dat you could sing at soite?"—"Yes, sir, says the printer, and so I can; but not at *first sight.*"

not so concerned with charitable matters. He gives a no-nonsense description of the advantages that turned Handel to the production of oratorios (document 4):

> Other considerations suggested to him the almost certain benefit of such an undertaking: the performance of a sacred drama would consist with the solemnity of the Lent season, during which stage representations in this as in other Christian countries are in general forbidden; but above all, this served to recommend it, that it should be

conducted at a small expense: no costly scenery was required, nor dresses for the performers, other than a suit of black, with which all persons that appeared in public were supposed to be provided. Instead of airs that required the delicacy of Cuzzoni, or the volubility of Faustina to execute, he hoped to please by songs, the beauties whereof were within the comprehension of less fastidious hearers than in general frequent the opera, namely, such as were adapted to a tenor voice, from the natural firmness and inflexibility whereof little more is ever expected than an articulate utterance of the words, and a just expression of the melody. . . . He knew also, that he could attach to him the real lovers and judges of music by those original beauties, which he was able to display in the composition of fugue and chorus; and these being once gained, the taste of the town was likely to fall in, as it frequently does, with the opinion of those who are best qualified to give a direction to it. To such a performance the talents of a second-rate singer, and persons used to choir service were adequate.

Each oratorio, including this one, consists of a series of essentially separate compositions, creating a pleasing variety of emotional impressions. The three ingredients are the same in opera and oratorio: recitatives, songs, and choruses, with an occasional duet or trio. When heard in sequence the individual numbers create larger patterns of alternation, intensification, and narration. Whereas in opera the song (or aria) is the backbone of the musical interest, with choruses serving only to close an act, in *Messiah* the chorus takes on a more important role.

Eighteenth-century theatergoers understood and expected that each aria would be preceded by a recitative with a simple chordal accompaniment. It is in recitatives that operatic plots progress: conversations take place, someone reports an occurrence, a character reacts to an event; such scenarios create an emotional state to be commented on in the aria to follow. Thus the recitative, although it is sung, is understood as representing speech; it is usually performed—or at least concluded—by the character who will sing the aria that follows.

Handel follows this pattern for the most part in *Messiah,* but with some variations. For example, there are no characters, so that the recitative need not be a prelude to the aria. In addition, the recitative accompanied by orchestra rather than by continuo features prominently in *Messiah;* these numbers tend to be more passionate, more expressive, and more changeable than the ordinary recitative and sometimes, as in "Comfort ye my people," almost take on the dimensions of an aria.

Handel used the shape of the standard da capo aria of the opera house for only a few songs in *Messiah.* In such an aria, a second musical section, featuring some sort of contrast—mood, key, theme—precedes a literal repetition of the main part, allowing for the opening sentiment to be viewed a second time in the light of the contrasting sec-

First Page of Handel's Autograph Score of *Messiah*

Handel's copy of *Messiah* was begun ("Angefangen") on Saturday, August 22, 1741, and finished on September 14. It was therefore entirely composed before he went to Ireland and before he knew very much about the abilities of the singers he would find there. His writing is clear but hasty; note in the opening *Sinfony* Handel's tendency to group bars in pairs, a practice abandoned after a few bars. This manuscript, along with a copy made by his assistant, John Christopher Smith, was used in the first performance in Dublin.

tion and permitting, even demanding, vocal embellishments by the singer. Handel had written hundreds of da capo arias in his operas, but in *Messiah* he seeks a more concentrated form. Perhaps, too, he is expecting less flourish from the singers, who after all will probably not be opera stars. Remember Hawkins: "He hoped to please by songs, the beauties whereof were within the comprehension of less fastidious hearers than in general frequent the opera." The da capo arias in Messiah are among the major pieces of the oratorio: "He was despised"; "The trumpet shall sound"; "Rejoice greatly" (at least as it was originally composed, though Handel, perhaps even before the first performance, revised it greatly and reduced its length by about half).

The variety of ways in which Handel avoids the length but simulates the effect of the da capo aria—having the opening music and mood return after a contrasting section—is brilliant. Possibilities include having the chorus continue instead of returning to the beginning of the aria: this is what happens in "O thou that tellest good tidings" and in "Why do the nations," which moves directly into the chorus "Let us break their bonds asunder" (Handel may have first conceived the latter aria as a da capo, but he soon revised it).

Musical style in the arias, of course, is what distinguishes Handel from his lesser operatic contemporaries. These songs are inventive, varied, and characteristic, and they imprint themselves on the memory. Mostly they are arranged as duets between the singer and the instrumental group, who share the same melodies and develop them alternately or together. Occasionally, however, the aria has a characteristic accompaniment that is not taken up by the singer, such as the angry string figure of "Thou shalt break them" or the raging repeated notes of "Why do the nations."

The choruses are what give Handelian oratorio its particular flavor. They are grand, majestic, alive, and they often speak for the listener, making the audience feel like a participant in the drama. In other oratorios the chorus takes on roles—Israelites, worshipers of Baal, and the like. The nearest Handel comes to this in *Messiah* is "Glory to God," where the chorus repeats the message of the celestial angels, who fade away into heaven at the end. More often in *Messiah* the chorus's role is that of a Greek chorus, enlarging the commentary of a single voice into that of all humankind.

In terms of musical style there are three types of chorus. Fugues ("He trusted in God," "Amen," "And with his stripes") are contrapuntal movements in which a single melody, associated with the short text, begins in one voice and is imitated successively by others, the whole composition being essentially based on a single musical idea. Second are the wonderful choruses developed from chamber duets that Handel had recently been composing ("All we like sheep"; "For unto us"; "His yoke is easy"). These are astounding examples of transformation. A little duet whose text says "No, I don't want to trust you, blind Cupid!" is transformed into "For unto us a child is born" ("Cieco amor, crudel beltà" becomes "unto us"—pause—"a son is given"); Handel adds the magnificent tutti exclamation "Wonderful Counselor" which was not in the duet, and the result is a stunning chorus whose origin in an Italian love duet is hard to believe. The only thing that suggests the origin of these duet choruses is the fact that for most of their length only one or two choral parts sing at a time; they are versions of the voices of the original duet, and the lightness of texture in these choruses is one of the distinct pleasures of *Messiah*.

Then there are the choruses, usually the favorites, that are made from a series of characteristic utterances that succeed one another and are combined in various permutations: "Hallelujah," "And the glory," "Worthy is the lamb," and many more. In these, Handel uses each phrase of text to generate a new musical idea. Thus for anybody who knows the "Hallelujah" chorus, each line of text will immediately recall the musical idea that goes with it: (1) "Hallelujah!"; (2) "For the Lord God omnipotent reigneth"; (3) "The kingdom of this world is become the kingdom of our Lord and of his Christ"; (4) "And he shall reign for ever and ever"; (5) "King of Kings, and Lord of Lords." But in each chorus of this kind, Handel finds ways of combining the separate elements into polyphonic webs, using one phrase to accompany another or making ingenious combinations of three or more. In the "Hallelujah" chorus, as everybody knows, the opening "Hallelujah," with its characteristic rhythm and harmony, becomes a sort of refrain that recurs throughout. After Handel introduces "For the Lord God omnipotent reigneth," alternating it with interjections of "Hallelujah," he starts it again as a fugue and combines that melody with the "Hallelujah." At the end, the trumpetlike repetitions of "King of Kings" is accompanied by the repeated "Hallelujah." Such choruses are easy to follow, fun to sing, and infinitely varied in the way the successive phrases of text interact while maintaining their musical character.

An overall pattern can be seen in *Messiah* that differs slightly from what Handel had learned to do in the opera. On the stage, the model is generally a succession of recitative-aria pairs. A recitative, sometimes among several characters but almost always finishing with the thoughts of the person about to sing, is followed by the aria, delivered by the character downstage center, who often has a reason (unspeakable grief, rage, determination to do something immediately) to depart the scene at the end—provoking, of course, more applause.

In *Messiah* a pattern of triplets, recitative-aria-chorus, builds up a short scene to a choral climax before changing the focus and beginning another pattern with another recitative. In the first part, for example, everything between the overture and the *pifa* (that "pastoral symphony" that introduces the scene with the shepherds and the angels) is in triplets. Afterward, the pattern having been established, the structures become more varied.

The libretto for *Messiah* was created by the Reverend Charles Jennens, a careful craftsman and a serious theologian, if given somewhat to pedantry. He had helped Handel with the arrangement from Milton, with additions by himself, that became *L'allegro, il penseroso ed il moderato* (1740; Handel performed it in Dublin), and he would be of service to Handel again.

Jennens (perhaps with some help from Handel and others) arranged a selection of religious texts from the Bible and from the service book of the Church of England, all of which were well known and had been recited and sung in church for centuries. This was surely an advantage to the audience, who were hearing not only their own language but familiar texts in that language. Those texts, though not metrical and rhymed, have melodious and rhythmical aspects as a result of the rhetorical efforts of their translators, who intended these texts to be performed, to be read aloud. They invested them with balanced phrases, complementary or antithetical statements, crescen-

> **In 1754 the librettist Jennens was still unconvinced of the timeless excellence of Handel's work:**
>
> I shall show you a collection I gave Handel, call'd Messiah, which I value highly, & he has made a fine entertainment of it, tho' not near so good as he might & ought to have done. I have with great difficulty made him correct some of the grossest faults in the composition, but he retain'd his Overture obstinately, in which there are some passages far unworthy of Handel, but much more unworthy of the Messiah.

does of repetition, and a great variety of other rhetorical figures designed to make the hearing effective and impressive.

Jennens was not satisfied with Handel's *Messiah,* perhaps because he thought that his own efforts merited better music: "His Messiah has disappointed me," he wrote in 1742, "being set in great hast, tho' he said he would be a year about it, & make it the best of all his Compositions. I shall put no more Sacred Works into his hands, to be thus abus'd." Later he wrote: "As to the Messiah, 'tis still in his power by retouching the weak parts to make it fit for a publick performance; & I have said a great deal to him on the Subject; but he is so lazy and so obstinate, that I much doubt the Effect."

Jennens the librettist was also a theologian: he uses texts whose meanings are enriched by their juxtaposition. The passage "I know that my redeemer liveth, and that in my flesh shall I see God" is taken from the Book of Job, but Jennens places it so as to comment on the Resurrection of Christ and its significance to the individual believer. Texts from the Old and New Testaments, from the Prophets and Revelation, from the Psalms and the Gospels, are juxtaposed so as to give new meanings to familiar texts by their new contexts.

Jens Peter Larsen has written eloquently of the importance of the libretto in shaping of the oratorio, and his book entitled *Handel's Messiah* should be studied by anyone interested in exploring further the structure of the work. Two particularly important points bear repeating. First, *Messiah* is neither a life of Christ nor scenes from that life: it is the story of humanity's redemption through God's sending of his son, the Messiah. Although there are references to events in the life of Christ, the bulk of the text and its music deal with the relation of humans to God, the change made possible through the incarnation. The third part of *Messiah*—whose words appear almost in their entirety in the burial service of the Church of England—is a grand hymn of thanksgiving for the resulting triumph over death.

Second, everything in *Messiah* seems to be viewed obliquely. The nativity is told mostly through Old Testament prophecy ("For unto us a child is born") or through the indirect revelation of angels to shepherds. The Resurrection, surely the central fact of the Christian faith, is not a blazing chorus with trumpets; in fact, it is not easy to find as a moment in *Messiah:* it is certainly not the *Hallelujah* chorus, which comes well after references to the Ascension and to the continuing work of the church of Christ on earth. If there is a moment at which the Resurrection is the central event, it must be the aria "But thou didst not leave his soul in hell."

So *Messiah* was familiar and unfamiliar at the same time. Those who heard the first performance recognized the musical style of Handel and the conventions of the opera house and already knew most of the words by heart. But they had never heard an oratorio like this one, so directly related to the essence of Christianity yet performed for a paying audience at a public hall. *Messiah* is performed hundreds of times every year in such halls nowadays, but in Dublin of 1742 it was potentially a shocking thing.

Dublin in 1742

Dublin, capital of modern Ireland, the city of Yeats, Shaw, Joyce, and Beckett, was in 1742 a city dominated by England, a city full of new and elegant public buildings and private houses, the second city of the British Empire. Handel traveled across the Irish Sea from Chester to the natural harbor of Dublin Bay; the city itself stands on either side of the Liffey River as it flows east to the sea.

From the twelfth century, Anglo-Norman power had been restricted to a narrow band — the Pale — along the coast, including Dublin. Medieval Dublin, south of the Liffey, clustered around a castle and the two cathedrals. Eighteenth-century Dublin, however, accommodating the houses of the newly prosperous weavers and merchants, expanded to the north of the river, with stately squares and Georgian mansions. (Modern Dublin is just the reverse: as early as the second half of the eighteenth century, well-to-do Dubliners began to move south, and today the Liffey divides the haves to the south from the have-nots to the north.) The city became one of the architectural glories of Europe in the eighteenth century. Many of the grand edifices that can still be seen today, and that give the city its charm, are the products of an eighteenth-century boom, which resulted in the construction of many terraces of handsome brick houses with decorative fanlights and elegant interiors.

English culture had long been an important ingredient in Dublin. Trinity College, founded in 1592 by Queen Elizabeth I, provided sons of gentlemen an alternative to an English education and was intended as a bulwark against Catholicism. Oliver Cromwell had seized much of the best Catholic land for his Protestant soldiers; and Ireland, which had backed the Catholic James II against William of Orange, paid the price for supporting the defeated Catholic pretender by a long period of English dom-

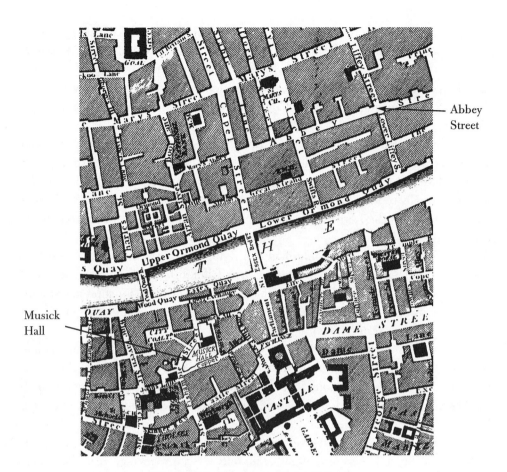

Abbey
Street

Musick
Hall

Map of Dublin, Showing the Musick Hall, 1797

In this detail of central Dublin, the Musick Hall is shown in a curve of
Fishamble Street above Copper Alley, from which there was evidently another
entrance into the hall. From the Musick Hall, Handel would cross the Essex
Bridge to reach his lodgings in Abbey Street, near the corner of Liffey Street.

ination. The Catholic majority was dominated for the whole of the eighteenth century
by a Protestant, English, and often absentee minority. Catholics were prevented from
holding office, practicing law, hiring more than two apprentices, joining a guild, own-
ing a weapon, or educating their children in Catholic schools.

In the first part of the eighteenth century, economic domination by England
had led to substantial unemployment and to an increase in crime. The Woolen Act of

1699 prevented the export of wool except as raw, unworked fiber, and then only to spec-
ified English ports, thereby crippling Ireland's most flourishing industry. Thousands
of workers either emigrated or starved. Jonathan Swift wrote that Ireland was "the only
Kingdom I ever heard or read of, either in ancient or modern Story, which was denied
the liberty of exporting their native Commodities and Manufactures, wherever they
pleased."

Ireland had its own Parliament, though its powers were so severely curtailed
that it was essentially a rubber stamp for laws enacted in England. Administration was
entrusted to the Lord Lieutenant of Ireland, who was nearly always an English noble-
man and usually resided in Dublin for only that part of the year when the Parliament
was in session. In the Lord Lieutenant's absence, administrative affairs were in the
hands of the Lords Justices.

Eighteenth-century Dublin had two cathedrals, both Anglican, as befitted a
city ruled from London. For centuries, Christ Church Cathedral, in the center of
the medieval city, and Saint Patrick's, outside the old walls, vied for supremacy; both
were in sad disrepair in the eighteenth century (and both were later given enthusiastic
nineteenth-century restorations).

Jonathan Swift (1667–1745) was dean of Saint Patrick's Cathedral at the time
of Handel's visit. The Dublin-born Swift, author of *Gulliver's Travels* and other political satires, had a keen social conscience and a deep concern for Irish poverty. His *Modest Proposal* (1729) had facetiously suggested that the children of poor parents be eaten
by the rich, in order to ease the burdens of the lower classes. At the time of Handel's
visit, Swift was in his final, cantankerous years. Loss of hearing, headaches, and dizzi-
ness all contributed to his conviction that insanity was approaching. He is cited in his
appreciation of Handel at the end of this chapter, and he is right in his estimation,
though his sort of enthusiasm perhaps alarmed his contemporaries.

Dublin was rich in theater, opera, and music, much of which was imported
from England or based on English models that corresponded to the tastes of Dublin society. Many well-known musicians resided in Dublin or played there regularly—for example, Francesco Geminiani, the Italian violin virtuoso, composer, and teacher, who
lived in London (where he had played with Handel) but visited and performed often in
the Irish capital; in the 1730s he had given a series of concerts in a concert room in
Spring Gardens, also called "Mr. Geminiani's Great Room," where he also sold paintings. He was prevented from becoming Master and Composer of the State Music in Ireland because he was Catholic; the post went instead to Geminiani's pupil Matthew
Dubourg, who was to lead Handel's Dublin orchestra for *Messiah*.

The Theatre in Smock Alley, or Theatre Royal, had been the center for drama,
music, and opera since its opening, in 1661. A visiting company from London had a regular season there. The theater in Aungier Street provided competition for the Smock
Alley theater, since it was relatively new (having opened in 1734) and had a larger stage.

View of Dublin from Capel Street, Looking over Essex Bridge,
by James Malton, 1799

Turning left at the end of Abbey Street, Handel enjoyed this view as he
crossed the bridge toward Parliament Street (the first of the wide boulevards
laid out by the Commission for Making Wide and Convenient Streets)
and made his way to the Musick Hall, on Fishamble Street. The domed
Royal Exchange, visible in the distance and now the City Hall, had not
yet been constructed. At that time the Lucas Coffee House and the
Eagle Tavern stood on the site.

Italian opera was presented in Dublin almost as soon as it became fashionable in early eighteenth-century London, and as in London its performances featured famous Italian singers. The success of *The Beggar's Opera* in London (1728) spawned a host of Irish ballad operas—essentially comedies with songs set to well-known tunes. The Crow Street Music Hall, which opened in 1731 (known as "The musical Academy for the practice of Italian Musick"), had until recently been the only venue specially intended for music.

Aside from commercial theaters, much of the musical life of Dublin was promoted by charitable institutions. Music and benevolence were symbiotically entwined: charity helped draw audiences, and music helped draw charitable givers. In this way, benefactors were elevated musically while at the same time accomplishing good works. Such affiliations have often been successful, and not only in Dublin. There is something about the combination of aesthetic pleasure and moral satisfaction that has always worked. But in Dublin the connection between music and charity was particularly close, and a number of important institutions combined both interests.

The Charitable Music Society on College-Green, for the relief of imprisoned debtors, was responsible for the construction of the New Music Hall (in which *Messiah* would have its first performance) and had its meetings in a small room in the building. The society traditionally gave weekly concerts and in 1741 succeeded in liberating from debtor's prison 188 "miserable persons of both sexes."

The Philharmonic Society of Dublin was particularly allied to Mercer's Hospital for the poor, founded in 1734 by the rich spinster Mary Mercer. With headquarters in Fishamble Street, near the New Music Hall, the society was the organization through which one applied for permission to have the choir of Saint Patrick's sing at Handel's performances (document 5): "Order'd [by the Governors of Mercer's Hospital] That John Rockfort John Ruthland & Richd Baldwin Esq^rs be desir'd to apply in the name of the Governors of Mercer's Hospital to the Rev^d the Dean [Jonathan Swift] & Chapter of St Patricks Dublin for their leave that such of their Choir as shall be Willing may assist at the Phil-Harmonick Society Performances which are principally intended for the Benefit of the said Hospital and to notifie to them that the Dean & Chapter of Christ Church have been pleas'd to grant them the same request."

The Great Music Hall in Fishamble Street, designed by the Dublin architect Richard Castle, opened in autumn 1741, just before Handel arrived for his season of concerts. It was there that Handel organized and conducted his two series of concerts and the first performance of *Messiah*. The music hall was often referred to as "Mr Neale's Hall," after the music publisher William Neale, who also led the Charitable Music Society. The hall was turned into a theater in 1777, closed at the end of the eighteenth century, and was later demolished. Although few pictures of it have survived, a 1794 engraving of the interior shows the renovations carried out for the hall's reopening as a private theater in 1793 and gives the general shape of the house. There were two rows of boxes, with a slanted parterre. A low wall or curtain separated the floor from the orchestra pit; the stage had two side doors and a back curtain decorated with a wreathed lyre. A "poetic description on the occasion of the opening of the New Music Hall" (document 14) gives the only contemporaneous impression. The hall could hold as many as seven hundred spectators and was used by a variety of charities and by private entrepreneurs for musical and other activities. Beginning in October 1741, Mrs. Hamilton and Mrs. Walker gave a public dance in the Music Hall every Saturday night.

Preparations for Messiah

After giving his second series of six concerts in the winter and spring of 1742, Handel undertook a special charitable performance of his new oratorio. He had managed the previous concerts himself, selling subscriptions at his house, but this new con-

The Interior of the Great Music Hall in Fishamble Street, 1794,
from *The Hibernian*

This seems to be the only surviving picture of the interior of the Music Hall,
which is widely reproduced as the room in which *Messiah* was first
performed. Unfortunately, this view shows the room after substantial
renovations were undertaken in 1791 to convert the dilapidated building into a
private theater. Only the general shape and dimensions were retained.

cert was a special benefit for the three charities that together sponsored the event; in
this case the organizations themselves controlled the sale of tickets. The performance
was announced, in essentially the same words, in the *Dublin Journal* and the *Dublin
News-Letter* (document 7):

> For Relief of the Prisoners in the several Gaols, and for the Support of
> Mercer's Hospital in Stephen's Street, and of the Charitable Infirmary
> on the Inns Quay, on Monday the 12th of April, will be performed at
> the Musick Hall in Fishamble Street, Mr. *Handel's new Grand Orato-
> rio, call'd the* MESSIAH, in which the Gentlemen of the Choirs of both
> Cathedrals will assist, with some Concertoes on the Organ, by Mr.
> Handell. Tickets to be had at the Musick Hall, and at Mr. Neal's in
> Christ-Church-Yard, at half a Guinea each. N.B. No Person will be ad-
> mitted to the Rehearsal without a Rehearsal Ticket, which will be
> given gratis with the Ticket for the Performance when pay'd for.

The performance, however, was postponed a day, to April 13. On April 3, rehearsals and performances were announced in the *Dublin Journal* (document 8): "On Thursday next being the 8th Inst. at the Musick Hall . . . will be the Rehearsal of Mr. Handel's new Grand Sacred Oratorio called *The* MESSIAH, in which the Gentlemen of both Choirs will assist: With some Concertos on the Organ by Mr. Handel."

A single rehearsal was surely not the only preparation needed for the performance of *Messiah*, but the *public* rehearsal was an important event, like the *répétition générale,* or dress rehearsal, that is so often a semipublic event in France (most press reports of Stravinsky's *Le sacre du printemps* discussed the rehearsal, not the performance). By now, however, Handel knew his performers well, having been in Dublin for several months and directed numerous concerts. His musical style in *Messiah* was not so different that it required any extraordinary skill on the part of the performers. The music probably was put together by Handel working with the singers, by Matthew Dubourg with the orchestra, and perhaps by a reading or two of the choruses.

As usual, Handel altered his music to accommodate the special strengths—and in this case the weaknesses—of the performers in this provincial capital. Handel customarily composed his music with specific performers in mind; he was happy to rearrange, transpose, or even recompose solo arias to suit the vocal ranges and the technical abilities of particular performers. The many alternative versions of later *Messiah*s, and of many other works by Handel, make this flexibility clear. Handel was a man of the theater: he wanted his music to be effective and his singers to shine.

But *Messiah* was not composed with specific forces in mind. Not knowing what he would find in Ireland, Handel composed an all-purpose oratorio suitable for performance by competent professional musicians. What is remarkable is how little he chose to change after meeting the musicians of Dublin.

Of the solo singers in the first *Messiah,* Mrs. Cibber was by far the best known—or most notorious. Susanna Maria Cibber was one of the most famous actresses of her day. She had triumphed in London as Polly in *The Beggar's Opera,* and the furor that arose between her and her rival, the actress Kitty Clive—and between rival camps of supporters—did much to keep her name before the public. She is one of few actresses buried in Westminster Abbey; at her death, the great dramatist David Garrick said, "Then tragedy expired with her."

Like other actresses, Mrs. Cibber had a reputation tinged with scandal. From a family of theatrical musicians, she had married Theophilus Cibber, son of the famous actor and playwright Colley Cibber. But Cibber was a manipulating and abusive husband who orchestrated a liaison for his wife with a certain Mr. Sloper, with whom Susanna ran off; as a result, she had been in a sort of forced retirement for some time. She was already in Dublin when Handel arrived, acting at the Aungier Street Theatre.

Mrs. Cibber's chief talent was dramatic rather than musical. Burney said that

Pieter van Bleeck, *Mrs. Cibber as Cordelia*, Mid-eighteenth Century

Mrs. Cibber was one of the most famous, and notorious, actresses on the
British stage. Married to the son of the Poet Laureate Colley Cibber, she
ran off with another man and had been in Dublin for several months
when Handel engaged her to sing in *Messiah.* Her light voice, clear
diction, and sensitive expression made her performance of the aria "He
was despised" particularly memorable.

Handel was "very fond of Mrs Cibber, whose voice and manners had softened his
severity for her want of musical knowledge." Handel had worked with her in London
and had been willing to spend long hours teaching her to sing her parts. Two songs
("He shall feed his flock" and "If God be for us") were transposed to suit Mrs. Cibber's
voice: when he composed *Messiah*, Handel of course did not know what voices would
be available in Dublin, but he must surely have been glad to have the services of so famous and dramatic a person as Mrs. Cibber.

Her light alto, according to Burney, had a "native sweetness and power of expression." Her voice was no more than "a mere thread, and [her] knowledge of Music,
inconsiderable; yet, by a natural pathos, and perfect conception of the words, she often
penetrated the heart, when others, with infinitely greater voice and skill, could only
reach the ear." When she sang "He was despised," according to an agreeable tradition,
the Reverend Dr. Delaney, chancellor of Saint Patrick's, was so moved, despite what he

may have felt about Mrs. Cibber's moral history, that he shouted, "Woman, for this be all thy sins forgiven thee!"

Christina Maria Avolio, the Italian soprano, had sung Handel's music as early as 1729, in a performance of his opera *Giulio Cesare* in Hamburg. For the Dublin concerts Handel brought her with him from London and employed her further in future London seasons. He was evidently satisfied with her abilities on the stage and in oratorio. In the week before *Messiah* she gave herself a benefit concert, and afterward another.

Mrs. Maclaine (we do not know her first name), the wife of the organist who also performed with Handel in Dublin, sang in *Messiah* as a soprano. She and her husband had been engaged by Handel when he was delayed by unfavorable winds at Chester on his way to Dublin. She was not, so far as we know, employed by Handel in any other venues; we can assume that she performed creditably, but she made no career for herself, in London or elsewhere. Indeed, the review published in the *Dublin Journal* (document 11) does not mention her at all, though it does seem to mention the other female soloists, as well as all the male soloists by including them among the "Gentlemen of the choirs." Mrs. Maclaine is named in a surviving copy of the wordbook that has the names of soloists penciled in, though it is possible that this wordbook might derive only from the second performance on June 3.

Other soloists included the altos William Lamb and Joseph Ward (men had for centuries sung the alto parts in church choirs by combining high tenor with falsetto ranges). Like all the tenor and bass singers, they were members of one or both of the Dublin cathedral choirs.

Lamb sang a substantial portion of the solo music for alto, including "Behold, a virgin shall conceive" and the aria "O thou that tellest good tidings to Sion." He also performed "Thou shalt break them with a rod of iron," though Handel gave him a recitative version to sing instead of the rather difficult aria he had composed. Lamb had been recommended for his job as vicar-choral by no less than the poet Alexander Pope, who in a letter to Dean Swift admits that he does not know Lamb's abilities firsthand ("I presume he is qualified for that which he desires"). Lamb had a fault perhaps common to many singers: Bishop Synge wrote to Swift about another singer who "has one good quality, not very common with the musical gentlemen, *i.e.* he is desirous to improve himself. If *Mason* and *Lamb* were of his temper, they would be as fine fellows as they think themselves."

John Mason, who also thought himself a fine fellow, sang a number of the bass solos. Mason had been recommended to Swift for the Saint Patrick's choir in 1729 by John Arbuthnot, who wrote, "I recommend one Mr Mason son of Mason Gentleman of the Queens Chappel, a Baritone Voice, for a vacancy of a Singer in your Cathedral. . . . I believe you will hardly get a better. He has a pleasant mellow voice and has sung several times in the Kings chappel this winter, to the satisfaction of the Audience." But as with Lamb, Handel remade splendid arias he had composed into simple recitatives for Mason: they were perhaps too much to learn for a singer who also had to sing "The people that walked in darkness" and "The trumpet shall sound." Or perhaps Handel was simply not satisfied with his abilities; in any case we know that "But who may abide the day of his coming" and "Thou are gone up on high" were sung as recitatives.

Other solo singers included the tenor James Bailey and the bass John Hill. These vicars-choral of the cathedral choirs were not the great singers Handel was used to working with. Handel's regular tenor, John Beard, and his bass, Thomas Reinhold, were voices worth hearing, voices for whom Handel wrote special arias. The Dublin gentlemen were undoubtedly worthy choirmen, able to manage the solos that came their way. Handel seems to have been particularly pleased with Bailey, since he remarks in a letter to Jennens that "I have form'd an other Tenor Voice which gives great satisfaction." But we shall also see that some of the revisions in his original conception of *Messiah* reflected not only his wish to tighten up the structure but also perhaps to avoid surprising the limited ability of the Dublin men.

The chorus consisted entirely of cathedral singers: the combined choirs of Saint Patrick's Cathedral (thirteen men and eight boys in 1742) and of Christ Church Cathedral (twelve men and eight boys). Choir members were allowed to participate in entertainments of this kind only with the permission of the dean and chapter of each cathedral, but the charitable purposes of many musical events made this possible in most circumstances. When Mercer's Hospital applied to the dean and chapter of Saint Patrick's, permission was at first given, then refused.

Swift ultimately relented and the choirs sang. The cathedrals shared not only a single choirmaster (Mr. Ralph Roseingrave) but many of the same singers, with the re-

> **Jonathan Swift, whose incipient insanity must have affected his memory, wrote to the subdean and chapter of Saint Patrick's on January 28:**
>
> And whereas it hath been reported, that I gave a licence to certain vicars to assist at a club of fiddlers in Fishamble Street, I do hereby declare that I remember no such licence to have been ever signed or sealed by me; and that if ever such pretended licence should be produced, I do hereby annul and vacate the said licence; intreating my said Sub-Dean and Chapter to punish such vicars as shall ever appear there, as songsters, fiddlers, pipers, trumpeters, drummers, drum-majors, or in any sonal quality, according to the flagitous aggravations of their respective disobedience, rebellion, perfidy, and ingratitude.

sult that the actual number available from the combined choirs is about sixteen men (for alto, tenor, and bass parts) and eight boys. The three female soloists, who also sang the choruses, add two sopranos and an alto to the choir, for a total of about twenty-seven singers, ten sopranos (remember that they need to divide for "Glory to God") and five or six for each of the other parts. Not all the available cathedral singers, however, may actually have sung. Handel was pleased with the results, as he wrote to Jennens: "The Basses and Counter Tenors are very good, and the rest of the Chorus Singers (by my Direction) do exceedingly well."

Thirty-eight-year-old Matthew Dubourg led the orchestra for Handel's Dublin performances. Dubourg's job included some of the duties of a modern conductor: with Handel at the harpsichord leading the performance (but directing very little with his hands), Dubourg kept the orchestra together through his demonstrative violin playing. No one waved a baton.

Matthew Dubourg was born in London, the natural son of a dancing master named Isaacs. As a young boy he had performed (while standing on a stool) a difficult solo by Corelli in the concerts of Thomas Britton. A pupil of Francesco Geminiani, Dubourg had worked with Handel in London as early as 1719, playing one of Handel's concertos. Handel's friend Mrs. Pendarves (later Mrs. Delaney) wrote about a concert she heard in London in 1727: "Dubourg was first fiddle, and everybody says he exceeds all the Italians, even his master Geminiani."

Dubourg had been Master and Composer of the State Music of Ireland since

1728 and would keep the position for another ten years (until 1752). Although he performed mostly in Dublin, he kept his Handelian connections: he played in Handel's next London season, which included the premiere of *Samson*. He often played concertos between the acts of Handel's performances and organized and led many Irish performances of Handel oratorios in the 1740s. Handel retained an attachment to Dubourg throughout his life, leaving him a hundred pounds in his will.

The quality of Dubourg's band in Dublin must have been fairly good, even though Swift referred to them disparagingly as "a club of fiddlers in Fishamble Street." Handel wrote to Jennens that "as for the Instruments they are really excellent, Mr Dubourgh beeing at the Head of them, and the Musick sounds delightfully in this charming Room."

Handel evidently had the best of Dublin's instrumentalists for his concerts: Monsieur de Rheiner ("a distress'd foreign gentleman") was, according to Faulkner's *Dublin Journal,* "obliged to put off his Day [his benefit performance announced for March 4, 1742], which was to have been on Tuesday next, on account of all the best Musick being engaged to Mr. Handel's Concert."

We have little specific information about the players in the orchestra, but to judge from the autograph score, there were to be strings and continuo, with a solo trumpet in "The trumpet shall sound" and two trumpets with kettledrums in four of the choruses. No oboes, no bassoons, no horns. But the strings are marvelously varied. Two of the hallmarks of Handel's greatness are the energy of his music and the remarkable inventiveness of the instrumental writing. The arias sometimes have only a bass line and a single tune played by the violins—for example, "O thou that tellest" and

---

Charles Burney describes Dubourg's excessive taste for ornament:

One night, while Handel was in Dublin, Dubourg having a solo part in a song, and a close [i.e., a cadenza] to make, *ad libitum,* he wandered about in different keys a great while, and seemed indeed a little bewildered, and uncertain of his original key … but, at length, coming to the shake [the trill that ends the cadenza], which was to terminate this long close, Handel, to the great delight of the audience, and augmentation of applause, cried out loud enough to be heard in the most remote parts of the theatre: "You are welcome home, Mr. Dubourg."

"Rejoice greatly." Sometimes all the strings together provide a texture against which the voices or chorus stand out: "Surely he hath borne our griefs" and "For he is like a refiner's fire." And sometimes the strings themselves are orchestrated, the full group alternating with duets from the violins, as in "Ev'ry valley" and "He was despised."

Some scholars, like Paul Henry Lang, believe that this is the orchestra Handel used in Dublin: strings only, with trumpets—a club of fiddlers. But there is reason to believe that Handel generated wind parts from his score and used oboes and bassoons, and indeed even horns.

It was not unusual, indeed it was more common than not, for a copyist to derive wind parts from an apparently strings-only score. The bassoons are easy: they can play from a basso continuo part. All they need are instructions from the composer (or copyist) as to when they should play and when they should be silent and let the cello play alone.

The same can be done for the oboes by letting them play from violin parts. But here a difficulty arises, because there are two basic ways of employing the usual first and second oboes: in cases where a single melody in the first violins is harmonized by the rest of the strings (as is the case with almost all dance music and with many other musical forms as well), it is usually best to have both oboes play along with the first violin part, to give definition to the melody line; but in pieces composed more contrapuntally (fugues, imitations, and the like), it is preferable to have oboes doubling both the first and the second violins.

Separate oboe parts are, therefore, usually more effective, even though they are derived from the music already composed for the violins. Examples of this can in fact be found in the early sources for *Messiah*. The so-called "Matthews" orchestral parts, copied by John Matthews for a performance at Salisbury in 1761 and now in Dublin, have oboe parts that are somewhat more independent of the violins than is usual: some copyist has tried his hand as a composer. A more significant set of parts, and one more closely connected with Handel, is the score and the parts left by him to the Foundling Hospital in London. In these, the oboes are generally in unison and mostly follow the choral soprano. Only rarely do they deviate from this: in the overture they divide for the fugue, and they occasionally play the opening orchestral tutti of a chorus as well as the soprano part. They are, in short, typical Baroque oboe parts, perhaps less imaginative than what Handel himself would have created (they do not play in the pifa, which imitates reed instruments) but probably not too different from what the oboes played in Dublin.

Oboes were certainly available in Dublin. Handel used them for almost all the rest of the music he performed there: *Acis and Galatea, L'allegro, Imeneo,* various coronation anthems, and so on. And Handel used oboes in *Messiah,* in the duet "How beautiful are the feet of them . . . Break forth into joy," which was sung in Dublin and whose music is bound into the autograph score, though it hardly seems likely that

Performance parts left by Handel in his will to the Foundling Hospital:

3 first violin (one marked *concertino*)

3 second violin (one marked *concertino*)

2 viola

2 violoncello

2 bassoon

1 oboe 1

1 oboe 2

trumpet and kettledrums

4 soprano (A further soprano book, including the solos not in the surviving solo
   book, is now lost.)

3 alto (one marked *principale*)

3 tenor (one marked *principale*)

3 bass (one marked *principale*)

oboes were used for one movement only! The choral version of "Their sound is gone out," bound at the end of the autograph manuscript, has two oboe parts in Handel's hand. This is a later chorus not sung in Dublin, but it was surely not used in later performances that had oboes only for this one chorus; and if oboes were used throughout at later performances, it is improbable that the oratorio was originally conceived, and performed, without them.

For the Dublin performance we do not have parts detailing when these wind instruments play. We can presume that they play in the choruses, doubling either orchestral or vocal parts; but in the arias and recitatives there might be moments where the winds are omitted to allow a particular string sound to prevail: such moments as the string accompaniments to "Comfort ye" and "Why do the nations" would require a lot of composing to produce suitable, probably sustained, wind parts to go along with the string figurations.

As to the composition of the orchestra as a whole, we can obtain a good image of Handel's ideas, and perhaps his ideals, from the parts left to the Foundling Hospital. Although these parts may never have been played, they represent the product of

Handel's own copyists; and what is more, they match closely the performances of *Messiah* given by Handel at the Foundling Hospital.

The performances in 1758 and 1759 included twelve violins, three "tenors" (violas), three cellos, two basses, four oboes, four bassoons, two trumpets, two horns, and drums. The choir consisted of twelve or thirteen men and six trebles from the Chapel Royal.

Based on Handel's practice elsewhere, we can make a reasonable reconstruction of Dubourg's orchestra for *Messiah,* based essentially on that of the Foundling Hospital performances and parts. A few explanatory remarks will help clarify some details.

The use of four or more oboes is perfectly normal in Handel, at least for an orchestra of this size. The larger the string band, the more oboes would be wanted to provide the proper balance. Handel did not follow the modern orchestral practice of using only one wind player to a part. Likewise the use of several bassoons is normal. The existence of two identical bassoon parts for the Foundling Hospital implies four bassoons, a perfectly usual number.

Handel often used horns, and he may well have done so in Dublin. That there are no horn parts in the score means little. Although there are none in the Foundling Hospital score, Handel used horns in the Foundling performances: the simple solution, and the one usually employed by Handel, is to have the horns play with the trumpets, but one octave lower, making it easy for the two instruments to play from the same parts. Naturally no horn would have tried to duplicate the solo in the aria "The trumpet shall sound," but in the choral numbers with trumpets the addition of a pair of horns would be natural and seemly. The arrival on March 20 in Dublin of "Mr. Charles the Hungarian, Master of the French Horn," might have provided an opportunity to enrich the orchestra for *Messiah*. On May 12 of that year Charles gave a benefit concert that included a great deal of Handel's music.

The continuo consisted at least of organ and harpsichord. Handel had brought his own organ, on which he undoubtedly played the concertos featured between the parts of *Messiah,* as at his other concerts; but during *Messiah* the organ was played by Mr. Maclaine, while Handel directed from the harpsichord. The joint use of harpsichord and organ for continuo accompaniment, or their alternation for expressive or other purposes, is a standard practice with Handel, though not much observed nowadays; the creative possibilities of this combination deserve further exploration.

In the Music Hall, April 13

The audience, some seven hundred in number, likely found it difficult to get into the Great Music Hall, or to find room once they gained access. Fishamble Street was narrow, and an advertisement for an earlier concert had advised patrons to avoid traffic snarls : "Gentlemen and Ladies are desired to order their Coaches and Chairs to

Chamber Organ by Johann Snetzler, 1742

This organ is said by some to be the one that Handel brought with him to Dublin and on which he played concertos in the intervals between his oratorios. As he wrote to Jennens, "The Musick sounds delightfully in this charming Room, which puts me in such Spirits (and my Health being so good) that I exert my self on my Organ with more than usual Success."

come down Fishamble-street, which will prevent a great deal of Inconvenience that happened the Night before; and as there is a good convenient Room hired as an Addition to a former Place for the Footmen, it is hoped the Ladies will order them to attend there till called for."

There seems to have been only one entrance for the public, so that filling and emptying the hall must have taken considerable time. Anticipating the problem of fitting seven hundred people into a hall that usually accommodated only six hundred, the press urgently requested that gentlemen arrive without their swords and ladies without their hoops, "as it will greatly encrease the Charity, by making Room for more Company."

The audience began to arrive about eleven, when the doors were opened, for the scheduled performance at midday. Given the difficulty of lighting a hall in the evening, especially one that was not a theater, and the custom of having dinner at four in the afternoon, the starting hour of noon was almost inevitable: a complete *Messiah,* with two intermissions during which Handel played organ concertos, ought to have finished a little after three, permitting time for the audience to exit the hall, get into a coach or sedan chair, and arrive home to dinner by four.

"The Audience," wrote Handel about his earlier subscription series, is "composed (besides the Flower of Ladyes of Distinction and other People of the greatest Quality) of so many Bishops, Deans, Heads of the Colledge, the most eminents People in the Law as the Chancellor, Auditor General &tc." (document 3). On this occasion the Lord Lieutenant, the duke of Devonshire, had already left Dublin for London; the Lords Justices were the highest-ranking members of the audience. Dublin society was small enough that many in the audience would have known one another. They would also have been familiar with the performers, most of whom played regularly in Dublin; the few who were visitors would have been recognized from Handel's two

The Dublin Wordbook, Pages 2 and 3

For sixpence a concertgoer could acquire a copy of the words sung in *Messiah*. As is standard in such wordbooks, the nature of the music is also indicated: "Recitative," "Song," and so on. In this particular copy, now in the British Library, the names of Dublin singers have been penciled in beside portions of the text, providing much information about the arrangements Handel made in Dublin. Mr. Mason, a vicar-choral in the cathedral choirs, sang a recitative version of "But who may abide the day of his coming?"

series of subscription concerts. This was not an event designed to show off a visiting virtuoso or a dazzling soprano castrato, though there were certain performers with international reputations: the attraction was Handel and his new oratorio.

Arriving at the theater, audience members could buy a printed wordbook ("price a British sixpence") containing all the texts to be sung and indicating whether they were done as recitative, as song, or as chorus. In one copy of this booklet, the now-anonymous purchaser penciled in the names of the singers as the text proceeded; how fortunate that this copy has survived!

Handel arrived in Dublin with his new oratorio already composed (his composing score survives, as does a copy of it also used in the Dublin performances and for many later performances; this latter score includes some names of singers in the Dublin performances). In the course of rehearsals, however, he made changes: he omitted a few of the more difficult arias, substituting recitatives more suitable to the singers' abilities; and he abridged several pieces, making the oratorio flow more quickly (and also perhaps easing the strain on the local singers).

The choruses Handel composed in London were not changed in Dublin: the singers were evidently adequate. He had made choruses that could be managed by competent choir singers, and he had no second thoughts as to their form.

Most of the revisions Handel made were concessions to local voices. Three arias ("But who may abide," "Thou art gone up on high," and "Thou shalt break them") were replaced by recitatives, to judge from the indications in the wordbook. Of these, two recitatives survive that may be the ones used in Dublin, but the recitative version of "Thou art gone up" has apparently been lost. It seems possible that Messrs. Mason and Lamb, who sang these texts, were not quite up to the demands of the score. Or Handel may have wished to streamline the oratorio, but if so he must have changed his mind afterward, because he never abbreviated the oratorio at these places again.

A number of abridgements indicated in the score produce a tightening up, a quickening of the pace; they make the oratorio as a whole, and individual numbers in it, speak more forcefully. (They also have the effect of relieving the singers involved.) We cannot be certain of when the abridgements were made, in that the score had been in use for so long, but it seems probable that they had already been incorporated for the Dublin performances. The abridgements include shortening the longer da capo version of "Rejoice greatly" and abbreviating "Why do the nations," probably a concession to Mr. Hill; the duet "O death, where is thy sting?" has a shortened form pasted into the conducting score that may have been used at Dublin to accommodate Ward and Bailey. The slight retouching of the pifa and of the accompaniment figures to "Ev'ry valley" was also probably adopted for Dublin.

At the keyboard, Handel not only directed the performance but, between sections of *Messiah*, also played concertos on the organ he had brought with him. These compositions, filled with his virtuosic improvisations, were a favorite with audiences all through his career as a producer of oratorio.

Handel was also legendary on the harpsichord. Charles Burney described his mastery of the instrument : "Indeed, his hand was then so fat, that the knuckles, which usually appear convex, were like those of a child, dinted or dimpled in, so as to be rendered concave; however, his touch was so smooth, and the tone of the instrument so much cherished, that his fingers seemed to grow to the keys. They were so curved and compact, when he played, that no motion, and scarcely the fingers themselves, could be discovered."

Always worth watching, "Handel wore an enormous white wig," said Burney, speaking of the London performances, "and, when things went well at the Oratorio, it had a certain nod, or vibration, which manifested his pleasure and satisfaction. Without it, nice observers were certain that he was out of humour. At the close of an air, the voice with which he used to cry out, CHORUS! was extremely formidable indeed." We can suppose that the white wig, with its nod, was in evidence in Dublin and that Handel had matters arranged so that he could see and direct all the performers.

Dublin Journal, April 6–10, 1742, Page 2 (detail)

This four-page newspaper, printed by George Faulkner (who also printed the wordbook for *Messiah*), provided commercial notices, local news, and all available international news. In the first column (which begins with the news of a hanging at Kilmainham) is the notice of the rehearsal of *Messiah*. At the bottom of column two, Faulkner notes the publication of a poem to Mrs. Cibber, and at the top of column three, the publication of Jonathan Swift's new *Dunciad*.

This would have been possible only if they were arranged on the stage. Even though there appears to have been a pit in the Great Music Hall, Handel could hardly have had the solo singers near him at a place where they could be audible; and the orchestra near enough for his continuo accompaniments to match what other instrumentalists were doing; and Mr. Dubourg near enough to wish him a welcome home after a cadenza—unless all were at one level. We do not know the precise arrangement of the performers, but surely Handel and the solo singers were near the front of the platform. The only real question is the relation of orchestra to chorus. Because the soloists were expected to sing the choruses as well, the chorus could not have been too distant. Perhaps they even stood in front of the orchestra (as was to be typical in Beethoven's Vienna), but this seems less likely than an arrangement of chorus to the side and rear of the orchestra. The singers were expected to dress in black, if Handel's later practice (described above by Hawkins) is any guide.

The English sung by most of the singers was probably better than that usually heard at Handel's oratorio performances in London, because in Dublin the singers were mostly native English speakers rather than Italian opera singers; the exception is Signora Avolio, who may have reminded listeners of the criticism expressed by a London cynic (see the epigraph to this chapter).

The many infelicities that the Dublin singers found in their parts had to be dealt with somehow. Did Mrs. Maclean sing the word "were" as two syllables both times Handel set it to two notes in the recitative "There were shepherds"? Did the chorus sing "Surely" to three syllables? Did Mr. Mason worry about the number of times he was asked to accent "incorruptible" on its second and fourth syllables in "The trumpet shall sound"? There must have been some tacit adjustments made here and there: Handel himself, with his incomplete command of English, would probably not have noticed foreign pronunciations and errors of accentuation.

The singers were, for the most part, not opera singers and may have had neither the skill nor the desire to add the sort of vocal ornamentation that was part of the attraction of opera. Cathedral singers would have been trained to do much less, and the little evidence we have suggests that Handel disapproved of elaborate extempore embellishment by singers. The nearly complete absence of full da capo arias removes one temptation to embellish. Nevertheless, a few surviving manuscripts—not Handel's but those done by other scribes for later performances—contain evidence of adornments and cadenzas, though none of them is directly related to Dublin.

Press reports of the rehearsal and performance of *Messiah* are fulsome but not very informative (documents 9, 10):

> Yesterday Mr. Handell's new Grand Sacred Oratorio, called, The *MESSIAH*, was rehearsed . . . to a most Grand, Polite and crouded Audience; and was performed so well, that it gave universal Satisfaction to all present; and was allowed by the greatest Judges to be the finest Composition of Musick that ever was heard, and the sacred Words as properly adapted for the Occasion.
>
> [*Dublin Journal,* April 10]

> Yesterday Morning, at the Musick Hall . . . there was a public Rehearsal of the Messiah, Mr. Handel's new sacred Oratorio, which in the opinion of the best Judges, far surpasses anything of that Nature, which has been performed in this or any other Kingdom. The elegant Entertainment was conducted in the most regular Manner, and to the entire satisfaction of the most crowded and polite Assembly.
>
> To the benefit of three very important public Charities, there will be a grand Performance of this Oratorio on Tuesday next in the forenoon.
>
> N. B. At the Desire of several Persons of Distinction, the above Performance is put off to Tuesday next [April 13th]. The Doors will be opened at Eleven, and the Performance begin at Twelve.
>
> [*Dublin News-Letter,* April 10]

It is gratifying to know that the rehearsal went well, that it was conducted in a most regular manner; and it is hard to disagree with the reviewer about the quality of the music. But one could wish for a bit more detail in describing the rehearsal. This sort of minimalist criticism, however, is characteristic of journalistic writing of the time.

These accounts come not from musical or artistic journals but from the local papers that also report shipping news and advertise upcoming horse races. Reports of Handel's other performances are much like these, and although there is no reason to doubt that they *were* superlative performances, it seems in the nature of the reviewing standards of Dublin to report the good qualities without requiring the niceties of individual characterization. The same unqualified praise, lacking in description, is used in reporting the performance (document 11):

> On Tuesday last Mr. Handel's Sacred Grand Oratorio, the MESSIAH, was performed at the New Musick-Hall in Fishamble-street; the best Judges allowed it to be the most finished piece of Musick. Words are wanting to express the exquisite Delight it afforded to the admiring crouded Audience. The Sublime, the Grand, and the Tender, adapted to the most elevated, majestick and moving Words, conspired to transport and charm the ravished Heart and Ear. It is but Justice to Mr. Handel, that the World should know, he generously gave the Money arising from this Grand Performance, to be equally shared by the Society for relieving Prisoners, the Charitable Infirmary, and Mercer's Hospital, for which they will ever gratefully remember his Name; and that the Gentlemen of the two Choirs, Mr. Dubourg, Mrs. Avolio, and Mrs. Cibber, who all performed their Parts to Admiration, acted also on the same disinterested Principle, satisfied with the deserved Applause of the Publick, and the conscious Pleasure of promoting such useful, and extensive Charity. There were above 700 People in the Room, and the Sum collected for that Noble and Pious Charity amounted to about 400*l.* out of which 127*l.* goes to each of the three great and pious Charities.
>
> [*Dublin Journal,* April 17; the same report, minus the last sentence, was printed in the *Dublin Gazette* and the *Dublin News-Letter*]

A certain Dr. Quinn was among the few who give eyewitness accounts; his observations read rather like the *Journal*'s:

> The *Messiah* was performed in Dublin for the first time, and with the greatest applause. Mrs. Cibber and Signora Avolio were the principal performers. These, with the assistance of the choiristers of St. Patrick's cathedral and Christ-church, formed the vocal band; and Dubourg, with several good instrumental performers, composed a very respectable orchestra. There were many noble families here, with whom Mr. Handel lived in the utmost degree of friendship and familiarity.... I had the pleasure of seeing and conversing with Mr. Handel, who, with his other excellences, was possessed of a great stock of hu-

mour; no man ever told a story with more. But it was requisite for the hearer to have a competent knowledge of at least four languages, English, French, Italian, and German, for in his narratives he made use of them all.

Dr. Edward Synge, bishop of Elphin, heard *Messiah* in Dublin, and Handel forwarded the bishop's praise of it to Jennens (document 12):

> As Mr. Handel in his oratorio's greatly excells all other Composers I am acquainted with, So in the famous one, called The Messiah he seems to have excell'd himself. The whole is beyond any thing I had a notion of till I Read and heard it. It seems to be a Species of Musick different from any other, and this is particularly remarkable of it. That tho' the Composition is very Masterly & artificial, yet the Harmony is So great and open, as to please all who have Ears & will hear, learned & unlearn'd. . . . A Third reason for the Superior Excellence of this piece, 'Tis this there is no Dialogue. In every Drame there must be a great deal & often broken into very Short Speeches & Answers. If these be flat, & insipid, they move laughter or Contempt."

How did the performance go? We don't really know. But Handel's alterations in the music, which make it more suitable for the limited abilities of the Dublin singers, give hints that he might have wished for more. According to his report to Jennens, however, he did seem pleased with *Messiah*'s reception (document 3):

> Without Vanity the Performance was received with a general Approbation. Sig^ra Avolio, which I brought with me from London pleases extraordinary, I have form'd an other Tenor Voice which gives great Satisfaction, the Basses and Counter Tenors are very good, and the rest of the Chorus Singers (by my Direction) do exceeding well, as for the Instruments they are really excellent, Mr Dubourgh beeing at the Head of them, and the Musick sounds delightfully in this charming Room, which puts me in such Spirits (and my Health being so good) that I exert my self on my Organ with more than usual Success. [Handel is speaking of his concerts in general, not of *Messiah* in particular.]

And when Handel was pleased, everybody in range of his white wig knew it, as Burney reports: "HANDEL's general look was somewhat heavy and sour; but when he *did* smile, it was his sire the sun, bursting out of a black cloud. There was a sudden flash of intelligence, wit, and good humour, beaming in his countenance, which I hardly ever saw in any other."

Anonymous, *The Charming Brute,* 1754

This engraving is derived from a pastel caricature done by Goupy, who was
once a friend of Handel. The artist mocks Handel for his gluttony (the boar
seated on a wine cask), his vanity (the mirror), and his fondness for loud music
(the trumpets and drums). Handel was renowned for his enormous white wig
and his keyboard playing.

The first performance of such a famous work holds a special fascination for us,
but it is one of many performances of a work that Handel continued to revive and revise
as he saw fit. If there is now a "standard" form of *Messiah,* that standard usually de-
pends on one's copy of the vocal score or one's favorite recording. Handel himself re-
ordered and rearranged the oratorio many times throughout his career according to his
changing needs, tastes, and circumstances. When a star singer rose on the horizon, as
did the countertenor Gaetano Guadagni in 1750, Handel was happy to transpose arias
for him (e.g., "Why do the nations" and others) and to recompose other pieces to suit
the voice (he added the prestissimo version of "But who may abide" for Guadagni).

But in Dublin in 1742, there was only one version of *Messiah,* heard for the first time in the New Music Hall.

A concert given at noon on a Tuesday in the hall filled with the cream of Dublin society: what was it like to be in that audience? What was the effect of the performance of *Messiah* on its Dublin hearers? Although we cannot be sure, we can attempt to be in tune with Handel's ideas by considering what such an audience was used to hearing, what they expected, and what was new.

Nothing about the music of *Messiah* was revolutionary. The recitatives, songs, and choruses were all in the musical style with which the audience was familiar, not only from two decades of opera performances in Dublin but also from Handel's earlier series of performances there. This was the regular fare of the patrons of high culture in the 1740s. Whereas the performing forces may seem puny when compared to some of the titanic performances of *Messiah* given in the nineteenth and twentieth centuries, they were entirely usual for Dublin, and for Handel. He did not want enormous choirs and orchestras.

The few remarks we have about the performance suggest that it was entirely acceptable, or even an unusually good version of something familiar. There is nothing wrong with a performance being acceptable; more than a beginning point for appreciation, acceptance is a welcome thing for any piece of music. For many, surprises and novelty are desirable only in the very limited context of a style that is well understood and not in need of any tinkering. Terms used in the published reports suggest such an attitude: "conducted in the most regular Manner"; "to the entire satisfaction of the most crowded and polite Assembly"; "a very respectable orchestra"; "performed their Parts to Admiration."

What, then, distinguished *Messiah* from other concerts, or indeed from other performances given by Handel at about that time? Principally it was an exceptionally good example of a known type. Dr. Synge: "He seems to have excell'd himself. . . . It seems to be a Species of Musick different from any other." Likewise the *Dublin Journal* reports on the performance in such general terms that we cannot be sure it is *Messiah* being described; nonetheless, the language is one of appreciation.

"Exquisite delight" for which "words are wanting." The power and pleasure of music can be exquisite and different from any pleasure that can be expressed in words. "The Sublime, the Grand, and the Tender"—here the author is speaking of *musical* effects, moods, passions. These are states of the soul, emotional moments, passions—things felt by the human heart. Each such moment, in an opera aria or a song in an oratorio, achieves its effect by the combination of words ("majestick and moving") that set the scene and music that expresses the emotion of that scene. It is the combination of these two that gives each musical moment—each such moment usually lasting for an entire song or chorus—its characteristic individuality.

The audience could be expected to have had a substantial backlog of experience in this kind of music. They had been to the opera house, they had heard other oratorios, and they knew what effects to expect; they could be delighted at a new varia-tion on a familiar theme or bored when a composer added nothing to a customary form of expression. Many standard emotional states were regularly expressed in music, which was expected to call up in the listener a recognition of the passion being ex-pressed and to add something new to our understanding of this particular state of the soul. Nobody at *Messiah* would have failed to recognize from the beginning that "Why do the nations" is a rage aria for bass. They exist by the dozens in opera, very often sung by a bass, and always accompanied by some sort of furious orchestral accompa-niment like that in *Messiah*. Nor would the audience have missed the pastoral refer-ences in "He shall feed his flock": the bagpipe drone of the bass line, the lilting *siciliano* rhythm of the melody. Indeed, they would have been surprised if an aria about flocks had lacked such characteristics.

All this backlog of experience in a shared musical style provided Handel's au-dience with a means of appreciating his particular skill in adapting stock emotional ef-fects to new purposes, doing a better job than others at what was expected. The music is Sublime, Grand, and Tender; and equally important, it is adapted to "majestick and moving Words."

What is relatively new in *Messiah* is the setting of words from Scripture to this sort of music—a combination that must have seemed a bit risky to Handel. Only later did he present *Messiah* in London, where he perhaps feared that religious criticisms might be more severe.

The idea that religious words and music have no place in a theatrical setting—and its obverse, that music for religious purposes needs to have a certain religious char-acter—has always been a subject of contention. Swift's refusal to let his singers partic-ipate surely reflects a related attitude. No wonder that Handel avoided the title *Messiah* in his early London performance of the oratorio. Clearly a very special religious inter-est was attached to *Messiah*, which uses biblical words to recount the central Christ-ian message. Even the librettist, himself a member of the clergy, used religion to criti-cize *Messiah*, though in another way: "I have with great difficulty made him correct some of the grossest faults in the composition, but he retain'd his Overture obstinately, in which there are some passages far unworthy of Handel, but much more unworthy of the Messiah." It is not clear exactly what Charles Jennens was criticizing about the music, but it seems to have involved the *quality* of the music with respect to the im-portance of the text. Not all clergy were shocked, however. Dr. Synge thought very well of it, as we have seen, and seemed not to be worried about the inappropriateness of per-forming such words in a theatrical setting. Indeed, he thought that attending *Messiah* might have a salutary effect on religious sentiments: "They seem'd indeed throughly engag'd frome one end to the other. And, to their great honour, tho' the young & gay of both Sexes were present in great numbers, their behaviour was uniformly grave & decent, which Show'd that they were not only pleas'd but affected with the perform-

> **The *Universal Spectator*, in a 1743 article signed Philalethes (Greek for "lover of the true"), criticizes the use of religious subjects in oratorio:**
>
> An *Oratorio* either is an *Act of religion,* or it is not; if it is, I ask if the Playhouse is a fit *Temple* to perform it in, or a Company of *Players* fit *Ministers* of *God's Word,* for in that Case such they are made....
>
> In the other Case, if it is not perform'd as an *Act of Religion,* but for *Diversion* and *Amusement* only (And indeed I believe few or none go to an *Oratorio* out of *Devotion*), what a *Prophanation* of *God*'s Name and Word is this, to make so light Use of them?

ance. Many, I hope, were instructed by it, and had proper Sentiments inspir'd in a Stronger Manner in their Minds."

There is not much evidence of anti-Catholic sentiment in *Messiah.* Although the majority of Ireland's population was Catholic, members of the English ruling class of Dublin were the audience for *Messiah;* Protestantism could be assumed, and the Church of England was the provider of the librettist, the choirs, and the texts of much of the oratorio. Even though the entire oratorio has biblical words (thereby not limiting it to Protestants or Catholics), the use of the authorized, or King James, translation for most of the text was a clear sign of its Anglican origins, and the audience would surely not have overlooked the fact that part 3, starting with the song "I know that my Redeemer liveth," begins with words from the opening of the funeral service of the Book of Common Prayer.

What is exceptional about this piece is the quality of Handel's music, which has certainly proved itself in the two and a half centuries since its performance in Dublin; but many seem to have noticed and felt this from the beginning. "The best Judges allowed it to be the most finished piece of Musick"—not the most novel or revolutionary: the most *finished,* that is, carefully crafted in every detail, refined. As Dr. Synge reflected on his experience, he thought, "It seems to be a Species of Musick different from any other, and this is particularly remarkable of it. That tho' the Composition is very Masterly & artificial, yet the Harmony is So great and open, as to please all who have Ears & will hear, learned & unlearn'd." Handel had achieved an immediate and universal appeal, mostly through grandeur and simplicity.

After a performance of *Saul* on May 22, again the object of superlatives ("it was agreed by all the judges present, to have been the finest performance that hath been heard in this Kingdom"), a second performance of *Messiah,* on June 3, was Handel's last concert in Ireland. It was advertised in the same terms as the first, but because it took place at seven in the evening it was announced that "in order to keep the Room as cool as possible, a Pane of Glass will be removed from the Top of each of the Windows."

Before leaving Ireland, Handel undoubtedly also attended the concert by Mrs. Cibber and her sister-in-law, Mrs. Arne, whose duet concert on July 21 featured many works of Handel, though none from *Messiah*. He said farewell to Jonathan Swift, saw Garrick play Hamlet at the Smock Alley theater, and sailed for England on August 13.

Documents: Handel, *Messiah*

1. Handel performances in Dublin:

December 23, 1741, *L'allegro, il penseroso, ed il moderato,* with concertos
January 13, 1742, *L'allegro, il penseroso, ed il moderato,* with concertos (2d night of Mr. Handel's Musical Entertainments by Subscription)
January 20, 1742, *Acis and Galatea, Ode for St. Cecilia's Day,* several concertos
January 27, 1742, *Acis and Galatea, Ode for St. Cecilia's Day*
February 3, 1742, *Esther,* with Additions, and several concertos
February 10, 1742, *Esther,* repeated

February 6, a new series of six concerts is announced (see document 2):

February 17, 1742, *Alexander's Feast,* with Additions and several concertos
March 2, 1742, *Alexander's Feast,* with Additions and several concertos
March 17, 1742, *L'allegro ed il penseroso,* with Concertos on the organ

March 24, 1742, a new Serenata called Hymen (Handel's opera *Imeneo*)
March 31, 1742, *Hymen*
April 7, 1742, *Esther,* with concertos on the organ
April 13, 1742, *Messiah,* with concertos
May 25, 1742, *Saul,* with concertos
June 3, 1742, *Messiah,* with concertos

2. Announcement of Handel's second series of concerts, February 6, 1742:

By the Desire of several Persons of Quality and Distinction there will be a new Subscription made for Mr. Handel's Musical Entertainments, for Six Nights more, on the same Footing as the last. No more than 150 Subscriptions will be taken in, and no Single Tickets sold, or any Money taken at the Door. Subscriptions will be taken in at Mr. Handel's House in Abby-street near Lyffee-street, on Monday next, being the 8th Day of February from 9 o'clock in the Morning till 3 in the Afternoon. The Performances are to continue once a Week, till the 6 Nights are over.

[Otto Erich Deutsch, *Handel: A Documentary Biography* (New York: Norton, 1955), 538]

3. Handel to Charles Jennens, 29 December 1741:

Dublin Decem^br 29. 1741
S^r

it was with the greatest Pleasure I saw the Continuation of Your Kindness by the Lines You was pleased to send me, in Order to be prefix'd to Your Oratorio Messiah, which I set to Musick before I left England. I am emboldened, Sir, by the generous Concern You please to take in relation to my affairs, to give You an Account of the Success I have met here. The Nobility did me the Honour to make amongst themselves a Subscription for 6 Nights, which did fill a Room of 600 Persons, so that I needed not sell one single Ticket at the Door. and without Vanity the Performance was received with a general Approbation. Sig^ra Avolio, which I brought with me from London pleases extraordinary, I have form'd an other Tenor Voice which gives great Satisfaction, the Basses and Counter Tenors are very good, and the rest of the Chorus Singers (by my Direction) do exceeding well, as for the Instruments they are really excellent, Mr Dubourgh beeing at the Head of them, and the Musick sounds delightfully in this charming Room, which puts me in such Spirits (and my Health being so good) that I exert my self on my Organ with more than usual Success. I opened with the Allegro, Penseroso, & Moderato and I assure you that the Words of the Moderato [written by Jennens] are vastly admired. The Audience being composed (besides the Flower of Ladyes of Distinction and other People of the greatest Quality) of so many Bishops, Deans, Heads of the Colledge, the most eminents People in the Law as the

Chancellor, Auditor General, &tc. all which are very much taken with the Poetry. So that I am desired to perform it again the next time. I cannot sufficiently express the kind treatment I receive here, but the Politness of this generous Nation cannot be unknown to You, so I let You judge of the satisfaction I enjoy, passing my time with Honnour, profit, and pleasure. They propose already to have some more Performances, when the 6 Nights of the Subscription are over, and My Lord Duc the Lord Lieutenant (who is allways present with all His Family on those Nights) will easily obtain a longer Permission for me by His Majesty, so that I shall be obliged to make my stay here longer than I thought. One request I must make to You, which is that You would insinuate my most devoted Respects to My Lord and my Lady Shaftesbury, You know how much Their kind Protection is precious to me. Sir Windham Knatchbull will find here my respectfull Compliments. You will encrease my obligations if by occasion You will present my humble Service to some other Patrons and friends of mine. I expect with Impatience the Favour of Your News, concerning Your Health and wellfare, of which I take a real share, as for the News of Your Opera's, I need not trouble you for all this Town is full of their ill success, by a number of Letters from Your quarters to the People of Quality here, and I can't help saying but that it furnishes great Diversion and laughter. The first Opera I heard my Self before I left London, and it made me very merry all along my journey, and of the second Opera, call'd Penelope, a certain noble man writes very jocosely, il faut que je dise avec Harlequin, nôtre Penelôpe n'est qu'une Sallôpe. but I think I have trespassed too much on Your Patience, I beg You to be persuaded of the sincere Veneration and Esteem with which I have the Honnour to be
S^r

      Your

          most obliged and most humble Servant
          George Frideric Handel
          [Deutsch, *Handel,* 530–31]

4. Sir John Hawkins describes Handel's choice of oratorio:

Other considerations suggested to him the almost certain benefit of such an undertaking: the performance of a sacred drama would consist with the solemnity of the Lent season, during which stage representations in this as in other Christian countries are in general forbidden; but above all, this served to recommend it, that it should be conducted at a small expense: no costly scenery was required, nor dresses for the performers, other than a suit of black, with which all persons that appeared in public were supposed to be provided. Instead of airs that required the delicacy of Cuzzoni, or the volubility of Faustina to execute, he hoped to please by songs, the beauties whereof were within the comprehension of less fastidious hearers than in general frequent the opera, namely, such as were adapted to a tenor voice, from the natural firmness and inflexibility whereof little more is ever expected than an articulate utterance of the words, and a just expression of the melody. . . . He knew also, that he could attach to him the real lovers and judges of music by those original beauties, which he was able to display in the composition of fugue and chorus; and these being once gained, the taste of the town was likely to fall in, as it frequently does, with the opinion of those who are best qualified to give a direction to it. To such a performance the talents of a second-rate singer, and persons used to choir service were adaquate.

[Sir John Hawkins, *A General History of the Science and Practice of Music,* 5 vols. (London, 1776), rpt. in 3 vols (New York: J. L. Peters, 1875), rpt. in 2 vols., with a new introd. by Charles Cudworth (New York: Dover,1963), 2:889]

5. From the minutes of the Governors of Mercer's Hospital, January 4, 1742:

Order'd [by the Governors of Mercer's Hospital] That John Rockfort John Ruthland & Richd Baldwin Esq^rs be desir'd to apply in the name of the Governors of Mercer's Hospital to the Rev^d the Dean [Jonathan Swift] & Chapter of St Patricks Dublin for their leave that such of their Choir as shall be Willing may assist at the Phil-Harmonick Society Performances which are principally intended for the Benefit of the said Hospital and to notifie to them that the Dean & Chapter of Christ Church have been pleas'd to grant them the same request.

[Deutsch, *Handel,* 534]

6. Jonathan Swift to the subdean and chapter of Saint Patrick's Cathedral, January 28, 1742:

And whereas it hath been reported, that I gave a licence to certain vicars to assist at a club of fiddlers in Fishamble Street, I do hereby declare that I remember no such licence to have been ever signed or sealed by me; and that if ever such pretended licence should be produced, I do hereby annul and vacate the said licence; intreating my said Sub-Dean and Chapter to punish such vicars as shall ever appear there, as songsters, fiddlers, pipers, trumpeters, drummers, drum-majors, or in any sonal quality, according to the flagitous aggravations of their respective disobedience, rebellion, perfidy, and ingratitude.

[Deutsch, *Handel,* 537]

7. From the *Dublin Journal* and the *Dublin News-Letter,* March 27, 1742:

For Relief of the Prisoners in the several Gaols, and for the Support of Mercer's Hospital in Stephen's Street, and of the Charitable Infirmary on the Inns Quay, on Monday the 12th of April, will be performed at the Musick Hall in Fishamble Street, Mr. *Handel's new Grand Oratorio, call'd the* MESSIAH, in which the Gentlemen of the Choirs of both Cathedrals will assist, with some Concertoes on the Organ, by Mr. Handell. Tickets to be had at the Musick Hall, and at Mr. Neal's in Christ-Church-Yard, at half a Guinea each. N.B. No Person will be admitted to the Rehearsal without a Rehearsal Ticket, which will be given gratis with the Ticket for the Performance when pay'd for.

[Deutsch, *Handel,* 542–43]

8. From the *Dublin Journal*, April 3, 1742:

On Thursday next being the 8th Inst. at the Musick Hall . . . will be the Rehearsal of Mr. Handel's new Grand Sacred Oratorio called *The* MESSIAH, in which the Gentlemen of both Choirs will assist: With some Concertos on the Organ by Mr. Handel.

[Deutsch, *Handel,* 544]

9. From the *Dublin Journal*, April 10, 1742:

Yesterday Mr. Handell's new Grand Sacred Oratorio, called, The MESSIAH, was rehearsed . . . to a most Grand, Polite and crouded Audience; and was performed so well, that it gave universal Satisfaction to all present; and was allowed by the greatest Judges to be the finest Composition of Musick that ever was heard, and the sacred Words as properly adapted for the Occasion.

[Deutsch, *Handel,* 545]

10. From the *Dublin News-Letter*, April 10, 1742:

Yesterday Morning, at the Musick Hall . . . there was a public Rehearsal of the Messiah, Mr. Handel's new sacred Oratorio, which in the opinion of the best Judges, far surpasses anything of that Nature, which has been performed in this or any other Kingdom. The elegant Entertainment was conducted in the most regular Manner, and to the entire satisfaction of the most crowded and polite Assembly.

To the benefit of three very important public Charities, there will be a grand Performance of this Oratorio on Tuesday next in the forenoon.

[Deutsch, *Handel,* 544–45]

11. Messiah reviewed in the *Dublin Journal*, April 17, 1742:

On Tuesday last Mr. Handel's Sacred Grand Oratorio, the MESSIAH, was performed at the New Musick-Hall in Fishamble-street; the best Judges allowed it to be the most finished piece of Musick. Words are wanting to express the exquisite Delight it afforded to the admiring crouded Audience. The Sublime, the Grand, and the Tender, adapted to the most elevated, majestick and moving Words, conspired to transport and charm the ravished Heart and Ear. It is but Justice to Mr. Handel, that the World should know, he generously gave the Money arising from this Grand Performance, to be equally shared by the Society for relieving Prisoners, the Charitable Infirmary, and Mercer's Hospital, for which they will ever gratefully remember his Name; and that the Gentlemen of the two Choirs, Mr. Dubourg, Mrs. Avolio, and Mrs. Cibber, who all performed their Parts to Admiration, acted also on the same disinterested Principle, satisfied with the deserved Applause of the Publick, and the conscious Pleasure of promoting such useful, and extensive Charity. There were above 700 People in the Room, and the Sum collected for that Noble and Pious Charity amounted to about 400*l*. out of which 127*l*. goes to each of the three great and pious Charities.

[Deutsch, Handel, 546]

12. Dr. Edward Synge, bishop of Elphin, heard *Messiah* in Dublin, and his praise of it was forwarded by Handel to Jennens:

As Mr Handel in his oratorio's greatly excells all other Composers I am acquainted with, So in the famous one, called The Messiah he seems to have excell'd himself. The whole is beyond any thing I had a notion of till I Read and heard it. It seems to be a Species of Musick different from any other, and this is particularly remarkable of it. That tho' the Composition is very Masterly & artificial, yet the Harmony is So great and open, as to please all who have Ears & will hear, learned & unlearn'd. Without a doubt this Superior Excellence is owing in some measure to the great care & exactness which Mr Handel seems to have us'd in preparing this Piece. But Some reasons may be given why He has Succeeded better in this than perhaps He could with all his skill, fully exerted, have done in any other.

> 1 one is the Subject, which is the greatest & most interesting. It Seems to have inspir'd him.
> 2 Another is the Words, which are all Sublime, or affecting in the greatest degree.
> 3 a Third reason for the Superior Excellence of this piece, 'Tis this there is no Dialogue. In every Drame there must be a great deal & often broken into very Short Speeches & Answers. If these be flat, & insipid, they move laughter or Contempt.

Whereas in this Piece the attention of the Audience is Engag'd from one end to the other: And the Parts Set in Recitativo, being Continu'd Sentences, & Some times adorn'd with too much applause, by the audience as the rest.—

They seem'd indeed throughly engag'd frome one end to the other. And, to their great honour, tho' the young & gay of both Sexes were present in great numbers, their behaviour was uniformly grave & decent, which Show'd that they were not only pleas'd but affected with the performance. Many, I hope, were instructed by it, and had proper Sentiments inspir'd in a Stronger Manner in their Minds.

[*Autograph Letters of George Frideric Handel and Charles Jennens: Property of Earl Howe, C. B. E.* Sold by Christie, Manson and Woods (Christie's), July 4, 1973. Illustrated catalogue; quoted in Hogwood, *Handel,* 179, in a shortened version. The text here is from Richard Luckett, *Handel's Messiah: A Celebration* (New York: Harcourt Brace, 1992), 129–30.]

13. Excerpts from the correspondence of Charles Jennens:

His Messiah has disappointed me, being set in great hast, tho' he said he would be a year about it, & make it the best of all his Compositions. I shall put no more Sacred Works into his hands, to be thus abus'd. . . .

As to the Messiah, 'tis still in his power by retouching the weak parts to make it fit for a publick performance; & I have said a great deal to him on the Subject; but he is so lazy and so obstinate, that I much doubt the Effect....

I shall show you a collection I gave Handel, call'd Messiah, which I value highly, & he has made a fine entertainment of it, tho' not near so good as he might & ought to have done. I have with great difficulty made him correct some of the grossest faults in the composition, but he retain'd his Overture obstinately, in which there are some passages far unworthy of Handel, but much more unworthy of the Messiah.

[First two passages: H. C. Robbins Landon, *Handel and His World* (London : Weidenfeld and Nicolson, 1984), 172; third passage: Deutsch, *Handel,* 622]

14. A poetic description by Laurence Whyte on the occasion of the opening of the New Music Hall:

As Amphion built of the old the Theban wall,
So Neal has built a sumptuous Musick Hall:
The one, by pow'rful touches of his lute;
The other, by the fiddle and the flute.
Join'd with some others of harmonic sound,
He rais'd this lofty fabric from the ground;
Where heaps of rubbish in confusion stood,
Old walls, old timber, and some rotten wood;
From their old chaos they new forms assume,—
Here stands the Hall, and there the drawing-room,
Adorn'd with all that workmanship can do
By ornaments and architecture too.
The oblong area runs from east to west,
Fair to behold, but hard to be exprest;
At th' eastern end the awful throne is plac'd,
With fluted columns and pilasters grac'd,
Fit for the noblest President to rest,
Who likes the arms of Ireland for his crest.
In diff'rent classes, at the western end,
Musicians with their instruments attend;
While they diffuse their harmony around,
The concave arch reverberates the sound.
The architect has here display'd his art,
By decorations proper for each part:
The cornice, dentills, and the curious mould,
The fret-work, and the vaulted roof behold;
The hollow arches, and the bold design,
In ev'ry part with symmetry divine.

There stand fine mirrors to reflect the fair,
Lest they forget themselves, or where they are;
The precious curl and lappets to adjust,
And to remind them that they are but dust.

[rpt. in John T. Gilbert, *A History of the City of Dublin* (Dublin: J. McGlashan,
1854–59; rpt., Shannon: Irish University Press, 1972), 3 vols., 1:72–73]

15. From the *Dublin Journal*, April 20, 1742:

On Mr. *Handel's* Performance of his *Oratorio*, call'd the *Messiah*, for the Support of Hospitals,
and other pious Uses, at the Musick-Hall in Fishamble-street, on Tuesday, April 13th, 1742, before the Lords Justices, and a vast Assembly of the Nobility and Gentry of both Sexes. By Mr.
L.[aurence] *Whyte*.

What can we offer more in *Handel's* praise?
Since his *Messiah* gain'd him groves of Bays;
Groves that can never whither nor decay,
Whose *Vistos* his Ability display:
Here *Nature* smiles, when grac'd with *Handel's* Art,
Transports the Ear, and ravishes the Heart;
To all the nobler *Passions* we are mov'd,
When various strains repeated and improv'd,
Express each different Circumstance and State,
As if each Sound became Articulate.
　　　None but the Great *Messiah* cou'd inflame,
And raise his Soul to so sublime a *Theme*,
Profound the Thoughts, the Subject all divine,
Now like the Tales of *Pindus* and the *Nine;*
Or Heathen Deities, those Sons of Fiction,
Sprung from old *Fables,* stuff'd with Contradiction;
But our *Messiah,* blessed be his Name!
Both Heaven and Earth his *Miracles* proclaim.
His Birth, his Passion, and his Resurrection,
With his Ascension, have a strong Connection;
What Prophets spoke, or Sybels could relate,
In him were all their Prophecies compleat,
The *Word* made Flesh, both God and Man became;
Then let all Nations glorify his Name.
Let Hallelujah's round the Globe be sung,
To our *Messiah,* from a Virgin sprung.

[Deutsch, *Handel,* 546–47]

3

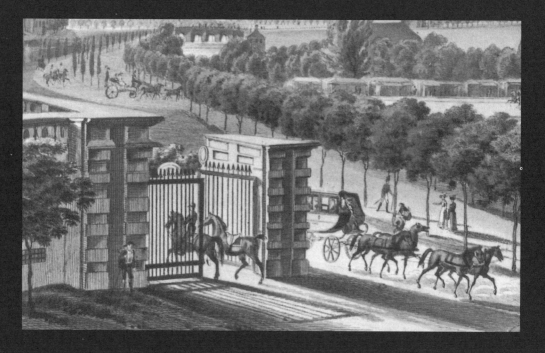

Ludwig van Beethoven, Ninth Symphony

Friday, May 7, 1824, 7:00 P.M.

After talks and discussions lasting for six weeks I now feel cooked, stewed and roasted. What on earth is to be the outcome of this much discussed concert, if the prices are not going to be raised? What will be left over for me after such heavy expenses, seeing that the copying alone is already costing so much?

—Beethoven to Schindler, April 1824

*L*udwig van Beethoven began planning a concert (or, as he called it, an "Academy") of his music in the spring of 1824. He had not given a concert for a decade, even though he was now famous: the king of France had awarded him a medal, the Philharmonic Society of London was courting him, and a group of distinguished residents of Vienna had just published an open letter to him entreating him to present his music in Vienna, not abroad.

Despite his fame, however, Beethoven could not possibly have known that his latest symphony would become perhaps the most famous piece of classical music in Western culture. The Ninth Symphony has fascinated listeners, critics, and analysts since the moment of its first performance. It has generated pop songs, hymn tunes, television theme music, and a variety of cultural phenomena to an extent matched only by Handel's *Messiah*. In Japan, performances of the Ninth are a crucial part of New Year's Eve celebrations: choral societies rehearse the piece diligently, and every year performances of the symphony on December 31 number in the dozens. Indeed, the format of the modern CD was determined by a Japanese firm's insistence that the symphony fit on a single disk.

Many later composers were guided by this symphony, which was both a milestone and a millstone. "He was an artist," said Franz Grillparzer at Beethoven's funeral, "and who shall arise to stand beside him?" The opening sound of the symphony's first movement, ambiguous as to key and meter, a figuration of chaos out of which order comes only gradually, gives a sense of the breadth of the symphony to follow; this general plan has been imitated by many subsequent composers, and not just second-rate imitators. It is difficult not to hear echoes of Beethoven, and of this symphony in particular, in a number of very long symphonies, sometimes with vocal participants, that seek a combination of personal and universal expression.　•

Portrait of Beethoven, 1824

This engraving is based on a chalk drawing by Stefan Decker reportedly made by the artist a few days after Beethoven's concert of May 1824. Perhaps it shows the haircut that Schuppanzigh praised in the conversation books. It certainly does not show Beethoven's dark complexion, his pockmarked face, or his often slovenly appearance.

Beethoven asks to use the Redoutensaal for his concert; he is given a bureaucratic answer:

To Count Moritz Dietrichstein

Vienna, March, 1824

Your Excellency!

I have been approached from various quarters with the suggestion that I should give a grand concert. I request you, therefore, to grant me permission to give it in the Grosser Redoutensaal and on the evening of April 8th. Duport is entirely in favour of it. About the Mass for His Majesty I must still beg to be excused. The next time I see you I shall enlighten you about everything concerning that work—I know that you will forgive me for not calling on Y(our) E(xcellency) in person. But I have an enormous amount to do; and I know that that is the case with Y(our) E(xcellency) as well. And you too do not stand on ceremony.

Your Excellency's

most devoted servant

L. Van Beethoven

Memorandum in the Imperial Royal High Steward's office, on Beethoven's request to give a concert in the Redoutensaal:

(Vienna: March 16, 1824)

Van Beethoven, musician, requests permission to hold a musical *Akademie* on the evening of April 7, in the I[mperial] R[oyal] Redoutensaal.

dated March 13th; rec'd. 16, 1824

Decree

Since the permission for holding a musical *Akademie* in the I. R. Redoutensaal does not rest with us, the I. R. Lord High Steward's Office, the petitioner has to apply for the granting of the same to the I. R. High Police Director's Office; then regarding the securing of the hall to the lessee of the I. R. Kärntnertor Theater, Domenico Barbaja.

By the I. R. Lord High Steward's Office

Mayrhofer

Carl Czerny on Beethoven's concert:

There is surely no more significant musical news that I can write you about from our dear old Vienna than that Beethoven finally gave repeated performances of his long-awaited concert, and in the most striking manner astonished everyone who feared that after ten years of deafness he could now produce only dry, abstract works, bereft of imagination. To the greatest extent, his new Symphony breathes such a fresh, lively, indeed youthful spirit; so much power, innovation and beauty as ever [came] from the head of this ingenious man, although several times he certainly gave the old wigs something to shake their heads about.

The Ninth Symphony has a unique place in Western culture and brings with it so many associations, so much critical and analytical history, and so much significance retrospectively that it is not easy to imagine this composition in Beethoven's Vienna. Whereas Viennese society of the time has passed into memory and museums, the Ninth Symphony has remained alive and seems more a part of our own time (or perhaps of all times) than of Beethoven's. In a sense, of course, it is one of the joys of music that this should be so. But our perception is inevitably different from that of the first audience, and our purpose here is to put ourselves in their place, in the Vienna of 1824, to consider the Ninth Symphony as a part of its own culture. In this way we may gain a new perspective on an old friend and perhaps enrich our understanding of Beethoven's genius and of this symphony's unique qualities.

To nineteenth-century Viennese, a symphony was a piece of concert music, though not a significant one. Mozart's forty-one symphonies and Haydn's 104 or so are certainly notable music—they are now played by orchestras everywhere—but they are of another world. The symphony of the late eighteenth century had been essentially a curtain-raiser played at the beginnings of musical events—a sort of wallpaper music that prepared the way for more important things to come: operas, concerti, oratorios. Thus a review of 1805: "The concert opened with a Haydn symphony which, as is usual with the opening pieces of concerts, was only half heard." Or again in 1800: "First a quartet or a symphony, which basically is viewed as a necessary evil (you have to start with something!) and therefore to be talked through."

A symphony was expected to begin loudly. Standard symphonies used in concerts (as opposed to those used for operas) consisted of several (usually four) movements, each having a different mood. The opening movement, occasionally preceded by a slow introduction, was generally the most substantial: it had a lively tempo and contrasted two sets of themes and two different keys. These themes were then developed in various ways—combined, transposed, divided into constituent elements—before being repeated in the original key. A slower, more lyrical movement followed, providing a contemplative or passionate contrast to the usually extroverted opening movement. Most symphonies by Mozart and Haydn had a minuet as the third movement, the clear phraseology and regular rhythm of the familiar dance offering a moment of relaxation. The symphony closed with a lively finale, a fourth movement, usually lighter and briefer than the opening movement. The whole thing lasted perhaps fifteen minutes.

Symphonies were much in demand in Vienna. Virtuoso soloists needed two or three for a concert: one to open the concert, one to close it, and perhaps one to call for attention after an intermission. Every oratorio opened with a symphony; and many, complete or partial, were used as intermission fillers in the theaters ("I was very attentive, not only in the *Singspiele,* but also to the symphonies between the acts, which the audience pays so little attention to").

By the time of Haydn and Mozart, symphonies had already begun to gain a new musical importance. As symphonies got larger and musically more significant, concert programs might include only parts of a symphony, or split its performance (as Mozart did with his "Haffner" symphony), presenting part at the beginning of the concert, the rest at the end. By the time of Beethoven's Ninth Symphony, the role of curtain-raiser was being taken over by concert overtures.

Beethoven's Third ("Eroica," 1803) and Seventh (1813) symphonies had expanded enormously the traditional weight and function of the symphony. Beyond physical scope, Beethoven's symphonies, especially the Fifth and Sixth, had created a sense of the multiple movements as a single work that possessed a psychological sequence through the several segments, a progression that generally represented struggle leading to triumph and transcendence.

Many of the unusual aspects of the Ninth Symphony were not entirely new in Beethoven's thinking. The Fifth Symphony, which begins in C minor but ends in a triumphant C major, saves the highest and lowest instruments—piccolo and contrabassoon—for the C-major finale; and the Ninth begins in a spooky not-quite D minor buts ends in a blaze of D major (with the piccolo and contrabassoon again entering only in the last movement, in the "Turkish March" of the finale).

Whereas a classical symphony had formerly consisted of a substantial first movement to which several shorter movements were appended, in the Ninth Beethoven shifts the weight from the first movement toward the end. This is not accomplished, however, by lightening the beginning; the first movement is grand, solemn, and perhaps tragic music, whose nebulous opening creates both doubt about the key (is it

Beethoven's Score of the Ninth Symphony

The score is not easy to read, and it is little wonder that the copyists
preparing the orchestral parts (see p. 158) had difficulty deciphering the
manuscript. The instruments are listed at the left: woodwinds at the top, brass
in the center, and strings at the bottom. Not included on this first page are the
vocalists and instruments that will enter later: soloists and chorus, trombones,
piccolo, contrabassoon, bass drum, and cymbals. His notations at the top—
"All[egr]o. Ma non troppo. Un poco mosso"—indicate tempo.

major? minor?) and a sense of timelessness that immediately signals the listener that
this is a work of cosmic proportion.

    The shift of weight is achieved partially by the reordering of the movements.
The Scherzo, here as elsewhere in Beethoven replacing the Mozartean minuet, is
moved to the second position; its humorous—or sinister—kettledrum solos and its
rhythmic tricks do not serve as relief after the slow movement; the outer sections of this
Scherzo are themselves in first-movement forms. The slow movement comes third, a
lovely and passionate series of variations on two themes in two keys; the first theme—
beginning much like the beautiful slow movement of the "Pathétique" piano sonata
—is in the key of B-flat, representing the dark side of this work (B-flat is significant in
the first movement and returns for the "Turkish March"), while the alternating theme
is in a celestial D major, the key toward which the symphony as a whole is moving.

But Beethoven produces the main shift of weight through a final movement of gigantic proportions: a chorus and a quartet of vocal soloists break into song, singing Beethoven's version of Schiller's ode to joy, *An die Freude*. Everything has been leading up to this: the last movement opens by reviewing and rejecting the music of the foregoing movements. Beethoven had experimented with interlocking movements in his Fifth Symphony, where the minor-key Scherzo leads without interruption into the triumphant C-major finale (with piccolo and contrabassoon), and this contrast is revisited when music from the Scherzo returns at the end of the development of the Finale. In the Ninth Symphony, however, the triumph comes not with a blazing start but in the course of the finale itself.

Nobody has succeeded in describing in analytical terms all the complexities and balances of this titanic finale. It is like a concerto, in which the soloists and chorus take the role of the solo instrument; it is like a symphony in itself, with varying moods, tempos, and movements; it is like an oratorio, with solo singers and choir; it is like a French revolutionary cantata, culminating in a great passionate outburst. But it is mostly the statement of a personal credo: "All men shall be brothers," centered around a folklike melody of such grandeur and simplicity that nobody ever forgets it.

This symphony is neither a curtain-raiser nor an intermission feature; and it is not what one was used to listening to in Vienna of 1824.

Life in Vienna

Vienna today still looks in many ways as it did to Beethoven. The Danube still flows past the edge of the city. The center is still dominated by the Steffl, the great Gothic spire of Saint Stephen's Cathedral. The magnificent Baroque buildings of Fischer von Erlach and others continue to give an imperial majesty to the city. One can still linger, have a good meal, and do a lot of reading in the many cafés and restaurants. The traditional four-wheeled, two-horse fiacre is still used for transport, although now it often moves on rubber tires and carries tourists.

In 1824 Vienna was still a fortified city, with eight main gates and twenty-seven bastions in its massive city walls. Just outside the walls, an open defensive ring, the glacis, on which no permanent building was allowed to stand, separated the center of the city from the newer suburbs. The glacis was some nineteen hundred feet across, roughly the range of a late seventeenth-century cannon (the last Turkish invasion had been in 1683). An outer ring of defenses and customs houses, the Linien, stood beyond the suburbs and defined the city limits.

The major buildings announce that Vienna was the capital of a great empire: the central complex of the Hofburg Palace; the Versailles-like Schönbrunn Palace, built by Maria Theresia, used at the Congress of Vienna, and once occupied by Napoleon; the Belvedere, built in the early eighteenth century for Prince Eugene of Savoy in grat-

Vienna, by Jacob Alt, ca. 1820

Viewed from the suburbs, the tower of the Gothic cathedral in central
Vienna (left) can be seen in the distance; the Rampe of the Schwarzenberg
Palace and the Karlskirche are in the foreground. The approach to Vienna
in Beethoven's day involved crossing the glacis, a defensive area as wide as
the range of a seventeenth-century cannon; no permanent buildings were
allowed to be erected on this open parkland.

itude for his victory over the Turks, but now owned by the Imperial family. The Prater, an Imperial hunting preserve, and the smaller Augarten now stood open to the public as parklands.

Vienna is an aristocratic city, full of palaces of the wealthy and the noble: Rasumofsky, Kaunitz, Metternich, Liechtenstein, Schwarzenberg—these are names connected with Beethoven, but to a Viennese they also speak of great families with palatial residences. Vienna is also a Catholic city: in addition to the Stefansdom and the many other churches, there were large monastic establishments—almost cities in themselves—such as the Schottenhof and the Mölkerhof.

Life in Vienna could be agreeable, but it was seldom long. Many children died (only two of Mozart's children survived infancy), and according to a contemporary guidebook, the average life span during the period 1801–25 was thirty-six to forty years for men, and forty-one to forty-five years for women. So Schubert (who died at thirty-one) and Mozart (at thirty-five) were not cheated of much of their lives; Beethoven, at

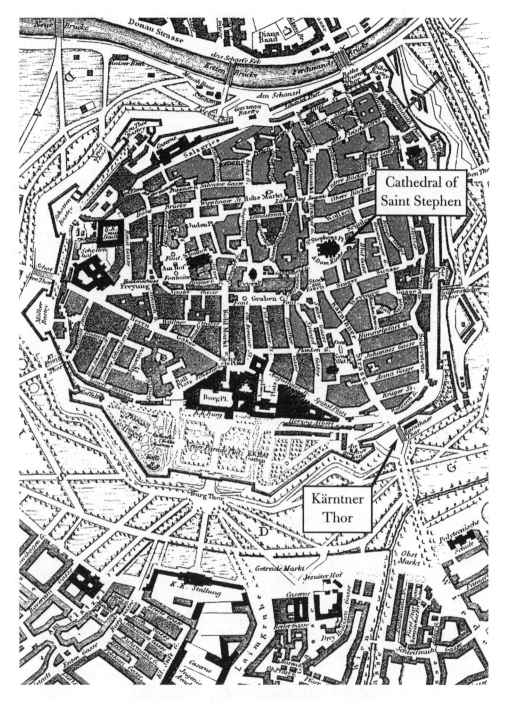

Map of Vienna (detail), Showing the City Center, 1823

The medieval city below the Danube has narrow streets and two major
monuments, the Cathedral of Saint Stephen and the polygonal Imperial
palace. The Kärntner Strasse leads south and a little east from the
cathedral and passes through the Kärntner Thor, the gate leading to the
province of Carinthia. Just inside this gate is the Kärntnertor Theater,
the opera house of Vienna and the site of Beethoven's concert.

The English physician Richard Bright described Vienna in 1814:

My apartment was large and desolate, without a carpet but provided with an earthen stove in one corner, and a little wooden bedstead in another. Such are the miserable accommodations in most of the inns at Vienna. . . . After some time I walked into the streets,—a service of danger; for most of them are narrow, and the sides, which are paved with flat stones for the convenience of walking, and are, on that account, greatly praised throughout the whole empire, are so little elevated above the carriage tract, that the foot passenger has no safety but in the judgment of the charioteer, who frequently risks an encounter with your feet, rather than with the wheels of a passing carriage. The coachmen, however, give some warning of their approach by a species of unintelligible roar, a little in accent like the language in which a Lancashire carter converses with his team; but not less peremptory than the rapid "by your leave" of a Bath chairman. When, by courage or good luck, I could snatch an opportunity to cast a look upwards, I observed that many of the houses were large, and handsomely built, and all of them very high; but, owing to the narrowness of the streets, there is a prevailing gloom, and it is only in a few of the more open parts that the real beauty of the buildings can develop itself. The shops display a considerable variety of goods, though frequently a square glazed case of patterns hanging at the door is the only mark by which the nature of the shopkeeper's dealings is indicated. Besides this, a small board, projecting into the street from above each door, bears some painted sign, as the Golden Fleece, the Scepter, the Schwarzenburg Head, or the Holy Ghost.

fifty-three, was an old man when he premiered his Ninth Symphony, and he lived another three years. Haydn, who died at seventy-seven, was extraordinary.

Cold, damp winters and hot, dusty summers led to chronic illnesses. In hot weather, the rich retreated to summer homes or spas (sometimes taking musicians with them); others, like Beethoven, often retired to villages such as Heiligenstadt. Large segments of the population were killed by periodic epidemics: smallpox in 1806, scarlet fever in 1822, cholera in 1831. The most common ailments were lung diseases, which went under a variety of names; impure water caused other types of disease (Beethoven died of a gastric ailment). Venereal diseases (from which Beethoven and Schubert probably both suffered) must have induced anguish about sexual encounters.

Family life was precious, crowded, and potentially dangerous. And married life was expensive; persons were forbidden to wed unless they had the requisite education, financial solidity, and political orthodoxy. Men unable to afford marriage remained bachelors, and many couples lived in common-law marriages, which added significantly to the official count of illegitimate births. Death from childbirth was common; the widowers left behind often remarried, and the orphaned children of those who did not were raised by relatives.

Living standards for the middle class centered on the high cost and the poor quality of housing. The first two stories of an apartment building were considered desirable, but not the ground floor, because of noise and dust, or the top floor, because of heat. Apartments were rented by the season, rents being due on Saint George's Day (April 24) and Saint Michael's (September 29). Beethoven's conversation books often reflect worries about housing at these times of year. In 1824 he considered several second-floor apartments with from three to five rooms, at rents ranging from 250 to 600 florins per year (a good meal might cost 1 florin, a box seat at the opera 8).

Viennese apartments were crowded, which explains the popularity of cafés and restaurants. Many people took at least one meal per day outside the home; this may be why food was usually the largest living expense, even though it was abundant and cheap. Other major living expenses included heating (firewood was expensive) and clothing (also expensive, though the right clothes were important); in 1824 these expenses required an average annual income of perhaps fifteen hundred to two thousand florins.

Vienna had undergone a great deal of political turmoil in recent years. The Holy Roman emperor Franz II (dedicatee of Haydn's most famous melody, later sung as "Deutschland über Alles") saw it all. The French Revolution, so encouraging to enlightened thinkers and so upsetting to absolute monarchs everywhere, cast a shadow that contributed to the repressive laws, the spies, the censorship, and the police surveillance that characterized Austrian life in Beethoven's day. The rise of Napoleon inspired the first dedication of Beethoven's "Heroic" Third Symphony, but this was angrily erased when Bonaparte made himself consul for life and then emperor. The political and economic consequences of Napoleon's European domination were disastrous to Vienna. The French occupied Vienna after the battle of Austerlitz in 1805; Franz II abdicated under pressure and became Emperor Franz I of Austria. Napoleon entered Vienna in 1809, residing in Schönbrunn Palace. The following year Napoleon cemented his dynastic position by marrying (in absentia) Marie Louise, the daughter of Franz I.

The Paradeplatz, Vienna, by Leopold Beyer, 1805

As one approaches the center of Vienna across the glacis, the Burgtor
(palace gate) leads to the parade ground and the Imperial palace, whose
symmetrical façade masks the fact that it is a vast complex of medieval,
Renaissance, and modern buildings.

By 1811 the Austrian state was effectively bankrupt. An enormous economic
collapse led to a devaluation of the currency and hard times for all. The political and
economic power of the aristocracy was much diminished. An annuity that Beethoven
was paid by a group of aristocrats was reduced to less than a third of its original value.
Commercial and bourgeois interests gradually reestablished a newly oriented society
in a period that would come to be called the Biedermeier era; these social and economic changes contributed to Beethoven's need and desire to fashion a career independent of state or individual patronage.

In 1824 Ludwig van Beethoven had been in Vienna for thirty-two years. In his
native Bonn he had worked as a keyboard player and an orchestral violinist and had
studied composition with Christian Gottlob Neefe. In Vienna he was one of the many
foreign musicians who sought to make a career at this international crossroads. He began by studying with Haydn and moved on to lessons in counterpoint with the cathedral kapellmeister Johann Georg Albrechtsberger.

Soon Beethoven established himself independently as a piano virtuoso and
composer, two roles that were almost always connected: a soloist did not generally play ·

the music of others. He became the darling of aristocratic salons owing to his spectacular keyboard skill, his improvisations, and his sharp tongue directed at his social superiors. By 1800 he was well enough established to give a concert, which included his First Symphony, for his own benefit in one of the major theaters. He was among those musician-composers who managed, not without great personal effort, to establish an independent career as performer, teacher, and composer, and his reputation soon spread beyond Vienna as a result of the publication of his sonatas, quartets, and chamber and orchestral music.

Beethoven's career depended to some extent on his being a public figure—a virtuoso performer and a composer able to lead the performance of his own works. But about 1800, his growing deafness precipitated a personal crisis. Such a calamity in the life of a highly charged and independent musician might have been overwhelming, but instead of giving in, Beethoven managed to concentrate even more deeply on his compositions. The beginnings of what some call his heroic style—the compositions that display the greatness, the struggle, the triumph, and the monumental proportions characteristic of the Ninth Symphony—are to be found in the music that Beethoven wrote after his decision to overcome his handicap. The "Eroica" symphony, the opera that became *Fidelio* (a heroic rescue), the "Waldstein" piano sonata, and many other works trace their beginnings to this period.

During this difficult time, Beethoven was forced to piece together a career from commissions, publications, proceeds from benefit concerts, and all the other sources of income available to a musician. Eventually unable to appear in public as a virtuoso because of his deafness, he gave himself to composition. At an agonizing and critical time he had given up his long-held desire to marry and live a domestic life. His now-famous letter to an "Immortal beloved," found after his death but written in 1812, is addressed to one whom he longs for but cannot attain. It seems that Beethoven soon resigned himself to a life of solitude; his protective concern for the welfare of his ward and nephew Karl in the years that followed is his only other deeply felt personal attachment, perhaps connected to his earlier matrimonial turning point. Composition and publication gradually led to Beethoven's rising reputation, not only in Vienna but in the larger world. By 1824 he was widely regarded as the world's greatest composer, but in Vienna itself he was more respected than heard. A revered and honored senior citizen, Beethoven was entirely out of sympathy with the new rage for Rossini's operas and was largely cut off from society by his own idiosyncratic gruffness and by the deafness that forced him to carry on all conversations in writing. His concert of 1824 was designed both to raise money and to present to the Viennese public his latest works: the Ninth Symphony and the *Missa Solemnis*.

By 1824 Beethoven had in many ways successfully dealt with the vicissitudes of a musician's life in Vienna. Musicians did then what they do now: perform, teach, compose. But in 1824 there were no university music faculties, no public concert orchestras or standing chamber ensembles. Musicians often looked for regular employment, but positions were not available to all, not easy to get, and not easy to keep. The safest and surest approach was to work for the state, which employed orchestras and singers for the state theaters; chamber musicians; a regular complement of instruments and voices for the Imperial chapel; and regularly salaried kapellmeisters and court composers. Appointment often depended as much on the candidate's politics and financial status as on his (or in the case of opera singers, her) musical ability. Some performers, especially the better ones, thought that work for the state was too taxing and too poorly paid.

Many aristocratic families also retained musicians; a few had whole orchestras, some had salaried chamber musicians, and many more full-time music teachers. This patronage had been of central importance for musicians in the eighteenth century but was less so now as a result of the post-Napoleonic financial collapse and the reduced circumstances of the aristocracy. A musician working for an aristocrat was clearly a servant, and getting a position was usually a matter of influence and connection as well as of talent. Beethoven is famous, of course, for his rude treatment of aristocratic patrons; this, combined with his virtuosity at the keyboard, seems to have made him, for a time, the indispensable favorite of aristocratic salons.

Then as now, salaried or not, musicians often assembled their income on an ad hoc basis. For much of his career, Beethoven, like Mozart, was valued more as a performer than as a composer; and performers at concerts, recitals, salons, and benefits earned fees. Many amateurs paid for music lessons, but schedules could be unpredictable and teachers were numerous. In 1804 Beethoven wrote, "Vienna is swarming with teachers who try to make a living by giving lessons." As a result, teachers had to work hard. Carl Czerny, the virtuoso student of Beethoven and teacher of Franz Liszt, reported that he gave eleven or twelve lessons a day, from eight in the morning till eight in the evening, for more than twenty years! Teachers in the conservatory founded in 1817 by the Gesellschaft der Musikfreunde did not fare well either, although professors of violin and singing did substantially better than others and had a steady, if not large, income. A composer could add to his coffers gifts from the dedicatees of compositions and fees from publishers; in Beethoven's case these were important.

Beethoven's income was relatively large in 1824. His annuity, which had been guaranteed by a group of noble patrons, had fallen off during the period of general economic disaster but was reestablished in 1811 at 1,360 florins a year. With the sale of only a little music he could have 1,500 florins a year. Still he complained of debts; of course, his ample living style, his two servants (and sometimes two apartments), and the expenses of educating his nephew Karl certainly had something to do with Beethoven's financial burdens. Nevertheless, Beethoven accumulated a substantial estate, which, by the time of his death, in 1827, had amounted to about 10,000 florins. In his concert of May 1824 Beethoven hoped, optimistically as it turned out, to realize a profit of some 2,000 florins—a good annual income.

J. F. Reichardt on the Viennese theater:

In the city and the suburbs five theaters of the most varied sort give performances all the year round. At the two court theaters in the city itself, one sees everything outstanding in the way of grand and comic opera, comedy, and tragedy that Germany produces—and, in some measure, Italy and France as well. . . . On days when no play is scheduled, all these theaters give great concerts and performances of the most important ancient and modern music for church and concert hall. Aside from this, all winter long there are frequent public concerts, by local and visiting musicians, and excellent quartet and amateur concerts by subscription. . . . All the great public diversions and amusements are enjoyed by all classes without any abrupt divisions or offending distinctions—in those respects, Vienna is again quite alone among the great cities of Europe.

Theater and opera served many purposes in Viennese life. Only at the theater could large groups assemble for entertainment, and theatergoing was the only social activity that included all classes. The theater was a public meeting place, a place for business, for fashion, for conversation, sometimes for assignations, and sometimes for listening to music or the spoken word.

Performances generally began at six or seven. Because seats were usually unreserved before the 1830s, it was customary for theatergoers to arrive early or, if possible, to send servants to buy and occupy seats for their employers. The rush for seats had its physical dangers, however. Nobles often sent their strongest chair bearers, and a law of 1800 forbade children under the age of sixteen from being sent for theater seats.

Rules concerning public decorum prohibited the presence of dogs in the theater and required gentlemen to remove their hats. Applause was also limited by decree: audiences were forbidden to request encores or repetitions, and performers were prohibited from appearing before the curtain to bow or to speak. But rules apply only to what *ought* to happen; in fact, audiences were loud and demonstrative, happily cheering between movements, and reprises were a regular feature of concert life. Performers were certainly applauded and were seldom prevented from taking individual bows. Applause in the theater may have served as a healthy outlet for repressed emotions in a highly regulated society charged with censorship and rigid etiquette.

Audiences felt less constrained in the smaller suburban theaters, which operated without direct court supervision or subvention. Of these only one was important for music: the Theater an der Wien (that is, along the banks of the Wien—or Wieden—River, which flows into the Danube from south and east of the city center). The theater had been opened in 1801 by Emanuel Schikaneder, who had also operated its predecessor, the old Freihaus Theater, where he had given the first performance of *The Magic Flute* and many another singspiel and comic play. The Theater an der Wien was billed as the largest and most beautiful in Vienna; it had a vast stage, said to hold five hundred men and fifty horses, and was equipped with elaborate and complex machinery for mounting the spectacles, melodramas, and *Zauberstücke* (magic operas) for which the house was famous. Like other theaters, it was sometimes available for concerts, and it had already premiered Beethoven's Fifth and Sixth symphonies, as well as the first two versions of *Fidelio*.

Of the two other lesser suburban theaters, one was the "small and dirty" Theater in der Leopoldstadt, renowned for Viennese folk comedies, a favorite venue among the working classes. The tiny (but charming) Theater in der Josephstadt had governmental permission to present opera, ballet, and drama, but it was always in difficult financial straits and came into its own only in the 1830s; notable among its premieres are the German version of Carl Maria von Weber's *Oberon* (1827) and Gustav Lortzing's *Zar und Zimmermann* (1837). Beethoven composed his overture "Die Weihe des Hauses" for the 1822 reopening of the theater (and he would use the overture again at the beginning of the concert that included the Ninth Symphony).

The two government-operated court theaters were in principle the private theaters of the emperor, though they had long been administered by a bureaucracy and were available to the upper reaches of society. One, the Burgtheater, got its name because it was attached to the palace; Mozart had often performed there, but now it presented mostly classic German drama; built in 1741, it had become, as Frances Trollope noted in 1838, "dingy, ugly, and inconvenient in form." Its prices were moderate, and most seats, as elsewhere, were unreserved. It was demolished in 1888, as its sister, the Kärntnertor Theater, had been twenty years earlier.

At the outer end of the Kärntnerstrasse stood the Royal and Imperial Theater, next to the Kärntnertor (the Carinthia Gate), the other official court theater, this one reserved mostly for opera and ballet. Built in 1763, the Kärntnertor Theater had an elegant interior with five tiers of balconies. Famous singers were on the payroll, and its ballet troupe was renowned. Italian opera commanded doubled ticket prices—Rossini could always pack the house. The first performance of the final version of *Fidelio* had been presented there in 1814 and the premiere of Weber's *Euryanthe* in 1823. In 1824 it was the venue for Beethoven's concert.

Beethoven chose the Kärntnertor Theater only partly because of the privilege associated with the court; theaters are not ideal places for orchestral music, but in 1824

Exterior of the Kärntnertor Theater, by Eduard Gurk, ca. 1815

The Kärntnertor Theater, one of two official court theaters in Vienna, was
used mainly for opera in 1824. It was rebuilt in 1763 after a fire, and the
covered entrance was added in 1766. The city wall is to the right, and the
noise of traffic passing through the nearby Carinthia Gate sometimes
interfered with listening to quiet music in the theater.

Vienna had no concert hall. Music was heard in private houses, in churches, and in
such other locations as could be obtained. Nor was there a standing orchestra in Vienna to play concert music or a series of orchestral concerts; instead, orchestras were
associated with a specific church or theater. The theaters themselves, even the court
theaters, could be rented and used for concerts on days when theatrical performances
were forbidden by law. These official Spielfreie Tage included Advent, Lent, certain
holidays and their eves, and the anniversary of the last emperor's death.

Most public concerts were single events organized by an individual. By the
early nineteenth century, however, there were a few regular concert series, often with a
charitable purpose. The Tonkünstlersozietät (Society of Musical Artists), founded in
1772, gave two concerts per year, usually of large-scale oratorios, for the benefit of the
widows and orphans of musicians; these well-attended concerts, performed by Vienna's professional forces, had been an important part of musical life since Mozart's
day.

The most substantial concert organization in Beethoven's Vienna was the

> **A concert in Vienna, 1808:**
>
> The *Liebhaberconzerte* have begun here for the winter, and the one I have just attended was nearly the death of me, for all that the company was very agreeable. In three rather small rooms, the like of which I have scarcely seen here before, a great crowd of listeners of all classes and an almost equally great one of musicians were so crammed together that I lost both my breath and my hearing. Fortunately, however, I did not also lose my sight, for a part of the company consisted of very attractive fine ladies, some of whom also sang very nicely. But even excellent things by Beethoven, Romberg, Paër, and others could have no effect, since in the narrow space one was quite deafened by the noise of the trumpets, kettledrums and wind instruments of all sorts.

Gesellschaft der Musikfreunde (Society of the Friends of Music), founded in 1814. Its large membership combined amateur and professional musicians with listeners and supporters. From 1814 to 1816 the society gave annual large-scale oratorio performances similar to the 1812 performance of Handel's *Alexander's Feast* (see page 148). In 1824 the society's activities included four major concerts and some sixteen smaller *Abendunter-haltungen*, or evening entertainments. At the larger concerts, held in the Redoutensaal (the great ballroom of the Imperial Palace), the repertory focused on serious music from earlier generations, excluding the modern vogue for the operatic music of Rossini and his imitators and shunning the spectacular virtuosi who were the mainstays of the commercial concert. Soloists and conductors were rotated; there were few concerti, and none for piano. Much vocal music was presented at these concerts, however, including music from oratorios by the local kapellmeister (including, of course, Mozart and Haydn). These concerts, probably of reasonable quality, brought together amateur and professional performers. The Abendunterhaltungen were essentially chamber music concerts, held on Thursdays throughout the season, usually in the Landeshaus (the County Hall) or the Rote Igel (the Red Hedgehog Inn) in the Tuchlauben; they included at least one string quartet or quintet, a vocal solo, an instrumental solo, and a number of vocal ensembles.

  Another musical series, the Concerts Spirituels, named after the famous Parisian series and led by Franz Xavier Gebauer until 1822 and then by Ferdinand

The Grosser Redoutensaal, by Joseph Schütz, ca. 1815

The larger of the two Redoutensaals, a great ballroom used primarily for
dancing, was occasionally the site of concerts as well. The second
performance of Beethoven's Ninth took place there on Sunday, May 23, 1824.

Piringer, was held twice a month—on Fridays at four o'clock—in the Landeshaus. Programs included symphonies and choral works but excluded virtuoso concerti and Italian opera. The quality of these must have been dreadful at times, because the singers and instrumentalists were largely amateur and usually performed at sight, though occasionally a single rehearsal was held.

The real spice of Viennese musical life was the variety of single-event commercial concerts. Some tickets benefited charitable organizations, perhaps the Institute for the Blind or the Bürgerspital, which received funds from the annual Saint Stephen's Day concert; more often, musical gatherings known as *Academien* were organized to benefit an individual musician who also served as impresario, making the necessary arrangements and taking responsibility for rentals, musicians' fees, and music copying, all with the hope of turning a profit from ticket sales. It is easy to understand why an individual could not undertake such concerts often. Mozart had produced Academien in which many of his piano concerti were performed; and many other local or touring singers or instrumental virtuosi gave Academies for the public, usually in one of the largest spaces available: the Kärntnertor Theater, the Theater an der Wien, or the large Redoutensaal.

Novelty, variety, virtuosity, the latest operatic tunes—that is what attracted a Viennese audience. An exotic instrument was always an attraction: soloists concertized on mandolin, harp, harmonium, czakan (a walking-stick instrument), and other instruments. Among the concerts organized in 1830 for the relief of flood victims, one included, in addition to works by Rossini played by the orchestra of the Gesellschaft der Musikfreunde, Czerny's arrangement of Rossini's overture to *Semiramide* for sixteen aristocratic dilettantes at eight pianos.

A virtuoso's concert generally began with a symphony or an overture and continued with a concerto; after a vocal solo or ensemble, the soloist might perform variations of his own composition; then another vocal solo or ensemble preceded a lighter piece of improvisation; the concert concluded with another symphonic movement. Paganini's concerts in Vienna in 1828 were perhaps the most dazzlingly effective, but certainly not the only examples of their genre.

Public concerts usually began around midday in that few premises were available for rent in the evening, given the risk of upsetting public order at night. In addition, the government did not want competition for its theaters. Renting concert spaces, especially theaters, was not cheap. Often there was little money left to pay for rehearsals, which as a result were few, and a performer's or composer's musical friends often contributed their services gratis.

In these circumstances, sight reading must have been indispensable, particularly when the ink on a performer's part was still wet or when his music was locked up until the last minute to avoid piracy. For the performance of Louis Spohr's cantata *Das befreyte Deutschland* in 1819 in the large Redoutensaal, Alice M. Hanson reports that the amateur chorus, all from the Gesellschaft der Musikfreunde, had four rehearsals; soloists and certain sections of the orchestra had a single sectional rehearsal; there were the usual *Grossprobe* (the general rehearsal for all participants) and the *Generalprobe* (dress rehearsal), held in the hall on the day before the performance: in all, six rehearsals for the chorus, two for the orchestra. In this context, the preparations for Beethoven's concert were in the Viennese tradition.

Preparing for the Ninth

When Beethoven began to plan for a concert that would include his Ninth Symphony, along with his new Mass, he first considered the Theater an der Wien, in many ways the largest and most up-to-date of the major theaters. Its stage might have attracted him for its ability to accommodate the large performing forces, and its seating capacity must have appealed to his business sense. However, Count Palffy, the theater manager, was unwilling to accept certain of Beethoven's stipulations, among them that the conducting be confided to Michael Umlauf and the leadership of the orchestra to Ignaz Schuppanzigh. The leader of the theater's orchestra was Franz

Clement, the dedicatee and first performer of Beethoven's Violin Concerto; he would probably have been willing, had matters been put to him delicately, to stand aside for Schuppanzigh, but the professional musicians of the theater were unwilling to play under musicians from outside when they had perfectly good players and leaders of their own (this is a common attitude even today), and it soon became clear that it would not be possible to come to terms.

The Kärntnertor Theater was chosen only in mid-April (see document 6), that is, about three weeks before the concert, although Anton Schindler, Beethoven's would-be confidant and his first biographer, had made earlier contacts with its manager, Louis-Antoine Duport, who managed the theater under the direction of the famous Italian impresario Domenico Barbaja. Proud to have Beethoven's concert under his roof, Duport was as obliging as possible. In his broken German, and more often in his native French, Monsieur Duport ("the little Napoleon," Schindler called him) gave clearer and more direct answers than most impresarios.

The relatively late choice of the Kärntnertor Theater made it difficult to do the careful planning that might have made for a more polished performance, but careful planning was not characteristic of Beethoven or of most of his contemporaries when preparing for concerts in which they served as impresario, manager, composer, and performer.

The program was long and ambitious, but not as long as concerts Beethoven had given in the past (his famous concert of December 22, 1808, included, among other things, the Fifth and Sixth symphonies, two movements of the C-major Mass, a piano concerto, a fantasy for piano, and the Choral Fantasy for piano, orchestra, and chorus, a program about twice as long as that of a modern symphonic concert). It is clear from the 1824 conversation books that many ideas were considered: that there be keyboard music, perhaps a movement from a piano concerto (this was rejected for lack of a suitable virtuoso); that there ought not to be two symphonies; that there be arias or duets ("which are so pleasing to the public"); that Beethoven perhaps be advertised as improvising at the piano, if not at the first concert then at a repetition.

As finally decided, the concert began with the Overture to *Die Weihe des Hauses,* originally composed for the reopening of the Josephstadt Theater two years earlier. Then followed the Kyrie, Credo, and Agnus Dei of the *Missa Solemnis,* which were called "hymns" in the program to circumvent government censors, who did not permit the performance of masses at concerts (see document 9). Beethoven had actually intended to perform the entire mass, but the difficulty of rehearsing so much music and the projected length of the concert led to the abandonment of the Gloria and, later, the Sanctus. The concert concluded with the symphony.

Beethoven had not only to compose the music but to provide it in a form from which the performers could sing and play; obtaining performance materials by a set date continued to be a pressing worry and was a contributing factor to the repeated postponement of the event.

Anton Schindler's official request for the Kärntnertor Theater:

Vienna; April 24, 1824

Dear Sir,

As agent for Herr Ludwig van Beethoven, I have the honor to notify you herewith of his wish, since he intends to hold his grand musical Akademie in the I[mperial] R[oyal] Theater near the Kärntnertor, that you will kindly let him have for this purpose all the solo singers, the entire orchestral and choral personnel, as well as the necessary lighting for the sum of 400 fl. C. M. Should the success of this Akademie occasion Herr van Beethoven to repeat it once or twice in the next week or at most ten days, he wishes in addition to obtain the I[mperial] R[oyal] Theater near the Kärntnertor again under the above conditions. Further, Herr van Beethoven has decided to entrust the leadership of this Akademie to Messrs. Umlauf and Schuppanzigh; therefore he also wishes that all that is necessary will be decreed on the part of the administration, so that no difficulties will hereby be made for him by the orchestra.

Herr van Beethoven wishes to give the solo parts to Mademoiselles Sontag and Unger, and to Herr Preisinger, and hopes that the administration will also accede to his wish in this respect.

As a favor to Herr Beethoven, the Musical Society has undertaken to supplement the orchestra with its most superior members, so that, all together, this comes to 24 violins, 10 violas, 12 basses and violoncellos, as well as doubled winds. Therefore it is also necessary to place the whole orchestra on the stage, as is generally the case with large oratorios.

Finally, I have yet to add only that the earlier arrangement with His Excellency, Count von Palffy, has come to nothing because, with the current shortage of capable singers [at Palffy's Theater] an der Wien, the solo parts could not be filled according to the wishes of Herr van Beethoven; also His Excellency expressly wished that Herr Clement should direct the orchestra, which Herr van Beethoven had long ago intended for Herr Schuppanzigh, and which he must insist upon for many reasons.

I now request you most urgently to declare yourself in writing about all this immediately, also to reserve the first evening for this Akademie as soon as possible, and only not to postpone it past the 3d or 4th of May.

I have the honor to remain

Your most obedient,

Anton Schindler

Beethoven writes to a copyist about details of the symphony:

Vienna, April, 1824

My Dear Herr Gläser!

    I asked you to copy exactly what I had written. But alas! I find that the words are written out in the very way I did not want, just as if it had been done on purpose. Hence I insist once more that most particular attention be paid to the way the words are entered under the notes. It is not a matter of indifference if the consonants are added immediately to the vowels, which should be drawn out, as I showed you and explained to you and, what is more, told S(chindler) to remind you. I really do insist that the score be written out exactly as it stands. In regard to the words, such as "so—ft", for example, the consonant should not be added until after the end of the lengthening. It is quite clearly written; and you can see that in the copy of the score similar instances have always been corrected in order that the words should be written exactly as I consider they should be, i.e., in accordance with my principles; and two vowels, such as "ei," for instance, even when the word ends with consonants, should be joined together. But the consonants must not be added until the lengthening is over; and this procedure should be adopted in the case of one or two consonants.

    Please carry on with your copying. I don't need your copy of the score, as I have my own, from which Schlemmer and others, who are immensely superior to M(aschek), have copied out both scores and (parts)—I am sending you the second movement too, so that the coda may be added as well. The coda has not been altered; it was only due to my forgetfulness that it was not added at once. Besides, in this matter I am of the same opinion as some great men such as Haydn, Mozart and Cherubini who never hesitated to delete, shorten or lengthen and so on—*Sapienti pauca.*

    I most earnestly request you not to inflict on me a third and fourth task. You will see from the enclosed parts that, once and for all, I will never abandon my method of composition in regard to lengthened vowels; nor can I ever deviate from it since I am far too strongly convinced that I am right—

    Your most devoted servant

    Beethoven

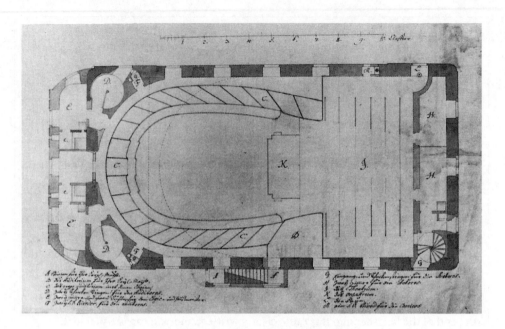

Floor Plan of the Kärntnertor Theater, 1784

This plan shows the curved arrangement of boxes in the theater, the
relatively small entrance hall, and the two curved staircases that lead to
the upper balconies. The location of sliding panels used for opera settings
is shown in the stage area. The orchestra pit is indicated by the letter K.
The space available for Beethoven's performance, using the apron and
the stage, measured about twenty-four feet wide at the narrowest point and
about thirty-seven feet deep.

Like printers, copyists are sometimes overoptimistic; in March a team of copyists estimated that the symphony would take about two weeks to finish, provided the finale did not prove too difficult, and Beethoven's friend the publisher Tobias Haslinger
volunteered to provide lithographed parts for the chorus at cost (see document 8). But
it was not to be so simple: on April 11 the symphony was still not finished, and the
copyist Peter Gläser undertook to finish it by the nineteenth (which would not leave
much time for rehearsals); copyists were still working to provide parts for the solo
singers just two weeks before the performance; and the conducting score was still not
ready in the last days of the month.

Once the theater and the music were decided, there were musicians to recruit.
The orchestra of the theater was engaged, but Beethoven intended to use many more
players than were in the normal complement of the opera orchestra.

The orchestra of the Kärntnertor Theater was one of very few professional
groups in Vienna, and possibly the best. Its forty-five instruments included twenty-six

strings (of which eight were first violins and six seconds); four violas, cellos, and basses; pairs of flutes, oboes, clarinets, bassoons, trumpets, and trombones; four horns; two percussion instruments; and a harp. Beethoven would use all but the harp in his concert. But he would need still more players.

Because of the purpose and placement of the orchestra for this academy, Beethoven wanted to increase its size considerably. Acoustics, placement, and space mattered substantially and were the object of considerable discussion. In the early stages of planning it was pointed out to Beethoven that the smaller orchestra at the Theater an der Wien (with thirty-eight players) had more impact than a larger one at the Redoutensaal. And despite his having increased the size of the orchestra considerably, the effect was not perfect, as we shall see.

To meet his orchestral needs, Beethoven had to call on the pool of amateur musicians in Vienna. Ferdinand Piringer, the director of the Concerts Spirituels, undertook the task of selecting and appointing additional players for the orchestra, inviting volunteers to participate through a public notice.

According to a reference in a conversation book, Piringer evidently selected the six best from each of twelve amateur first and second violins. A list elsewhere in the books indicates the written parts needed for the symphony:

> 6 times V[iolin]: P[rincipale]
> 6 —— V[iolin] S[econdo].
> 4 —— Alti
> 5 —— Violoncell.
> Doubled Harmonie

This suggests an orchestra of twelve each of first and second violins, eight violas, and ten cellos. There is no mention of basses in this list, but an earlier reference in Schuppanzigh's hand confirms these numbers and adds the eight missing basses: "12 on each [violin] part; 10 Violoncellos; 8 Contrabassi."

The phrase "Doubled Harmonie" refers to the duplication of the winds, evidently including the brasses. The doubling of wind instruments was not as rare then as it is today. The modern orchestra has one first oboe and one second oboe, and each plays a separate part; the same is true of all the winds and brasses. Documents from Beethoven's time indicate that the duplication of wind players was a fairly regular occurrence. In a letter (probably of 1816), he had mentioned a set of orchestral parts, including two for each wind instrument. Moreover, the Gesellschaft der Musikfreunde evidently used doubled winds from time to time. We see it in the seating for Handel's *Alexander's Feast*, and we note Beethoven's markings "tutti" and "solo" in a set of parts for the Fourth Symphony. Players of the "second harmony" were recruited by Schindler; among them were several professional brass players who volunteered their services in order to honor the composer.

If the full theater orchestra performed, then to reach the numbers mentioned in the conversation book Piringer would have needed to add ten violins, six violas, four cellos, and four basses; and to double the winds, another four horns, pairs of flutes, oboes, clarinets, and bassoons, two trumpets, three trombones, and perhaps a second timpanist. The result is an orchestra of eighty-two players, of whom forty-four are professionals from the theater and thirty-eight are either amateurs from the Gesellschaft der Musikfreunde or other volunteers.

The chorus, too, was augmented by the Gesellschaft der Musikfreunde. Leopold von Sonnleithner, a lawyer and a member of a distinguished musical family, saw to the recruiting of the choral singers. (Sonnleithner was also a friend of Schubert's and was later instrumental in getting Schubert's famous Opus 1, the song *Der Erlkönig*, published.) As a high official of the musical society, he was well placed to choose and enlist the best of the volunteer singers. A notation in a conversation book indicates that "twenty to twenty-four for each part are already on hand." This suggests that the intended size of the chorus was larger still, though exactly how much larger is difficult to say. Sonnleithner's recruiting took place before the change to the Kärntnertor Theater, whose chorus was substantial: it included thirty-two boys singing soprano and alto (all of whom were students at the singing school attached to the theater) and thirty-four men; if they all sang, and if Sonnleithner's volunteers were added, the total for the chorus would have been some 150 singers. But Beethoven seems to have ordered only ten of each chorus part; if two singers used each part, the chorus could not have numbered more than eighty; if three singers could see a single part, the number might have been as high as 120. It seems, though, that the volunteers were fewer than those originally recruited; at one point Schindler reported that the tenors of the theater chorus were a little weak and that Joseph Gottdank, a singer and *régisseur* at the theater, thought it might have been a good idea to add three or four from the Gesellschaft der Musikfreunde; at another point Sonnleithner is reported to have been glad that no volunteer singers were needed(!) in that the sopranos' high B would pose problems for anybody. But at least some amateurs must have been involved, for there is a mention of "several dilettantes" in the choir who wanted tickets, presumably for friends; at a later point, after rehearsals had already begun, Schindler noted that the solo singers of the Gesellschaft der Musikfreunde would sing but not those who were part of the theater. All this suggests that the volunteers were few and that the size of the chorus was nearer eighty than 120.

There were not many rehearsals, but no fewer than such concerts in Vienna were generally thought to require. Ignaz Dirzka, the chorus master of the Kärntnertor Theater, led five or six choral rehearsals, to judge from notations in the conversation books. This allowed for the learning of three movements of the Mass and the finale of the Ninth Symphony: about a rehearsal and a half per movement.

Ignaz Schuppanzigh, who was to lead the orchestra and who had collaborated with Beethoven all along in the planning of the concert, held a small number of re-

Interior of the Kärntnertor Theater, 1784

The interior of the theater where the Ninth Symphony was first performed
had two levels of seating on the first floor and five tiers of galleries. Although
many scholars feel that Beethoven's concert may have taken place before the
closed curtain, it seems almost certain that the curtain was raised and that the
soloists, chorus, and orchestra were all on the stage.

hearsals for the strings in the rehearsal rooms attached to the Redoutensaal in the Hofburg. During the same period, Beethoven, along with Michael Umlauf, led rehearsals
for the vocal soloists at his home.

It was not uncommon for singers to expect that operatic arias be written with
their voices in mind, and so it should not surprise us that singers asked Beethoven for
"changes that would lighten their labors," according to Alexander Wheelock Thayer.
Henriette Sontag, the soprano, called him a tyrant when he refused, turned to her colleague Caroline Unger, as Schindler tells it, and said, "Oh, all right! Let's struggle on
with it for God's sake." Dirzka asked for changes, and he too was refused. The only
change documented is one accorded to Joseph Preisinger, the bass, who in fact could
not sing the high F-sharp in the recitative of the symphony's finale—he was laughed
at in rehearsal. As it turned out, Preisinger could not manage the part and did not sing
in the concert.

The two full rehearsals were both held in the theater. A third was planned but

Poster Announcing Beethoven's Academy of May 7, 1824

"Grand Musical Academie of Herr Ludwig van Beethoven" (for the full translation, see page 137).

had to be canceled because of a ballet rehearsal. At the second—and final—rehearsal, on May 6, Beethoven stood at the door and greeted all the amateur performers, thanking them with an embrace for their participation.

In the Hall

Members of the audience arrived at the theater early, as was the custom in Vienna, where theater seats were often unreserved. They had undoubtedly read the official notice of the concert, listing the program and the ticket prices.

Seats in Viennese theaters came in a variety of configurations, not all of them comfortable. The most expensive seats, and the safest, were in boxes, really little open-sided rooms that held as many as ten people (see page 138); most of the audience sat in these. Boxes were sold as an entity, usually to aristocrats and rich bourgeoisie. Of the five tiers of galleries, the next-to-lowest, on the level with the Imperial box at the back,

Translation of poster announcing Beethoven's Academy of May 7, 1824:

Friday the [7th of May]

R[oyal] I[mperial] Court Theater beside the Kärntnertor.

Grand Musical Academy

by

Herr L. van Beethoven

Honorary Member of the Royal Academy of Arts and Sciences of Stockholm and
Amsterdam, and Honorary Citizen of Vienna

The musical pieces to be performed are the latest works of Herr Ludwig van Beethoven.

First: A Grand Overture.

Second: Three Grand Hymns with Solo and Chorus Voices.

Third: A Grand Symphony with Solo and Chorus Voices entering in the finale on Schiller's Ode to Joy.

The solos will be performed by the Demoiselles Sontag and Unger and the Herren Haizinger and Seipelt. Herr Schuppanzigh has undertaken the direction of the orchestra, Herr Kapellmeister Umlauf the direction of the whole, and the Music Society the augmentation of the chorus and the orchestra as a favor.

Herr Ludwig van Beethoven will himself participate in the direction of the whole.

(Prices of admission as usual.)

Free passes are not valid today.

The beginning is at 7 o'clock.

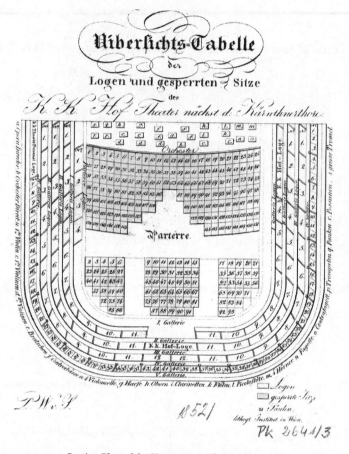

Seating Plan of the Kärntnertor Theater, ca. 1820

This floor plan is typical of large theaters of that time. The floor is divided
into two sections. The front, or noble, parterre had numbered seats—and
probably, as in the Burgtheater, backs that could be added for an additional
fee. The rear parterre, at a higher level, was unusual in having numbered
seats where most theaters had only unreserved benches. Of the five levels
of galleries, the lower three consisted of boxes rented for the season,
usually by noble families. The top two galleries had benches and standing
room. With approximately 650 seats and standing room, the theater
held nearly one thousand people.

was the most desirable; prices descended with distance from that level. The two highest galleries, as in most theaters of the day, were very high indeed and offered either
benches or standing room. On the parterre were the *gesperrte Sitze*—individual, reserved seats near the front of the theater to which backs could be added for those who
wished to recline and were willing to pay for it. Behind these was an open area of standing room, where those who wanted to circulate, or save money, could watch, converse,

and move about. At the back were rows of benches sold as unreserved seating to people willing to try to see over the heads of those standing in the middle of the theater. This back section was often crowded and noisy; in the Kärntnertor Theater, even these benches were divided into individual spaces that could be reserved in advance and claimed by an individual ticket holder.

The house for this concert was extremely full: "crowded to excess," said the reporter from the *Harmonicon;* "very filled," said the *Wiener Allgemeine Theater-Zeitung;* "unusually numerous audience," said the *Wiener Allgemeine musikalische Zeitung.* Perhaps we can conclude that the comments of diarist Joseph Carl Rosenbaum ("not very full"; "many boxes empty, no one from the Court") reflect either a faulty recollection or a lack of enthusiasm. Rosenbaum was right, though, about the absence of the Imperial family, despite Beethoven's strenuous efforts. It was just too late in the season, even for so honored a composer as Beethoven, to expect the members of the Imperial family to delay their summer departure.

The audience had come primarily to see and honor Beethoven and to hear his music. But the performers, which included some of the finest artists in Vienna, were attractions in their own right.

Among the singers was eighteen-year-old Henriette Sontag, perhaps the most famous soprano of that period and surely the performer who achieved the highest fame afterward. Although other singers had been recommended to Beethoven, such as Therese Grünbaum and Katharina Anna Wranitzky, his fondness for Sontag, combined with her stellar reputation, made her the evident choice. After only two professional seasons in Vienna, she was already singing leading operatic roles. Within a few years she would become the cause of "Sontag fever" in Berlin and would have a stunning début at the Théâtre-Italien in Paris. In 1830, owing to her marriage to an aristocratic diplomat, she announced her retirement from the stage, which lasted almost twenty years. In 1852 she traveled to America (where her cigar smoking raised eyebrows), and during a Mexican tour in 1854 she contracted cholera, from which she died. Sontag had a light, brilliant voice and was known for her technical skill.

Henriette Sontag

Sontag, then eighteen, sang the solo soprano part in the concert of May 7; this included three movements of the *Missa Solemnis* and the Ninth Symphony. Already an opera star in Vienna and a favorite of Beethoven, she went on to the sort of international career that is today characteristic of rock musicians.

Alphonse de Pontmartin recalled Henriette Sontag as he saw her in 1830 and gives us a view of the symptoms of Sontag fever:

Mademoiselle Sontag offered the most perfect type of Germanic beauty, as we dream about it from the poets without finding it in reality; what made her incomparable in the terrible role of Donna Anna [in Mozart's *Don Giovanni*] is that she opposed to the sensual fury of Spanish passion all that in Northern poetry is most ethereal and chaste. Svelte without being thin, the elegance of her waist matched perfectly the regularity of her features and the expression of her physiognomy, with her hair of an ashen blond that could light many a fire beneath the ash; with the tea-rose nuance of her forehead, the somewhat sad sweetness of her periwinkle-colored eyes, and the fine arc of her lips which seemed now to smile at something invisible, and now to speak to the unknown. The ideal, our dear twenty-year-old ideal, vague like a dream without an awakening, sweet as the caresses of a sister, fresh as April dew, pure as Himalayan snow, timid as the bird that we surprise in its nest and which slips between our fingers leaving us only a feather from its wing, melancholy as the premonition of a storm in the middle of the splendors of a spring morning, the ideal revealing itself in the most delicate form and singing with a celestial voice, that is how I remember Mademoiselle Sontag from long ago.

Sontag's friend Caroline Unger, less delicate and more down-to-earth, was the contralto. Three years older than Sontag, Unger, too, had just begun an operatic career in Vienna and was to make a name for herself, though she never achieved Sontag's international fame. Unger had just sung Dorabella in Mozart's *Così fan tutte;* she studied with Aloysia Weber, Mozart's sister-in-law, and with J. M. Vogl, the great friend and interpreter of Schubert. She went on to a career in Italy under the guidance of the powerful impresario Domenico Barbaja, singing roles written for her by Bellini and Donizetti. François-Joseph Fétis, the journalist and lexicographer (whom we shall meet again in connection with Berlioz) praised her fine, broad tone, though he perceived some harshness in her upper register. Unger was a large and attractive woman; Schindler suggested in Beethoven's conversation books that she was changeable and unstable and did not pay enough attention to herself, especially in matters of food and

Caroline Unger, by F. von Lütgendorf

Sontag's friend Caroline Unger, twenty-one years old, sang the alto solos on May 7. She was a generous, hearty, and outgoing person and was reported to have turned Beethoven around so that he could see the audience cheering. She later had an important international career.

drink: Sontag, Schindler thought, was more prudent. Unger evidently worked hard but had troubles with her part. She was a droll character, full of jokes and banter, though the upright Schindler did not share her views as to when pleasantry was appropriate. It was Unger, according to some reports, who turned Beethoven around during the concert so that he could see the applause of the audience. She later wrote of her experience:

> I still see that simple room in the Landstrasse [district] where a rope served as a bell-pull, and in the middle a large table on which the excellent roast and that capital sweet wine were served. I see the room next door, piled to the ceiling with orchestra parts. In the middle of it stood the piano that Field [actually Broadwood] had sent to Beethoven from London.
>
> Jette Sontag and I entered that room [in Beethoven's house] as though entering a church, and we attempted (alas in vain) to sing for our beloved master. I remember my insolent remark that he did not know how to write for the voice, because one note in my part in the symphony lay too high. He answered, "Just learn it! The note will come." His words spurred me on to work from that day on.

The tenor was twenty-eight year-old Anton Haizinger. He had been a *primo tenore* at the Theater an der Wien since 1821, where, among other roles, he had sung Florestan in *Fidelio* and was therefore well known to Beethoven. He later sang in Paris and London; settling in Karlsruhe, he and his wife founded a singing school that achieved considerable renown. When he sang in London, his voice was described as "very beautiful," though Henry Chorley found it "throaty and disagreeable." At first it

Haizinger, twenty-eight years old, was a
regular tenor at the Theater an der Wien,
where he had created the role of Florestan in
Beethoven's *Fidelio*. He later organized a
touring opera company, which Berlioz heard
in Paris.

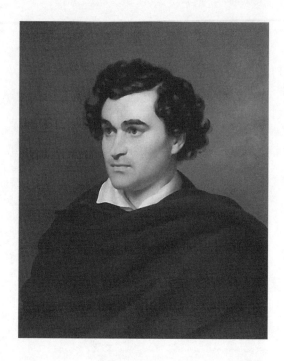

was intended that the tenor be Franz
Jäger, also at the Theater an der Wien.
Jäger was a fine singer and would
have been part of the bargain Beethoven was arranging with that theater. But he studied the part and
found it low for his voice, and when
the concert was moved to the Kärntnertor Theater, he felt compelled to
withdraw because of political relations among the tenors and the theaters of the city.
The next choice seems to have been Joseph Barth, a singer in the Imperial chapel, who
was the choice of Schuppanzigh, though it was admitted that Barth was no Jäger; only
when it appeared that Barth would be unavailable owing to a trip to Bohemia did the
choice fall on Haizinger. Haizinger would have to study hard, suggested Schindler,
since he was not as solid as Jäger, though his voice was as sonorous.

Joseph Seipelt, then thirty-seven, was the bass; for two years he had been a
member of the company at the Kärntnertor Theater. Seipelt must have been an experienced performer with a better than average ability as a sight reader, but he was not
Beethoven's original choice. Singers considered at first included Anton Forti and
Joseph Preisinger, both singers at the Kärntnertor Theater: Preisinger was chosen as
being more suitable for this sort of music. It was Preisinger who attended most of the
rehearsals and who managed to wring out of Beethoven the alteration of the famous
high F-sharp (Schindler had said to Beethoven that no other bass then in Vienna had
an F-sharp either). Seipelt replaced Preisinger at the last minute over the matter of high
notes and sang the performance on the strength of only one rehearsal. The last-minute
choice of Seipelt may have been more practical than aesthetic; Schindler describes
Seipelt's voice as being "extremely nasal." (We shall never know whether Seipelt sang
the high F-sharp: by then Beethoven had provided an alternative, and nobody reports
the version Seipelt used.)

Most of these singers were well enough known to be described by the correspondent for the newly founded magazine *Caecilia,* whose first issue (1824) included a major article on the musical scene in Vienna:

> In singing, the Italians have always been the model for the Germans, and rightly so. This time also our domestic talents form themselves after them with the most splendid success, especially Demoisellen Sonntag and Unger. Dem. Sonntag first studied in Prague and she possesses, by nature, a not especially strong, but gently sweet and exceedingly flexible voice. For the moment she has been able to please. Dem. Unger is a high alto, almost a mezzo-soprano; very industrious and very pleasant. Both these young, attractive singers also have been used in Italian opera with the happiest results. . . . Of our male singers, Hr. Forti, with his deep baritone, is the most excellent. Hr. Jäger and Hr. Haizinger are tenors whose voices do not please at all. Both have unusual high registers. Jäger's voice is occasionally muffled in the lower range, but he performs very pleasantly and with expression. Herr Haizinger's voice is more even in the entire range, but is more piercing, and his methodology has not improved by his aping of David [Giacomo Davide, the flexible and histrionic Rossinian tenor].

As was usual in the case of large-scale performances involving solo singers, chorus, and orchestra, several conductors, rather than an individual, were needed, each responsible for leading some aspect of the performance or some group of the performers. The *Anführer,* or chief conductor, of the performance was Michael Umlauf, a forty-three-year-old violinist and composer who held the position of Fourth Kapellmeister at the Imperial Court Theaters (one of six such positions). Umlauf was closely connected with Beethoven, who had wanted him in particular for this performance, as witnessed by the composer's willingness to insist on him at the Theater an der Wien.

Two years earlier, Umlauf had been "assisting" Beethoven in the direction of the fateful performance of *Fidelio* during which Beethoven was forced to stop conducting owing to his deafness. More than once Umlauf had had to take over the direction of a Beethoven concert, using both musical skill and what must have been a gift for diplomacy.

When Beethoven conducted in the theater the same thing happened: the stage manager and theater chronicler Georg Friedrich Treitschke reports that for the 1814 opening of *Fidelio* "the opera was capitally prepared; Beethoven conducted, his ardor often rushed him out of time, but Kapellmeister Umlauf, behind his back, guided everything to success with eye and hand."

The orchestra was led by Ignaz Schuppanzigh, a portly forty-eight-year-old virtuoso violinist. In his twenties Schuppanzigh had managed the mostly amateur concerts in the Augarten, with which Mozart had previously been involved; there he over-

The singer Franz Wild gives a vivid, if overstated, description of Beethoven conducting and Umlauf picking up the musical pieces, at a concert on January 2, 1814:

[Beethoven] mounted the conductor's platform, and the orchestra, knowing his weakness, found itself plunged into an anxious excitement which was justified only too soon; for scarcely had the music begun before its creator offered a bewildering spectacle. At the *piano* passages he sank upon his knee, at the *forte* he leaped up, so that his figure, now shrivelling to that of a dwarf, disappeared under the desk and anon stretched up far above it like a giant, his hands and arms working as if with the beginning of the music a thousand lives had entered every member. At first this happened without disturbance to the effect of the composition, for the disappearance and appearance of his body was synchronous with the dying away and the swelling of the music; but all at once the genius ran ahead of his orchestra and the master disappeared at the *forte* passages and appeared again at the *piano*. Now danger was imminent and at the critical moment Kapellmeister Umlauf took the commander's staff and it was indicated to the orchestra that he alone was to be obeyed. For a long time Beethoven noticed nothing of the change; when he finally observed it, a smile came to his lips which, if ever a one which kind fate has permitted me to see could be called so, deserved to be called "heavenly."

saw several important Beethoven performances. Schuppanzigh had also led at least two major string quartets: the first gave subscription concerts of some renown; the other he formed at the invitation of Count Razumovsky, who had asked Schuppanzigh to assemble the best quartet in the world. The latter group subsequently played, among many other pieces, the Beethoven quartets (Opus 59) dedicated to Razumovsky. (Members of both quartets played in the 1824 concert.) When Razumovsky's Viennese palace burned in 1814, Schuppanzigh accompanied his patron to Saint Petersburg. He had only recently returned after an absence of several years and, though he had gained a position in the Imperial chapel orchestra, Schuppanzigh was eager to reestablish his reputation and his standing in Vienna. At the time of this concert he was vying for the job

Ignaz Schuppanzigh

Schuppanzigh, an old friend of Beethoven's and a superb solo violinist and chamber musician, led the orchestra for the Ninth Symphony. He had led Count Razumovsky's famous string quartet and had collaborated with Beethoven on many premieres. Beethoven and others gave him the nickname "Falstaff."

of concertmaster at the Kärntnertor Theater, so he must have been particularly happy to lead the Ninth there. Later (probably having advanced his career through this concert) Schuppanzigh led the orchestra of the Imperial opera and remained an admired figure in Viennese musical life. He had previously been involved in many Beethoven first performances and later premiered the Schubert octet; Schubert dedicated his famous A-minor quartet to Schuppanzigh. Beethoven, among others, referred to Schuppanzigh as "Falstaff," owing not only to his girth but also to his good humor, and perhaps to his potatory prowess as well.

But Beethoven, Umlauf, and Schuppanzigh were not the only leaders of the ensemble. The piano virtuoso Sigismond Thalberg recalled attending this concert as a twelve-year-old and noted that Conradin Kreutzer, the recently appointed forty-four-year-old kapellmeister of the Kärntnertor Theater, was at the piano. Other observers do not mention Kreutzer, and one wonders whether Thalberg is simply wrong or the presence of a leader for the soloists is so natural as to be assumed, like the presence of a prompter. In any case, Kreutzer, the composer of light operas, and his piano, presumably at the front of the stage, would doubtless have been very helpful both for the chorus and the soloists, providing pitches and cues as needed.

The presence of such distinguished performers in this concert says much about the importance of the event in Viennese musical life and about the significance of Beethoven in the city's musical culture. Joseph Böhm played among the first violins; the twenty-nine-year-old virtuoso, professor of violin at the new Vienna Conservatory (1814), had recently returned from a concert tour, during which Schuppanzigh had replaced him in Böhm's own string quartet; perhaps Böhm was not entirely pleased with

The composer and critic Johann Friedrich Reichardt on Schuppanzigh:

Today I must speak to you about a very fine quartet series that Herr Schuppanzigh, an excellent violinist in the service of Prince Rasoumowsky, the former Russian envoy to the Imperial court, has opened by subscription for the winter.... Herr Schuppanzigh himself has an original, piquant style most appropriate to the humorous quartets of Haydn, Mozart, and Beethoven—or, perhaps more accurately, a product of the capricious manner of performance suited to these masterpieces. He plays the most difficult passages clearly, although not always quite in tune, a consideration to which the local virtuosi seem in general to be superior; he also accents very correctly and significantly, and his cantabile, too, is often quite singing and affecting. He is likewise a good leader for his carefully chosen colleagues, who enter admirably into the spirit of the composer, though he disturbed me often with his accursed fashion, generally introduced here, of beating time with his foot, even when there was no need for it .

Schuppanzigh's return to Vienna. The twenty-nine-year-old violinist Leopold Jansa, another well-respected Viennese musician and teacher, also played that evening. Joseph Mayseder, thirty-five years old, had played second violin in the Schuppanzigh quartet and was again playing with his old colleague, presumably leading the second violins. Mayseder became an institution in Vienna in his own right, playing in the opera orchestra for decades.

Joseph Linke, another member of Schuppanzigh's Razumovsky quartet, presumably led the cellos. Schuppanzigh must have felt considerable comfort at having as part of the string section men he had trained and played with for years.

The names of some of the wind players appear in conversations with Beethoven. Among them are Karl Hieronymus Nikolaus Scholl (flute), Joseph Friedlowsky and Wenzel Sedlak (clarinets), and the two Swiss players, Theobald Hürth (first bassoon) and Eduard Constantin Lewy (solo horn at the theater)—might Lewy have played the famous fourth-horn passages in the slow movement?

It is often assumed that this performance, like many others, took place before a closed theater curtain, with the orchestral musicians in the pit. It seems clear, how-

Almost thirty years after Beethoven's concert, Henry Chorley remarked on Joseph Mayseder's artistry in unflattering circumstances:

Among the special musical attractions that Vienna possessed in 1844 (and happily still possesses in 1852) was the violin-playing of Herr Mayseder. This was a pleasure all the more choice because it has been rarely, if ever heard, except in the Austrian capital. . . . When I was in Vienna this exquisite artist might be heard playing a *solo* every night when a *ballet* was transacted by the elderly and bony crew, who in 1844 figured as Nymphs, Beauties, Graces, and Muses, at the *Kärnther Thor* Opera House. There was no great stimulus at such a time of year, and with such forms and gesticulations on the stage to accompany, for a *virtuoso* to play his best. . . . Yet those *solos* by Herr Mayseder are among the best exhibitions of their kind, that I ever enjoyed. The ease, the precision of accent—totally distinct from French piquancy or Italian intensity—the gamesome and delicate grace, and the sufficient exhibition of the violin thrown into them, were as delightful as the pleasantest scene in one of M. Auber's operas, or the most finely-finished and fantastically-decorated *aria* sung by a Cinti Damoreau or a Sontag.

ever, that at least for this event, and probably quite a few others, the performers were onstage. For one thing, Schindler says that Caroline Unger turned Beethoven around toward the proscenium so that he could see the audience's applause; had Beethoven been in the pit, turning him toward the proscenium would have turned him away from the audience, not toward it. Beethoven had evidently always wanted the performers onstage: in a letter of April 24 that Schindler sent to Duport, it was made clear that room would have to be provided on stage for the orchestra. Indeed, Friedrich August Kanne, editor of the *Wiener Allgemeine musikalische Zeitung* and a friend of Beethoven's, makes clear in his review that the performance was onstage and that the placement hampered the sound: "The effect that so heavy an orchestration ought to have brought forth was so weakened by the bare spaces between the wings in which the sound faded away and dissipated itself, that we could hardly take in half of the noteworthy effect in the moving masses of tone" (document 33). Writing about the second performance

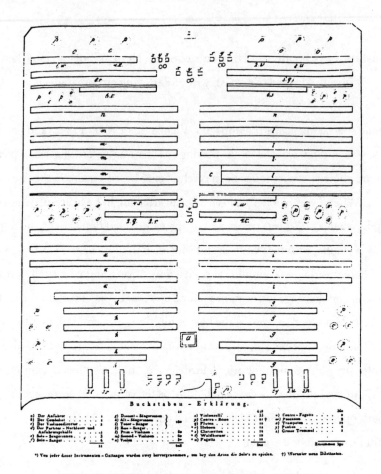

Seating Plan for a Performance of Handel's *Alexander's Feast*,
Orchestrated by Mozart, 1812

This enormous performance, given to benefit the victims of a fire, contributed to
the formation of the Gesellschaft der Musikfreunde. Here the chorus is arranged
in rows in front of the orchestra, with the chief conductor placed near, but not at,
the front of the chorus. Solo singers stand even farther forward, with the result
that they cannot see the conductor, though they have the assistance of a keyboard
player at the very front who can. The strings are in front, first and second violins
on the right and left, and winds and brass in the rear; groups of cellos and double
basses are scattered throughout the area.

(which took place on May 23), Kanne says he prefers the acoustics of the first performance: "The performance of this composition was far more successful in the Theater by
the Kärntnertor that entirely suppressed the reverberation of sound (it is understood
because the orchestra was placed on the stage) than in the large Redoutensaal, because
there [the theater] the staccato and pointed tones appeared far better rounded as individual bodies of sound and threw no reverberating shadows to darken the contour.

There the large crowd of the orchestra, augmented by the participation of many dilettantes, greatly enhanced the sound" (document 35).

The exact disposition of the performing forces for this occasion is not known, but a hypothetical arrangement is given in the accompanying diagram, based on other, better-documented performances. For example, it seems clear that in concerts involving choral works, the chorus was always placed in front of the orchestra, with solo singers either farther forward or between the chorus's first rows. The Anführer (in this case Umlauf) was placed not entirely at the front, but near it, with a few rows of chorus, and all the solo singers, out of his line of vision. This explains in part the occasional presence of a keyboard instrument at the edge of the stage, its lid opened toward the performers: such an arrangement allows the player to see the Anführer and to cue the solo singers discreetly. The layout for an 1812 performance of Handel's *Alexander's Feast,* as orchestrated by Mozart and performed in the Winterreitschule (the indoor riding ring of the Imperial palace), was similar (see page 148).

A remark of Schindler's ("Der chor sitzt unten") might suggest that the choir for the Ninth Symphony was placed in the orchestra pit or on the floor of the theater. But this observation was made at a rehearsal held away from the theater, and he probably means "downstage." The absence of references to lost seats in the parterre and the fact that Frau Grebner (whom we shall soon meet) was in the chorus near Beethoven, who had to be turned toward the proscenium to see the audience, argue that the chorus was on stage as well.

There was no standard plan of orchestral seating in Vienna. Sometimes the strings were placed on one side and all the winds on the other, as in a seating for the Concerts Spirituels of about 1825 (see page 150); and sometimes the strings were in front and the winds behind, which seems to be the general plan behind the enormous performance diagrammed on page 148; the shallowness of the Kärntnertor's orchestra pit puts the strings in the center, with winds right and brass left.

The Violindirektor in the pit of the Kärntnertor Theater performed at a raised desk in the center, facing the stage; but in a concert a Violindirektor plays from a raised desk at the end of the front row of first violins. In a concert with a large chorus, the Anführer might find himself at a considerable distance from the Violindirektor, though the sightlines and the cooperation between these two are of real importance.

The reconstruction presented here generally follows the plan of the Concerts Spirituels (see page 150) in the placement of the violins and violas to one side, with cellos and basses in the center, just as they are in the theater. The winds are doubled, and they have been arranged in such a way that the secondary winds, who play to reinforce tuttis, are in the back; the regular Kärntnertor Theater winds and brasses are seated together, leaving the additional recruits apart. A similar arrangement is evident in the 1812 performance (see page 148), where one set of winds is seated in front of the strings, and another is in the back.

Diagram of the Choir and Orchestra for the Concerts Spirituels, ca. 1825

The Spiritual Concerts, directed by Ferdinand Piringer, who also recruited
and trained the chorus for the Ninth Symphony, presented sacred music twice
a month on Fridays. This engraving, from a treatise published by Dr. F. S.
Gassner in 1844, shows the arrangement of performing forces around 1825.
The chorus stands in front of the orchestra, and the solo singers, at the front,
have their backs to the Kapellmeister. The orchestra is seated around the
organ: the violins and violas to the left, the cellos and double basses front
center, and the woodwinds, brass, and kettledrums to the right.

Umlauf is near, but not at, the front, with Beethoven at his elbow to set tempi;
Conradin Kreutzer is at the piano, which is on the front edge of the stage with the lid
open toward the performers. The solo singers, near the front of the stage, are placed so
that they can see Kreutzer and perhaps catch an occasional sidelong glimpse of Umlauf, and not so far that Caroline Unger cannot easily step to Beethoven's side to call his
attention to a cheering audience.

The effect of a chorus in front of the orchestra, combined with the ample side
wings typical of an early eighteenth-century opera house, surely contributed to the dis-
persal and muffling of the orchestral sound noticed by Kanne. There may have been

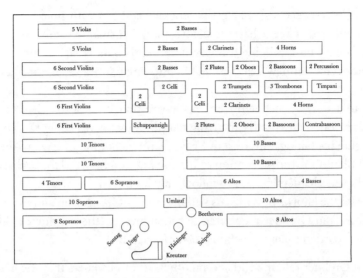

Hypothetical Arrangement of Performers for the Academy of May 7, 1824

The performing forces for Beethoven's concert of May 7 may have been
arranged in this manner. Based on other Viennese arrangements of orchestral
and choral forces (see pp. 148 and 150), the chorus is placed in front of the
orchestra, and solo singers are center front; the pianist, Conradin Kreutzer, is
at the front edge of the stage, the lid of the piano open toward the
performers. Kreutzer can therefore see Umlauf, the conductor (which the
soloists cannot). Beethoven is slightly behind and to the right of Umlauf so
as to indicate the tempi of the various movements. The orchestra is
arranged, as in the Concerts Spirituels (p. 150), with the violins and violas to
the left, winds and brass to the right, and cellos and double basses in the
center. A second set of woodwind players (probably amateurs) is placed at
the rear behind the brass to reinforce tutti passages.

some arrangement of risers, however, for at least part of the orchestra: a note from
Schindler to Beethoven before the concert says that he is going to see Duport and
Stubenrach (the manager and the stage designer at the theater) to get the scaffolding in
order (his word is *Gerüst,* which means some sort of framework or scaffolding).

Naturally we can't reconstruct every moment of this important musical performance. But from what we know of customary practices, and from a few hints and details, we can get an idea of how the music sounded and how it was perceived.

The performance went well enough, it seems. At no time did the music have to
be stopped because of miscues (as had happened in other Beethoven concerts).
Beethoven appeared wearing a green dress coat, and Schindler turned out to be right:
he had told Beethoven before the concert that, in the dim candlelit theater, no one
would notice that he was not dressed in formal black attire (which would not be ready
for another week). The green coat apparently fooled Thalberg, who noted that Beethoven was wearing a "black dress coat, white neckerchief, and waistcoat, black satin

smallclothes [knee-breeches], black silk stockings, shoes with buckles." Beethoven had also troubled to have a haircut before the performance—an event that must have been relatively rare, judging from the amount of commentary in the conversation books (Beethoven's nephew Carl wrote, "Schuppanzigh praises the master who cut your hair!").

By that time even Beethoven was aware that he was too deaf to conduct, though he was nonetheless active in giving tempi. Knowing his energy as a conductor, we can imagine his taking a more active role than Umlauf might have wished; we do know that Umlauf took the precaution of instructing the choir and the orchestra to disregard Beethoven's leadership and to follow only him.

One of the chorus provides us with her view of Beethoven and the concert. In her later years Frau Grebner recounted her memories to the conductor Felix Weingartner, who recorded them in his book *Akkorde* (1912):

> Frau Grebner told me and several other devout listeners that she had taken part in the first performance as a soprano in the chorus. Beethoven sat among the performers from the first rehearsal onwards, to be able to hear as much as his condition would permit. He had a stand in front of him, on which his manuscript lay. The young girl, who now sat before me as a venerable old lady, stood just a few steps away from that stand and thus had Beethoven constantly in view. Her description of him is the same as the one that has been handed down to us: a thick-set, very robust, somewhat corpulent man, with a ruddy, pock-marked face and dark, piercing eyes. His grey hair often fell in thick strands over his forehead. His voice, she said, was a sonorous bass; he spoke little, however, for the most part reading pensively in his score. One had the tragic impression that he was incapable of following the music. Although he appeared to be reading along, he would continue to turn pages when the movement in question had already come to an end. At the performance a man went up to him at the end of each movement, tapped him on the shoulder and pointed to the audience. The motions of the clapping hands and the waving handkerchiefs caused him to bow, which always gave rise to great jubilation. Altogether, the effect made by the work at its first performance was quite prodigious. At times there was a burst of applause during a movement. One such moment, Frau Grebner recalled, was the unexpected entrance of the timpani in the Scherzo.
>
> This had the effect of a bolt of lightning and produced a spontaneous show of enthusiasm.

[document 30]

Although we know that Beethoven was an energetic conductor, Frau Grebner suggests that he was more an observer at this performance. Her account is at odds with others, too, in the matter of turning Beethoven around. Thalberg reports Beethoven's being turned around by Caroline Unger at the end of the Scherzo, perhaps in connection with the applause that Frau Grebner remembered; others, including Schindler and Unger herself, report this event at the end of the concert.

How was the performance? Evidently a little underrehearsed and a little weak-sounding. Rehearsals had not gone well, and Umlauf had lost his temper at one of the last rehearsals. Everybody apparently tried hard, but the results were less than perfect.

Three journals carried extensive reviews (all of which are reproduced in the documents), but even though the critics sought to do Beethoven honor, they tried to find ways of suggesting that the concert could have gone better and sounded fuller:

> From *The Harmonicon:* "The impracticability of devoting sufficient time to the number of rehearsals that were necessary in order to do justice to music which is at once new, and of so lofty a character, made it impossible to give it with that precision, and with those delicate shades of *forte* and *piano,* which are required to do them justice."
>
> [document 36]

> From the *Wiener Allgemeine Theater-Zeitung:* "All parts of it made the most decided impact, especially the Scherzo, and this symphony would have distinguished itself even more by the striking fantasy which introduces the final chorus, which itself might have enhanced the work even more, had it been possible for the participants to have rendered this section as perfectly as it demanded.
>
> In regard to the orchestra one can say no more than that it is inconceivable how they were able to perform these uncommonly difficult compositions with three [actually two, of course] rehearsals, because they rendered them most worthily indeed. And this orchestra was composed for the most part of dilettantes; that one can only find in Vienna!
>
> The singers did what they could." [document 32]

> From the *Wiener Allgemeine musikalische Zeitung* [speaking of the Mass]: "Neither the chorus nor the solo singers were prepared well enough as demands so difficult and deeply intricate music. [The critic goes on to complain about the sound being muffled in the wings, as mentioned above, and then speaks hopefully of a second performance] in all particulars improved, . . . in another locale that is better

suited for music, thereby fulfilling all demands of the art in the accompaniment of the orchestra and in the precision of the execution."

[document 33]

The string players had rehearsed, but not enough. The parts were not easy for players accustomed to more routine operatic fare, and the dilettantes may have been baffled. Kanne, in his review of the second performance, had some telling things to say about the string playing, which applies even more fully to the first performance:

> One hardly needs to add that a composition such as this, created with the highest freedom of spirit and unchecked enthusiasm, often scarcely gives time to trained violinists to think out a good fingering, on account of which then, also normally weak players, that is those who readily play variations or concertos, but who are not accustomed to the fast passages of orchestral performances, would normally be horrified at first by such difficult places, set down their bows then and sit out so many measures, thus, in this case, disregard hard techniques until they once again join in easier passages and can mix anew with the orchestra in progress. The reliable ones with true artistic expression had to compensate during such passages by playing stronger for the players who swallowed their notes.   [document 35]

"The winds did very bravely," wrote Schindler in a conversation book, but these were the same players of whom, during rehearsals, Schindler had little good to say ("The *harmonie* of the theater is going to the devil; it is *sehr miserabel*"). Perhaps that bravery did not result in musical precision: undoubtedly the players tried hard and meant well, but the writer could not report at the same time that they had entirely succeeded in their effort.

The critic for the *Wiener Allgemeine Theater-Zeitung* hints at problems at the beginning of the last movement (document 32). Schindler wrote in the conversation book of March during the rehearsals: "How many contrabasses should play the recitative? — Will it be possible? All! — In strict time there would be no difficulty, but to give it in a singing style will make careful study necessary. — If old Grams were still alive one could let the matter go unconcernedly, for he directed 12 contrabasses who had to do what he wanted. — Good; then just as if words were under it? — If necessary I will write words under it so that they may learn to sing." Whether or not Schindler wrote words into the parts for double basses is doubtful, but the performance at that point was apparently not a great success; and Beethoven is later reported as having insisted to Sir George Smart that the recitative ought to go in strict time. Indeed, he seems to have insisted on strict time for Preisinger's opening recitative, to judge from Schindler's side of a conversation with the composer ("but what about Preisinger? Should he sing *ad libitum?* No? It would make such a better effect, are you sure? Ach! Herr Jesus!!!").

The trouble with the double basses is corroborated by Leopold von Sonnleithner, who in 1864 recollected: "I attended all (or most) of the orchestral rehearsals of the Ninth Symphony.... I can confirm from my own experience that Beethoven had the recitatives played quickly, that is, not exactly *presto* but not *andante* either. The whole symphony, especially the last movement, caused great difficulty for the orchestra, which did not understand it at first, although leading musicians (such as Mayseder, Böhm, Jansa, Linke) were playing in it. The double-bass players had not the faintest idea what they were supposed to do with the recitatives. One heard nothing but gruff rumblings in the bass, almost as though the composer had intended to offer practical evidence that instrumental music is absolutely incapable of human speech" (document 27).

Or, as Rosenbaum's diary put it privately, "for all the large forces, little effect."

The voices evidently had their own troubles. Rehearsals had been so minimal that the *Wiener Allgemeine musikalische Zeitung* critic felt the need to mention their unpreparedness. We know that the soloists repeatedly had trouble with the music in rehearsal and that Beethoven had refused to accommodate their requests for changes. And they were required to sing the solo parts of the Ninth Symphony immediately after performing three movements of the *Missa Solemnis!* Soloists still did not know their parts a few days before the performance (not a note, said Schuppanzigh; they don't know what they are singing, said Schindler, though he also remarked that Haizinger was doing remarkably well considering that he had just got the music). Both Sontag and Unger struggled with their parts; Sontag reported that she had never sung anything so difficult, and Schindler opined that their training in Italian "Gurgeley" was not sufficient for such sustained singing. On the eve of the concert, Umlauf still felt the need to shout ("Pfui Teufel!") at Sontag and Unger for not mastering their parts.

Thayer reports that trouble was inevitable: "The obvious thing happened;— the singers who could not reach the high tones simply omitted them." And this must have happened mostly in the symphony, when voices were tired. In addition the *Wiener allgemeine Theater-Zeitung* (document 32) hints that the performers were not at their best owing to underrehearsal: "The singers did what they could. Opera singers are accustomed to adapting themselves to their tasks over many rehearsals, especially if the style may be foreign to them. Herr Seipelt proved to be the best suited [and had the least rehearsal!]. Herr Haizinger had a more difficult assignment. In and of itself, the intonation makes this composition unusually difficult to sing, and beyond that the rhythm changes very frequently."

In addition to the usual applause for individual movements, the audience cheered loud and long at the end of the concert. The Scherzo was evidently interrupted by clapping in an attempt to secure a repetition (this is probably the same show of enthusiasm that Frau Grebner recalled); and at the end, according to Beethoven's friends in his conversation book, the people burst out four times with the cry "Vivat!" until the police commissioner finally had to call for silence. The acclaim was almost entirely for Beethoven himself. Schindler remarked that even Sontag and Unger received little of the applause they normally enjoyed.

The event was a triumph for Beethoven, both as a local hero and as a skilled composer. It was not, however, a triumph of musical execution, for even by the differing standards of that time, all did not go as well as it might have. Nor was it a financial triumph. Beethoven had hoped to make a substantial profit from the concert and was enraged to find that expenses had outstripped income. Indeed, even though the box office receipts had been carefully supervised by his nephew Karl, Beethoven turned on his friends at a dinner he had intended to give as a celebration: Schuppanzigh, Umlauf, and Schindler felt compelled to abandon him at the restaurant—the "Zum wilden Mann," in the Prater—because of his verbal abuse.

A second concert of the symphony had been planned, and Duport, the theater manager, managed to get Beethoven to agree to a change in the program, reducing the Mass to a single movement and adding an Italian vocal trio by Beethoven and an aria by Rossini, sung by the famous Herr David. Such an appeal to the public fashion surely did not appeal to Beethoven's taste, who in any case was no supporter of Rossini's music. Perhaps he was so disappointed by the receipts of the first concert that he no longer took an active interest.

This second concert—on Sunday, May 23, at half past noon—provided an occasion for a large audience to hear a second and possibly better performance of the symphony. But as it happened, the great Beethoven, the pride of Vienna, had to compete with an unusually beautiful day: the public stayed away, and the house was less than half full.

Beethoven's Audience: 1824 and Now

What are the main differences between this 1824 performance and those generally given at the turn of the millennium? Perhaps one should approach this question by asking what the Viennese audience might have wanted in a performance or what experience Beethoven wanted to convey to his listeners. Beethoven was of course providing music to be heard more than once—music to be published, music perhaps for the Philharmonic Society in London—and so his concern with its performance in Vienna was in a way a single manifestation of a piece whose longer career was already assured.

Beethoven cared a great deal about the details of orchestral practice. Ignaz von Seyfried, Beethoven's friend of many years, reported that "he was very particular about expression, the delicate nuances, the equable distribution of light and shade, as well as an effective *tempo rubato,* and without displaying vexation, would discuss them with individual players." Beethoven's attention to detail of performance around 1810 could obviously not be put to the same practical use in 1824, by which time he was entirely deaf; he must have relied on Schuppanzigh and on Umlauf, who undoubtedly did as much as possible with the time available and with the prevailing style of performance.

The orchestral playing was presumably typical of its time. Vienna, as a cultural and artistic crossroads, had a rich influx of musicians from countries such as Austria, Hungary, Czechoslovakia, Poland, Germany, and Italy. The orchestra certainly consisted of players who used a variety of bows and reflected the styles of many different teachers. Even among those who regularly played together in the theater orchestras, such a diversity of styles was entirely normal. The concern for uniformity in string playing and technique that is so characteristic of the modern orchestra did not exist.

Competent orchestral players would have avoided vibrato, portamento (sliding between notes), and certain other features of later nineteenth-century technique, and at the same time they should have avoided the ornamental details suitable for soloists. As Louis Spohr put it in his *Violinschule* of 1832, an orchestral violinist should "abstain from all superfluous appoggiaturas, turns, trills and the like, as well as all contrived position work, sliding from one note to another, changing the finger upon a note, in short from everything appertaining to the embellishment of solo playing, which would disturb the smoothness of ensemble if transferred to orchestral playing." Rubato seems, at the time, to have been considered a matter for solo performers, against a background of even rhythm in the accompanying orchestra; any use of rubato in this performance would normally have been the province of the solo singers only.

A Page from the Original Orchestral Parts

Some of the original orchestral parts used at the first performance of the Ninth
Symphony are in the possession of the Gesellschaft der Musikfreunde in
Vienna. This page, a first violin part, shows a passage from the Scherzo, in
the hand of a professional copyist working quickly; the second line bears
an alteration in Beethoven's hand (see document 16, a letter from Beethoven
to a copyist). Traces of the music on the other side of the sheet show
through the first four lines.

People listening to the Ninth Symphony at the end of the twentieth century, as played by leading symphony orchestras, would hear notable differences in the sheer sound. Modern orchestras have a precision, a blend, a smoothness, that is carefully cultivated, but Beethoven's orchestra might have sounded much like performances now available on period instruments. In these ensembles, the sound of the gut strings is leaner and lacks the constant vibrato of modern strings; the proportion of winds to strings is greater; the wind instruments do not have the uniform key systems that were invented later in the nineteenth century; and natural trumpets and horns are standard. The resultant sound is somehow rawer and less blended; winds and percussion are more evident as separate elements in the texture.

Beethoven performed his symphony for an audience he knew well and whose approbation he must have desired as much as he did their cash. Yet he provided a performance that was, by our standards, underrehearsed, full of amateur performers, probably awkward in its leadership because of Beethoven's presence, and part of a program so tiring for the singers that there were bound to be mishaps. He set before the players and singers music with technical and stylistic demands not easily mastered in so few rehearsals. Despite these obstacles, the critics perceived a wonderful composition, one whose "brave" performance let the glories of the piece be heard, even though it lacked the "details of light and shade" that would have revealed it fully.

As to musical style, a glance will confirm that Beethoven's music is difficult; everyone but trumpet players will say that Beethoven is technically more demanding than Mozart and Haydn, and all of the music of this period is technically much more difficult than Handel's late Baroque music of a few decades earlier. In a musical culture with a familiar style, more music in the same style poses far fewer problems than new music in a new style. Without taking anything away from Handel's genius, it is probable that the players Handel assembled in Dublin to play *Messiah* had no surprises: this was music they understood. The arias and choruses had a familiar ring, even if they were new and even if they surpassed much of the music these musicians usually played. One suspects that Handel's rehearsals went smoothly.

In Vienna, however, not only was Beethoven's late music relatively new and different, but so were the playing styles of the musicians, with their diverse backgrounds. No single playing style prevailed, as would have been the case had they all learned from the same teacher, studied in the same conservatory, or been longtime members of an ongoing orchestra. Doubtless there were basic elements of musicianship that required an attention to ensemble, to playing together, but at the same time the diversity of background and experience would have precluded the sort of orchestral perfection that we now take for granted.

The critics who hoped for a second performance of Beethoven's new symphony, "in all particulars better prepared," were indicating that not all was perfect; indeed, by our standards perhaps no Viennese orchestral performance was perfect. Yet the system seems to have worked: people continued to organize Academies with few rehearsals, to write orchestral music for such occasions, and to wish to hear such music.

What was it that composers, musicians, and listeners were looking for in 1824? Among players and singers there must have been a high premium on sight-reading, on being able to get the music right the first time, and on making rapid adjustments to the necessities of rhythm, tuning, and other such matters (modern studio musicians making television commercials or recording film scores know all about this). Among listeners there must have been a similar premium on "hearing at sight," on listening to new compositions with such keen ears that enjoyment could be gained as the music unfolded. This is always true for arts that develop in real time. When we hear a piece for the hundredth time, part of our pleasure may derive from imagining that we are listening for the first time, though we grasp and hold many more details than we could the first time. One imagines that Beethoven's listeners were used to hearing new music, though in a contemporary style with which they were comfortable, and that the musically aware public had skills in listening that are lost to most of us. Nineteenth-century listeners were more attuned to matters of style: the expected return of themes, the relationship of keys, the novelties and surprises that set one piece apart from another, and many other delicious details that would be perceived even in a mediocre performance. Listeners tolerated a foreground of imprecision in order to see the artistic vision. They were not merely listening to the performance but listening *through* it to the music itself.

Documents: Beethoven, Ninth Symphony

A Selection of Letters to and from Beethoven

Beethoven's letters are cited from the following two volumes: Emily Anderson, trans., *The Letters of Beethoven* (New York: Norton, 1985), pp. 1116–37; and Theodore Albrecht, ed. and trans., *Letters to Beethoven and Other Correspondence*, 3 vols., vol. 3: *1824–1828* (Lincoln: University of Nebraska Press, 1996).

1. *To Count Moritz Dietrichstein:*

Vienna, March 21, 1824

Your Excellency!

As I have heard that I am not to have April 7th for my concert, I most humbly beg Your Excellency to grant me the Grosser Redoutensaal for a concert on April 8th, and preferably at about noon, a time which will inconvenience neither the Theatres nor myself. I am deeply obliged to Your Excellency for the ready kindness you have always shown me and, what is even more flattering, for the fact that Your Excellency is not entirely unsympathetic to my art. I hope soon to have an opportunity of demonstrating to Your Excellency my very deep respect and admiration.

Your Excellency's
most obedient
Ludwig Van Beethoven

[Anderson, letter 1272]

2. To Count Moritz Dietrichstein:

Vienna, March, 1824

Your Excellency!

I have been approached from various quarters with the suggestion that I should give a grand concert. I request you, therefore, to grant me permission to give it in the Grosser Redoutensaal and on the evening of April 8th. Duport is entirely in favour of it. About the Mass for His Majesty I must still beg to be excused. The next time I see you I shall enlighten you about everything concerning that work—I know that you will forgive me for not calling on Y(our) E(xcellency) in person. But I have an enormous amount to do; and I know that that is the case with Y(our) E(xcellency) as well. And you too do not stand on ceremony.

Your Excellency's
most devoted servant
L. Van Beethoven

[Anderson, letter 1273]

3. Memorandum in the Imperial Royal High Steward's office, on Beethoven's request to give a concert in the Redoutensaal:

Vienna: March 16, 1824

Van Beethoven, musician, requests permission to hold a musical *Akademie* on the evening of April 7, in the I[mperial] R[oyal] Redoutensaal.

[dated March 13th; rec'd. 16, 1824]

Decree

Since the permission for holding a musical *Akademie* in the I. R. Redoutensaal does not rest with us, the I. R. Lord High Steward's Office, the petitioner has to apply for the granting of the same to the I. R. High Police Director's Office; then regarding the securing of the hall to the lessee of the I. R. Kärntnertor Theater, Domenico Barbaja.

By the I. R. Lord High Steward's Office

Mayrhofer

[Albrecht, 3:16]

4. Beethoven to Louis-Antoine Duport, late March 1824
(Beethoven wrote this draft in Duport's native French):

I learned of your kindness in granting me the small hall [the smaller Redoutensaal]; unfortunately, it is only suitable for solo players and for small dances ["pour petit polonaise"]. It is not the thing for me; my works require a large area, a hall to give what are called grand musical performances; naturally one cannot pay great sums for the hall for them [concerts], without the costs being really significant: the copying at least 600 florins, for the authorities 4,500. Here are already over 5,000 florins, and the the costs of a great number of performers, and what still remains [for me]. As for me, despite the simplicity of my character, it must be admitted that the most illustrious and the most enlightened patrons and protectors of Art invited me to do so, but it will not be a misfortune for the capital that I do not give an Akademie. I am very obliged to you though for the small hall, and despite all that, I shall not give an Akademie. I am always ready to serve.

[apparently an insert for the sentence above:]

naturally with a large chorus, large orchestra, one must expect a large audience, only it is not possible with the small hall. Providence will not patronize me unless I give an Akademie; it is not a kindness to have given me such a hall, for I need [. . .]

[Albrecht, 3:21]

5. To Peter Gläser:

Vienna, April, 1824

My Dear Herr Gläser!

I asked you to copy exactly what I had written. But alas! I find that the words are written out in the very way I did not want, just as if it had been done on purpose. Hence I insist once more that most particular attention be paid to the way the words are entered under the notes. It is not a matter of indifference if the consonants are added immediately to the vowels, which should be drawn out, as I showed you and explained to you and, what is more, told S(chindler) to remind you. I really do insist that the score be written out exactly as it stands. In regard to the words, such as "so—ft", for example, the consonant should not be added until after the end of the lengthening. It is quite clearly written; and you can see that in the copy of the score similar instances have always been corrected in order that the words should be written exactly as I consider they should be, i.e., in accordance with my principles; and two vowels, such as "ei", for instance, even when the word ends with consonants, should be joined together. But the consonants must not be added until the lengthening is over; and this procedure should be adopted in the case of one or two consonants.

Please carry on with your copying. I don't need your copy of the score, as I have my own, from which Schlemmer and others, who are immensely superior to M(aschek), have copied out both scores and (parts)—I am sending you the second movement too, so that the coda may be added as well. The coda has not been altered; it was only due to my forgetfulness that it was not added at once. Besides, in this matter I am of the same opinion as some great men such as Haydn, Mozart and Cherubini who never hesitated to delete, shorten or lengthen and so on—*Sapienti pauca.*

I most earnestly request you not to inflict on me a third and fourth task. You will see from the enclosed parts that, once and for all, I will never abandon my method of composition in regard to lengthened vowels; nor can I ever deviate from it since I am far too strongly convinced that I am right—

Your most devoted servant

Beethoven

[Anderson, letter 1275]

6. Anton Schindler to Louis Antoine Duport:

Vienna; April 24, 1824

Dear Sir,

As agent for Herr Ludwig van Beethoven, I have the honor to notify you herewith of his wish, since he intends to hold his grand musical Akademie in the I[mperial] R[oyal] Theater near the Kärntnertor, that you will kindly let him have for this purpose all the solo singers, the entire orchestral and choral personnel, as well as the necessary lighting for the sum of 400 fl. C. M. Should the success of this Akademie occasion Herr van Beethoven to repeat it once or twice in the next week or at most ten days, he wishes in addition to obtain the I[mperial] R[oyal] Theater near the Kärntnertor again under the above conditions. Further, Herr van Beethoven has decided to entrust the leadership of this Akademie to Messrs. Umlauf and Schuppanzigh; therefere he also wishes that all that is necessary will be decreed on the part of the administration, so that no difficulties will hereby be made for him by the orchestra.

Herr van Beethoven wishes to give the solo parts to Mademoiselles Sontag and Unger, and to Herr Preisinger, and hopes that the administration will also accede to his wish in this respect.

As a favor to Herr Beethoven, the Musical Society has undertaken to supplement the orchestra with its most superior members, so that, all together, this comes to 24 violins, 10 violas, 12 basses and violoncellos, as well as doubled winds. Therefore it is also necessary to place the whole orchestra on the stage, as is generally the case with large oratorios.

Finally, I have yet to add only that the earlier arrangement with His Excellency, Count von Palffy, has come to nothing because, with the current shortage of capable singers [at Palffy's Theater] an der Wien, the solo parts could not be filled according to the wishes of Herr van Beethoven; also His Excellency expressly wished that Herr Clement should direct the orchestra, which Herr van Beethoven had long ago intended for Herr Schuppanzigh, and which he must insist upon for many reasons.

I now request you most urgently to declare yourself in writing about all this immediately, also to reserve the first evening for this Akademie as soon as possible, and only not to postpone it past the 3d or 4th of May.

I have the honor to remain

Your most obedient,

Anton Schindler

[Albrecht, 3:28–29]

7. Beethoven to Anton Felix Schindler:

(Vienna, April 1824)

If there is anything to report, you may write, but do seal your letter. There are wafers and sealing wax on the table for this purpose—

Write down where Duport is living and at what time he is usually at home, whether he can be seen alone, or whether other people will be present—and, if so, what people?—I am not feeling well. Portes vous biens—I am still considering whether I shall have a word with Duport myself or write to him, a thing which I should not do without being rather bitter—

Don't think of waiting for me to dine with you, but I hope you will enjoy your meal. I am not coming, for the bad food we had yesterday has made me sick.

A carafe of wine has been put there for you.

[Anderson, letter 1276]

8. To Tobias Haslinger, music printer:

Dear Tobias   (Vienna, April, 1824)

We need no more parts except for those of my best club members. But the plates should be corrected from the parts I am sending you. If not, another set of proofs will have to be dealt with. Piringer has been instructed to select the eight best violinists, the two best viola-players, the two best cellists. . . . That is the number who are to augment the orchestra.

[Anderson, letter 1277]

9. To Herr von Sartorius, Imperial and Royal Censor:

Sir!   (Vienna, April, 1824)

As I am told that the Imperial and Royal Censorship will raise objections to the performance of some church works at an evening concert in the Theater an der Wien, all I can do is to inform you that I have been invited to arrange this performance, that all the compositions required have already been copied, which has necessitated considerable expenditure, and that the time is too short to arrange forthwith for the production of other new works—

In any case only three church works, which, moreover, are called hymns, are to be performed. I urgently request you, Sir, to interest yourself in this matter in view of the fact that, as it is, there are so many difficulties to cope with in any undertaking of this kind. Should permission for this performance not be granted, I assure you that it will not be possible to give a concert and that the entire cost of having the works copied will have been met to no purpose—

I trust that you will remember me—

I am, Sir, with kindest regards, your most devoted

Beethoven

[Anderson, letter 1278]

10. *To Ignaz Schuppanzigh:*

(Vienna, April, 1824)

Don't visit me anymore. I am not giving a concert

B—ven

[Anderson, letter 1279]

11. *To Anton Felix Schindler:*

(Vienna, April, 1824)

I request you to come to me tomorrow morning early, if possible, or at about 12 o'clock, for I have an oxygen acid to tell you about. Duport said yesterday that he had written to me. But I have not received the letter. What is best of all, however, he declared that he was satisfied. At the same time he is still waiting for the chief dive which will extend far beyond the proscenium.

From bottom C# to top F—

Beethoven

[Anderson, letter 1280]

12. *To Anton Felix Schindler:*

(Vienna, April, 1824)

After talks and discussions lasting for six weeks I now feel cooked, stewed and roasted. What on earth is to be the outcome of this much discussed concert, if the prices are not going to be raised? What will be left over for me after such heavy expenses, seeing that the copying alone is already costing so much?

[Anderson, letter 1281]

13. *To Anton Felix Schindler:*

(Vienna, April, 1824)

I request you not to come again until I send you word to do so. There will be no concert.

B—ven

[Anderson, letter 1282]

14. To Count Moritz Lichnowsky:

(Vienna, April, 1824)

I despise what is false—
Don't visit me any more. There will be no concert—
B—ven

[Anderson, letter 1283]

15. To Ferdinand Rzehaczeck:

(Vienna, April, 1824)

My Dear Herr Von Rzehaczeck!
Schuppanzigh has assured me that you are going to be so kind as to lend me the necessary instruments for my concert. Encouraged by this assurance I ask you to let me have them; and I hope that I shall meet with no refusal if I earnestly beg you to send them—
Your devoted servant
Beethoven

[Anderson, letter 1284]

16. To a copyist:

(Vienna, April, 1824)

Copy everything exactly as I have indicated; and use some intelligence here and there. For, of course, if bars are copied on pages differently from those of the manuscript, the necessary connections must be observed; and the smaller notes too; for almost half of your notes are never exactly on or between the lines. If all the movements of the symphony are going to be copied as you have copied the Allegro, the whole score will be useless—I need the solo vocal parts which have already been copied, and also the violin parts and so forth which have not yet been checked, so that instead of one mistake there may not be 24—As for the title-pages and end-pages I need these more urgently, that is to say, today or tomorrow. It is doubtful whether the Leopoldstadt is nearer than the Ungargasse. But it is obvious that things are more difficult to arrange in the L[eopoldstadt] than at my home.
Beethoven

[Anderson, letter 1285]

17. To Karl Friedrich Hensler:

(Vienna, end of April, 1824)

Esteemed Friend!
Please be so kind as to send me the parts of the overture which I composed for the opening of your theatre. I intend to have this work performed at a concert which I am giving. As this time I have a larger orchestra and must therefore have these parts copied in duplicate,

you will have them back neatly copied out instead of your present copies which were rather clumsily made at the time owing to the rapidity with which the work was done and to the great untidiness of the copyists. I am always hearing of your good health and prosperity, in which I take a real interest, even though I can see you only very seldom.

With kindest regards, your friend

Beethoven

[Anderson, letter 1286]

18. To Anton Felix Schindler:

(Vienna, early May, 1824)

Now to the Birne after 12 o'clock—with my bowels completely empty and feeling starved—then to the coffee house, then back here again and then off to Penzing immediately, for, if not, I shall lose those rooms.

[Anderson, letter 1287]

19. To Anton Felix Schindler:

(Vienna, shortly after May 7, 1824)

I do not accuse you of having done anything wicked in connexion with the concert. But stupidity and arbitrary behaviour have ruined many an undertaking. Moreover I have on the whole a certain fear of you, a fear lest some day through your action a great misfortune may befall me. Stopped-up sluices often overflow quite suddenly; and that day in the Prater I was convinced that in many ways you had hurt me very deeply—in any case I would much rather try to repay frequently with a small gift the services you render me, than have you at my table. For I confess that your presence irritates me in so many ways. If you see me looking not very cheerful, you say "Nasty day again, isn't it?" For owing to your vulgar outlook how could you appreciate anything that is not vulgar?! In short, I love my freedom far too dearly. I will certainly invite you occasionally. But it is impossible to have you beside me permanently, because such an arrangement would upset my whole existence—Duport has agreed to the concert taking place next Tuesday. For he has again refused to allow the singers to perform in the Land-ständischer Saal, which I could have had tomorrow evening. Moreover, he has again appealed to the police. So please take the notice and find out whether there is any objection to a second performance—I would never have accepted the kindnesses you have rendered me without re-turning them; and I will never do so—As for friendship, well, in your case that is a difficult mat-ter. In no circumstances would I care to entrust my welfare to you, because you never reflect but act quite arbitrarily. I have found you out once already in a way that was unfavourable to you; and so have other people too—I must declare that the purity of my character does not permit me to reward your kindnesses to me with friendship alone, although, of course I am willing to serve you in any matter connected with your welfare—

B.

[Anderson, letter 1288]

20. Beethoven's draft of a letter to the orchestra of the Kärntnertor Theater:

(Vienna, probably May 9, 1824)

I am obliged to thank most sincerely all those who showed me so much love and cooperation at my Akademie. Since I have been invited to give it one more time, I am convinced that I shall not commit an error—since, as a result of the invitation I am giving a second this coming Friday in the Landständischer Saal—if I request all of the participants once more to take part and to ennoble my work by their assistance.

[Albrecht, 3:33–34]

21. To Henriette Sontag:

(Vienna, May 12, 1824)

My Lovely and Precious Sontag!

I have always been intending to call on you sometime and thank you for your fine contribution to my concert. Well, I hope to be able in a day or two to visit you and to take you and Unger out to lunch in the Prater or the Augarten. For it is now the most beautiful season for that. I understand that the concert is to be repeated in about a week. . . . You will . . . support it, and for this I shall always be grateful to you. My very best wishes to you until I have the pleasure of seeing you.

> Your true friend and admirer
> Beethoven

[Anderson, letter 1289]

22. To Bernhard Schotts Söhne, Mainz:

(Vienna, May 20, 1824)

Gentlemen!

It was impossible to answer your letter sooner, for I have been far too busy. I have had the enclosed letter written by a business man, since I am not very well up in matters of this kind. If these proposals suit you, do let me know very soon, for other publishers want to have my works, i.e., each publisher would like to have one of them. But I must confess that this correspondence with publishers at home and abroad has become very heavy and that I should like it to be curtailed.—In regard to a quartet I cannot yet give you a definite promise. But, provided that you reply as soon as possible, I can certainly let you have the two works which I have mentioned.—I have not yet received a copy of your "Cäcilia", which must first pass our censorship!!!

All good wishes. The person you have recommended to me is to show me some of his compositions the day after tomorrow; and I will indicate to him in all sincerity the path which he can follow. — Please let me have an answer soon about the two works, for out of consideration for other people too I must reach a decision. Since I cannot live here on my income alone, I must pay attention to such matters more than I should other wise do—

Your most devoted

Beethoven

[Anderson, letter 1290]

23. To Bernhard Schotts Söhne, Mainz:

(Vienna, May 20, 1824)

Sir!

In reply to your esteemed communication of April 27th I have the honour to inform you that I am more or less willing to let you have my grand Mass and the new symphony. The price of the former is 1000 gulden A.C., and of the latter 600 gulden A.C., at the standard rate of 20 gulden. Payment can be arranged in the following way: you will send me three drafts on a reliable banking house in Vienna and this house will accept them; whereupon I shall send the works to you who will defray the cost of postage, or I shall deliver them to somebody here whom you will nominate for that purpose. The drafts can be made out for the following periods, e.g. one for 600 gulden for a month, one for 500 gulden for two months and another for 500 gulden for four months counting from the present date. If this arrangement suits you, I shall be glad if you will produce very handsome editions. Meanwhile I have the honour to remain with all due respect

your willing servant

Ludwig Van Beethoven

[Anderson, letter 1291]

Firsthand Reports Relating to the Concert

24. The violinist Joseph Böhm on the first performance of the Ninth Symphony:

The work was studied with the diligence and conscientiousness that such a huge and difficult piece of music demanded. It came to the performance. An illustrious, extremely large audience listened with rapt attention and did not stint with enthusiastic, thundering applause. Beethoven himself conducted, that is, he stood in front of a conductor's stand and threw himself back and forth like a madman. At one moment he stretched to his full height, at the next he crouched down to the floor, he flailed about with his hands and feet as though he wanted to play all the instruments and sing all the chorus parts. The actual direction was in Duport's [actually Umlauf's] hands; we musicians followed his baton only. Beethoven was so excited that he saw nothing that was going on about him, he paid no heed whatever to the bursts of applause, which his deafness prevented him from hearing in any case. He had always to be told when it was time to acknowledge the applause, which he did in the most ungracious manner imaginable.

[Friedrich Kerst, ed., *Die Erinnerungen an Beethoven* (Stuttgart: J. Hoffmann, 1913), 2:73, as translated in H. C. Robbins Landon, *Beethoven: A Documentary Study* (London: Thames and Hudson, 1970), 354–55]

25. Carl Czerny to Johann Peter Pixis, June 24, 1824:

There is surely no more significant musical news that I can write you about from our dear old Vienna than that Beethoven finally gave repeated performances of his long-awaited concert, and in the most striking manner astonished everyone who feared that after ten years of deafness he could now produce only dry, abstract works, bereft of imagination. To the greatest extent, his new Symphony breathes such a fresh, lively, indeed youthful spirit; so much power, innovation and beauty as ever [came] from the head of this ingenious man, although several times he certainly gave the old wigs something to shake their heads about.

[Albrecht, 3:37]

26. From the diary of Joseph Carl Rosenbaum:

Friday, 7 (may 1824). Warm . . . At the K. Th. van Bethowen's concert, with Sontag, Unger, Heitzinger and Seipelt singing, Umlauf conducting. He sympathizes with it. Overture and three Hymns with Kyrie and Ode to Joy; lovely but tedious—not very full—to the K. Th. Many boxes empty, no one from the Court. For all the large forces, little effect. B's disciples clamoured, most of the audience stayed quiet, many did not wait for the end.

[From the autograph in the Handschriftensammlung of the Österreichisches Nationalbibliothek, as translated in Landon, *Beethoven,* 355]

27. Leopold Sonnleithner's report of April 1864 on the performance of the Ninth Symphony:

You ask me to inform you, on the basis of my personal recollection, about the tempo Beethoven took in the double-bass recitatives in the last movement of his *Ninth Symphony.* I do not hesitate to comply with that request, and state first of all that in the spring of 1824 I attended all (or most) of the orchestral rehearsals of the *Ninth Symphony,* which was performed for the first time of 7 May 1824. Beethoven himself stood at the head of the forces, but the actual conducting of the orchestra was looked after by Umlauf, who beat time, and Schuppanzigh as first violin. I can confirm from my own experience that Beethoven had the recitatives played quickly, that is, not exactly *presto* but not *andante* either. The whole symphony, especially the last movement, caused great difficulty for the orchestra, which did not understand it at first, although leading musicians (such as Mayseder, Böhm, Jansa, Linke) were playing in it. The double-bass players had not the faintest idea what they were supposed to do with the recitatives. One heard nothing but a gruff rumbling in the basses, almost as though the composer had intended to offer practical evidence that instrumental music is absolutely incapable of speech. The more often this gigantic work was performed subsequently, the better the musicians and the audience came to terms with it.

On this occasion I cannot refrain from mentioning something my deceased friend Carl Czerny (a favorite pupil of Beethoven's) repeatedly related to me and which he confirmed as being reliably true. Some time after the first performance of the *Ninth Symphony,* Beethoven is supposed to have announced to a small group of his closest friends, among them Czerny, that he realized he had committed a blunder with the last movement of the symphony; he wanted, therefore, to eliminate it and write an instrumental movement without voices in its place; he already had an idea in mind for it.

Although the less favourable reception of the final movement with chorus was probably not entirely without influence on this statement of Beethoven's he was certainly not the man to waver in his views as a result of criticism of the day or less than customary applause. Therefore, it seems in fact that he did not feel quite comfortable on the new path he had taken. In any event it is greatly to be regretted that his announced intention was never carried out.

[*Allgemeine musikalische Zeitung* 16 (April 6, 1864); translated in Landon, *Beethoven*, 355–56]

28. *Joseph Huttenbrenner's account of Beethoven's reaction to the news that only 420 gulden had been realized from the concert of May 7, 1824, rather than the large profit the composer had anticipated:*

I handed him the ticket-office figures. He collapsed at the sight of them. We picked him up and laid him on the sofa. We stayed at his side until late at night; he did not ask for food or anything else, and did not speak. Finally, on perceiving that Morpheus had gently closed his eyes, we went away. His servants found him the next morning as we had left him, asleep and still in the clothes in which he had conducted.

[Kerst, *Die Erinnerungen*, 2:79; translated in Landon, *Beethoven*, 356]

29. *Anton Schindler's description of Beethoven's mistrustfulness:*

Beethoven believed that he owed Umlauf, Schuppanzigh and me some thanks for our efforts. A few days after the second academy, therefore, he ordered a meal at the Wilder Mann in the Prater. He arrived in the company of his nephew, his brow hung round with dark clouds, acted coldly, using a biting, carping tone in everything he said. An explosion was to be expected. We had only just sat down at the table when he brought the conversation round to the subject of the pecuniary result of the first performance in the Theatre, blurting out point-blank that he had been defrauded by the administrator Duport and me together. Umlauf and Schuppanzigh made every effort to prove the impossibility of a fraud of any sort, pointing out that every piece of money had passed through the hands of the two theatre cashiers, that the figures tallied precisely, and that furthermore his nephew, on the instructions of his apothecary brother, had superintended the cashiers in defiance of all custom. Beethoven, however, persisted in his accusation, adding that he had been informed of the fraud from a reliable quarter. Now it was time to give satisfaction for this affront. I went off quickly with Umlauf, and Schuppanzigh, after having to endure several volleys at his voluminous person, soon followed. We gathered at the Goldenes Lamm in the Leopoldstadt to continue our interrupted meal undisturbed. The furious composer, however, was left to vent his anger at the waiters and the trees, and as punishment had the opulent meal alone with his nephew.

[Anton Felix Schindler, *Biographie von Ludwig van Beethoven* (Munster: Aschendorff, 1840), 2:88; translated in Landon, *Beethoven*, 356–57]

30. Conductor Felix Weingartner's account of an eyewitness report:

Frau Grebner told me and several other devout listeners that she had taken part in the first performance as a soprano in the chorus. Beethoven sat among the performers from the first rehearsal onwards, to be able to hear as much as his condition would permit. He had a stand in front of him, on which his manuscript lay. The young girl, who now sat before me as a venerable old lady, stood just a few steps away from that stand and thus had Beethoven constantly in view. Her description of him is the same as the one that has been handed down to us: a thickset, very robust, somewhat corpulent man, with a ruddy, pock-marked face and dark, piercing eyes. His grey hair often fell in thick strands over his forehead. His voice, she said, was a sonorous bass; he spoke little, however, for the most part reading pensively in his score. One had the tragic impression that he was incapable of following the music. Although he appeared to be reading along, he would continue to turn pages when the movement in question had already come to an end. At the performance a man went up to him at the end of each movement, tapped him on the shoulder and pointed to the audience. The motions of the clapping hands and the waving handkerchiefs caused him to bow, which always gave rise to great jubilation. Altogether, the effect made by the work at its first performance was quite prodigious. At times there was a burst of applause during a movement. One such moment, Frau Grebner recalled, was the unexpected entrance of the timpani in the Scherzo.

This had the effect of a bolt of lightning and produced a spontaneous show of enthusiasm. Anyone who knows the Viennese public will not be surprised.

[Felix von Weingartner, *Akkorde* (Leipzig: Breitkopf & Härtel, 1912), 1–2; translated in Landon, *Beethoven*, 357]

31. Anton Schindler reporting on a Paris concert of the Ninth Symphony under the direction of François-Antoine Habeneck (see Chap. 4):

Herr Kapellmeister Conradin Kreutzer, who was at the rehearsals and performance under Beethoven's presence in Vienna in 1824, could not convince his contrabassists in Cologne *that Beethoven had this recitative performed so fast that its effect was like thunder,* and he was induced to refer the players to me when I came to the final rehearsals of this symphony in Cologne. The character of melancholy was incontestably the least that Beethoven desired in that recitative, although he might appear motivated by the words of the solo bass: "Freunde, nicht diese Töne" etc. He knew the nature of the instruments too well not to feel that such a long recitative of contrabasses would become boring, and, to a certain degree, ludicrous.

[From Anton Felix Schindler, *Beethoven in Paris* (Munich: Aschendorff, 1842), 45–46; translation adapted from David Benjamin Levy, "Early Performances of Beethoven's Ninth Symphony: A Documentary Study of Five Cities" (Ph.D. diss., University of Rochester, 1979), 348–49]

Reviews of the Performance

32. From the Wiener allgemeine Theater-Zeitung *58 (May 13, 1824): 230–31:*

On May 7 a musical high feast took place in the I[mperial]. R[oyal]. Court Opera Theater. Beethoven gave a grand musical Academy and performed from his compositions a grand Overture, three Hymns (parts of his new Mass), and a grand Symphony with solo and choral voices on Schiller's Ode to Joy entering in the finale.

The solo voice parts were performed by Demoisellen Sonntag [*sic*] and Unger, and Herren Haitzinger [*sic*] and Seipelt. Herr Schuppanzigh directed the orchestra, Herr Kapellmeister Umlauf had the general direction, and the Musikverein undertook the strengthening of the chorus and orchestra. The composer himself was active in the direction of the whole.

The ticket prices were the customary ones, the house was very filled. The public received the tone-hero with the most respectful sympathy, listened to his wonderful, gigantic creations with the most intent attentiveness and broke out in jubilant applause, often during sections, but repeatedly after each of them.

After one hearing of these immense compositions, one can scarcely say more than that he has heard them. To engage in an illuminated discussion, is, for anyone who only attended the production, impossible. Therefore one should be satisfied with the promise that these pages will return again to these artworks by Beethoven with respect to the more precise details.

Imagine the highly inspired composer, the musical Shakespeare, to whom all means of his arts are readily available at the slightest nod, how he glowed from devotion and how, in the innermost belief in the holy work of redemption, he sings the praise of God and the hope of Mankind. Then one has, perhaps, a slight notion of the impact of this Kyrie, Credo, and Agnus Dei!

The opening Overture was a real treat indeed. Only when one remembers the Hymns and the immense Symphony does this masterpiece seem somewhat ordinary.

Beethoven has long shown through his symphonies so high a level of artistic creation in this branch of composition, that since then it has become difficult for any composer to succeed in the wake of this helicon. This newest symphony however is certainly the greatest work of art that Beethoven, with his full Titan's strength, has brought into existence.

All parts of it made the most decided impact, especially the Scherzo, and this symphony would have distinguished itself even more by the striking fantasy which introduces the final chorus, which itself might have enhanced the work even more, had it been possible for the participants to have rendered this section as perfectly as it demanded.

In regard to the orchestra one can say no more than that it is inconceivable how they were able to perform these uncommonly difficult compositions so fully with three rehearsals, because they rendered them most worthily indeed. And this orchestra was composed for the most part of dilettantes; that one can find only in Vienna!

The singers did what they could. Opera singers are accustomed to mastering their performances over many rehearsals, especially if the style may be foreign to them. Herr Seipelt proved to be the best suited. Herr Haizinger had a more difficult assignment. In and of itself, the intonation makes this composition unusually difficult to sing, and beyond that the rhythm changes very frequently.

Hr. Schuppanzigh and Hr. Umlauf have long been famous as directors, but through his achievement today, Umlauf has made himself unforgettable to all Viennese friends of music.

The most ardent wish of a large public is that these works of art that so beautifully manifest the divine in human nature be heard again soon. May this wish be fulfilled!

[Translation adapted from Levy, "Early Performances," 48–49]

33. *From the* Wiener Allgemeine musikalische Zeitung 8, no. 30 (May 12, 1824): 120:

The performance . . . finally took place on May 7 in the Theatre by the Kärntnertor with an unusually numerous audience.

Beethoven's genius seemed to us to be entirely in its youth and original strength again in these grand, gigantic compositions. His rich, powerful fantasy rules with lofty freedom in its familiar realm of tones, and raises the listeners on its wings into a new world that excites amazement.

The great realm of instrumental music in which the celebrated master of so many beautiful creations has preferred to move during his entire life, has still many treasures to await from him because his lofty fantasy, which transcends time and taste, proves itself by each new product to be an inexhaustible source of beauty.

Even though it would have been preferable to hear the three pieces of his grand new Mass that we heard on this occasion in another locale, because once and for all the difference in the seating places also resulted in a large difference in perception with respect to the listeners, and further because neither the chorus nor the solo singers were as fully prepared as such difficult and deeply intricate music requires, yet still the grand style in which Beethoven produced the whole work showed itself in evident clarity.

The effect that so heavy an orchestration ought to have brought forth was so weakened by the bare spaces between the wings in which the sound faded away and dissipated itself, that we could hardly take in half of the noteworthy effect in the moving masses of tone.

The Overture and the grand symphony with the chorus entering in the finale, however, stood out more in their effect.

We therefore earnestly wish that the efforts of several worthy artists who are organizing a second performance, in all particulars better prepared, in a large space that is better suited for music, thereby fulfilling all demands of the art in the accompaniment of the orchestra and in the precision of the execution, may be crowned by a happy success.

It is well worth considering the circumstance that contemporaries of the great composer cannot possibly heed with an indifferent eye when the effort of bringing forth these grand works should not grant him at least some profit; though indeed it stands in no relation to that which he offers to the world, but which nevertheless is of great importance for the "artist's pilgrimage on earth."

The second performance will raise to the highest degree of joy the enthusiastic applause with which the great master, who took part personally in the general direction, was honored, and the composer will find therein anew the reward for his efforts.

The excellent Kapellmeister Umlauf, who directed this performance, has earned the grateful recognition of all friends of art in the highest degree for his zeal and skill.

[Translation adapted from Levy, "Early Performances," 53–54]

34. From the Leipziger Allgemeine musikalische Zeitung 26, no. 27 (July 1, 1824): cols. 437–42:

Grand musical Academy by Hrn. Ludwig van Beethoven, honorary member of the Royal Academies of Arts and Sciences in Stockholm and Amsterdam, also honorary citizen of Vienna, where his newest works were produced, namely: 1. Grand Overture; 2. Three Grand Hymns with solo and choral voices; 3. Grand Symphony with solo and choral voices on Schiller's "Ode to Joy" entering in the finale. The soloists were the Demoiselles Sonntag and Unger, Herren Haitzinger and Seipelt; the Musikverein augmented the orchestra and chorus. Hr. Schuppanzigh directed at the violin, Hr. Kapellmeister Umlauf directed with the baton, and the composer himself took part in the general direction of everything: he stood, that is, by the side of the presiding marshal and fixed the beginning of each tempo, reading in his original score, because a higher enjoyment sadly was denied him owing to the state of his hearing. But where can I find the words to relate to my readers about these giant works, and especially after a single performance which was not well-rounded enough, especially in the vocal sections, where also only three rehearsals could in no way suffice in view of such extraordinary difficulties; therefore there could be no question of an imposing power nor needed differentiation of light and shade, assured security of intonation, or fine shading and nuanced execution. And yet the effect was indescribably great and magnificent, the jubilant applause from full hearts was enthusiastically given the lofty master, whose inexhaustible genius revealed a new world to us and unveiled never-heard, never-imagined magical secrets of the holy art.

The Overture (C major) belongs unchallenged to Beethoven's most finished works. He who is even only somewhat familiar with his numerous works knows what is meant by that. The introductory Andante is developed most nobly, simply, and masterfully. The Allegro is based on a single, driving, rolling figure, inhibited by nothing commonplace, fashioned in free fugal style, one unified whole, flowing in a torrent of glowing fantasy, confining itself only to three scales, C, G, and e minor, but never becoming monotonous, always newly shaped, without the slightest abatement, captivating and raising the interest, and everything so flowing, natural, clear, and understandable, but also exceedingly strenuous and tiring for the performers. Thus would Handel have written had he had the orchestral resources of our time at his disposal, and only one deeply akin to his spirit could succeed in following in the footsteps of this giant.

The three Hymns are principal movements from the composer's newest Mass which he recently sent in copies to several illustrious Maecenas, and for which he just recently received a costly golden medallion from the King of France expressly minted as a remembrance.

The *Kyrie*, D major, is a ceremonious, truly religious Andante that returns with foreign harmonies after the *Christe*, b minor, in which the voices roll forward and wind about in uneven meter in strict contrapuntal art; and the whole seems less like a child-like devout song of prayer, and much more like a melancholy entreaty of a contrite people praying in dust.—The handling of the Credo is indeed unusual and most highly original. The basic key, B-flat major, as well as the tempo, changes often, perhaps, in fact, too often, and the ear scarcely has a chance to absorb the rapid changes. In the *consubstantialem patri* a short, but very energetic fugato begins: the pathetic, monotonic chorale on the words of the creed *et incarnatus est* has a chilling effect and the painfully moving cry of suffering, *passus et sepultus est,* with its dissonant violin accompaniment, cannot be described with words. The continuous figuration on the words *cujus regni non erit finis* is grandly conceived and significant, but one feels especially surprised to hear the *et vitam venturi saeculi* sounded as a slow fugue. Indeed, the motion at the entrance of a countersubject seems somewhat accelerated, but the first Moderato returns, the solo voices now offer a broad, richly ornamented phrase, *Amen,* and the whole ends softly with a likewise long, fading postlude in the orchestra. If it is permitted to speak of effect in a church composition, in the same sense as a tone-poem exercises its power over our spirit, then it cannot be denied that precisely this delayed, nervously awaited close weakens the earlier effects because there seem to be no imaginable grounds for it except the desire to go one's own way. In some cases it is more suitable to remain true to established forms. Who fails to feel himself greatly inspired, like being raised up towards heaven on Seraph's wings, by a fiery stately fugue by Naumann, Haydn, or Mozart?—the character of the *Agnus Dei* (b minor) is uneasily heavy-heartedness and deep mourning. The unusual use of four horns brings forth an entirely peculiar effect. The *Dona* begins as a pleasant Allegretto, D major, 6/8, which spins forth with beautiful imitations until the movement suddenly turns to B-flat major. The timpani, like distant thunder, begin to rumble on the dominant, the solo soprano again intones, recitative-like without fixed rhythm, *Agnus Dei, qui tollis peccata mundi,* a summons which the trumpets answer with a soft Intrada in B-flat, until the full chorus finally bursts out in the frightening, horrible *Miserere nobis.* It is difficult to decipher what the composer exactly had in mind with this section. No less sufficient ground can be found for why the instrumental section that follows, a fugal Presto in 2/4, is inserted here, in which all the voices are silent until they return to action in the recapitulation of the *Dona* as the concluding base of the entire movement. A fervent wish is for all to be somewhat more concise and less fragmented.—

The symphony may measure itself fearlessly with its eight sisters; it certainly will not be obscured by any. Only its originality reveals its father, otherwise everything is new and unprecedented. The first movement is a defiantly bold Allegro in d minor, most ingeniously invented and worked out with true athletic power. From the first chord (A major) until its gradual development into the colossal theme, expectation is kept in uninterrupted suspense, but is resolved most happily. It is impossible to give a sketch of it and it would provide only an insufficient portrayal. The wildest mischief plays its wicked game in the Scherzo (also d minor). All the instruments compete in the banter, and a brilliant march in the fresh major mode is, indeed, an unusually refreshing alternate section. He who sets out with the notion that there could be no Andante more enjoyable and delectable than that of the Seventh Symphony should hear this one (in B-flat major) and he will begin at least to question his opinion. What heavenly song; how overwhelming the variations and combinations of the motives; what artful and tasteful development, how natural everything in the most sumptuous fullness; what grandeur of expression and grand simplicity! The master demands, much, very much, nearly overstepping the human power of his instrumentalists, but he also thereby brings forth such magical effects after which others fruitlessly strive, even with similar means, but without Promethean flash of fire!— The finale (d minor) announces itself like a crushing thunderclap with the shrill cutting minor ninth over the dominant chord. Like in a potpourri, in short periods, all previously-heard principal themes are paraded before us once again in colorful succession, as if reflected in a mirror. Then the contrabasses growl a recitative that seems to ask the question: "What is to happen next?" and answer themselves with a soft, swaying motive in the major mode that develops by the gradual entrance of all the instruments in wonderfully beautiful connections, without Rossinian repeating basses and motion in thirds, into an all-powerful crescendo in measured gradations. Finally, after an invitation by the solo bass, the full chorus also intones in majestic splendor the song in praise of joy. Then the happy heart opens itself wide to the feeling of delight of the spiritual enjoyment and a thousand voices rejoice: "Hail! Hail! Hail! to the godly music! Honor! Praise! and thanks to its worthiest high priest!"

—The critic now sits with regained composure at his writing desk, but this moment will remain unforgettable for him. Art and truth celebrate here their most glowing triumph, and one could rightly say: *non plus ultra!*—Who in fact could succeed in excelling these unnameable moments? It therefore lies in the realm of the impossible for the remaining strophes of the poem, set partly for solo voices, partly for choral forces, in changing tempi, keys, and meters, to be capable of producing a similar effect, no matter how excellently the individual portions are handled. Even the most glowing adherents and the most inspired of the composer's admirers are fully convinced that this truly unique finale would be even more incomparably imposing in a more concentrated shape, and the composer himself would have agreed if cruel fate had not robbed him of his ability to hear his creations. Only one wish, only one request, is for the early repetition of these masterworks. Parenthetically: The revenue, since the subscription to the loges and to part of the orchestra were not cancelled, amounted to 2200 Fl. W. W. From that, the administration received as overhead for the evening, orchestral and vocal personnel, 1000 Fl.; the copying cost 700 Fl.; incidental costs: 200 Fl.; profit: net 300 Fl. W. W. or 120 Fl. in silver.

—Beethoven is occupied presently with the composition of Grillparzer's opera: *Melusine,* and a grand cantata with text by Bernard. It is not known how far both works have progressed, because it is a peculiarity of this artist not to speak about his activities.

[Translation adapted from Levy, "Early Performances," 59–63]

35. *From the* Wiener Allgemeine musikalische Zeitung 8, nos. 38, 40 (June 5, 7, 1824): 149–51, 157–59:

[In this lengthy, two-part article the editor, Friedrich August Kanne, analyzes Beethoven's music after hearing both concerts. This excerpt refers to the performance itself.]:

The performance of this composition was far more successful in the Theater by the Kärntnerthor that entirely suppressed the reverberation of sound (it is understood because the orchestra was placed on the stage) than in the large Redoutensaal because there [i.e., in the theater] the staccato and pointed tones appeared far better rounded as individual bodies of sound and threw no reverberating shadows to darken the contour. There the large crowd of the orchestra, augmented by the participation of many dilettantes, greatly enhanced the sound. One hardly needs to add that a composition such as this, created with the highest freedom of spirit and unchecked enthusiasm, often scarcely gives time to trained violinists to think out a good fingering, on account of which then, also normally weak players, that is, those who readily play variations or concertos, but who are not accustomed to the fast passages of orchestral performance, would normally be horrified at first by such difficult places, set down their bows then and sit out so many measures, thus, in this case, disregard hard techniques until they once again join in easier passages and can mix anew with the orchestra in progress. The reliable ones with true artistic expression had to compensate during such passages by playing stronger for the players who swallowed their notes.

[Translation adapted from Levy, "Early Performances," 88–89]

36. *From* The Harmonicon 2 *(London, 1824): 180–81:*

Accordingly, on the 7th of May, a grand musical performance took place at the Kärnthnerthor Theatre. The leaders of the music were Kapellmeister Umlauf and M. Schuppanzigh, and the great Composer himself assisted on the occasion. He took his place at the side of the principal leader, and, with his original score before him, indicated the different movements and determined the precise manner in which they were to be given; for, unfortunately, the state of his hearing prevented him from doing more. The theatre was crowded to excess, and the sensation caused by the appearance of this great man was a kind that is more easy to imagine than to describe. The arrangement of the pieces performed was as follows: 1st, Beethoven's Grand Overture in C major: 2nd, Three Grand Hymns, with solo and chorus parts from his new Mass, never before performed; 3rd, A grand New Symphony with a finale, in which are introduced a solo and chorus part, from Schiller's *Lied an die Freude* (Song of Joy). This also was performed for the first time, and is Beethoven's last composition—We shall offer a few observations on each of these in the order of their performance. . . .

With respect to the new symphony, it may, without fear, stand a competition with its eight sister-works, by none of which is the fame of its beauty likely to be eclipsed; it is evidently of the same family, though its characteristic features are different:

————facies non omnibus una,
Non diversa tamen, qualem debet esse sororum.—Ovid.

The opening passage is a bold *allegro,* in D minor, full of rich invention, and of athletic power; from the first chord till the gradual unfolding of the colossal theme, expectation is constantly kept alive, and never disappointed. To give a skeleton of this composition would be scarcely practicable, and, after all, would convey but a very faint idea of the body; we shall therefore only touch upon some of the more prominent features, among which is a *scherzo* movement (D minor) full of playful gaiety, and in which all the instruments seem to contend with each other in the whim and sportiveness of the passage; and a brilliant march in the vivid major mode, forms a delightful contrast with the passages by which it is introduced. Whoever has imagined, in hearing the *andante* of the 7th symphony, that nothing could ever equal, not to say surpass it, has but to hear the movement of the same kind in the present composition, in order to change his sentiments. In truth, the movement is altogether divine, the interchanges and combinations of the *motivos* are surprising, the tasteful conduct of the whole is easy and natural, and in the midst of the rich exuberance of the subject, the simplicity that prevails throughout is truly admirable. But it is in the finale that the genius of this great master shines forth most conspicuously. We are here in an ingenious manner presented with a return of all the subjects in short and brilliant passages, and which, as in a mirror, reflect the features of the whole. After this, a singular kind of recitative by the contra-basses, introduces a crescendo passage of the overwhelming effect, which is answered by a chorus of voices that bursts unexpectedly in, and produces an entirely new and extraordinary result. The passages from Schiller's "Song of Joy" are made admirably expressive of the sentiments which the poet intended to convey, and are in perfect keeping with the tone and character of the whole of this wonderful composition. Critics have remarked of the finale, that it requires to be heard frequently in order to be duly appreciated.

At the conclusion of the concert, Beethoven was unanimously called forward. He modestly saluted the audience, and retired amidst the loudest expressions of enthusiasm. Yet the feeling of joy was tempered by an universal regret, to see so gifted an individual laboring under an infliction, the most cruel that could befall an artist in that profession for which nature had destined him. We have no doubt but the master will consider this one of the proudest days in his existence, and it is to be hoped that the testimony of general feeling which he has witnessed will tend to soothe his spirit, to soften down some of its asperities, and to convince him that he stands upon a pinnacle, far above the reach of any and every malignant passion.

Both the singers and instrumental performers acquitted themselves on this interesting occasion, in a manner that is deserving of the highest praise. Of the worthy Kapellmeister Umlauf, who undertook the conduct of this great work, and who with M. Schuppanzigh, a master of known abilities, led the band, it is but justice to say, that his zeal, knowledge, and talents deservedly obtained him the most conspicuous place, and the merited thanks of his brother artists. The impracticability of devoting sufficient time to the number of rehearsals that were necessary in order to do justice to music which is at once new, and of so lofty a character, made it impossible to give it with that precision, and with those delicate shades of *forte* and *piano,* which are required to do them justice.

The deep and general feeling which this concert in honor of the great master of the modern art in Germany, excited, together with the disappointment experienced by many who were unable to obtain admission, induced the Director of the Theatre to make an offer to the composer, of a certain consideration, if he would condescend once more to appear in public, and assist at a repetition of the same music. With this request he complied, and in addition to the pieces before performed, he offered them a manuscript *terzetto,* with Italian words, which was accordingly performed, and considered by the numerous Italian amateurs in Vienna, as a kind of compliment paid by the composer to themselves. — The performance went off with still greater eclat than on the former occasion, and this new composition was hailed by all with no less enthusiasm than the other works.

Hector Berlioz, Symphonie fantastique

Sunday, December 5, 1830, 2:00 P.M.

Here is a young man, lanky, skinny, with long blond hair whose disorder has something that reeks of genius; all the traits of his bony form are drawn forcefully, and his large deep-set eyes, under a large forehead, dart jets of light. The knot of his cravat is tightened as though with rage; his suit is elegant because the tailor made it elegant, and his boots are muddy because his impetuous character refuses to sit still and be pulled along in a carriage, because the activity of his body must match the activity going on in his head. He runs about among the hundred musicians who fill up the stage of the Conservatoire, and although all these regulars in the Conservatoire orchestra make up perhaps the most admirable orchestra ever heard, he begs, he growls, he entreats, he excites each one of them. This man is Berlioz, he is the young composer who, despite his talent, has just carried away the prize at the Institute; and when the public applauds him, he does not advance to give an elegant bow and to let his arms fall servilely towards the parterre; he only stops where he is; he nods his head to acknowledge the applause which rings in the hall, and he continues the remark he was making to Launer [first violin at the Opéra] or to Toulou [first flute]. All that is what we saw at the concert which this young composer gave for the benefit of the wounded of the July Revolution.

—*Le Temps,* December 26, 1830

*I*n 1830 Hector Berlioz was twenty-seven years old and already becoming known in the musical world of Paris. Still, it was something of an accomplishment that he had the help of Paris's leading musicians for the concert that was to include the *Symphonie fantastique*. Although he did not have the stature of a Beethoven (many would say he still does not), the young, impetuous redhead (his hair must have looked blond to the journalist of *Le Temps*) had recently won the coveted Prix de Rome, the highest honor France could bestow on a young composer. The required residency at the Villa Medici, however, was not a welcome part of the prize for Berlioz, and he was determined to make his mark with a wider public before his departure.

For many listeners the *Symphonie fantastique* is an archetypal Romantic symphony: even though it comes only six years after Beethoven's last example of the genre, it somehow seems much more modern; it has a shocking effect even on modern audiences who have heard quite a lot of shocking music. Perhaps it is the overt descriptive quality, the written program detailing scenes in the tormented love life of an artist, that sets it apart (though Beethoven's Sixth Symphony is also programmatic); or the harmonic boldness that was once considered mere ineptitude; or the richness and inventiveness of the orchestration, a giant step beyond Beethoven. Whatever the reason, we often point to the *Fantastique* as the first great Romantic symphony; it definitively marks Berlioz's coming of age as a composer and is one of several events in the remarkable Parisian year of 1830 that we can now identify sagely as symbolic of the Romantic view of the world.

Paris in 1830 was the most important city in the world, especially for music. The city at that time contained many of the landmarks that we recognize with pleasure today: the cathedral of Notre-Dame stood on the Ile du Palais in the Seine, the University of Paris dominated the Left Bank, and the Louvre was the focal point of the Right (though the now open-ended U-shaped palace was then closed by the royal residence of the Tuileries Palace, which was burned by revolutionaries in 1871). Despite its antiquity, however, Paris lacked much that we now take for granted. The river had no stone embankments, so that its sometimes muddy banks served as landing stages, laundry centers, and ferry landings. The Arc de Triomphe (then called the Arc d'Angoulême) at the top of the muddy Avenue des Champs-Elysées had been started but was far from finished; there was no white Sacré-Coeur atop the hill in the outlying village of Montmartre; no Eiffel Tower; no Opéra at the top of its avenue, which did not yet exist (nor, of course, was there an Opéra Bastille—the opera house in 1830 was tucked away in the rue Le Peletier). The great railway stations that now serve as cornerstones of Parisian geography were yet to be built, along with the railways and the metro.

Hector Berlioz, by Auguste Hussener, 1847

This engraving shows Berlioz as a successful
composer, with the ribbon of the Prix de
Rome in his lapel. He is no longer the young,
impetuous composer of 1830 described at his
concert: "Here is a young man, lanky, skinny,
with long blond hair whose disorder has
something that reeks of genius" (*Le Temps,*
December 26, 1830). Berlioz described
himself a little differently as he received the
prize: "I doubt that anyone noticed the blush
of modesty on my forehead as I did so, for so
far from being freshly shorn it was buried
beneath a forest of red hair—a feature which,
in conjunction with other characteristic
points, tended to place me unmistakably in
the owl category."

Paris still had its medieval walls
(as did Vienna), which enclosed a
much smaller area than the twenty arrondissements of Paris that became
official after 1845. There were few
wide paved boulevards, but a great
many narrow unpaved streets with
foul-smelling gutters running down
the middle; the city was not especially well lit, though gas was beginning to be used in
street lamps.

The population had increased from about half a million at the beginning of the
century to about three-quarters of a million by 1830: Paris was more than twice the size
of Vienna. Domestic life, for most, centered around apartment houses with shops on
the street level; the better apartments were on the second and third floors, and spaces
on higher floors decreased in size, comfort, and expense. The garrets under the mansard
roofs provided space for servants, members of the working class, shop assistants and,
to be sure, Romantic artists. Life expectancy was much shorter than it is today: those
not carried off by childhood diseases could expect to live into what is now considered
middle age: the average lifetime was thirty-nine years. The polluted Seine, garbage in
the streets, and the rudimentary medical treatment available contributed to unsanitary
living conditions and to outbreaks of cholera and other epidemics. Women married
early (at twenty-five one more or less officially became an old maid), though men, there
as in Vienna, often married ten years later than their female counterparts.

The better-dressed Parisian men compelled themselves to wear high collars,

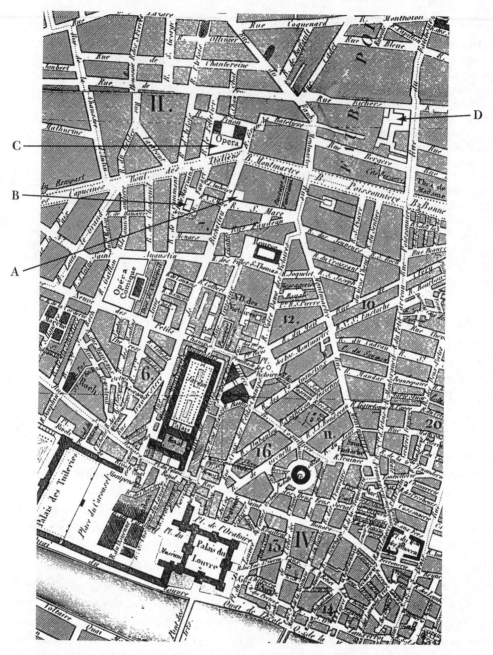

Map of Paris (detail), Showing the Conservatoire, the Opéra, and Berlioz's House

Berlioz's apartment, at 96 rue de Richelieu (A), is centrally located for an active musician. The Théâtre-Italien in the Salle Favart (B) is just a street away, and the Opéra house in the rue Le Peletier (C) is not much farther. Almost all the theaters were located on the grand boulevards, including the Nouveautés, where Berlioz sang in the chorus and where his first plan to perform his symphony came to a disastrous end. The Conservatoire (D), where the symphony was finally performed, is one street beyond the Boulevard Poissonière.

trousers pulled tight by a strap underfoot, high hats, and clean-shaven faces that might be complemented by substantial side-whiskers. Women, like men, wore their hair quite high, and their waists very small.

People of fashion might be seen at a restaurant or café, at the opera or a boulevard theater, or in one of the many *cabinets de lecture,* the neighborhood libraries where, for a fee, one could spend time reading papers and journals. The many fashionable salons, each presided over by a lady (less often by a gentleman) of high standing, gathered a regular élite for literary, artistic, and political conversation. Sometimes the gatherings were for music; the young Alfonse de Pontmartin remembers being invited to a memorable evening at the baronne de la Bouillerie's, where Madame Malibran and Mademoiselle Sontag, the reigning stars of the Opéra, sang to Rossini's accompaniment (for his description of Sontag's singing, see page 140).

Women were prominent not only as leaders of salons, however. In the 1830s George Sand was publishing important journalism; the countess d'Agoult, under the name of Daniel Stern, was likewise a major author (in addition to her literary activities, she ran away with Franz Liszt and bore him three children, one of whom, Cosima, would marry Richard Wagner).

Paris, then as now, attracted people from everywhere; artists, writers, musicians, all wanted recognition in the city. The artistic life in Paris of the 1830s has seldom been rivaled—either before or since. In 1870, Berlioz, the successful composer and conductor, was to write in his memoirs, "What immense resources we possess in this maelstrom that is Paris, to which the hopes and restless ambitions of all of Europe turn."

The uneasy ambitions of the young Hector Berlioz tended in the same direction. The son of a well-to-do physician from the provinces, he ostensibly went to Paris to study medicine, though he was certain that he wanted to succeed as a composer—and only in Paris could that be achieved. It was necessary, however, to find other means of support while waiting for fame to arrive, particularly when his irate father reduced his allowance. In September 1826 Berlioz shared rooms in the rue de la Harpe, where expenses were only thirty francs a month, with his compatriot the pharmacy student Antoine Charbonnel. Eventually Berlioz found various jobs that provided him not only with income but with musical experience: he read musical proofs for the publisher Troupenas (this was one of his introductions to the music of Beethoven); he worked almost nightly as a singer in the chorus of the Théâtre des Nouveautés, earning fifty francs per month; he taught the guitar; and he began to write as a musical journalist, developing a style that would make him one of the most entertaining writers on music. When his father restored his allowance in 1827, Berlioz was able to give up the theater chorus and to move into more dignified lodgings at 96 rue de Richelieu. His real recognition as a composer was not to come until 1830.

Berlioz's House, at 96 Rue de Richelieu

Berlioz lived in this building in 1830, in the fifth-floor mansard apartment
on the left. Perhaps he knew that from his window he could see the building
in which Harriet Smithson, the Shakespearian actress and the inspiration
for the *Symphonie fantastique*, lived for a time.

Revolution and Romanticism

Politically, the year 1830 is a milestone in French history. The Bourbon monarchy, restored fifteen years earlier at the fall of Napoleon, had generated tensions that became a crisis with the promulgation of new laws on censorship in July; three days of
fighting in the streets ("les Trois Glorieuses"), the paving stones being used yet again
to make barricades, led to the abdication of Charles X (king of France) and the acces-

sion of his cousin Louis-Philippe (king of the French). Louis-Philippe, a well-meaning and middle-of-the-road gentleman, was before long regularly and roundly mocked—we picture him with his umbrella—by the very middle-class press that ought rightly to have given support to a monarch who respected the bourgeoisie. Eugène Delacroix's painting *July 28, 1830*, subtitled *Liberty Leading the People*, represents the glories of the July Revolution and, since its creation shortly afterward, has been a symbol not only of the hard-won freedom to which liberty guides the French but of the enduring values of the French people themselves.

For many, 1830 marks the birth of the Romantic movement—and not just the year but the premiere on February 25 of *Hernani*, a drama in verse by the young Victor Hugo (only a year older than Berlioz but infinitely better known). The very first line of the play makes a "forbidden" *enjambement*—a connection to the next line through the incompleteness of the sense; during the performance, this touched off loud discussions among the audience on the wisdom of going beyond established and accepted techniques. Less Romantic, perhaps, but a milestone in the history of literature was the publication in November 1830 of Stendhal's *Le rouge et le noir*, by the young Henri Beyle, a passionate lover of music (though not so much of Berlioz).

In music, of course, the performance of the *Symphonie fantastique* on December 5 announced the new musical Romanticism that was to be of such importance to succeeding decades.

The Romantics broke out beyond previous boundaries of the arts—in drama and versification (*Hernani* is the classic case), in musical style (the *Symphonie fantastique*), in painting (Delacroix's *Death of Sardanapalus*). They looked for wider subject matter: other places and times became attractive (particularly the exotic and colorful); they were fascinated by the supernatural (Goethe's *Walpurgisnacht* is related to the witches in Berlioz's symphony); they revalued the Middle Ages and began the long rehabilitation of medieval monuments, which have been preserved for our day. There was an interest in politics and in history (Berlioz, Delacroix, and Hugo had all been involved, as were Keats and others, in supporting the Greek uprising against the Turks).

The word *romantic* is used in popular jargon to refer to amorous love, a usage that preserves an important aspect of Romanticism: the conception of a single, overpowering love. The *Symphonie fantastique* demonstrates this Romantic passion in musical terms, and Berlioz's second version of the program for the symphony expresses it in words (document 17): "A young musician, afflicted with that moral disease that a well-known writer [Chateaubriand] calls the sickness of the soul, sees for the first time a woman who embodies all the charms of the ideal being he has imagined in his dreams, and he falls hopelessly in love with her." The symphony goes on to describe "the passage from this state of melancholy reverie, interrupted by a few fits of groundless joy, to one of frenzied passion, with its movements of fury, of jealousy, its return of tenderness, its religious consolations." The Romantic's love is not sickly sweet, nor is it

Estelle Fornier, ca. 1864

It is not easy to discern in this photograph the eighteen-year-old girl with whom the twelve-year-old Berlioz had been infatuated. A song he composed while longing for Estelle survives as the melody played by the violins in the slow introduction to the first movement of the *Symphonie fantastique*.

necessarily reciprocal, but it is felt with such a driving force that it is capable of engendering passionate behavior, suicide, or great works of art.

Berlioz is surely included among the Romantics not only because he lived during the period but also because the *Symphonie fantastique* was inspired in such a romantic fashion by two great loves: the beloved Estelle of his youth and the great Shakespearian actress Harriet Smithson. Estelle Dubeuf lived near Berlioz's grandfather in the village of Meylan, near Grenoble; Berlioz reports that at the age of twelve he fell instantly in love with Estelle (with particular emphasis on her pink boots): "This Estelle, however, was a girl of eighteen with a tall, elegant figure, large eyes ready primed for the attack (though they were always smiling), a head of hair that would have graced Achilles' helmet, and the feet, I will not say of an Andalusian, but of a pure-bred Parisian. And she wore pink half-boots. I had never seen such things before. You may laugh; but although I have forgotten the colour of her hair (I believe it was black), I cannot think of her without seeing before me, dazzling as those great eyes of hers, the little pink boots."

As a young man Berlioz tried his hand at composition, and among his early efforts was a sad song on a text from Florian's *Estelle et Némorin,* in which he pours out his despair at leaving Estelle; it was to become the melody, says Berlioz, played by the violins at the start of the *Symphonie fantastique* to express the hopeless sadness of the lovesick artist. And indeed the words he cites do fit the melody played twice by muted violins: "Je vais donc quitter pour jamis mon doux pays, ma douce amie" (So I will leave forever my sweet homeland, my sweet love).

Harriet Smithson was a more proximate influence on the symphony, and on Berlioz's life. The combination of the power of Shakespeare and the sudden pangs of love at first sight produced in Berlioz an overpowering desire to attract the attention of the actress. That Berlioz ultimately did so is owing in part to the *Symphonie fantas-*

Harriet Smithson and Charles Kemble in *Romeo and Juliet*, 1827

The English actress had a profound effect on literary Paris when her
Shakespeare Company presented *Romeo and Juliet, Hamlet*, and other works in
English. Berlioz, among others, was much affected by his discovery of
Shakespeare and by Smithson's performances. His passion for Smithson is the
inspiration for the *Symphonie fantastique*, and the romantic beloved of the
symphony eventually became Madame Berlioz.

tique. Smithson was a twenty-eight-year-old English actress playing Ophelia when
Berlioz first saw her in *Hamlet* at the Odéon Theater in 1827; he was thunderstruck:
"The impression made on my heart and mind by her extraordinary talent, nay her dramatic genius, was equalled only by the havoc wrought in me by the poet she so nobly
interpreted. That is all I can say." Actually he said a great deal more; when he saw
Smithson in *Romeo and Juliet* four days later, he remembers that "by the third act,
hardly able to breathe—as though an iron hand gripped me by the heart—I knew that
I was lost." He worked hard to bring himself to Miss Smithson's attention, but with little success at first. Berlioz later heard gossip about Smithson and her manager, which
led him for a time to feel as strongly against her as he had toward her at first: in this
turnabout is a key to the passions depicted in the *Symphonie fantastique*.

Literary influences, in addition to personal ones, affected Berlioz in the production of the symphony, as is well known. Berlioz discoverered Goethe's *Faust* in the 1827 translation by Gérard de Nerval and commented in his memoirs that "the marvellous book fascinated me from the first. I could not put it down, I read it incessantly, at meals, at the theatre, in the street." He himself says he was still under the influence of Goethe, and especially of *Faust,* when he wrote the *Symphonie fantastique,* and more than one scholar has wondered whether the symphony may not contain some music originally intended for his opera on the subject, of which all we have now is the *Huit scènes de Faust.* Victor Hugo's "La ronde du sabbat" (1825), together with the Witches' Sabbath in *Faust,* surely inspired the last movement of the symphony.

Shakespeare, and not just his spectacular interpreter Miss Smithson, had captivated Berlioz since his first encounter (in 1827 he also attended a performance of *Othello* that impressed him as much as it left another member of the audience unmoved: the philosopher Hegel). He also read Alfred de Musset's translation of De Quincey's *Confessions of an Opium Eater,* another story of doomed love in which Musset has the hero see his beloved at a ball and later imagine (under the influence of the drug) that he is sentenced to death.

It was the discovery of Beethoven that turned Berlioz toward the idea of writing a symphony; recent performances of Beethoven symphonies by the Conservatory orchestra had affected him deeply. Although he had not yet heard the Ninth Symphony, he had evidently seen the score, in that he discussed it in an article published in 1829. We know how profound an effect it had on him, even from superficial resemblances: he was to write a symphony with chorus (*Roméo et Juliette*) and a symphony in which the themes of previous movements are recalled at the beginning of the last (*Harold en Italie*); later, of course, he conducted the Ninth Symphony himself, notably in his London concerts of 1852 with the New Philharmonic Society. In 1829 Berlioz had heard *Fidelio,* presented that year by a company with Anton Haizinger (who had sung the tenor solo at the premiere of the Ninth Symphony in 1824).

The program of the symphony, the written explanation of the sentiments expressed in the music (document 17), describes situations in the life of an artist (for which we can read the Romantic Berlioz), or at least the musical portions of such situations. The young musician, affected by the *vague des passions* (introduction: Estelle melody), sees and falls in love with a young woman; her melody, the idée fixe, begins the Allegro of the first movement and recurs whenever the artist sees her or thinks of her. He sees her at a distance at a ball (second movement), and he meditates on her in the country (third movement: Scene in the Fields). Realizing that she has deceived him, he takes opium, but the miscalculated dose is strong enough only to provoke visions, not to kill him: he imagines that he has killed his beloved and that he is marching to his own execution (fourth movement: March to the Scaffold). He sees himself at a witches' sabbath (fifth movement), assembled for his macabre funeral, when *she* appears in convoluted mocking form, having lost her nobility (Berlioz's view of Smithson at the time?). The funeral chant *Dies irae* is heard; bells; the sabbath contradance. It is a whirl of events stirring up all the passions.

The program of the *Symphonie fantastique* has provoked endless debate about "program" music and "absolute" music—whether music can reasonably and clearly represent physical objects, actions, sensations, and emotions or, whether, on the other hand, there can be an "absolute" music that lacks any external descriptive content for the hearer and achieves emotional effect purely by the organization of sounds.

In fact, Berlioz saw this symphony as an instrumental drama, for which the program serves more or less as a libretto. As he himself put it in the preface to the program: "The composer's purpose has been to develop, in what they have that is musical, different situations in the life of an artist. The plan of the instrumental drama, lacking the help of words, needs to be explained in advance. The following program should thus be considered as the spoken text of an opera, serving to introduce the musical movements, whose character and expression it motivates." For the first performance of 1830, the program was printed and distributed to the audience, though it had also been published in several newspapers, arousing much interest before the premiere.

But the fact that Berlioz several times changed the relation of the program to the symphony without changing the music makes it clear that the music has an independent existence. The program certainly affects our perception of the music, but without the program the symphony is still a symphony, not a series of pictures whose captions are lost.

Further changes in the program arose from a later composition by Berlioz entitled *Lélio* (he referred to it as a monodrama), in which the same artist—now played by an actor—wakes from his opium dream and meditates further. Berlioz considered the two symphonies to be parts of a single work called *Episode de la vie d'un artiste* and revised the program for use whenever the two parts were to be performed together: in such a circumstance he recommended that the orchestra be placed behind a curtain, extended the opium dream to involve all five movements of the *Symphonie fantastique*, and removed the artist's anger at the beloved. He suggested that when the Fantastic Symphony was to be played by itself in a concert, the curtain would not be necessary, and indeed that the program could also be dispensed with, since the symphony, Berlioz says, offers in itself a musical interest independent of any dramatic intention. All this, of course, brings us back to the question of absolute music: if Berlioz changed his mind about the meaning of the program, its wording, and whether it ought to be a part of a performance, it must surely remind us that the program is neither invariable nor inseparable from the piece.

It also brings us back to 1830 and to the effect that the program had, and was intended to have, on the musical public and musical life of Paris in that year.

Berlioz describes Paris in his memoirs:

Paris is where music one moment lies moribund and the next moment seethes with life; where it is sublime and second-rate, lordly and cringing, beggar and king; where it is at once glorified and despised, worshipped and insulted. In Paris music has its loyal and intelligent followers; in Paris music too often speaks to morons, barbarians and the deaf. You see it walking freely and without restraint, or barely able to move for the clammy fetters with which the witch Routine shackles its powerful limbs. In Paris music is a god — so long as only the skinniest sacrifices are required to feed its altars. The god is granted temples laden with splendid trophies — on condition that he turn man, and clown too on occasion. In Paris you see Art's scrofulous bastard brother, Commerce, flaunting his bourgeois finery in the public eye, and Art, naked and unadorned as the Pythian Apollo, lost in contemplation, hardly deigning to glance down on him with a smile of remote contempt. You may even see Commerce obtain unbelievable favours from this too unworldly brother, creeping into the great chariot of the sun, seizing the reins and attempting to turn the immortal car round; whereupon the true driver, startled into activity by such mad presumption, tears him off the seat and hurls him from his presence.

Music in Paris

The musical world of Paris in 1830 was highly active and highly stratified. At the top of the musical hierarchy, in terms of both art and commerce, stood the Académie Royale de Musique — the Opéra — and it was fully understood that the height of achievement for a composer was to have an opera produced there, and for a performer to be regularly employed there.

The opera house in the rue Le Peletier, considerably grander than the Kärntnertor Theater in Vienna, had for the previous four years been the site of annual premieres of works by Rossini, most recently *Guillaume Tell* (1829). Another important production of late had been Esprit Auber's *La muette de Portici*, based on a libretto by Eugène Scribe (1828); this opera about a popular uprising concluded with a famous eruption of Vesuvius. Both productions featured memorable music with political over-

A Performance of *La muette de Portici* at the Opéra

The opera house in the rue Le Peletier was the principal venue for opera
until Garnier's grand building was constructed in the 1870s. This scene
shows the famous third act of *La muette de Portici,* in which Vesuvius erupts.
This piece may be the reason that Habeneck refused to repeat the "March
to the Scaffold" at the first performance of the *Symphonie fantastique,* in
that the players needed to finish the concert in time to get to the Opéra
for a special performance of *La muette.*

tones—a significant aspect of the theater in those days: *La muette,* well known for the
number "Amour sacré de la patrie," actually touched off a revolution in Belgium; *Guillaume Tell* contained a trio celebrating "la liberté." After the July Revolution, the management of the Opéra was entrusted to the remarkable Louis Véron, who made the
Opéra profitable for virtually the only time in its history, owing almost entirely to the
success in 1831 of Giacomo Meyerbeer's *Robert le diable.* Véron, a quack doctor and a
strong apologist for his importance in the history of opera, created a sort of star system
whereby the fees for famous singers increased while those for rank-and-file musicians
shrank. The Opéra had a very important orchestra, as we shall see.

In principle, the second theater of the realm was the Opéra-Comique. The
company had just opened a new theater near the Place de la Bourse, where musical
works with spoken dialogue were performed. These were the only two venues for new
French operas, and composers were eager for their compositions to be performed on
either of these stages. Limited to performing works in French, the Opéra-Comique was

prevented from participating in the lucrative Rossini fever. In 1828–29, the leading composers were Boieldieu and Auber (each of whom had eight works produced), but no one was as well represented onstage as Eugène Scribe, the librettist of nine shows.

The Théâtre-Italien, in the rue Favart, was the opera house for Italian works; its purpose was to present to the French public the foremost Italian operas—in Italian. Under the direction of Ferdinando Paër, it had done so from 1812 until 1824, when Rossini was made codirector after the production of two of his operas. Rossini brought Meyerbeer to Paris in 1825; although he turned his attention to the Opéra at the end of the 1820s, Rossini still influenced the subsequent directors of the Théâtre-Italien. The repertory in 1828–29, though it did include one work by Halévy (*Clari*) and one by Mozart (*Don Giovanni*), was otherwise entirely devoted to nine works by Rossini. In the 1830s its directors put on new works by modern Italian composers such as Bellini (*I Puritani,* 1835), Donizetti (*Marino Falieri,* 1835), and Mercadante (*I Briganti,* 1836). The Théâtre-Italien boasted a group of superb singers, especially in the 1830s; but despite Rossini's considerable interest and influence (he almost succeeded in convincing the famous François-Antoine Habeneck to become its conductor in 1830), it remained subsidiary to the Opéra. Its orchestra, smaller than that of the Opéra and somewhat less experienced, was nevertheless known for its first-rate abilities in Italian operatic style and in the accurate accompaniment of singers.

Music was to be heard as well in the many boulevard theaters, so called for their location around the series of grand boulevards that extended from the church of the Madeleine to the Place de la Bastille along the site of medieval walls.

Melodramas were played in the Théâtre de l'Ambigu-Comique, the Théâtre de la Gaité, and the Théâtre de la Porte Saint-Martin. The grand master of the melodrama, Guilbert de Pixérécourt, had developed a dramatic formula that never failed to please. Each play features impressive scenery, local color, and passionate emotional thrills within predictable dramatic contexts, a handsome tableau at the end of each act, and rich music and dance. Musically one could expect an overture and entr'actes, as well as tender or passionate airs (often on familiar or borrowed melodies), and—the hallmark of melodrama—the interruption of spoken words with musical punctuations or the simultaneous musical accompaniment of spoken monologues or dialogues. Dancing too was indispensable, fitted into the action under the guise of a village wedding, a court ceremonial, or an exotic pageant. The combination of spectacle, drama, dance, and orchestral music gave to the boulevard audiences all the ingredients that others looked for at the Opéra. And the Opéra was not slow to borrow the dancers, the set designers, and the special-effects technicians of the boulevard theaters to create the spectacle of the Grand Opera.

On the boulevards the *comédie-vaudeville* had entertained the public for years, especially at the Madame, the Vaudeville, the Variétés, and the Nouveautés theaters. At the famous Gymnase Theater, Eugène Scribe had produced dozens of popular works before taking his talents into the lyric theater, first in collaboration with Auber in *La muette de Portici* and then in many other aspects of French Grand Opera. But it was on the boulevards that Scribe first showed his skill in making a play full of dramatic tension, delayed revelations, and mistaken identities; he was concerned with Romantic passions, exotic subject matter, historical events of recent importance. After seeing one of Scribe's pieces in 1832, Mendelssohn wrote that the vaudeville was a "genre eminently French . . . where the end of every scene brings on a well-known tune."

The Variétés Theater also presented comedies and burlesques, like *Le comte Odry,* a parody of Rossini's *Le comte Ory* and of the Rossini phenomenon. The Nouveautés, whose recently hired chorus included the young Hector Berlioz, had been developing a repertory of "pièces mêlées de couplets"—essentially plays with songs— and more ambitious pieces along the lines of the Opéra-Comique. Among their latest productions was *Canon d'alarme, ou les classiques et les romantiques,* in which an old husband and his "ultra-Romantic" wife have to call on Figaro to cure their capricious daughter. (The boulevard attractions available on the day of Berlioz's concert are listed in document 8.)

Other entertainments beckoned too. The Cirque-Olympique was famous for its "mimodrames" involving music, spectacle, and horses. The theaters of the Acrobates and the Funambules provided ropewalking, acrobatics, pantomime, and harlequinade. There were two marionette theaters and a children's theater. Eleven establishments offered *bals publics,* where the latest in dance music could be enjoyed. Monsieur Daguerre's Diorama, where such scenes as the eruption of Vesuvius or the Holyrood Chapel by Moonlight were to have their effect on Grand Opera, had many imitators (the Néorama, Géorama, Cosmorama, Peristréphorama, and so on). The menagerie of M. Martin included "two lions, one Bengal tiger, the hyena of Asia and the llama of Peru; each animal is tamed, and plays with its master."

In the face of such a wealth of opportunities for entertainment, is it hardly surprising that Pierre Marie Baillot's famous series of chamber music concerts (1827–40), at which Berlioz heard Beethoven's Opus 131 in 1829, took place in such a small room (150 seats) in the rue Saint-Lazare. Smaller venues, such as the salons of the piano makers Erard, Pleyel, Pape, Duport, Petzold, and Bernhard, often served for musical events on a rental basis; following Baillot's example other chamber series sprang up. Individual concerts, such as that given by Chopin in the salons of Erard in 1832, made the rental of such halls a reasonable business.

The orchestras of Paris were relatively numerous and in general quite accomplished, thanks to the Conservatoire, which for years had been producing first-rate instrumentalists to fill orchestral positions within the city. The Paris Conservatoire was founded in 1794 as the Ecole Royale de Chant. Converted into a national conservatory charged with furnishing musicians for the fourteen armies of the republic, it has remained an important and influential institution to this day. In 1830 the director was

Some Parisian Orchestras, circa 1830:

	Opéra 1830	Conservatoire 1830	Théâtre-Italien 1827	Gaité 1828	Ambigu 1828	Porte St-Martin 1828
Violin 1	12	15	8	2–3	5	5
Violin 2	12	14	8	2–3	4	4
Viola[a]	8	7	4	2	2	2
Cello	9	12	4	2	3	2–3[b]
Bass	8	8	7	2	3	2–3[b]
Flute	3	4	3	1	2	1
Oboe	3	3	2	1	—	1
Clarinet	3	4	2	1	2	2
Bassoon	4	4	2	2	1	2
Horn	4	4[c]	4	2	2	2
Trumpet	2	2	2	—	—	1
Trombone	3	4[d]	3	1	—	1
Ophicleide	1[e]	—	—	—	—	—
Harp	2	1	—	—	—	1
Percussion	5[f]	3[g]	1	1	1	1

[a] Called "quinte" at the Opéra, a term dating from the five-part string writing of Lully.

[b] The sum of the basses (cellos and double basses) is 5.

[c] There were also two "supplementary" horns.

[d] There was also a fifth "external" trombone. One of the players also played ophicleide; one also played bass drum.

[e] Player also played trombone.

[f] Two timpanists, bass drum, cymbals, triangle.

[g] Two timpani (one player also sang bass) and a bass drum, whose player was drawn from the trombones.

Luigi Cherubini (whose music Beethoven admired and whose administration Berlioz deplored; Cherubini had only to wrinkle his eyebrows, it was said, and the whole Conservatoire trembled); Berlioz had studied there with, among others, the Czech composer Anton Reicha and the composer of operas Jean-François Le Sueur.

As in Vienna, Parisian orchestras accompanied operatic and stage spectacles—with the single and important exception of the Conservatoire orchestra, whose sole purpose was to perform concert music.

Of the various theatrical orchestras, that of the Opéra was preeminent in that its instrumentalists were the highest paid and it enjoyed the most prestige. This orchestra was the direct descendant of the one founded by Jean-Baptiste Lully, the chief musician of Louis XIV in 1669, and had not changed drastically since the operas of Gluck in the 1770s: in 1830 it featured triple woodwinds, except for an additional bassoon, which was a peculiarity of the Opéra and what the now-Parisian Berlioz used in the *Symphonie fantastique*.

Recruitment in the opera orchestra was by competition; successful applicants were usually taken on as supernumeraries and got regular places as they became available. In 1830 the majority of the players had been trained at the Conservatoire, where more than half, particularly among the first violins, had received a First Prize. The strings were a strong complement, with real depth, and the wind players were renowned far and wide.

The musicians of the Opéra were paid according to a hierarchical scale that ranged from six hundred francs annually for the bass drum to three thousand francs for Pierre Marie Baillot—the famous first-chair violin, professor at the Conservatory, and organizer of the well-known chamber music series. (An average violinist, by contrast, was paid about twelve hundred francs.) The two leading wind players, Jean-Louis Tulou, the flutist who had moved up from the Théâtre-Italien, and the first oboist Gustave Vogt made three thousand francs a year. Other wind players had salaries similar to those of the strings, though horn players were paid something above the average. As is true in most opera houses, the singers did rather better. Madame Cinti-Damoreau, the famous soprano, received a contract of sixteen thousand francs a year. After 1830 the gap widened with the loss of the royal subsidy, and the management reduced salaries for the rank and file and increased the high fees for big names. (Berlioz's allowance from his father put him in the same category as the bass drum and obliged him to look for additional work; the monthly wage for the lowest-paid workers was about five hundred francs.)

Players at the Opéra had regular contracts, but not particularly advantageous ones, since they could be broken by management; but a player could not leave until a year after he had given notice of his resignation. The work involved three or four performances a week, not counting rehearsals and occasional obligatory concerts; 182 performances were officially scheduled a year. Discipline was strict, and repeated absences

François-Antoine Habeneck

Habeneck, in addition to being a violinist and professor at the Conservatoire, was conductor of the opera and of the renowned Conservatoire concerts. He conducted the first performance of the *Symphonie fantastique,* probably using his usual violin bow. "At every wrong note, he turned around and pointed out the culprit to the vindictive public with his violin-bow" (Charles de Boigne).

were not tolerated. Members of the orchestra could not play for other operas or perform as soloists without express permission, which was rarely granted. Despite their distinction, they were more employees than artists.

The paramount musical authority in Paris was François-Antoine Habeneck, conductor of both the Opéra and Conservatoire orchestras. The fifty-year-old Habeneck was one of two professors of violin at the Conservatoire; and his influence was as far-reaching in his time as that of Lully in the seventeenth century or of the composer and conductor Pierre Boulez in our own day. Only he could get his Conservatoire pupils into the orchestra without having them pass through the audition process. It was Habeneck who introduced the symphonies of Beethoven to the Parisian public (and hence also to Berlioz) and who, as a champion of the music of younger composers, was to conduct the premiere of the *Symphonie fantastique.* At twenty-three Habeneck had entered the Opéra orchestra as a rank-and-file violinist; between 1821 and 1824 he was to serve as its concertmaster and first assistant conductor and indeed as general director of the Opéra. From 1824 until 1844 he was chief conductor, during which time he took on numerous other offices and posts that allowed him to exert extraordinary influence on the musical life of the capital.

It was Habeneck who, in the Opéra pit on August 28, 1828, at the premiere of Rossini's *Le Comte Ory,* conducted for the first time facing the musicians and using a violin bow rather than the large baton of the time beater (the *batteur de mesure*). Up until that time both the orchestra and the time beater had faced the stage, with the time beater nearest the stage; this can be seen in the illustration of the Paris Opéra (page 193), where the time beater leans on the front edge of the stage, obviously establishing communication with the players not through eye contact but through the sound the baton makes when it is struck on the floor of the pit. Such pounding, however discreet, had always been a part of operatic performance in France; it is hard to imagine that Habeneck could have conducted such a score as the *Symphonie fantastique* by pounding on the floor. At the Opéra, however, even though Habeneck now conducted with a bow, he continued for years to rely on audible beats when necessary, striking on the prompter's box with his bow.

Habeneck was an expressive and highly respected conductor; he continued to use his violin bow (though he did not play while conducting), and he conducted generally from a first violin part; he helped to keep the players on their toes, and his audience aware of the score, by calling attention to "clams" in the orchestra. Charles de Boigne, in his 1857 *Petits mémoires de l'Opéra,* wrote that "Habeneck had the bad habit of letting the audience in on the secret of the clams [*couacs*] that occurred in his orchestra. At every wrong note, he turned around and pointed out the culprit to the vindictive public with his violin-bow." In the arrangement of performing forces for concerts in the Conservatoire (see page 215) Habeneck placed himself, much like his Viennese counterparts when there was a chorus, near but not at the front, so that a portion of the chorus could not see him directly. One wonders whether many performers were singled out for special attention when Habeneck conducted the *Symphonie fantastique.*

Among Habeneck's most important achievements was the foundation of the Société des Concerts du Conservatoire (the Conservatoire orchestra). It may be that Habeneck tired of the routine of the operatic repertory, and it is certainly true that he had a fondness for recent Germanic symphonic music and a special passion for Beethoven. He began by inviting orchestral players (one can imagine a musician's difficulty in refusing) to a dinner preceded by a play-through of the "Eroica" Symphony.

Saint-Saëns on Habeneck:

All the women had their backs to him, so that whenever a dangerous passage arrived there were almost always accidents. On such occasions Habeneck turned around towards the unfortunate choristers, or rather towards the audience, and made grimaces; and since he was very ugly, the only result he obtained was an outburst of hilarity in the auditorium.

"Gentlemen," he said to the exhausted players, among whom the double-bass players were making cannibal sounds, "in the name of a grateful Beethoven you are invited to the table for dinner." This was the legendary beginning that led two years later to the formation of the Conservatoire orchestra, which had its first season in 1828. These concerts—six a season, with an occasional one or two extra—were given on Sunday afternoons in the spring in the same Grande Salle of the Conservatoire that was to be the venue two years later for Berlioz's symphony.

The Conservatoire orchestra was organized by and for the participating musicians, all of whom were professionals who assembled for their common benefit and for the making of music. In the social history of music it is an extraordinary event. Its elaborate constitution, drawn up in 1828, provided for recruitment of players from the graduates of the Paris Conservatoire through an executive committee. There were 112 members of the society—sixty-four in the orchestra, thirty-six in the choir, and twelve soloists, mainly singers. Any extra players were chosen from the current students at the Conservatoire; given the title of "aspirants," these young musicians took over regular places in the society when they became vacant.

The financial health of the Conservatoire orchestra depended on income from the sale of tickets, the profits from which were divided among the performers. Ticket prices ranged from two to nine francs; at first there was a royal subsidy of two thousand francs a year, though this varied with the political situation.

The concert programs of the orchestra were conservative—the Constitution said nothing about championing modern music. A typical concert might have been familiar, in its shape and length, to a Viennese concertgoer. Beginning with a symphony of Haydn, Mozart, or Beethoven, there generally followed choral movements from masses or oratorios by the same classical masters or by Cherubini; then might come operatic extracts and a concerto (or a virtuosic piece composed and played by a soloist); an orchestral piece—an overture or another symphony—concluded the program. The repertory was limited: not until the 1840s was older music (Rameau, Handel, Bach) programmed. Besides Mendelssohn, Cherubini was the only living composer regularly represented (of course he was the director of the Conservatoire in which the concerts were held).

In a sense these concerts mark the beginning of the modern orchestral canon. They were given by an expert orchestra assembled to play concerts, not operas; they were produced in a subscription series; the programs concentrated on orchestral music; and they featured music by a variety of highly respected, mostly deceased composers, from Haydn to those of the recent past.

Habeneck had some habits regarding programming that are no longer much in vogue. When a symphony was too long or too difficult to rehearse, for example, he was perfectly willing to play only part of it or to divide it into parts separated by other music. Thus the famous French premiere of Beethoven's Ninth Symphony, in 1832,

Seats and prices at concerts of the Conservatoire orchestra:

	Places	Price (francs)
Orchestra	180	6
Parterre	150	3
Stalles (balcony)	68	9
Loges de rez-de-chaussée (30)	176	6
Premières loges (30)	157	9
Deuxièmes loges (32)	177	6
Troisièmes loges (4)	25	3.50
Stalles d'amphithéâtre	38	3.50
Amphithéâtre	51	3
Corridors (orchestra and balcony)	32	6
Stage boxes (2)	24	2
Total	1,078	

was split in half by the inclusion of Cherubini, Weber, and a quartet movement of Beethoven. The second performance, two years later, divided it differently: the concert began with the first three movements, continued with music of Auguste Franchomme, Weber, and Rossini, and concluded with the final choral movement.

Habeneck also liked to show off the skill and precision of his string section by performing movements of string quartets by Haydn or Beethoven using the entire forty-eight string players of the orchestra. In this way he presented music otherwise little known. Chopin, who felt the effect was not always felicitous, wrote to a friend in 1832, "You think you're hearing four gigantic instruments: the violins like a palace, the viola like a bank, and the cello like the Protestant Church."

The orchestra was made up of the best instrumental players of Paris, most of whom also played in the orchestra of the Opéra. A few also performed with the Opéra-Comique or the Théâtre-Italien, where the cellist Franchomme and the flutist Jean-Louis Tulou were considered stars. The prestige of the Conservatoire orchestra was enormous, and it rapidly gained an international reputation.

Berlioz was planning for the concert before he began composing the symphony. His plans for a performance had begun in January 1830, when he intended to give a concert to include this symphony on the Sunday after Ascension, May 23, 1830. By April 16 the symphony was ready; the date of the proposed concert was postponed one week to Whitsunday, May 30 (a day when the theaters would be dark, allowing them to be used for nontheatrical events). Plans were advanced enough that the program of the symphony was printed in *Le Figaro* of May 21 and the *Journal des Comédiens* on May 23 (see documents 1 and 2). The concert was to include the eminent soprano Wilhelmine Schroeder-Devrient and Anton Haizinger (an "incredible singer," according to Berlioz).

The Théâtre des Nouveautés, where Berlioz had sung in the chorus, had a modest orchestra of its own. Through his acquaintance with Nathan Bloc, the theater's conductor, Berlioz managed to arrange a first play-through, designed to convince the theater management that this symphony would attract public attention. The rehearsal was a disaster: at the distance of 170 years it seems amusing, particularly as Berlioz recounts it in his memoirs, but it was probably not so hilarious to the young composer, or to Bloc and his colleagues, at the time:

> The Théâtre des Nouveautés had for some time been performing opéras-comiques, and now had a reasonably good orchestra under the command of Bloc. He persuaded me to offer my new work to the directors of the theatre; we should jointly organize a concert and give the work a hearing. The directors consented, for the sole reason that the symphony's unusual programme had caught their fancy; they thought a lot of people would come out of curiosity. But I wanted a performance on a really grand scale, so I engaged a further eighty players. When added to Bloc's, they formed an orchestra of a hundred and thirty. The theatre had no normal provision for an army of performers on this scale; the necessary physical conditions, the platforms for the different levels, even the desks, were lacking. To all my inquiries the directors replied with the imperturbable calm of men who have no conception of the difficulties involved: I had no need to worry, everything would be seen to, they had a scene-shifter who was a very clever fellow. But when the day came for the rehearsal, and my orchestra of a hundred and thirty tried to arrange themselves on the stage, there was nowhere to put them. The tiny pit, when pressed into service, barely accommodated the violins. From all over the theatre an uproar arose that would have driven a much more sanguine composer demented. People were calling for desks, while the carpenters strove to knock together something that would do instead. The scene-shifter went about swearing and searching for his flats and his struts. There were cries for chairs, for instruments, for candles; the double basses

were out of strings; there was no place anywhere for the drums. The orchestral attendant did not know where to begin. Bloc and I were in thirty-seven different places at once; but it was all to no avail. The situation had got beyond control. It was a rout, a musical Crossing of the Beresina.

However, despite the confusion, Bloc insisted on trying a couple of movements, "to give the directors an idea of the symphony." We rehearsed the Ball and the March to the Scaffold as well as was possible with our forces in disarray; and the March created a perfect furore among the players. But the concert never took place. The directors recoiled before such tumult, and the enterprise was abandoned. It would involve, they said, too much elaborate preparation; they "had no idea so much was required for a symphony."

My plan had been wrecked for want of desks and a few benches. The extreme care which I now take over the practical details of concert-giving dates from then. I know too well what disasters the least negligence in this respect can lead to.

The chaos resulting from inadequate preparation was enough to convince the theater, despite Bloc's friendship with Berlioz, that this undertaking was too risky. Berlioz must have lost his young shirt, even if the orchestra performed (or tried to) as part of its regular duties: eighty invited musicians could not all have been such friends of Berlioz that they could provide professional services free of charge. But the performance was canceled. Berlioz, in writing to his father, suggested that the date was unsatisfactory—in that two competing events would deprive him of an audience—and made no reference to the misfire at rehearsal; indeed, he says that there were two rehearsals, during which the entire symphony was evidently rehearsed, and that it was just as he had imagined it.

In the few months that separated this first attempt to perform the symphony from the second, successful plan that resulted in a concert on December 5, much had happened in the fortunes of Berlioz—and in the history of France. In particular, the July Revolution had changed the political landscape of the country. Berlioz, who must have heard the noise from his room under the dome of the Institut de France, found out about the Three Glorious Days only on the second of them, when he emerged from the institute to find rioting in the streets. He had just finished composing a cantata in competition with other composers in the hope of winning the Prix de Rome.

This prestigious award sent young painters, sculptors, architects, engravers, and composers to the Villa Medici in Rome for two years and included a further subvention (to allow them to develop their creative talents) of three thousand francs annually for the next three years—a sizable sum compared to Berlioz's allowance from his fa-

The Théâtre des Nouveautés, Probably as It Appeared in the Early
Nineteenth Century

One of many boulevard theaters presenting vaudeville, melodramas, and other
popular dramatic and musical entertainments, the Nouveautés was in 1830
presenting substantial comic operas. Berlioz was employed there as a member
of the chorus, and through this connection he undertook the first, disastrous
attempt to perform the *Symphonie fantastique.*

ther. The prize was essential to artists who aimed to make their mark in France, and
Berlioz had failed to win it several times before. The composer-contestants were locked
in rooms and given the text of a cantata they were to compose for voice and orchestra
(Berlioz liked to mock the standard hack-literary opening of such texts: "Scarcely had
rosy-fingered Dawn touched the mountains with her tint") within the space of twenty-

five days. The results were evaluated by a jury of the Académie des Beaux-Arts, and the winning cantata, selected by the members of the academy as a whole, was performed with orchestra at a formal prize-giving ceremony in the Institut de France.

Berlioz found that the academic requirements did not conform to his new ideas, but he played a trick that won him the prize: he left out of his submitted score the great conflagration scene with which he really meant the cantata to end, fearing that it would be too much for the judges. And after winning the prize (he was officially notified on August 21), it was that very conflagration that caused Berlioz great triumph and great disaster. Berlioz the raconteur makes a hilarious spectacle of the public performance of his cantata, which features also in his concert of December 5:

> The Permanent Secretary, holding in one hand the wreath of artificial laurels which will crown the victor's brow and in the other the solid gold medal which will pay his rent until he leaves for Rome (it is worth a hundred and fifty francs, as I discovered), reads out in a loud and clear voice the name and Christian names of the composer. The laureate rises:
>
> > Upon his candid forehead freshly shorn
> > A blush of manly modesty appearing
> > (Boileau, *Le lutrin* ["The Lectern"]).
>
> He embraces the Permanent Secretary (polite applause). The laureate's distinguished master is sitting a few feet from the Permanent Secretary's rostrum. The pupil embraces his distinguished master (more polite applause). On a bench at the back, behind the academicians, the laureate's parents sit weeping tears of silent joy. The laureate vaults over the intervening benches, treading on someone's toe, trampling another's coat and, reaching the top, flings himself into the arms of his father and mother, who by now are sobbing unashamedly (no applause; but people are beginning to laugh). To the right of this touching group a young person is signalling to the hero of the hour. He responds by leaping in her direction and, after tearing a woman's dress and crushing a dandy's hat, contrives to reach his cousin. He embraces his cousin. Sometimes he embraces his cousin's neighbour (loud laughter). Another lady, sitting by herself in a distant corner of the hall, makes discreet signs of affection which our hero affects not to notice. Then he turns and flies to embrace his mistress—his betrothed, the woman who is to share his life and fame. This time, in his haste and confusion and blindness to all other women, he kicks one of them over, trips over a bench, falls with a crash, abandons all hope of

greeting the hapless girl, and regains his seat, bathed in perspiration (loud and prolonged laughter and applause). This is the crowning moment of the academic year, and I know many people who go along solely to witness it. I say this without any rancour against these jokers; for when my time came there was no father, mother, cousin, master or mistress for me to embrace. My master was ill, my parents disgruntled and elsewhere, and my mistress . . . So I embraced only the Permanent Secretary, and I doubt that anyone noticed the blush of modesty on my forehead as I did so, for so far from being freshly shorn it was buried beneath a forest of red hair—a feature which, in conjunction with other characteristic points, tended to place me unmistakably in the owl category.

I was, besides, in no mood to embrace anybody. I do not believe I have ever been in such a black fury in my life. The reason was this. Our subject that year was "The Last Night of Sardanapalus." The poem ended at the moment when the vanquished potentate gathers his most beautiful slaves around him and mounts the funeral pyre. My first impulse had been to write a kind of symphonic description of the scene: the wails of the reluctant victims, the great sensualist defying death in the midst of the encircling flames, the crash of the falling palace. Then I thought of the means that would be required in a purely orchestral piece to suggest a scene of this kind, and I restrained myself. The music section of the Academy would certainly have condemned the whole cantata after one look at such a finale, quite apart from the fact that, boiled down for the piano, it would have sounded nonsensical. So I waited. When the prize had been awarded and I was sure of not losing it, and sure of performance by a full orchestra, I wrote my conflagration. At the final rehearsal the piece produced such an effect that several academicians, who had been caught unawares, came up and congratulated me warmly and without any resentment at the trap I had set for their sacred beliefs.

The rehearsal in the Institute assembly hall was attended by a large number of artists and music-lovers who had come to hear this cantata by a young composer already notorious for his wild eccentricity. Most of them went off full of the extraordinary impression the conflagration had made on them. As a result of their enthusiastic accounts, the audience arrived next day in an unusual state of curiosity and expectation.

I was not altogether confident of the abilities of Grasset, ex-conductor at the Théâtre-Italien, who was in charge of the performance, and before it began I went and sat near him, manuscript in hand. Mme Malibran, whose interest had been aroused by the reports of the day before, but who had not been able to find a seat in the hall, was also accommodated nearby on a stool, sandwiched between two double basses. It was the last time I saw her.

My decrescendo began (for the first words of the cantata were "E'en now Nature in darkest night lies veiled," and I had therefore been obliged to compose a sunset in place of the traditional dawn; it seems I am doomed to be different, forever at odds with life and the Academy!). All went smoothly; Sardanapalus learnt of his defeat, resolved to die and summoned his women, and the pyre was kindled. Everyone listened intently. Those who had been at the rehearsal whispered to their neighbours, "Now it's coming. Wait till you hear it—it's fantastic."

Ten million curses on all musicians who do not count their rests! In my score the horn was supposed to give the cue to the timpani, the timpani to the cymbals, the cymbals to the bass drum; the first stroke of the bass drum was the signal for the final explosion. But the accursed horn-player failed to play his note. Without it, the timpanist was afraid to come in. In consequence, cymbals and bass drum also kept silent. Absolutely nothing happened. The violins and cellos went on with their futile tremolo; otherwise, not so much as a pop. The fire went out without a crackle; the much-heralded holocaust had turned into a damp squib—*ridiculus mus* [a silly mouse]. Only a composer who has himself been through such an experience can conceive the fury that possessed me. I could hardly breathe. A cry of horror burst from me. I hurled my score into the middle of the orchestra and sent the two nearest desks flying. Mme Malibran started back as if a mine had exploded at her feet. The whole place was in an uproar—the orchestra in confusion, the academicians scandalized, the audience mystified, the composer's friends in high indignation. Another musical catastrophe had overtaken me, the cruellest I had yet experienced. Would that it had been the last!

Berlioz's second plan for a concert was not so ill-fated: as a winner of the Prix de Rome, he had become a young musician of real stature. But although he could now make his way in Paris as a composer, he could not remain there, because he failed to get the residency requirement set aside. He planned a concert in the Grande Salle of the Conservatoire for November 7, with Habeneck conducting. Fired perhaps by patriotic emotion, Berlioz associated his concert with recent political events by making it a benefit for the wounded of the recent July revolution (see his letter to the king, document 7). The concert, as so often happens with single events organized by one overworked individual, was postponed by a week, to November 14, then to November 21, and finally to December 5, when it at last took place.

Berlioz had a great deal to do beyond preparing the orchestral parts and arranging for musicians, especially as the date approached. On November 19 he wrote to his friend Humbert Ferrand, "I am running around all evening on account of a rehearsal of my symphony which I am doing tomorrow" (document 9). Up to the very last minute, he was still arranging for the rental of instruments, strings, and mutes. In the early days of December, he had six hundred posters printed (which someone presumably saw to affixing around Paris) and 1,538 programs, far more than the capacity of the hall of the Conservatoire.

The first general rehearsal was on November 20, and we can imagine that under Habeneck's direction it went better than the disaster in the Théâtre des Nouveautés. Although, according to Berlioz's memoirs, two full rehearsals were held, it seems likely from letters and other materials that there were smaller sectional rehearsals, often under the direction of Berlioz.

The Grande Salle of the Conservatoire, though not large, could accommodate more than a thousand people. Inaugurated in 1811, it was decorated in Pompeian style (which was brilliantly restored in the 1980s). Lighting was provided by some small skylights, which let in scant daylight, and by a number of elegant chandeliers, which burned oil rather than gas to avoid the danger of an explosion that might harm the books in the nearby Conservatory library. The hall was heated by ceramic stoves on each of the three floors.

The ground floor was divided into orchestra (in the front, with seats) and parterre (in the back, with benches); there were four levels of boxes (the topmost of which, the amphitheater, seemed to touch the ceiling); the best seats were on the second level and included the first loges and the gallery seats in front of them; the worst (in addition to the amphitheater) were in the stage boxes and in a number of supplementary places that provided standing room in the corridors ("antechambers of musical purgatory," observed Antoine Elwart). A *loge d'honneur,* in the center of the first loges, was reserved for the sovereign. The hall itself is remarkably small by modern standards; for example, at the narrow point between the columns framing the stage boxes, the proscenium measures only about thirty feet across. An early plan shows the full stage with six sets of receding flats; however, the arrangement used for music (see page 210) involved a movable hemicycle of painted panels (*l'amphithéâtre mobile*) extending back from the proscenium opening and enclosing four stepped platforms on which performers were seated. These panels and platforms were constructed for the Conservatory in 1828 on Cherubini's instructions.

The hall has often been praised for its splendid acoustics, and its audiences,

The Auditorium of the Conservatoire, after Renovations

Built in 1811 by the architect Delannoy, this hall, as restored in the 1980s,
reproduces to some extent the look and the acoustic of the hall as Berlioz
knew it. Its small dimensions, not evident in this image, make for crowded
conditions but create an acoustic that allows every detail to be heard, even
when a large orchestra is playing the *Symphonie fantastique*.

especially for the Conservatoire concerts, were known for their rapt attention and silence. Even so, overcrowding and the tendency of some members of the audience to
leave during, rather than after, a concert sometimes caused disruptions. In addition,
overheating, especially in the amphitheater (a Turkish bath is refreshing by comparison, said one longtime concertgoer), and the hard benches made concerts seem long to
the uncomfortable listeners.

The five-part program for December 5 was as follows:

Overture to *Les Francs-Juges*
Two *Mélodies irlandaises* for chorus and piano
The cantata *La mort de Sardanapale*
A violin solo by Mayseder, played by Chrétien Urhan
The *Symphonie fantastique*

These pieces were arranged to make a suitable program, which meant offering choral and solo singing, instrumental virtuosity, and orchestral works at the begin-

View toward the Stage of the Hall of the Conservatoire, ca. 1990

Luigi Cherubini, director of the Conservatoire, ordered the decorative
wooden panels at the back of the stage. For orchestral concerts, tiered
risers at the back elevated the winds, brass, and percussion.

ning and end. This program was not unlike one that the Conservatoire orchestra might
present—except that almost all the music was by a single, contemporary composer.

The individual pieces deserve explanation. The opera *Les Francs-Juges* had
engaged Berlioz's attention for some time, and indeed the March of the *Symphonie fantastique* is a remnant of that project. The "Chant sacré" and the "Chant guerrier," from
Berlioz's *Neuf mélodies irlandaises*, call for tenor solos (sung by the young Pierre-
François Wartel); a chorus of sopranos, tenors, and basses, each divided into firsts and
seconds; and a piano. The cantata, which had had such a disastrous public performance under Monsieur Grasset, finally caught fire as intended; the tenor soloist, here as
at the awards ceremony at the institute, was the tenor Alexis Dupont, who was later to
sing the title role of Berlioz's *Benvenuto Cellini*.

A violin solo played by the well-known Chrétien Urhan provided the necessary soloistic virtuosity in a concert of this kind. It was a composition by Joseph Mayseder, the Viennese violinist who had played in the Schuppanzigh quartet and at the

premiere of Beethoven's Ninth Symphony and who was a mainstay of the Vienna opera (for a description of his playing, see page 147). It was normal for a soloist giving a concert to provide fantasies or other pieces of his or her own composition to show off, and Berlioz may have wanted such a showpiece in his concert (even if it did not show off his own playing) to please an audience used to such musical treats; he may also have needed to offer a solo to procure the services of the renowned Monsieur Urhan, whose presence added distinction to the concert.

The fifty-year-old Urhan had joined the Opéra in 1816 as a violist and now played first violin in both the Opéra and the Conservatoire orchestras. He was later to play the viola solo in Berlioz's *Harold en Italie* (a solo written for Paganini, who did not find it difficult enough) as well as the famous viola d'amore solo in Meyerbeer's *Les Huguenots,* written with Urhan in mind. Urhan was known for his deeply religious character; although he had sought, and received, dispensation from the archbishop of Paris to play in the Opéra, he nonetheless played facing the audience so as not to be tempted to look at the legs of the dancers. He was a regular collaborator with the violinist Pierre Baillot in the latter's series of concerts of chamber music, and with other string quartets, where he played viola. He was to take part in Chopin's Paris concerts of 1832 and 1833; at Berlioz's instigation he played in a benefit concert for Harriet Smithson (at which Chopin and Liszt played a duet); with Liszt and the cellist Alexandre Batta he gave a famous series of concerts in 1837 that included all the Beethoven piano trios. Urhan was organist at the church of Saint Vincent de Paul, where Liszt often heard him. Liszt praised Urhan's seriousness, his dignity, his talent and individuality. Urhan was also something of a critic, writing in 1832 an "analysis" of Beethoven's Ninth Symphony in *Le Temps*.

That afternoon, a printed program of the *Symphonie fantastique* was distributed to members of the audience. The contents of the program had had a complicated history, in that Berlioz had fiddled with the text until the very last moment.

The previous May, Berlioz had sent out to the press the initial version of the program, its text derived from a surviving, handwritten draft; the printed version survives only in the papers that ran it: *Figaro*, on May 21, and *Journal des comédiens* (which left out the introductory paragraph), two days later.

Shortly before the December concert, Berlioz made a few revisions to the symphony and changed the program, again sending it to the press. This time it was printed verbatim by the *Revue musicale*, with the following modifications: (1) the title of the first movement was changed from "Rêveries—existence passionée" to the title we know now, "Rêveries—passions"; (2) a description was added of the new coda of the slow movement: "At the end, one of the shepherds takes up the *ranz de vaches* again; the other no longer answers. . . . Distant sound of thunder . . . Solitude . . . silence . . ."; and (3) information was added to the end of the last movement (perhaps reflecting recent musical changes). The earlier version, which had read "Funeral ceremony; sabbath

Episode

DE

LA VIE D'UN ARTISTE,

SYMPHONIE FANTASTIQUE, EN CINQ PARTIES,

Par Hector Berlioz,

EXÉCUTÉE POUR LA PREMIÈRE FOIS LE 5 DÉCEMBRE 1830,

Au Conservatoire de Musique de Paris.

Programme.

Le compositeur a eu pour but de développer, DANS CE QU'ELLES ONT DE MUSICAL, différentes situations de la vie d'un artiste. Le plan du drame instrumental, privé du secours de la parole, a besoin d'être exposé d'avance. Le programme suivant doit être considéré comme le *texte parlé d'un opéra*, servant à *amener* des morceaux de musique dont il *motive le caractère et l'expression* (1).

RÈVERIES. — PASSIONS.

(Première partie.)

L'auteur suppose qu'un jeune musicien, affecté de cette maladie qu'un écrivain célèbre appelle le *vague des passions*, voit pour la première fois une femme qui réunit tous les charmes de

(1) Il ne s'agit point en effet, ainsi que certaines personnes ont paru le croire, de donner ici la reproduction exacte de ce que le compositeur se serait efforcé de rendre au moyen de l'orchestre; c'est justement, au contraire, afin de combler les lacunes laissées nécessairement dans le développement de la pensée dramatique par la langue musicale, qu'il a dû recourir à la prose écrite pour faire comprendre et justifier le plan de la symphonie. L'auteur sait fort

First Page of the Program of the *Symphonie fantastique*, as Quickly Revised before the Performance

Owing probably to criticism of the advance program in the press, Berlioz at the last moment printed a revised version of the symphony's program, featuring a long footnote responding to criticism of his process of musical depiction (see his bill for this, p. 214). He also took the opportunity to tone down his criticism of Harriet Smithson, about whom he had heard false reports. The original beginning for the fourth movement ("Convinced that not only does she whom he adores not respond to his love, but that she is incapable of understanding it, and that, moreover, she is unworthy of it . . .") becomes "Convinced that his love is unappreciated . . ." (see document 17).

round-dance," now read "Funeral knell, burlesque parody of the *Dies irae,* sabbath
round-dance. The sabbath round-dance and the *Dies irae* together."

Meanwhile, Berlioz sent the program, with only one tiny change, to the printer;
this version was printed on cheap pinkish-brown paper, for use at the concert.

The influential and opinionated François-Joseph Fétis, however, not only
printed the program he received but strongly criticized Berlioz's intentions as he understood them, particularly with reference to pictorial music. Berlioz, surely upset by
criticism before his concert, rushed to print *another* version of the program—this one
on pink paper—which includes a long footnote responding to the criticism of "certain
persons." He took the opportunity to include a reference, at the end of the first move-

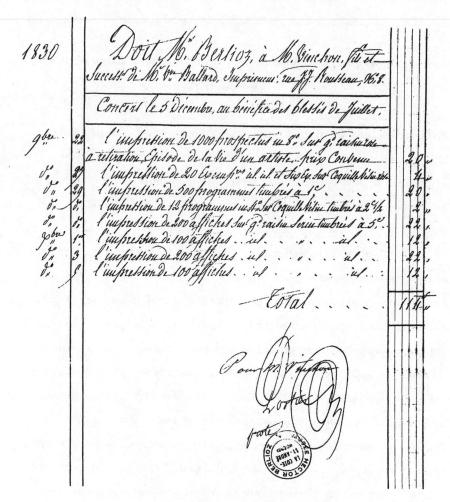

Berlioz's Bill from the Printing Firm of Vinchon

Among the many details Berlioz looked after was the printing of tickets,
posters, and programs for his concert. On November (9bre) 22 he was billed for
"1000 prospectus," the first version of the program. On November 29, two days
after Fétis's criticism was published (document 6), Berlioz printed "500
programmes," surely the revised version.

ment, to religious consolations, and he toned down the reasons for the young musician's decision to take opium: his beloved is no longer unworthy but merely misun-
derstands him. This version of the program was printed in at least two press runs, perhaps for reasons of speed: two versions survive, with somewhat different layouts. A
third printing of the same text, completely reset and on yellow paper, may also have
been used for the premiere.

The orchestra in the Grande Salle on December 5 was assembled for the oc-

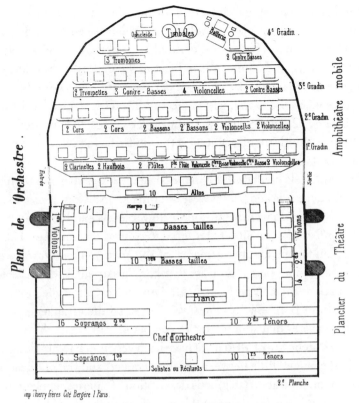

Plan de 'Orchestre .

Amphithéâtre mobile

Théâtre

Plancher du

Osmcleide   Timbales   Batterie   4ᵉ Gradin .

3 Trombones   2 Contre Basses

2 Trompettes   3 Contre - Basses   4 Violoncelles   2 Contre Basses   3ᵉ Gradin

2 Cors   2 Cors   2 Bassons   2 Bassons   2 Violoncelles   2 Violoncelles   2ᵉ Gradin

1ᵉ Gradin

2 Clarinettes 2 Hautbois   2 Flûtes   Pᵗᵉ Flûte Violoncelle Cᵗᵉ Basse Violoncelle Cᵗᵉ Basse 2 Violoncelles

Entrée   Sortie

10   Altos

Harpe

1er Violons

10 2ᵉˢ Basses tailles

Violons

10 1ʳᵉˢ Basses tailles

2ᵈ

14

Piano

16 Sopranos 2ᵈˢ   10 2ᵈˢ Ténors

Chef d'orchestre

16 Sopranos 1ᵒˢ   10 1ʳˢ Ténors

Solistes ou Récitants

2ᵉ Planche

imp Thierry frères Cité Bergère 1 Paris

Seating Plan of the Conservatoire Orchestra, ca. 1828

This plan is from a book by Antoine Elwart, one of Berlioz's competitors for the Prix de Rome of 1830. It shows Habeneck's arrangement of performing forces for the Conservatory concerts and probably corresponds to the arrangements for Berlioz's concert of December 1830. As in Vienna, the chorus is in front of the orchestra. First and second violins face each other across the bass singers, behind which are the violas. The cellos and double basses (right) and the woodwinds and brass (left) are raised on tiers.

casion. Berlioz himself invited the performers, organized rehearsals around their schedules, and arranged for payment and for the use of instruments. He drew most of the musicians from the pool of the Opéra and Conservatoire orchestras—after all, Habeneck was conducting and presumably had a hand in the recruiting—along with a few from the Théâtre des Nouveautés, where Berlioz had tried out two movements earlier in the year. This was not the precision orchestra of the Conservatoire, but given Habeneck's direction and the fact that it included many of that orchestra's members, we can presume that the *Symphonie fantastique* got as good a reading as was possible under the circumstances.

    A diagram of Habeneck's method of seating the orchestra in the Grande Salle (page 215) and an engraving of a concert in the hall show that the players were placed partly on the stage, which projected well beyond the proscenium arch, and partly on the four raised platforms. The chorus, divided into sopranos, tenors, and basses, like most French choruses at the time, was in front of the orchestra. Sopranos and tenors were on either side of Habeneck (making it necessary for him to turn toward the audience when he rebuked the sopranos!); in the middle on the stage were the bass singers. Around the basses, still on the stage, were the upper strings; the first violins, to the conductor's left; the seconds, to his right; and the violas, facing directly ahead with their backs to the raised platform.

The four levels of platforms contained all the lower strings and the winds. On the right-hand side, cellos and basses were intermixed on all four levels; to the left were the winds and brass, with woodwinds on the lower levels and brass and percussion at the back. Only a few adjustments are required to convert this into a probable, and perfectly suited, plan for the first performance of the *Symphonie fantastique*. We would merely need to add more percussion, another harp, a serpent, and a place for the bells (if bells were used as the first performance!). Our concert also called for a chorus and a piano, to perform Berlioz's *Mélodies irlandaises,* so the arrangement on page 215 probably approximates that adopted for December 5.

Berlioz's orchestra of 1830 must have been very much to his liking, because his orchestral ideal changed little between this first concert and the publication of his famous treatise on orchestration (1843); his description of a perfect concert orchestra and its seating (reproduced as document 20) is very close to the way Habeneck seated the orchestra for the *Fantastique*.

This orchestra provided Berlioz's audience with new sounds. He was perhaps the first modern orchestrator to use the orchestra not as a medium of four- or five-part writing but as the source of sounds, timbres, relationships, and colors that could be an important part of the music itself. He created novel instrumental effects: in the last movement, by striking the violin strings with the wood of the bow and sliding notes on the flute and horn; and at the end of the third movement, by using the four kettledrums to create chords. There were also the wonderful moments when Berlioz created a magical carpet of accompaniment out of a variety of instrumental figures: the idée fixe in the middle of the first movement and some of the variations in the third movement. The audience would surely have noticed such innovations.

Well-traveled listeners might have recognized certain aspects of the orchestra as typically Parisian. Although he used only double winds, Berlioz did avail himself of the four Parisian bassoons. He was careful to give a prominent place to the English horn (in the second movement), an instrument that in 1830 would have been rare outside of Paris; the use of not one but two harps was unusual in symphonic literature, though not uncommon in the pit of the Opéra.

Berlioz's audience, people used to listening to the Conservatoire orchestra,

Berlioz's opinion of the serpent:

The essentially barbaric sound of this instrument was much better suited to the ceremonies of the bloody cult of the Druids than to those of the Catholic Church, where it is still found, a monstrous monument to the lack of intelligence and to the grossness of feeling and taste which, since time immemorial, have directed in our temples the employment of music in divine service. One must allow an exception only for the use of the serpent in masses of the dead to double the terrifying plainchant of the *Dies irae*. Then its cold and abominable howling is doubtless appropriate.

was familiar with some aspects of orchestral sound that might seem strange to us. Most important is how much smaller the hall is than the concert halls of today; in that space even a large orchestra can give something of the effect of chamber music. The orchestra that played there in 1830 produced a lighter sound, owing mostly to the stringed instruments, strung with gut and played with bows somewhat lighter than those used now. In particular, the double basses, three-stringed instruments that only went down to G, were needed in large numbers, both for this concert and for the theater orchestras, because they produced so little sound.

The brass section for the *Symphonie fantastique* differed remarkably from what we are accustomed to. The ophicleide, a keyed instrument serving as the bass of the brass family, was well known in Paris: each of the twelve legions of the Garde Nationale had a military band, and each had at least three or four ophicleides. Despite the relative weakness of its sound and its association with military bands, this was the usual choice when a bass instrument was needed for the orchestral brass.

In the last movement Berlioz calls for the addition of a serpent, an ancient bass instrument made of wood and snakelike in shape (it is a relative of Monteverdi's cornetto); its brass mouthpiece and fingerholes make it a hybrid of the brass and woodwind families. The serpent was used extensively in French churches to accompany the singing of plainchant ("In all of Paris," wrote Mendelssohn in 1831, "you can hear no Sunday Mass that's not accompanied by serpents"), and Berlioz surely uses it to accompany the *Dies irae* because of that association; the serpent and the ophicleide together must have produced a sound suitable for a witches' sabbath.

Even the more familiar members of the brass section, the trumpets and the horns, were in an important period of transition, having evolved from the valveless instruments of the eighteenth century into those with pistons or rotary valves that permitted one to play a variety of chromatic notes with relative ease: the less tension of the lips, the less risk of missing the note.

In 1830, the valveless trumpet was still in regular use in Parisian orchestras (as elsewhere). Whereas in 1824 Beethoven used only natural trumpets in the Ninth Symphony, by the 1830s it had become possible, and indeed almost normal, to add valved instruments, either cornets or piston-trumpets, to the traditional pair of natural trumpets. (The *cornet à pistons* was apparently used for the first time in the Opéra orchestra for Rossini's *Guillaume Tell* in 1829.) In such combinations, the valved instruments can play whole melodies, such as the grand C-major statement of the idée fixe in the middle of the first movement or the fortissimo blast in the March to the Scaffold, while the natural instruments provide the harmonic and rhythmic accompaniment that their limitations so often dictate. When Berlioz was preparing the *Symphonie fantastique*, however, he felt no need for natural trumpets; instead the score uses one *trompette à pistons* in E-flat in the march and two in the last movement. If he had been writing for a standing orchestra, he would surely have provided parts for everybody, including the old-fashioned natural trumpets; the published version of the symphony, with two natural trumpets and two cornets, is more an acknowledgement of reality—of what the standard orchestra is likely to have had on hand—than a statement of preference.

The horns, too, were in a period of change from natural to valved. In the first concert of the Conservatoire orchestra, in March 1828, Monsieur Meifred, who taught at the Conservatoire alongside a professor of natural horn, played a solo for *cor à pistons*. The *Symphonie fantastique* is written so as to be playable on natural horns with no valves; this required the use of interchangeable crooks, which, by altering the horn's length, enabled one to play in different keys. Thus pairs of horns are found in C, E-flat, E-natural, F, and B-flat in the course of the score. Berlioz, however, anticipated the possibility that valved horns might be available: although the score at the start of the fourth movement mentions horns "natural or with valves," the players are instructed to make the stopped sound with the hand (and not to use their valves), to ensure that they will produce the characteristic covered sound so necessary for the spooky effect at the beginning of the March to the Scaffold. Later in the same movement, at the triumphant passage in C major, Berlioz has another instruction for anybody whose horn may have valves: "avec les cylindres, tous les sons ouverts"—that is, those who have valves should see to it that all sounds are played as open (unstopped) notes, even though stopping might be more convenient.

The timpani were smaller instruments than those in use today. With calfskin drumheads and the looser tension needed to produce a deep note on a small instrument, the sound was more percussive and less long-lasting—more a thunk than a boom. The bass drum was deeper but smaller in circumference than modern ones, and

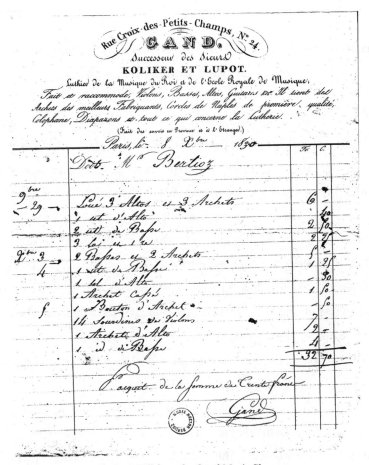

Berlioz's Bill from the Gand Music Shop

Before his concert Berlioz was enormously busy buying and renting
equipment for his players. Among his purchases are fourteen violin mutes
(tenth item), acquired the day of the concert (5 Xbre, December 5); perhaps he
decided at the last minute to have the opening melody of the symphony played
by muted violins.

it was played on a stand with its head flat, like the kettledrums; Berlioz has two of his
four drummers play the bass drum in the last movement.

In short, Berlioz's symphony was written at an important moment in orchestral history. Berlioz knew that superb orchestral playing was possible but also that there
were technical difficulties to be overcome. He composed just as the symphony orchestra was beginning its career as a virtuoso ensemble and anticipated many of the changes
in instrumental manufacture and technique that characterize the growth of orchestral
sound and style.

Although Berlioz was a relative newcomer to the concert world of Paris, the au-

Felix Mendelssohn describes the Conservatoire orchestra to his friend the composer Carl Friedrich Zelter in 1832:

The school of Baillot, Rode, and Kreutzer [current or past teachers of violin at the Conservatoire] furnishes them with violinists, and it is a joy to behold the young people coming to the orchestra en masse with their instruments, and then commencing, all with the same bowing, in the same style, with the same serenity and fire. Last Sunday there were fourteen on each side with Habeneck leading them, giving the beats with his violin bow. . . . The worst drawbacks are the double basses, which having only three strings can only go as far as G; they are lacking in power and tone, so that whenever there is a *forte* the real support pillars are lacking. Moreover the first clarinet is shrill and has a stiff and unpleasant delivery and tone. Also the trumpets are unsure in the high notes and modify the difficult passages and lastly the tympani have a hollow, muffled kettle sound, somewhat like drums. The latter and the basses do the most damage to the overall effect.

On the other hand, there is never the slightest question of hesitation or wrong notes, nor of even the slightest disunity; it is the most precise ensemble that can be heard in the world today, and at the same time they manage to play quite comfortably and calmly. One hears how each member completely fulfills his role, is in full mastery of his instrument, how each has his own part and knows everything which is demanded of him by rote, in short how the entire orchestra is made up not of individual musicians, but of an ensemble.

dience that Sunday afternoon included some major musical figures: opera titans of the past (Gaspare Spontini) and the future (Meyerbeer); keyboard virtuosi such as Johann Peter Pixis, the German pianist and composer (he had traveled to England in 1828 with Henriette Sontag, soloist for Beethoven's Ninth Symphony), and the nineteen-year-old Franz Liszt, already well known (he had met Berlioz for the first time the day before the concert and took him out to dinner after the performance); the musical press, notably in the person of François-Joseph Fétis, editor of the *Revue musicale* and soon to become

Camille Moke, by Marie-Alexandre Alophe, ca. 1830

The eighteen-year-old Camille Moke was a teacher of piano in Madame d'Aubrée's school for disabled young women, where Berlioz taught the guitar. It was Camille who reported to Berlioz the compromising information about Harriet Smithson that provoked his rage. After winning the Prix de Rome, Berlioz became engaged to Camille Moke, but while he was absent in Rome, she married the piano manufacturer Camille Pleyel.

Berlioz's enemy; and the German satirist and political writer Ludwig Börne (see document 16).

Also present were two women of great personal importance to the composer: Camille Moke, his fiancée, and her recalcitrant mother. Berlioz had fallen in love again. The eighteen-year-old Camille was a teacher of piano in Madame d'Aubrée's school for disabled young women, where Berlioz taught the guitar. Berlioz was charmed by her keyboard playing, and she in turn was enchanted by his red hair. It was Camille who had reported to Berlioz the compromising information about Harriet Smithson (it was not true: did she perhaps know this?) that provoked Berlioz's rage and inspired his vehemence toward the beloved ("she is now only a prostitute, fit to take part in such an orgy"), as expressed in the earliest version of the program. Camille's protective and aspiring mother had long resisted the idea of her daughter's marriage to Berlioz, but with the prestige of the Rome Prize (and perhaps knowing that Berlioz would be out of the way for at least a couple of years), she softened considerably.

Berlioz's composition teacher Le Sueur was ill (as he had been for the prize ceremony and would be again for Berlioz's second performance in 1832) but was represented by his wife and daughter. Luigi Cherubini refused to attend because of animosity between the two; he was to be the butt of many jabs in Berlioz's memoirs. When asked whether he were going to hear Berlioz's music, the Italian-born composer is reported to have said, in his strongly accented French, "Zé n'ai pas besoin d'aller voir comment il né faut pas faire" ("Zere is no need to go to see how NOT to write ze musique"). He had the air, writes Berlioz, "of a cat about to be given a dose of mustard. (When the concert turned out to be a success, he looked like a cat that has had a dose of mustard.)"

Notably absent also was Harriet Smithson—who was as yet unaware of Ber-

Berlioz Conducting the *Symphonie fantastique*, 1840s

This German caricature, related to one of Berlioz's many conducting tours,
suggests that the symphony is too loud. The orchestra apparently includes
only brass, double basses, and cannon (note the enormous ophicleide on the
upper right). Its effect on the listeners is evident, and one wonders if the
audience in Paris in 1830 had a similar reaction.

lioz's adoration and would have been astounded to know that she was the inspiration
for the symphony. Nonetheless, Smithson may have been responsible for one event in
the concert: Habeneck's refusal to repeat the March to the Scaffold despite the audience's outbreak of spontaneous applause. Habeneck, and many of the players in that
afternoon concert, had an evening engagement at the Opéra and could not risk being
late: at 7 P.M. they were to be part of a special performance of Auber's *La muette de Portici,* the role of Fenella, the young mute girl around whom the action turns, to be played
by Smithson, the dedicatee of the benefit performance for the July Revolution.

The *Symphonie fantastique* was received with shouts and the stamping of feet
(though this might, of course, have been a response to the concert as a whole, since the
symphony came last). The audience applauded after each movement, as was customary (consider Berlioz's remark on the first performance of his symphony *Harold in
Italy:* "Only the first movement received little applause"); intense applause and shouting signaled a request for a repetition. The audience liked the march in particular—

Spontini was overheard to say that only Beethoven could equal it. Berlioz himself, who we know was on stage (from the account in *Le Temps)*, probably performed in the percussion section, as he later often liked to do; from the top of the orchestra, he would have had a good view of the proceedings.

Two days after the concert, Berlioz was euphoric in his letter to Humbert Ferrand: "I had a furious success. The *Symphonie fantastique* was welcomed with shouting and stamping; they demanded a repetition of the March to the Scaffold; the Sabbath destroyed everything with satanic effect" (document 9). Berlioz's rather calmer description of the concert, told from a distance of many years in his memoirs, suggests that the symphony went well enough to give a true impression:

> I organized a concert at the Conservatoire at which the academic offering [the prize cantata] figured along with the Fantastic Symphony, a work that had not yet been heard. Habeneck undertook to conduct and all the players, with a generosity for which I shall always be profoundly grateful, for the third time gave their services.
>
> On the day before the concert, Liszt called on me. It was our first meeting. I spoke of Goethe's *Faust,* which he confessed that he had not read, but which he soon came to love as much as I. We felt an immediate affinity, and from that moment our friendship has grown ever closer and stronger. He came to the concert and was conspicuous for the warmth of his applause and his generally enthusiastic behaviour.
>
> The performance was by no means perfect—it hardly could be, with works of such difficulty and after only two rehearsals. But it was good enough to give a reasonable idea of the music. Three of the movements of the symphony, the Waltz, the March to the Scaffold and the Witches' Sabbath, created a sensation; the March especially took the audience by storm. The Scene in the Country made no impression at all. But it bore little resemblance to the present version. I made up my mind at once to rewrite it. . . .
>
> The cantata was well performed; the conflagration caught fire at the appointed time, the palace crashed in ruins. Altogether it was a great success.

It may be that Berlioz's later revisions of the symphony, and his subsequent career as a conductor of his own works, of which the *Symphonie fantastique* was a mainstay, led him to look back on the premiere as something of a trial run of, or apprenticeship for, the symphony, a version that ultimately was replaced with the score we know today.

A somewhat more vivid description of the premiere is given by the author of a review published in *Le Temps* on December 26 (document 12), the first few lines of which are cited at the beginning of this chapter. It continues: "At precisely two o' clock, Habeneck, the chief of this marvelous troupe, in which there is not a soldier who has not commanded somewhere or who is not worthy of command, Habeneck struck his stand with the point of his bow, and the profoundest silence immediately reigned in the hall, where a swarm of brilliant young women of taste had been listening loudly only a short time before."

The reviewer mentions the Overture and the cantata but makes no mention of the *Mélodies irlandaises* or the violin solo; unfortunately, his discussion of the *Symphonie fantastique* addresses essentially the program but says very little about the performance and nothing that would give us an idea of how its shape might have been different from the one we know. Like many another critic, he admires Berlioz's orchestration, though he says that Berlioz is weak in the tender and lyrical movements and comes into his own only in the fantastic, the lurid, and the ferocious. The audience was affected, though: "How we shivered in horror before the scaffold, rendered by such beautiful images of such startling veracity that they aroused, right in the middle of the execution, a thunder of applause that nothing could stop, and how everyone laughed at the sabbath at the laugh of the monsters, and how we looked at each other struck with surprise listening to this truly infernal music, these cries, these wailings, the outbreaks of laughter and these efforts of rage! . . . Mr Berlioz, if he matches this beginning, will one day be worthy to take his place alongside Beetowen."

It should not be too surprising that press coverage of the concert was minimal. Berlioz had not yet taken his place alongside Beethoven—indeed, Beethoven himself was still being discovered—and the attention given to this concert was in keeping with Berlioz's place as a young man of promise. It is disappointing that the novelty of the symphony's program seems to have distracted most journalists from commenting on the details of the concert.

The *Revue de Paris* published a review (document 13) that railed against the outrages of program music as perpetrated in the *Symphonie fantastique* but said nothing about the concert itself, except to complain of "that terrible fracas which is still punishing the vaults of the Conservatoire." The result of Berlioz's pictorial efforts, writes the reviewer, "despite traits which show talent, even genius, is confusion, chaos, tedium, a lack of planning, all painful." The pain, though, may not have been direct: the reviewer goes on to quote an early version of the program (probably the one distributed to the press in May), not the one printed for the premiere; it is easy to wonder whether the *Revue de Paris* is reporting secondhand information.

Fétis's *Revue musicale* gave the concert only a couple of paragraphs (document 14). The anonymous writer, surely Fétis himself, liked the same movements as everybody else: the ball and the march. He respects Berlioz's genius for new effects, but he concludes that "this music arouses astonishment rather than pleasure; it lacks charm."

Two single-paragraph notices, singularly lacking in detail, give views as opposed as could be imagined. *Figaro* called the piece "the most bizarre monstrosity one can possibly imagine," whereas *Le National* reported that this was "a great concert which will be a milestone in the memory of lovers of true music." Both papers regretted that they had no space for a full report (documents 11, 15).

Five years after the first performance, Fétis wrote an appreciation of the *Symphonie fantastique* in which he recalls his presence at the concert:

> At last came the day when M. Berlioz gave a concert to let us hear his compositions; it was, I believe, about eight years ago [actually five] that the concert took place—there have been many others of the same kind since then. The audience at that one was small, and there was scarcely anyone in the hall who was not either a friend or a guest. It was here that we heard for the first time the *Fantastic Symphony*. The audience thought it was having a nightmare during the whole performance; but they did notice the *Marche du supplice* for its novel effects and applauded it. From this moment I began to form my opinion of M. Berlioz: I saw that he had no taste for melody and but a feeble notion of rhythm; that his harmony, composed by piling up tones into heaps that were often monstrous, was nevertheless flat and monotonous.

The concert must surely have cost Berlioz more than he could afford. When he wrote to his father that he hoped to make a thousand francs, he must have been trying to impress him with his business sense and chance of success. His expenditures seem to have been around seven hundred francs, which covered heating and lighting; personnel; instrument rental; printing of posters, tickets, and programs; and so on. Not included in this is the enormous expense of producing orchestral parts (copying had run to twenty-three hundred pages). Although these parts were an investment in the future, in that they remained the property of the composer, copying was a tremendous expense that profits could not possibly cover.

The concert had at least one desired effect. After dining with Liszt (who loved the symphony), Berlioz went to see the Mokes, in the Faubourg Montmartre, and found that all had changed: Madame Moke, who for so long had hoped that young Camille might do better than marry the son of a provincial physician, now found herself confronted with a winner of the Prix de Rome and a composer applauded by a roomful of distinguished persons at the Conservatoire. She was now willing to give her approval of Camille's engagement to Berlioz. On December 12 the composer wrote to his friend Ferrand (document 9), "It is my music which extorted the consent of Camille's mother. Oh! My dear symphony, I owe my fiancée to it. . . . Oh, I am in a drunken state! Camille, ever since she heard my *Sabbath*, calls me only 'her dear Lucifer, her dear Satan.'"

Hearing the Symphony in 1830

As Fétis wrote, "The audience at that one was small, and there was scarcely anyone in the hall who was not either a friend or a guest," Berlioz having papered the Grande Salle for this benefit performance. Members of the press, whom he had worked hard to cultivate, were also present. Berlioz was a rising star, the Prix de Rome composer, and his music deserved attention.

The audience was probably not unaware of the purely musical values in the symphony; the lovely melodies, the balance of shapes and forms, the well-wrought developments, the fascinating orchestration. But they were no doubt most entranced by the story. They had perhaps read an advance version of the program in the press, but they now held the program in their hands and were curious as to how the music they were about to hear would depict, or reflect, the sadness, the passion, the drug-induced nightmares of a Romantic artist. They must have listened carefully for the idée fixe and enjoyed following it through the scenes in the fields and at the ball. Berlioz recollected that the March to the Scaffold, with its memorable guillotine stroke at the end, took the audience by storm. But surely the Witches' Sabbath had the greatest effect. Referring to this final movement, Fétis joked that "the audience thought it was having a nightmare during the whole performance." Similarly, *Le Figaro* called it "the most bizarre monstrosity."

Perhaps the religious overtones caused some in the audience to wonder; the hero's "religious consolations," expressed by the slow chords at the end of the first movement, are contrasted with the use of a plainchant from the burial service in the last. The *Dies irae* is transformed before our eyes from a solemn slow dirge into a mocking dance. On the day before the concert, *Le Figaro* concluded its article on the forthcoming concert by noting, "We have religious music, and plenty of it; but impious music: has anybody composed any before Berlioz? we think not. A subject for weeping and gnashing of teeth for the *Gazette*." The *Gazette* was the official organ of the government, and *Figaro* was suggesting that official circles might not be pleased with what might be perceived as sacrilege.

Berlioz was not, of course, making a personal statement about religion but showing the relation of the diabolical sabbath to the world of morality and true emotions by transforming both religion and love, in the form of their themes, into a fiendish dance.

Of all the pieces in this book, the premiere of the *Symphonie fantastique* is in some ways the most difficult to imagine, because the version Berlioz performed in 1830 has been lost. Over the next fifteen years, he made numerous revisions and alterations to the original version before publishing a definitive score in 1845. That is the score that generally gets performed today, for two reasons: first, it is all we have; and second, it represents Berlioz's final, mature thoughts as to what the symphony ought to be.

Berlioz himself admits that much of the music was recomposed after the performance, some of it in Italy; in many ways the symphony, he says, did not take its final form for years: "The adagio (the Scene in the Country), which nearly always affects the public and myself so keenly, cost me nearly a month's arduous toil; two or three times I gave it up. On the other hand, the March to the Scaffold was written in a night. But I continued to make considerable changes to both movements, and to the rest of the work, over the course of several years."

In 1833 Franz Liszt published a piano transcription, which was the only available version of the symphony until 1845; this is the version on which Schumann's famous analysis is based, and it represents a somewhat earlier state than the published score.

There exists a score of the symphony in Berlioz's hand, now in the Bibliothèque nationale de France. But even this document, precious as it is, does not represent the 1830 performance. In the manuscript the movements are separate fascicles, written at different times on a variety of papers. In addition to the clean copies of each of the movements, the manuscript has corrections, erasures, and additions, sometimes made on *collettes* (pieces of paper pasted over the music below). Although the combination is difficult to unravel, the eminent Berlioz scholars D. Kern Holoman and Hugh Macdonald have greatly clarified what this important document represents. What we now know about the symphony that was heard in 1830 must be deduced from the materials that survive.

The development section of the first movement underwent substantial changes; a section after the present measure 184 and another later section that combines the first and second themes (we know this because a piece of it survives) have been removed from the manuscript and lost. Berlioz added the "galloping" dominant chords and the passage that follows them, including the rising and falling chromatic series of first-inversion chords and the three bars of silence just before the return of the idée fixe in G major. What is not certain is whether these revisions were made before or after the December 1830 performance. Berlioz also worked on revisions of the sections leading up to the tutti C-major statement of the idée fixe at the end of the movement; most noticeably, the strikingly beautiful oboe solo (tempo primo), which accompanies the development of the beginning of the idée fixe in the lower strings, was not present in 1830 (the fact that it makes many parallel octaves with the wind accompaniment may be a hint that it is a subsequent layer); and much of this section has been rewritten and perhaps shortened. The movement once ended at measure 491, before the ritardando and the *religiosamente* that make a general dynamic and rhythmic decrescendo; here are the "religious consolations" that were added to the program between May and December of 1830.

The second and third movements in Berlioz's manuscript, after being substantially revised, were written down during or after Berlioz's stay in Rome. The ball movement is on Italian paper, and its 1830 form is lost to us. A particularly interesting

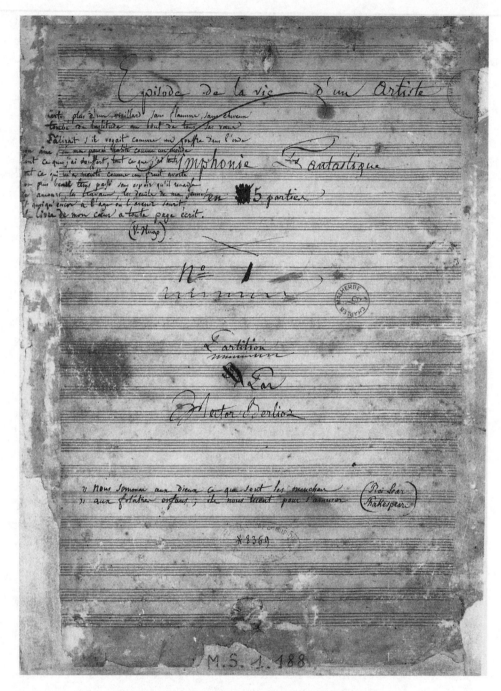

Title Page of Berlioz's Autograph of the *Symphonie fantastique*

Many of the sources of Berlioz's inspiration can be seen on the title page of
this autograph score of the *Symphonie fantastique*. The full title is "Episode of
the Life of an Artist: Fantastic Symphony in Five Parts." Shakespeare is
quoted ("As flies to wanton boys are we . . ."), as is Victor Hugo. Berlioz
originally writes "by Hector Berlioz" rather than "par" (Shakespeare's
influence), and his notations here would indicate that the number of
movements in the original score was not five.

story is attached to this movement: while in Italy Berlioz heard that his supposed fiancée, Camille Moke, had married the well-to-do piano manufacturer Camille Pleyel, and in a explosive fit of jealousy he determined to murder her, her interloping husband, and her meddlesome mother and then to commit suicide. Guns and disguises and a hilarious series of misadventures justify the full price of Berlioz's memoirs. However, at the time he was preparing to leave Rome disguised as a maid and intent on doing himself in, the redrafting of the movement remained unfinished. He describes this moment in his memoirs: "Next I took the score of the Ball Scene, and, as the coda was not completely orchestrated, wrote across it, 'I have not had time to finish this. If the Conservatoire Concert Society should happen to want to perform the work during the composer's *absence,* I beg Habeneck to double the flute passage at the last entry of the theme with clarinets and horns at the lower octave and to score the chords which follow for full orchestra. That will do for the ending.'"

The actual inscription written across the top of the page in the manuscript score ("I haven't time to finish myself; let it be finished according to my other copy; all the parts have to be recopied because of the changes") is not quite as dramatic as Berlioz reports in his memoirs, but it does suggest the existence of another, earlier score, presumably the version used in 1830 or a descendant of it. As it happens, two fragments of that earlier version survive—pieces of the title page and the final page—whose blank versos were used for pasted-in corrections in the first movement. They show that the second movement originally ended at about the present bar 335, without the thirty bars of *animez* and *serrez* sections of coda added in Rome; this version has no clarinet part and only a single pair of horns (which partly explains Berlioz's note about reorchestrating the movement). A cornet part, which is not in the printed score and parts, had been added to the present manuscript at some later date, perhaps for a particular performer. Just before the final printing of the 1845 score, Berlioz revised the passage in which the idée fixe first appears, adding the reminiscences of the waltz theme that so enhances the movement (by 1845 the combination of two themes had become a Berlioz hallmark).

The 1830 form of the third movement is lost. Berlioz says that he revised it drastically ("The Scene in the Country made no impression at all. But it bore little resemblance to the present version"); the fair copy that is now in the autograph manuscript may have been written out on Berlioz's way back to Paris in the spring of 1832, since it is written on a French paper resembling the paper that he used in his native La Côte St. André to copy out some music composed in Rome. The autograph has been altered to remove a passage of about fifteen measures from this version; but we cannot know whether they were in the 1830 version. This was the only movement so heavily altered that it needed to be fully recopied (the second movement was evidently recopied mostly because of changes in scoring), and Berlioz himself reminds us that in 1830 it was nothing like what it finally became. The original form of the movement can be sur-

Paris in the 1840s, Showing the Seine and the Tuileries

This image is among the earliest photographs of the city as Berlioz knew it,
long before the stone embankments along the river and the grand boulevards
engineered by Baron Haussmann.

mised, at least partially, from the Gratias of Berlioz's early *Messe solennelle,* rediscovered
in 1991, which uses the same theme.

The fourth movement (which Berlioz says he composed in a single night) was
originally a march intended for *Les Francs-Juges:* its former title page is still in the manuscript of the symphony. Berlioz had only to add the "head"—the first few notes—of
the idée fixe at the end (so that it could be chopped off) to make it a perennially successful part of the symphony. The march came into the symphony fully composed, and
Berlioz's revisions are minimal: the manuscript is scored for a single trompette à pistons in E-flat instead of the two later cornets in B-flat; a few slight changes enrich the
accompanimental texture in the strings at the second outbreak of blazing B-flat major
(measures 89f); and the snare drum, so effective in the final chords, is absent in the
manuscript. Maybe the applause that began right at the deathblow in 1830 suggested
the drumroll, as a sort of built-in crowd noise.

About forty measures of the fifth movement are missing in the manuscript,
though they may have been performed in 1830. Otherwise the movement is probably

similar to what was played in 1830, with only minor changes made later: Berlioz abandons the serpent (never very musical, the instrument was not usually found in orchestras outside of France) for a second ophicleide; and, as elsewhere, his original valve trumpets get changed in the score to the more normal cornets.

As for the bells, did Berlioz in 1830 have access to actual bells offstage, or did he use pianos in triple octaves, the alternative that he recommends in the score and that he often resorted to on concert tours? David Cairns has pointed out that in the 1790s the Opéra was known to have owned a pair of bells in C and G—exactly those Berlioz calls for. If they still existed, and if the administration was on good enough terms to lend them (the Opéra had performed Berlioz's fantasy on *The Tempest* in 1829), then perhaps the ecclesiastical parody was complete even at the first performance and the pianos (at least one was generally available in the hall; see page 215) remained silent. But no reviewer mentions them, and bells were no more common on concert platforms in 1830 than they are today.

In the matter of orchestration Berlioz was already a pioneer, even in this first work of his maturity. He was to become a noted conductor and to write a treatise on orchestration that, with revisions by Richard Strauss, continues to be a bible of the possibilities of the Romantic orchestra. Berlioz ultimately rejected certain effects tried in the first performance, when experience or practicality proved them undesirable. For example, the resounding pedal tones in the trombone that contribute to the great blast in B-flat (fourth movement, measure 62 and elsewhere) are not in the manuscript score. At the time of the premiere, Berlioz called for alto, tenor, and bass trombone, the last of which was not capable of these pedal tones; this special sound must have been a discovery between 1830 and the time of the publication of the score. The alto trombone is used very little today, its part usually being taken by a tenor trombone (most modern players can manage the high E-flat in measure 122 of the march). The result is that neither Berlioz's original trombone section nor the revised group in the published score (alto and two tenors) is generally heard today.

The autograph score calls for muted horns (at the beginning of the fifth movement), but the published version does not. Berlioz never again called for muted horns and does not mention the mute in his treatise on orchestration: perhaps he learned that a stopped note with the hand is easier to control. Another technique tried in the autograph but later abandoned is the muffle (created by a cloth laid across the drumhead) used for the timpani (at the coda of the Scene in the Country and at the beginning of the march) and for the bass drum (at the beginning of the last movement); in 1830 Berlioz did not yet know as much about drumsticks as he did in 1845. In the printed score the muffles are gone, and in their place is a variety of drumsticks, each giving a special sound: wooden-headed sticks, sponge-headed sticks (used where the autograph had used muffles) and, where not otherwise marked, presumably the normal leather-covered sticks. Many modern drummers play the entire symphony with felt-covered sticks: something has perhaps been lost in doing so. On the other hand, Berlioz's general abandonment of the piston trumpet in favor of the cornet may not be a matter of preference but of practicality, to judge from his continuing low opinion of the cornet: orchestras just didn't have piston trumpets, and he intended his score to be played by orchestras, presumably on occasions when he would not be present.

Berlioz was a young man, full of genius, talent, and ambition; he was eagerly acquiring knowledge about musical repertory and experience of musical performance. But the depth of his information about orchestras and orchestration was limited to his own recent experiences in Paris.

It should not surprise us that Berlioz's speedy and passionate fashioning of a symphony for 1830, made partly from reused materials, shows signs of youthful passion and exuberance—perhaps even inexperience. That earlier symphony was the one heard in 1830, though it is no longer heard today.

The Second Performance: 1832

Although our purpose here is to study the first performance of the *Symphonie fantastique,* it would be a pity to pass over the remarkable performance of December 9, 1832, not only because it represented a distinct version of the symphony reflecting the changes Berlioz made in Rome but also because its personal significance for the composer is told so well in the memoirs.

The 1832 performance included the *Symphonie fantastique* as part of the larger work entitled *Episode de la vie d'un artiste,* which begins with the symphony and continues with the new "monodrama" *Lélio, ou le retour à la vie.* The program was changed again to include all of the symphony within the opium dream from which Lélio awakes. This is the version of the symphony that Franz Liszt transcribed for piano. Berlioz made considerable revisions in the first movement (using pages from the earlier version of the second movement to paste in corrections); he used his revised versions of the second and third movements and made a substantial cut in the last movement.

The setting for this concert was again the Conservatoire, and again Habeneck conducted. The hall was full and noisy, and Berlioz tells us of how a certain Shakespearean actress happened to be present.

> The programme consisted of my Fantastic Symphony followed by its sequel *Lélio* or *The Return to Life,* the monodrama which forms the second part of the "Episode in the Life of an Artist." The subject of this musical drama, as is known, was none other than my love for Miss Smithson and the anguish and "bad dreams" it had brought me. Now consider the incredible chain of accidents which follows.

A Concert in the Conservatoire

This image gives a picture of a concert conducted by Habeneck in the hall
of the Conservatoire. It does not make clear how crowded those concerts
usually were, nor how hot the hall became. The engraver here has a violinist
playing a left-handed violin!

Two days before the concert—which I thought of as a farewell to
art and life—I was in Schlesinger's music shop when an Englishman
came in and almost immediately went out again. "Who was that?" I
asked Schlesinger, moved by a curiosity for which there was no rational motive. "That's Schutter, who writes for *Galignani's Messenger.*
Wait a moment," he added, striking his forehead, "I have an idea. Let
me have a box for your concert. Schutter knows Miss Smithson. I'll
ask him to take her the tickets and persuade her to come." The suggestion made me shudder, but I lacked the strength of mind to reject
it. I gave him the tickets. Schlesinger ran after Schutter, caught him
up, and doubtless explained what a stir the presence of the famous actress would create. Schutter promised to do everything he could to get
her there.

While I was occupied with rehearsals and all the other preparations, the unfortunate director of the English company [Smithson] was busy ruining herself. The guileless actress had been counting on the continued enthusiasm of the Parisians and on the support of the new school of writers who three years earlier had lauded both Shakespeare and his interpreter to the skies. But Shakespeare was no longer a novelty to the feckless and frivolous public. The literary revolution demanded by the romantics had been achieved; and not only were the leaders of the movement not eager for any further demonstration of the power of the greatest of all dramatic poets: unconsciously, they feared it. It was not in their interests that the public should become too familiar with works from which they had borrowed so extensively.

The result was that the English company excited little response, and receipts were low. It had been an expensive venture. The season showed a deficit which absorbed the imprudent director's entire capital. This was the situation when Schutter called on Miss Smithson and offered her a box for my concert, and this is what ensued. She herself told me long afterwards.

Schutter found her in a state of profound despondency, and his proposal was at first badly received. At such a moment it was hardly to be expected she should have time for music. But Miss Smithson's sister joined with him in urging her to accept: it would be a distraction for her; and an English actor, who was with them, on his side appeared anxious to take advantage of the offer. A cab was summoned, and Miss Smithson allowed herself, half willingly, half forcibly, to be escorted into it. The triumphant Schutter gave the address: "The Conservatoire," and they were off. On the way the unhappy creature glanced at the programme. My name had not been mentioned. She now learnt that I was the originator of the proceedings. The title of the symphony and the headings of the various movements somewhat astonished her; but it never so much as occurred to her that the heroine of this strange and doleful drama might be herself.

On entering the stage box above a sea of musicians (for I had collected a very large orchestra), she was aware of a buzz of interest all over the hall. Everyone seemed to be staring in her direction; a thrill of emotion went through her, half excitement, half fear, which she could not clearly account for. Habeneck was conducting. When I came in and sat breathlessly down behind him, Miss Smithson, who until then had supposed she might have mistaken the name at the head of the programme, recognized me. "Yes, it is he," she murmured;

"poor young man, I expect he has forgotten me; at least . . . I hope he has." The symphony began and produced a tremendous effect. (Those were days when the hall of the Conservatoire, from which I am now excluded, was the focus of immense public enthusiasm.) The brilliant reception, the passionate character of the work, its ardent, exalted melodies, its protestations of love, its sudden outbursts of violence, and the sensation of hearing an orchestra of that size close to, could not fail to make an impression—an impression as profound as it was totally unexpected—on her nervous system and poetic imagination, and in her heart of hearts she thought, "Ah, if he still loved me!" During the interval which followed the performance of the symphony, the ambiguous remarks of Schutter, and of Schlesinger too—for he had been unable to resist coming into her box—and their veiled allusions to the cause of this young composer's well-known troubles of the heart, began to make her suspect the truth, and she heard them in growing agitation. But when Bocage, the actor who spoke the part of Lélio (that is, myself), declaimed these lines:

> Oh, if I could only find her, the Juliet, the Ophelia whom my heart cries out for! If I could drink deep of the mingled joy and sadness that real love offers us, and one autumn evening on some wild heath with the north wind blowing over it, lie in her arms and sleep a last, long, sorrowful sleep!

> "God!" she thought: "Juliet—Ophelia! Am I dreaming? I can no longer doubt. It is of me he speaks. He loves me still." From that moment, so she has often told me, she felt the room reel about her; she heard no more but sat in a dream, and at the end returned home like a sleepwalker, with no clear notion of what was happening.

Berlioz married Harriet Smithson within a year, thereby consummating the dreams and passions he had expressed musically in the *Symphonie fantastique*. The two led an increasingly bitter and unhappy life together and eventually separated.

Documents: Berlioz, *Symphonie fantastique*

The (Abandoned) Concert of May 30, 1830

1. From Figaro, *May 21, 1830, 1–2:*

Grand concert
given at the Théâtre des Nouveautés, Sunday May 30, the day of Pentecost.
Episode of the life of an Artist.
Fantastic symphony in five movements,
by M. Hector Berlioz

It often happens that a composer sets himself in front of his piano, torments the keys, plays some chords, throws some notes on a staff, without having had the slightest hint, during all of his work, of what in artistic terms is called an idea.

And is it not still more frequent that he gathers, with a great effort of invitations or posters, friends, lovers of music, an orchestra; that he has his scribblings performed loudly, and that his audience does find an idea in it all, or mistakes the nature and the significance of the idea, if by chance the musician has had one?

M. Hector Berlioz, a young composer with an original imagination, wants to play a more open game: he does not want to rely on the hazards of being interpreted. It is he himself who analyzes his inspirations. The symphony whose program he has composed has not yet been performed in public. What effect will it have? We can only guess in advance; but the program of the different movements which comprise it is already a bold and bizarre act which is truly striking.

What is more, M. Berlioz has assembled a great troop of forces to give his effort the best possible chance of success. The orchestra of the Nouveautés, whose reputation has been made and consolidated in such a short time, reinforced with the élite of the performers of the Conservatoire, is charged with the performance of the fantastic symphony. All these musicians, whose number will reach a hundred, will be arranged on the stage and conducted by M. Bloc.

One can only expect an immense effect from this constellation of artists who have made their mark with such éclat in the Conservatory concerts, and who have given to their orchestra the reputation of the best performing orchestra in Europe.

[Then follows a version of the program, with these notable features: (1) the first movement is called "Rêveries—existence passionnée"; (2) there is no mention of religious consolation in the first movement; (3) there is no mention of the timpani thunder at the end of the adagio; (4) the strong criticism of the beloved ("and what is more, she is unworthy") preceding the dose of opium is toned down.]

This concert, in which M. Haitzinger and Mme Devrient will be heard, will conclude with the overture to *Les Francs-Juges* by M. Berlioz.

It will take place next Sunday, May 30, at half past eight in the evening, at the Nouveautés theatre.

2. *From* Journal des Comédiens, *May 23, 1830:*

Concert of M. Hector Berlioz

This will take place next Sunday, at the Théâtre des Nouveautés, at eight o'clock in the evening. Not for a long time has any musical evening offered such piquant attractions to the curious: first, M. Haitzinger, Mme Schroeder-Devrient and several other distinguished artists will be heard; but for a certainty M. Hector Berlioz himself will furnish the most curious inter-mezzo. In this memorable evening, performed by the excellent orchestra of the Nouveautés, reinforced with the élite of the forces of the Conservatoire, he will offer the public a piece on which he has lavished all his attention, and which is distinguished, we are assured, by the warmest originality.

This piece is designated under the title of *Episode of the Life of an Artist, fantastic symphony in five movements.* M. Berlioz, wishing to put all his listeners in a position to under-stand it, has drawn up himself a sort of *scenario,* a dramatic sketch of his musical novel, for it truly is one, with all the luxuriance of emotion and incident of modern literature. Here it is, ex-plained in prose: we shall see whether, at the performance, it will be as clear and as interesting as the promise of this bizarre tale.

[Then follows a version of the program, which matches that printed in *Figaro,* except that it lacks the opening explanatory paragraph.]

3. *Berlioz's description of his first attempt at performing the* Symphonie fantastique:

The Théâtre des Nouveautés had for some time been performing opéras-comiques, and now had a reasonably good orchestra under the command of Bloc. He persuaded me to offer my new work to the directors of the theatre; we should jointly organize a concert and give the work a hearing. The directors consented, for the sole reason that the symphony's unusual pro-gramme had caught their fancy; they thought a lot of people would come out of curiosity. But I wanted a performance on a really grand scale, so I engaged a further eighty players. When added to Bloc's they formed an orchestra of a hundred and thirty. The theatre had no normal provision for an army of performers on this scale; the necessary physical conditions, the plat-forms for the different levels, even the desks, were lacking. To all my inquiries the directors replied with the imperturbable calm of men who have no conception of the difficulties in-volved: I had no need to worry, everything would be seen to, they had a scene-shifter who was a very clever fellow. But when the day came for the rehearsal, and my orchestra of a hundred and thirty tried to arrange themselves on the stage, there was nowhere to put them. The tiny pit, when pressed into service, barely accommodated the violins. From all over the theatre an up-roar arose that would have driven a much more sanguine composer demented. People were calling for desks, while the carpenters strove to knock together something that would do in-stead. The scene-shifter went about swearing and searching for his flats and his struts. There were cries for chairs, for instruments, for candles; the double basses were out of strings; there was no place anywhere for the drums. The orchestral attendant did not know where to begin.

Bloc and I were in thirty-seven different places at once; but it was all to no avail. The situation had got beyond control. It was a rout, a musical Crossing of the Beresina.

However, despite the confusion, Bloc insisted on trying a couple of movements, "to give the directors an idea of the symphony." We rehearsed the Ball and the March to the Scaffold as well as was possible with our forces in disarray; and the March created a perfect furore among the players. But the concert never took place. The directors recoiled before such tumult, and the enterprise was abandoned. It would involve, they said, too much elaborate preparation; they "had no idea so many arrangements were required for a symphony."

My plan had been wrecked for want of desks and a few benches. The extreme care which I now take over the practical details of concert-giving dates from then. I know too well what disasters the least negligence in this respect can lead to.

[*The Memoirs of Hector Berlioz,* ed. David Cairns (New York: Alfred A. Knopf, 1969; rpt., New York: Norton, 1975), 126–27.]

4. Berlioz's description of his experience at the award ceremony for the Prix de Rome:

The Permanent Secretary, holding in one hand the wreath of artificial laurels which will crown the victor's brow and in the other the solid gold medal which will pay his rent until he leaves for Rome (it is worth a hundred and fifty francs, as I discovered), reads out in a loud and clear voice the name and Christian names of the composer. The laureate rises:

> Upon his candid forehead freshly shorn
> A blush of manly modesty appearing.
> (Boileau, *Le lutrin* ["The Lectern"].)

He embraces the Permanent Secretary (polite applause). The laureate's distinguished master is sitting a few feet from the Permanent Secretary's rostrum. The pupil embraces his distinguished master (more polite applause). On a bench at the back, behind the academicians, the laureate's parents sit weeping tears of silent joy. The laureate vaults over the intervening benches, treading on someone's toe, trampling another's coat and, reaching the top, flings himself into the arms of his father and mother, who by now are sobbing unashamedly (no applause; but people are beginning to laugh). To the right of this touching group a young person is signalling to the hero of the hour. He responds by leaping in her direction and, after tearing a woman's dress and crushing a dandy's hat, contrives to reach his cousin. He embraces his cousin. Sometimes he embraces his cousin's neighbour (loud laughter). Another lady, sitting by herself in a distant corner of the hall, makes discreet signs of affection which our hero affects not to notice. Then he turns and flies to embrace his mistress—his betrothed, the woman who is to share his life and fame. This time, in his haste and confusion and blindness to all other women, he kicks one of them over, trips over a bench, falls with a crash, abandons all hope of greeting the hapless girl, and regains his seat, bathed in perspiration (loud and prolonged laughter and applause). This is the crowning moment of the academic year, and I know many people who go along solely to witness it. I say this without any rancour against these jokers; for when my time came there was no father, mother, cousin, master or mistress for me to embrace.

My master was ill, my parents disgruntled and elsewhere, and my mistress . . . So I embraced only the Permanent Secretary, and I doubt that anyone noticed the blush of modesty on my forehead as I did so, for so far from being freshly shorn it was buried beneath a forest of red hair—a feature which, in conjunction with other characteristic points, tended to place me unmistakably in the owl category.

I was, besides, in no mood to embrace anybody. I do not believe I have ever been in such a black fury in my life. The reason was this. Our subject that year was "The Last Night of Sardanapalus." The poem ended at the moment when the vanquished potentate gathers his most beautiful slaves around him and mounts the funeral pyre. My first impulse had been to write a kind of symphonic description of the scene: the wails of the reluctant victims, the great sensualist defying death in the midst of the encircling flames, the crash of the falling palace. Then I thought of the means that would be required in a purely orchestral piece to suggest a scene of this kind, and I restrained myself. The music section of the Academy would certainly have condemned the whole cantata after one look at such a finale, quite apart from the fact that, boiled down for the piano, it would have sounded nonsensical. So I waited. When the prize had been awarded and I was sure of not losing it, and sure of performance by a full orchestra, I wrote my conflagration. At the final rehearsal the piece produced such an effect that several academicians, who had been caught unawares, came up and congratulated me warmly and without any resentment at the trap I had set for their sacred beliefs.

The rehearsal in the Institute assembly hall was attended by a large number of artists and music-lovers who had come to hear this cantata by a young composer already notorious for his wild eccentricity. Most of them went off full of the extraordinary impression the conflagration had made on them. As a result of their enthusiastic accounts, the audience arrived next day in an unusual state of curiosity and expectation.

I was not altogether confident of the abilities of Grasset, ex-conductor at the Théâtre-Italien, who was in charge of the performance, and before it began I went and sat near him, manuscript in hand. Mme Malibran, whose interest had been aroused by the reports of the day before, but who had not been able to find a seat in the hall, was also accommodated nearby on a stool, sandwiched between two double basses. It was the last time I saw her.

My decrescendo began (for the first words of the cantata were "E'en now Nature in darkest night lies veiled," and I had therefore been obliged to compose a sunset in place of the traditional dawn; it seems I am doomed to be different, forever at odds with life and the Academy!). All went smoothly; Sardanapalus learnt of his defeat, resolved to die and summoned his women, and the pyre was kindled. Everyone listened intently. Those who had been at the rehearsal whispered to their neighbours, "Now it's coming. Wait till you hear it—it's fantastic."

Ten million curses on all musicians who do not count their rests! In my score the horn was supposed to give the cue to the timpani, the timpani to the cymbals, the cymbals to the bass drum; the first stroke of the bass drum was the signal for the final explosion. But the accursed horn-player failed to play his note. Without it, the timpanist was afraid to come in. In consequence, cymbals and bass drum also kept silent. Absolutely nothing happened. The violins and cellos went on with their futile tremolo; otherwise, not so much as a pop. The fire went out without a crackle; the much-heralded holocaust had turned into a damp squib—*ridiculus mus*. Only a composer who has himself been through such an experience can conceive the fury that possessed me. I could hardly breathe. A cry of horror burst from me. I hurled my score into the middle of the orchestra and sent the two nearest desks flying. Mme Malibran started back as if a mine had exploded at her feet. The whole place was in an uproar—the orchestra in confusion, the academicians scandalized, the audience mystified, the composer's friends in high indignation. Another musical catastrophe had overtaken me, the cruellest I had yet experienced. Would that it had been the last!

[*Memoirs of Hector Berlioz,* 136–37]

Announcements of the Concert of December 5, 1830

5. *From* Figaro, *December 4, 1830, 3:*

Episode of the life of an artist.
Symphonie fantastique.

If we must believe the rumors of the musical world, and the hopes which M. Berlioz's talent inspires, a concert announced for tomorrow, Sunday, will be one of those rare solemnities which attract the musical dilettantes to the temple in the rue Bergère. We will find there, they say, something to console us for the degradation of our lyric theatres. Let us not speak of the first pieces in the concert: an overture of the *Francs-Juges* already applauded, a cantata of *Sardanapalus* which earned its author the great Prix de Rome. Let us move on to the *Fantastic symphony,* which seems to us to be the main work.

This is the first time that one has tried to give an exact meaning to instrumental music. Until now, a symphony has been a development, more or less successful, of a melodic idea without a specific signification, and where the composer's only perceptible purpose has been to make a pleasing piece of music. M. Berlioz's symphony is a novel. It tells you with instruments a story like that of René, that of Werther. A young musician falls in love, and all the joy and sadness of love are developed in the first three scenes of the drama. By a singular curiosity, the cherished image appears to the mind of the artist always linked to a musical thought which recurs like an idée fixe in the course of the work. The young man poisons himself. Instead of death, he finds himself in an opium nightmare, he dreams that he has killed his beloved, and that he attends his own execution. The death-blow interrupts a final tender and sad thought of the beloved.

A witch's sabbath begins. Gathered for the funeral of the executed, shadows, phantoms, and all the monsters arrive, from those that groan and croak in the swamps to those who laugh a laugh lost on the height of the air.

The bells ring. The devils very gravely intone the *Dies irae,* and others take it up in quicker time, and the holy canticle, thus reduced to the smallest dimensions, is transformed into a grotesque contradance.

We have religious music, and plenty of it; but impious music: has anybody composed any before Berlioz? we think not. A subject for weeping and gnashing of teeth for the *Gazette.*

6. From Revue Musicale, Publiée par M. Fétis *10 (November 27, 1830): 89–90:*

M. Hector Berlioz will give, on Sunday, December 5, in the great hall of the Conservatoire, a concert in which one will hear various works of his composition. The orchestra, composed of more players than the Conservatoire orchestra, will be directed by M. Habeneck. Tickets of admission may be had from all the music shops.

M. Berlioz's principal aim in giving this concert is to present a symphony he has composed on a new plan. It has as its title: *Episode of the life of an artist: fantastic symphony in five parts.* The subject of this work is a sort of novel which M. Berlioz has imagined, and which he has felt he needed to print, to facilitate the understanding of his composition. It is perhaps a misunderstanding of the aims of art to want to apply oneself to painting material facts or to express abstractions, and to need to resort to explanations is enough proof of its inability to do these things: still, M. Berlioz had an example of a similar attempt in the *Pastoral symphony* of Beethoven; however, he has thought he could find more resources in instrumental music than that great musician had attributed to it. We will thus not insist on our opinion before hearing M. Berlioz's work, and we will content ourselves with presenting its program, which is truly curious.

[Then follows a version of the program almost identical to that which Berlioz first prints for the concert.]

7. A letter from Berlioz to King Louis-Philippe:

To His Majesty the King of the French
    Sire,
        Eager to associate myself with the public gratitude towards the heroes of the national cause, I am preparing a concert for the benefit of the July wounded; a group of distinguished artists is flocking to assist my efforts.

Recently honored by the Institute, I could not enter the profession under more auspicious circumstances. If Your Majesty should deign to honor this musical ceremony with Your Majesty's august presence, it would be yet another proof of Your Majesty's concern for our liberators and at the same time it would give me the most powerful of encouragements.

Sire, the fine arts have also their part to play in the glory of the fatherland. The enlightened favor which in all times Your Majesty has given to them gives me the confidence that my entreaty will not be found indiscreet, even though it can only be justified by honorable intentions.

I am with profound respect, Sire, Your Majesty's most humble and most obedient servant and subject,

Hector Berlioz, pensioner of the Académie.

[Paris, Archives Nationales o⁴. 1327; rpt. in *La musique à Paris en 1830–1831,* ed. François Lesure et al. (Paris: Bibliothèque Nationale, 1983), 38. Berlioz received three hundred francs from the royal accounts.]

Offerings of the Parisian Theaters on December 5, 1830

8. "Spectacles du 5 décembre 1830," from Le National, *a four-page daily paper founded in 1830:*

Académie Royale de Musique [the opera] (for the benefit of Mlle Smithson): La jeune femme en colère; La Muette de portici; L'Ours et le Pacha

Théâtre Français: Les trois quartiers; le Barbier de Séville; l'Avocat patelin

Opéra-Comique: Aline; la Dame Blanche

Odéon: Marino Faliero; ma Place et ma Femme

Vaudeville: Bonaparte; la Ligue des Femmes; la Succession

Variétés: Voltaire; la Monnaie de singe; le Moulin de Jemmapes; les Brioches

Gymnase: Louise; le Collège de * * *; Jeune et Vieille; la Seconde Armée

Nouveautés: Le Couvreur; les trois Catérine; l'École

Gaité: l'Amour et les Poeles; Fénélon; Napoléon; le Chiffonier

Ambigu: Cartonele; les Alcides; Napoléon

Porte Saint-Martin: les Victimes cloîtres; la Chanoine; la Fille du musicien

Cirque olympique [dark]

Monsieur Comte: la Pendule; un Coup d'état; la Dinde du Mans; le vieux Garçon

Luxembourg: 14 ans de la vie de Napoléon; Don Quichotte

Berlioz on His Concert

9. Excerpts from letters of Berlioz to Humbert Ferrand:

[November 19, 1830]

I am running around all evening on account of a rehearsal of my symphony which I am doing tomorrow. On the 5th of December, at two o'clock, I am giving an immense concert at which will be performed the overture of the *Francs Juges,* the *Chant sacré* and the *Chant guerrier* from the *Mélodies,* the scene of *Sardanapalus* with a hundred musicians for the CONFLAGRATION, and finally the *Symphonie fantastique.*

Come, come, it will be wonderful. Habeneck will conduct the giant orchestra. I count on you. . . .

Come, come!

The 5th of December . . . a Sunday . . . an orchestra of 110 musicians . . . *Francs Juges* . . . Fire . . . *Symphonie fantastique* . . . Come, come!

[December 7, 1830]

This time you absolutely must come; I had a furious success. The *Symphonie fantastique* was welcomed with shouting and stamping; they demanded a repetition of the March to the Scaffold; the Sabbath destroyed everything with satanic effect. I have been begged to repeat the concert on the 25th of this month, the day after Christmas [*sic*], and I will do so.—So, you will be there, won't you?—I expect you.

Farewell; I am totally overwhelmed.

[December 12, 1830]

I can't give my second concert; there are several reasons which prevent me. I leave Paris at the beginning of January. My marriage is set for the season of Easter 1832, provided that I do not lose my pension and that I go to Italy for a year. It is my music which extorted the consent of Camille's mother. Oh! My dear symphony, I owe my fiancée to it. . . .

Oh, I am in a drunken state! Camille, ever since she heard my *Sabbath,* calls me only "her dear Lucifer, her dear Satan."

[Hector Berlioz, *Lettres intimes,* with a preface by Charles Gounod, 2d ed. (Paris: Calmann-Levy, 1882), 83 (letter of November 19), 84 (December 7), 85 (December 12)]

10. Berlioz's description of the concert in his memoirs:

I did not want to go away, however, without giving a public performance of my *Sardanapalus* cantata, whose finale had come to so inglorious an end at the Institute prize giving. So I organized a concert at the Conservatoire at which the academic offering figured along with the Fantastic Symphony, a work that had not yet been heard. Habeneck undertook to conduct and all the players, with a generosity for which I shall always be profoundly grateful, for the third time gave their services.

On the day before the concert, Liszt called on me. It was our first meeting. I spoke of Goethe's *Faust,* which he confessed that he had not read, but which he soon came to love as much as I. We felt an immediate affinity, and from that moment our friendship has grown ever closer and stronger. He came to the concert and was conspicuous for the warmth of his applause and his generally enthusiastic behaviour.

The performance was by no means perfect—it hardly could be, with works of such difficulty and after only two rehearsals. But it was good enough to give a reasonable idea of the music. Three of the movements of the symphony, the Waltz, the March to the Scaffold and the Witches' Sabbath, created a sensation; the March especially took the audience by storm. The Scene in the Country made no impression at all. But it bore little resemblance to the present version. I made up my mind at once to rewrite it. . . .

The cantata was well performed; the conflagration caught fire at the appointed time, the palace crashed in ruins. Altogether it was a great success.

[*Memoirs of Hector Berlioz,* 139–40]

Reviews and Reports of the Concert of December 5

11. From Figaro, December 7, 1830, 3–4, in the column Bigarrures (meaning "medley" or "variety"):

M. Berlioz has kept his word: his fantastic symphony is truly a musical novel. This composition is the most bizarre monstrosity one can possibly imagine. We will try to take account of it. In the meanwhile, let us say that its success was complete. Five or six salvos of applause and stamping of feet in admiration have compensated M. Berlioz for the innumerable obstacles with which routine harassed the early steps of his career.

12. *From* Le Temps, *Sunday, December 26, 1830, col. 5637:*

Here is a young man, lanky, skinny, with long blond hair whose disorder has something that reeks of genius; all the traits of his bony form are drawn forcefully, and his large deep-set eyes, under a large forehead, dart jets of light. The knot of his cravat is tightened as though with rage; his suit is elegant because the tailor made it elegant, and his boots are muddy because his impetuous character refuses to sit still and be pulled along in a carriage, because the activity of his body must match the activity going on in his head. He runs about among the hundred musicians who fill up the stage of the Conservatoire, and although all these regulars in the Conservatoire orchestra make up perhaps the most admirable orchestra ever heard, he begs, he growls, he entreats, he excites each one of them. This man is Berlioz, he is the young composer who, despite his talent, has just carried away the prize at the Institute; and when the public applauds him, he does not advance to give an elegant bow and to let his arms fall servilely towards the parterre; he only stops where he is; he nods his head to acknowledge the applause which rings in the hall, and he continues the remark he was making to Launer or to Toulou. All that is what we saw at the concert which this young composer gave for the benefit of the wounded of the July Revolution.

At precisely two o'clock, Habeneck, the chief of this marvelous troupe, in which there is not a soldier who has not commanded somewhere or who is not worthy of command, Habeneck struck his stand with the point of his bow, and the profoundest silence immediately reigned in the hall, where a swarm of brilliant young women of taste had been listening loudly only a short time before.

The overture of the *Francs-Juges,* with which the concert began, is a grand symphony, more remarkable still for its bizarre quality and the force of its thought than for the felicity of its expression. Its forms are gigantic, and I don't think that the trumpets of the last judgment have any more incisive effect than the thundering trombones which accompany; but this instrumentation, so good and so striking, is perhaps too melodramatic in character. After the overture, which was performed with a verve and a perfection which has no peer except at the Conservatoire concerts, came the scenes of Sardanapalus, and if one was a little unhappy with the singing which preceded the finale, if we can reproach it with weakness, doubtless because we expect much more from its author, what enthusiastic applause greeted the incineration of the palace of the voluptuary king; we saw the fire run, inflame the beams, roar under the long vaults, and we really heard everything collapse with a frightful fracas. This last part produced the greatest effect, and the connoisseurs could remember nothing except perhaps the overture *Le jeune Henri* to match this piece in novelty.

But we must speak of the fantastic symphony called *Episode in the life of an artist.* The author had developed in a program the subject of this strange composition; he supposes first that a young musician, affected by the illness of the *vague des passions* (in 1830 style) falls hopelessly in love with a woman, and that, by a bizarre happening, the image of this cherished woman never appears to him except in the form of a musical thought, remembered incessantly in the middle of all the situations he encounters. In the second movement, he admires her in the course of a ball, in the tumult of a celebration, and feelings of love and of jealousy alternate in agitating him. In the third, the scene in the country gives his ideas an unaccustomed calm, a more smiling color; and the musical idea, so ingeniously thrown into this conception for the information of the listener, returns more sweetly and tenderly than ever. In the fourth, he becomes certain that his beloved is unworthy of his love, and he poisons himself with opium: but the dose is too weak, and he only sleeps, accompanied by the most horrible visions. He dreams that he assassinates his mistress, that he is condemned to death, and that he attends his own execution. In the fifth, still in his dream, he is transported to a witches' sabbath, among a frightful group of spectres, sorcerers and monsters. There are cries, singing, laughter, gnashing of teeth, and the musical idea appears again, but degraded, vilified, changed into a grotesque dance tune, trivial, ignoble. (That is itself a sublime thought.) Finally this horrid scene finishes with a witches' dance where all the monsters dance in a parody of the *Dies irae*.

Such an invention is certainly mad, but it is dramatic and full of poetry. Clearly the audacious composer has not recoiled before the most difficult problems of performance.

Monsieur Berlioz's talent is eminently somber and fantastic; it seems that he aims at ferocity: his thought is in some sense always full of anger, and he excels only at painting violent scenes, the torturing of the soul and of nature. The dreams, the sweet passions of the first three movements were not successfully rendered. His orchestra, though always instrumentated with a rare facility, is generally confused, empty, and lacks imagination; but with what terrible uproar he returns in the last two movements! how everyone shivers under the impressions of that solemn march, funereal, through which we still hear at a distance, with an unaccustomed gladness, the weakened musical theme! how we shivered in horror before the scaffold, rendered by such beautiful images of such startling veracity that they aroused, right in the middle of the execution, a thunder of applause that nothing could stop; and how everyone laughed at the sabbath at the laugh of the monsters, and how we looked at each other struck with surprise listening to this truly infernal music, these cries, these wailings, the outbreaks of laughter and these efforts of rage! There is despair in this singular talent. There is Salvator Rosa, there is Hoffmann, there is blacker still. I am convinced that this symphony is of an inconceivable strangeness, and the schoolmasters will surely call anathema on this profanation of the beautiful; but, I am sure, for those who care little for the rules, M. Berlioz, if he matches this beginning, will one day be worthy to take his place alongside Beetowen.

13. *From* Revue de Paris 21 *(1830): 120–23:*

Concert given by M. Berlioz at the Conservatory of Music
All the arts are enclosed within certain limits which they are forbidden to transgress. Their charm, their power depend on this unity of purpose, on this complete purity; to confuse them is to lose them. In a decadent period one sees sculptors coloring their marbles, painters putting statues on their canvases and not men, poets aiming at musica! and picturesque effects, musicians pretending to an exact imitation of all that their art will never express and never im-

itate. Vain efforts to overstep the boundaries which the nature of things imposes on the artist! Barbarism is the result; the laws of the organism reject these innovations. This is not a matter of arbitrary rules, of codes planned in advance to shackle genius, of barriers placed by a La Harpe or a Le Batteux; nature herself requires that man remain man, that each species have its laws of reproduction and organization, that painting be painting and music music, at the risk of becoming nothing at all.

Hence look what our poets produce when they transform themselves into painters and only describe. Darwin in England, Delille in France. What has become of their glory? Ask the ages whether they admire or scorn those ivory busts with ebony eyes and silver hands, which have been worked with such an odd devotion and left to us by a degenerate sculpture. In the reign of Napoleon, did not the "Battle Sonata" ruin all the pianos of the empire? Did we not swoon with pleasure on hearing the arpeggios that represented an encampment, the dissonances that expressed the cries of the wounded, and those block chords over which the engraver wrote "The emperor's speech to the troops." Speech! What a sublime effort! In the guise of spoken eloquence, thirty measures of music! It is the masterwork, the last degree of ridicule one can attain in this system which tries to give music the attributes of poetry or rhetoric, and to poetry those of painting.

Doesn't each art have resources enough of its own? Mozart, Beethowen, Haydn, all keep within musical limits, but have they not brought forth new and sublime effects? It is not necessary, as M. Berlioz does, to transform a symphony into a poem, to give a meaning to each *da capo,* and a sense to every ritournelle. Essentially vague, striking the ear with a sound whose prestige is confused and limitless, music refuses this servile imitation. Music is infinite: that is her merit and her failing; she is lost in space, like the life of man in eternity, like the drop of water in the sea. Reverie, melancholy, religious sentiment, passionate ardor, these accord with music which is vague, immense, but imprecise, like these same emotions which she nourishes. How, I ask, can any musician of imagination and who knows his art propose to solve the following problem? We copy exactly the program of M. Berlioz's symphony:

Reveries.—Passions.

The author supposes that a young musician, affected by that moral disease called by a famous writer the *vague des passions,* sees for the first time a woman who has all the charms of the ideal being he has imagined in his dreams, and he falls hopelessly in love. By a singular curiosity, her dear image never appears to the artist except linked to a *musical idea* in which he finds a certain passionate character, but noble and timid like that which he assigns to the object of his love.

This melodic reflection and its model pursue him like a double *idée fixe.* That is the reason for the constant appearance, in every movement of the symphony, of the melody that begins the first *allegro.* The passage from this state of melancholy reverie, interrupted occasionally by a few fits of groundless joy, to one of delirious passion, with its moments of fury, of jealousy, its return to tenderness, its tears, etc., is the subject of the first movement. [Note here the absence of "religious consolations."]

Then come A Ball, A Scene in the Country, A March of the Scaffold, A Dream of a Witches' Sabbath.

To translate this poetic novel into music, what has M. Berlioz done? He has multiplied the effects, and regularly broken up the musical design; and fearing that the idiom he uses would not suffice to express so many different ideas, he has assembled together, but without succeeding, all the resources of his art. The result, despite traits which show talent, even genius, is confusion, chaos, tedium, a lack of planning, all painful. The result is a sort of delirious wandering which contrasts with the regularity of movement and the harmony of forms which are the first requirement of music. This did not have the depth of wisdom, the calculated originality, of Beethowen: it was the feeble effort of a young artist full of verve, and who is impelled to sterile efforts by the wish to stimulate an inattentive audience. Certainly a well-made air, a happily-fashioned melody, would have put the artist in a better light than that terrible fracas which is still punishing the vaults of the Conservatoire.

We are far from wishing to discourage talent in its first flight. Certainly there are ideas, spirit, audacity, poetry, in this mixture of literary music and harmonic elegy, whose details the bass drum and the cymbals tried to explain. But we cannot, for love of art and its progress, give any quarter to these attempts at effects outside the realm of art itself. The strangest musical whim will incur no blame; it is the travesty of music, it is melody become a childish game, a means of imitation both imperfect and false; it is this miserable borrowing of one art from another, depriving them of their character, which seems to hasten them to their doom.

14. *From* Revue Musicale, Publiée par M. Fétis *10 (December 11, 1830): 151:*

News from Paris

The concert that M. Berlioz gave last Sunday in the great hall of the Conservatoire attracted a large number of amateurs, of artists, and of the curious. This young musician, urged by his instinct in a new direction, has many partisans among the young, always avid for novelties. Several of the pieces announced on the program were already known; but the fantastic symphony of the second part excited lively curiosity because of its subject, and all the attention was concentrated on it.

It is a highly extraordinary composition, this symphony; the genius for new effects manifests itself in the most evident way, and two movements (*le bal* and *la marche du supplice*) herald a vast imagination; finally, one finds a truly individual physiognomy, well beyond the ordinary forms of art; but, in general, this music arouses astonishment rather than pleasure; it lacks charm, and while it shows its author to have a great ability, it leaves the regret that he does not use it in a manner more in conformity with the aims of art. For the rest, it must be said that there is unmistakable progress in the work of M. Berlioz; to convince oneself it is enough to compare the overture to *Les Francs-Juges* with the two pieces I have just cited. Let us hope that he will more and more feel the need to charm the ear as well as astonish the imagination. Without both these conditions, it is difficult to make a lasting reputation.

15. *From* Le National, *December 6, 1830, 3:*

[This is an untitled paragraph between reports on a newly established prize for overseers in industry and a new book on canal and river navigation.]

M. Hector Berlioz gave today, Sunday, at the Conservatoire, a great concert which will be a milestone in the memory of lovers of true music. We heard a symphony in five movements, composed by this young artist, which is no less remarkable for the boldness and the originality of its ideas than for the novelty of the form. The public gave this piece lively applause. We regret that lack of space prevents us from giving further details. M. Berlioz will be sufficiently compensated by the memory of the success he has obtained.

16. *From the published letters of Ludwig Börne, the German satirist and political writer:*

Paris, Wednesday, December 8, 1830

Sunday I attended a concert at the Conservatoire. A young composer named Berlioz, about whom I have already written to you, had some of his compositions performed; he is a Romantic. A whole Beethoven lies hidden in this Frenchman. But so wild that it needs restraint. Everything pleased me very much. A remarkable symphony, a dramatic one in five acts, naturally purely instrumental music, but so that we could understand it he had printed a text explaining the action as in an opera. It is the most dissolute irony, such as no poet has yet expressed in words, and all sacrilegious. In it the composer tells the story of his own youth. He poisons himself with opium and dreams that he has murdered his beloved and been condemned to death. He is present at his own execution. We heard an extraordinary march, the likes of which I have never heard. In the last movement he shows us the Witch's Sabbath, just as in [Goethe's] *Faust,* and it is as real as can be. His beloved, who has shown herself unworthy, appears also in the Walpurgisnacht, but not like Gretchen in *Faust,* but bold, witch-like. . . . In art and literature, as in politics, boldness precedes freedom. One must be able to appreciate that, in order not to condemn the contemporary French Romantics unfairly.

[*Börnes Werke: Historisch-kritische Ausgabe,* ed. Ludwig Geiger, with Jules Dresch, Rudolf Furst, Erwin Kalischer, Alfred Klaar, Alfred Stern, and Leon Zeitlin, 12 vols. (Berlin: Bong [preface 1911]), 6:88–89).

The Program of the Symphony

17. The version of the program as quickly reprinted for the concert of 1830:

Episode
of
The Life of an Artist,
Fantastic Symphony in five parts,
By Hector Berlioz,
performed for the first time December 5, 1830
At the Conservatory of Music of Paris.

————

Program

The composer's aim has been to develop, IN WHAT THEY HAVE THAT IS MUSICAL, various situations in the life of an artist. The plan of the instrumental drama, lacking the help of words, needs to be explained in advance. The following program should thus be considered as *the spoken text of an opera,* serving to *introduce* the musical movements, whose *character and expression it motivates.*[1] [See the footnote inserted by Berlioz, below.]

REVERIES.—PASSIONS.
(First Part.)

The author imagines that a young musician, afflicted with that moral disease that a well-known writer calls the *vague des passions,* sees for the first time a woman who embodies all the charms of the ideal being he has imagined in his dreams, and he falls hopelessly in love with her. Through an odd whim, whenever the beloved image appears before the mind's eye of the artist it is linked with a *musical thought* whose character, passionate but at the same time noble and shy, he finds similar to the one he attributes to his beloved.

This melodic image and its model pursue him incessantly like a double *idée fixe.* That is the reason for the constant appearance, in every movement of the symphony, of the melody that begins the first *allegro.* The passage from this state of melancholy reverie, interrupted by a few fits of groundless joy, to one of delirious passion, with its movements of fury, of jealousy, its return of tenderness, its religious consolations[a]—this is the subject of the first movement.

A BALL.
(Second Part.)

The artist finds himself in the most varied situations—in the midst of *the tumult of a party,* in the peaceful contemplation of the beauties of nature; but everywhere, in town, in the country, the beloved image appears before him and disturbs his peace of mind.

SCENE IN THE COUNTRY.
(Third Part.)

Finding himself one evening in the country, he hears in the distance two shepherds piping a *ranz de vaches* [a mountain melody] in dialogue. This pastoral duet, the scenery, the quiet rustling of the trees gently brushed by the wind, the hopes he has recently found some reason to entertain, all concur in affording his heart an unaccustomed calm, and in giving a more cheerful color to his ideas. He reflects upon his isolation; he hopes that his loneliness will soon be over. . . . But what if she were deceiving him! . . . This mingling of hope and fear, these ideas of happiness disturbed by black presentiments, form the subject of the *adagio*. At the end one of the shepherds again takes up the *ranz de vaches;* the other no longer replies. . . . Distant sound of thunder . . . Loneliness . . . Silence.

MARCH OF THE SCAFFOLD.

(Fourth Part.)

Convinced that his love is unappreciated,[b] the artist poisons himself with opium. The dose of the narcotic, too weak to kill him, plunges him into a sleep accompanied by the most horrible visions. He dreams that he has killed his beloved, that he is condemned and led to the scaffold, and that he is witnessing *his own execution*. The procession moves forward to the sounds of a march that is now sombre and fierce, now brilliant and solemn, in which the muffled noise of heavy steps gives way without transition to the noisiest clamor. At the end of the march the first four measures of the *idée fixe* reappear, like a last thought of love interrupted by the fatal blow.

DREAM OF A WITCHES' SABBATH.

(Fifth Part.)

He sees himself at the sabbath, in the midst of a frightful troop of ghosts, sorcerers, monsters of every kind, come together for his funeral. Strange noises, groans, bursts of laughter, distant cries which other cries seem to answer. The beloved melody appears again, but it has lost its character of nobility and shyness; it is no more than a dance tune, mean, trivial, and grotesque: it is *she,* coming to join the sabbath. . . . A roar of joy at her arrival. . . . She takes part in the devilish orgy. . . . Funeral knell, burlesque parody of the *Dies irae*,[2] sabbath round-dance. The sabbath round and the *Dies irae* combined.

---

[1][Footnote by Berlioz, which was printed at the bottom of the first page of the original program and continued on the second.] It is not at all a matter of copying exactly what the composer has tried to present in orchestral terms, as certain persons seem to think; on the contrary, it is precisely in order to fill in the gaps which musical language unavoidably leaves in the development of dramatic thought, that the composer has had to resort to written prose to explain and justify the plan of the symphony. The author knows very well that music can take the place of neither word nor picture; he has never had the absurd intention of expressing *abstractions* or *moral qualities,* but rather passions and feelings. Nor has he had the even stranger idea of painting *mountains:* he has only wished to reproduce *the style and the melodic forms* that characterize the singing of some of the people who live among them, or *the emotion* that the sight of these imposing masses arouses, under certain circumstances, in the soul. If the few lines of this program had been of such nature that they could be recited or sung between the movements of the symphony, like the choruses in ancient tragedies, then doubtless there could be no such misunderstanding of the sense they contain. But instead of being heard they must be read; and those who make the curious accusation against which the musician must defend himself fail to realize that if he really entertained the exaggerated and ridiculous opinions about the expressive power of his art that are laid at his door, then by the same token he would have thought this program to be merely a kind of duplication, and hence perfectly useless.

As for the imitation of natural sounds, Beethoven, Gluck, Meyerbeer, Rossini, and Weber have proved, by noteworthy examples, that it has its place in the musical realm. Nevertheless, since the composer of this symphony is convinced that the abuse of such imitation is quite dangerous, that it is of very limited usefulness, and that its happiest effects always verge on caricature, he has never considered this branch of the art as an end, but as a means. And when, for example, in the Scene in the Country, he tries to render the rumbling of distant thunder in the midst of a peaceful atmosphere, it is by no means for the puerile pleasure of imitating this majestic sound, but rather to make *silence* more perceptible, and thus to increase the impression of uneasy sadness and painful isolation that he wants to produce on his audience by the conclusion of this movement.

ᵃ[Author's note] Here in the earlier printed version, instead of "its religious consolations," was "its tears, etc."

ᵇ[Author's note] In the earlier printed version, "Convinced that not only does she whom he adores not respond to his love, but that she is incapable of understanding it, and that, moreover, she is unworthy of it."

²[Berlioz's note] Hymn sung in the funeral rites of the Catholic Church.

[Translation adapted from Edward T. Cone, *Fantastic Symphony: An Authoritative Score; Historical Background; Analysis; Views and Comments*, Norton Critical Scores (New York: Norton, 1971), 31–35]

Later Documents

18. Berlioz's description of his concert of 1832, at which Harriet Smithson was present:

The programme consisted of my Fantastic Symphony followed by its sequel *Lélio* or *The Return to Life*, the monodrama which forms the second part of the "Episode in the Life of an Artist." The subject of this musical drama, as is known, was none other than my love for Miss Smithson and the anguish and "bad dreams" it had brought me. Now consider the incredible chain of accidents which follows.

Two days before the concert—which I thought of as a farewell to art and life—I was in Schlesinger's music shop when an Englishman came in and almost immediately went out again. "Who was that?" I asked Schlesinger, moved by a curiosity for which there was no rational motive. "That's Schutter, who writes for *Galignani's Messenger*. Wait a moment," he added, striking his forehead, "I have an idea. Let me have a box for your concert. Schutter knows Miss Smithson. I'll ask him to take her the tickets and persuade her to come." The suggestion made me shudder, but I lacked the strength of mind to reject it. I gave him the tickets. Schlesinger ran after Schutter, caught him up, and doubtless explained what a stir the presence of the famous actress would create. Schutter promised to do everything he could to get her there.

While I was occupied with rehearsals and all the other preparations, the unfortunate director of the English company [Smithson] was busy ruining herself. The guileless actress had been counting on the continued enthusiasm of the Parisians and on the support of the new school of writers who three years earlier had lauded both Shakespeare and his interpreter to the skies. But Shakespeare was no longer a novelty to the feckless and frivolous public. The literary revolution demanded by the romantics had been achieved; and not only were the leaders of the movement not eager for any further demonstration of the power of the greatest of all dramatic poets: unconsciously, they feared it. It was not in their interests that the public should become too familiar with works from which they had borrowed so extensively.

The result was that the English company excited little response, and receipts were low. It had been an expensive venture. The season showed a deficit which absorbed the imprudent director's entire capital. This was the situation when Schutter called on Miss Smithson and offered her a box for my concert, and this is what ensued. She herself told me long afterwards.

Schutter found her in a state of profound despondency, and his proposal was at first badly received. At such a moment it was hardly to be expected she should have time for music. But Miss Smithson's sister joined with him in urging her to accept: it would be a distraction for her; and an English actor, who was with them, on his side appeared anxious to take advantage of the offer. A cab was summoned, and Miss Smithson allowed herself, half willingly, half forcibly, to be escorted into it. The triumphant Schutter gave the address: "The Conservatoire," and they were off. On the way the unhappy creature glanced at the programme. My name had not been mentioned. She now learnt that I was the originator of the proceedings. The title of the symphony and the headings of the various movements somewhat astonished her; but it never so much as occurred to her that the heroine of this strange and doleful drama might be herself.

On entering the stage box above a sea of musicians (for I had collected a very large orchestra), she was aware of a buzz of interest all over the hall. Everyone seemed to be staring in her direction; a thrill of emotion went through her, half excitement, half fear, which she could not clearly account for. Habeneck was conducting. When I came in and sat breathlessly down behind him, Miss Smithson, who until then had supposed she might have mistaken the name at the head of the programme, recognized me. "Yes, it is he," she murmured; "poor young man, I expect he has forgotten me; at least . . . I hope he has." The symphony began and produced a tremendous effect. (Those were days when the hall of the Conservatoire, from which I am now excluded, was the focus of immense public enthusiasm.) The brilliant reception, the passionate character of the work, its ardent, exalted melodies, its protestations of love, its sudden outbursts of violence, and the sensation of hearing an orchestra of that size close to, could not fail to make an impression—an impression as profound as it was totally unexpected—on her nervous system and poetic imagination, and in her heart of hearts she thought, "Ah, if he still loved me!" During the interval which followed the performance of the symphony, the ambiguous remarks of Schutter, and of Schlesinger too—for he had been unable to resist coming into her box—and their veiled allusions to the cause of this young composer's well-known troubles of the heart, began to make her suspect the truth, and she heard them in growing agitation. But when Bocage, the actor who spoke the part of Lélio (that is, myself), declaimed these lines:

> Oh, if I could only find her, the Juliet, the Ophelia whom my heart cries out
> for! If I could drink deep of the mingled joy and sadness that real love offers
> us, and one autumn evening on some wild heath with the north wind blow-
> ing over it, lie in her arms and sleep a last, long, sorrowful sleep!

"God!" she thought: "Juliet—Ophelia! Am I dreaming? I can no longer doubt. It is of me he speaks. He loves me still." From that moment, so she has often told me, she felt the room reel about her; she heard no more but sat in a dream, and at the end returned home like a sleepwalker, with no clear notion of what was happening.

[*Memoirs of Hector Berlioz*, 214–17]

19. Berlioz disinters the remains of Harriet Smithson:

[Harriet Smithson died in 1854, and ten years later Berlioz was charged with moving her remains to a new cemetery. His Juliet, his Ophelia, the inspiration for his symphony, is now a character in the gravediggers' scene.]

The grave had already been opened. On my arrival, the gravedigger jumped down into it. The coffin, though ten years in the ground, was still intact; only the lid had decayed from damp. Instead of lifting out the whole coffin, the gravedigger wrenched at the rotting planks, which came away with a hideous crack, exposing the coffin's contents. The gravedigger bent down and with his two hands picked up the head, already parted from the body—the ungarlanded, withered, hairless head of "poor Ophelia"—and placed it in a new coffin ready for it at the edge of the grave. Then, bending down again, with difficulty he gathered in his arms the headless trunk and limbs, a blackish mass which the shroud still clung to, like a damp sack with a lump of pitch in it. It came away with a dull sound, and a smell.

[Memoirs of Hector Berlioz, 496–97]

20. Berlioz's description of an ideal concert orchestra:

[Berlioz's ideal for an orchestra was described in his seminal treatise on orchestration. It seems clear that the seating plan he describes, the room he prefers, and the general disposition he sees as ideal are those of the Concerts du Conservatoire (cf. page 215). Although the orchestra here is slightly larger than that of the *Symphonie fantastique,* it is arranged almost exactly as Habeneck had begun seating the orchestra years before in the Conservatoire. Since a chorus was present at the first performance of the *Symphonie fantastique* (for the *Chant guerrier*), we can be sure that Berlioz still believed, thirteen years later, that the placement of the orchestra (if not the performance) at the premiere was nearly ideal.]

The space occupied by the musicians, their disposition on a horizontal plane or on an inclined plane, in an enclosure closed on three sides or at the center of a hall, with reflectors made of solid material suitable for reflecting the sound, or soft materials which absorb and break the vibrations, and more or less near the performers, have a great importance. The *reflectors* are indispensable; they are arranged differently in various closed spaces. The nearer they are to the origin of the sound, the more powerful is their effect. . . .

The best way to arrange the players, in a hall whose dimensions are appropriate to their number, is to place them, ones above the others, on a series of risers, put together in such a way that each row can send out its sounds to the listener without any intermediate obstacle.

Every well-arranged concert orchestra should be disposed in these ranks. If it is performing on a theatre stage, the stage should be perfectly closed behind, on the right and left, and above, by an enclosure of wooden panels. . . .

The finest concert orchestra, for a hall barely larger than that of the Conservatoire, the most complete, the richest in nuances, in variety of timbre, the most majestic, the strongest, and the smoothest at the same time, would be an orchestra composed as follows:

21 first violins; 20 seconds; 18 violas; 8 first violoncellos; 7 second violoncellos; 10 contrabasses
4 harps

2 piccolos; 2 flutes; 2 oboes; 1 english horn; 2 clarinets; 1 basset horn or a bass clarinet; 4 bassoons

4 cylinder-horns; 2 trumpets with cylinders; 2 cornets à pistons (or with cylinders); 3 trombones (1 alto and 2 tenors, or 3 tenors); 1 large bass trombone; 1 ophicleide in B-flat (or a bass tuba)

2 pairs of timpani and 4 timpanists; 1 bass drum; 1 pair of cymbals

If there were a piece to be performed with chorus and orchestra, one would need for an orchestra of this size:

46 sopranos (firsts and seconds)
40 tenors (firsts and seconds)
40 basses (firsts and seconds)

This mass of 248 performers placed on a stage at the end of the hall, would have at the rear five rows of risers each two and a half feet high, and they would be distributed as follows:

On the top riser (beginning from the back of the theatre) which is the highest and farthest removed from the audience, from left to right: the *Bass drum,* the *Cymbals,* the two pairs of *Timpani,*[1] the *Ophicleide,* the large *Bass trombone.*

On the second riser (also from left to right): 2 *Contrabasses,* 2 *Violoncellos,* 2 *Cornets à pistons,* 2 *Trumpets,* 3 *Trombones.*

On the third: 4 *Contrabasses,* 8 *Violoncellos.*

On the fourth: 2 *Contrabasses,* 2 *Violoncellos,* 4 *Bassoons,* 4 *Horns.*

On the fifth: 2 *Violoncellos,* 1 *Basset horn,* 2 *Clarinets,* 1 *English horn,* 2 *Oboes,* 2 *Piccolos,* 2 *Flutes.*

On the rest of the stage, or the horizontal plane much vaster than the raised amphitheatre portion: in the back, with their backs to the fifth riser and facing the public, in a single line if the theatre is wide enough: the 18 *Violas.*

In the middle and in front of the Violas: 1 *Contrabass,* plus another *Contrabass* and 1 *Violoncello* playing together from a single stand, as leaders of the mass of the basses.

On one side of the stage, in front of the Violas, in three rows, and presenting their profiles to the public: the 21 *First violins,* the leader of the first violins at the end of the front row.

On the other side of the stage, also in three rows: the 20 *Second violins,* facing the firsts; the leader of the seconds at the end of the front row.

In the empty space between these two groups of violins, and in front of the stand of the bass-leaders: the 4 *Harps.*

In front of the harps, near the first desk of first violins, and facing nearly the whole instrumental mass: the *Conductor.*

The *choir* should then be divided into three groups (each forming a complete choir), the first and smallest in the middle of the apron, in front of the conductor, facing the public; the other two to right and left, with their profiles to the public, should be raised on each side on three little risers a foot high, so that the emission of the voices may be as free as possible. On the front rows would be the *Sopranos,* behind them the *Tenors,* and finally, behind them, on the highest risers, the *Basses.*

---

[1][Berlioz's footnote] I said above that this orchestra would be for a hall *slightly larger than that of the conservatory* of Paris, and it is for that reason that I indicate here the placement of the percussion instruments at the greatest distance from the conductor; for on the contrary in cases where it is a question of an immense orchestra like the orchestras of festivals, one must be careful of relegating them to the extremity of the instrumental mass. Their effect on the rhythm is too great not to place them where they can receive, quickly and surely, the movements of the Conductor. Thus in such cases the percussion instruments must be placed almost in the center of the orchestra, not far from the Conductor.

[Hector Berlioz, *Grand traité d'instrumentation et d'orchestration modernes* (Paris: Schonenberger, 1843)]

5

Igor Stravinsky, Le sacre du printemps

Thursday, May 29, 1913, 8:45 P.M.

I think the whole thing has been done by four idiots: First, M. Stravinsky who wrote the music. Second, M. Roerich who designed the scenery and costumes. Third, M. Nijinsky who composed the dances. Fourth, M. Diaghilev who wasted money on it.

—Enrico Cecchetti, Diaghilev's ballet master

The choreography is ridiculous, the music sheer cacophony. There is some originality, however, and a certain amount of talent. But taken together, it might be the work of a madman.

—Giacomo Puccini

he most important single moment in the history of twentieth-century music might well be the first performance of Stravinsky's *Le sacre du printemps*. It certainly was one of the loudest unamplified moments. Are there other competing moments? The appearance of Schoenberg's *Pierrot lunaire?* Debussy's *Pelléas et Mélisande?* Probably nothing else is so clearly a focal point as *Le sacre;* no one would disagree that this is a seminal piece whose repercussions in the world of music are still being heard today and will continue into the future. Although *Le sacre* has attained a unique place in the musical pantheon, it is probably impossible to appreciate its initial conception as a theater piece, particularly since the choreography, unlike the score, was not written down. Although a great many details of that performance are known, others will forever keep us in suspense.

Those who attended the performance knew that what they had witnessed was important and prophetic. In 1918 Jean Cocteau wrote of *Le sacre* that "the work was and remains a masterpiece; a symphony impregnated with savage pathos, with earth in the throes of birth, noises of farm and camp, little melodies that come from the depths of the centuries, the panting of cattle, deep convulsions, prehistoric georgics." Cocteau was right about the place of *Le sacre* in twentieth-century musical life, and he was not the only prophet. When Léon Vallas wrote that Stravinsky "has offered us this year the music that we should really hear around 1940," he could surely not have known that Walt Disney would use *Le sacre,* or parts of it (albeit with a different visual accompaniment), to dazzle the eyes and ears of the world in *Fantasia* in 1950.

Stravinsky was thirty-one in 1913, the year *Le sacre* was performed, and he continued to compose until his death, in 1971. Despite numerous other compositions, however, *Le sacre* has remained his most famous piece; for the next sixty years of his life it was preferred—along with the earlier ballets, *The Firebird* and *Petrushka*—to all his later music.

One might expect a piece entitled *Le sacre du printemps* (*The Rite of Spring*) to have music akin to its title. The word *sacre* is used for the coronation of a monarch, for the consecration of a bishop: it denotes a ritual performed by high ecclesiastical authority, one rich in tradition and conducted for a specific purpose: before the ceremony the person is not a king or a bishop; after it he is. Ritual music ought to reflect aspects of the rite: solemnity, well-understood tradition, a direct relation to the purpose. When the ritual we observe is familiar to us, the results are easy to judge: the proper actions are carried out, the appropriate words said, the deity invoked. The trouble arises with strange rituals: there we are observers, not participants, and we cannot really say whether the job is done properly. The rituals depicted in *Le sacre* are intended to be those of a pagan and prehistoric Russia; they involve shamans, worship of the earth,

Igor Stravinsky, by Jacques Emile Blanche, 1915

Stravinsky was a natty dresser and kept himself fit. Often painted and sketched in these years, he always appears neat, stylish, and perhaps a bit aloof. "Monsieur Stravinsky is short and he seems tall because he carries his head in the air and his look dominates his interlocutor; he speaks from on high." Stravinsky is described here by Henri Postel du Mas, in a sort of puff piece for the upcoming ballet season, designed to arouse interest in *Le sacre*.

and the choice and execution of a sacrificial virgin; the music that accompanies them is nothing like the music we might hear at a coronation in Reims. *Le sacre* was evidently repugnant to many of its first hearers, probably in part because it was nothing like the ritual music they knew (and nothing like spring). The music is savage, repetitive, highly complex, static in many ways. Some of these aspects are not inconsistent with much ritual music, music that is intended not so much to please as to get the job done. That night in the Théâtre des Champs-Elysées, however, the audience was probably not making such connections.

One might also expect music on the theme of spring to be a little more pleasant. Such music is usually as predictable as music about the sunrise, the sea, or birdcalls: we know how it ought to go, and the interest is in hearing how the usual themes (rustlings of leaves, flowers, birds, returning warmth, surges of new energy) can possibly be presented in a way that is both new and musically satisfactory. But this musical rite of spring is aggressive, chaotic, inexpressive, ugly: it has nothing to do with spring as we know it. Stravinsky's music, as he himself put it, was intended to portray "the surge of spring, the magnificent upsurge of nature reborn." His is a completely new conception of spring—the awesome, frightening, post-Darwinian spring of rampant unchecked growth. Part of what is so wonderful about the music is just how apt a depiction it is.

From the beginning solo, so high in its range it was all but unrecognizable as a bassoon, through the rest of the prelude, the increasing number of melodies, rhythms, and instruments creates chaos of such melodic complexity that it seems as though all of creation were shouting for attention; this changes, after an ominous moment, into a music that has no melody at all, only a shifting pattern of rhythms in the famous eight-note chord insistently repeated in the strings as though the orchestra were being beaten like a drum. Here the dancing begins, and the story.

The ballet, subtitled "Pictures of Pagan Russia," has two parts, representing day and night, male and female, preparation and sacrifice. Each begins with ceremonial actions and games and concludes with a significant ritual moment: in the first part (entitled "The adoration of the earth"), a ritual kissing of the earth by the eldest and wisest of the sages; in the second ("The sacrifice"), the sacrificial dance itself, in which the chosen victim dances herself to death. There are seven titled sections in the first part, six in the second, making thirteen "numbers," thirteen essentially separate musical and choreographic units—much like many other ballets, in fact. But their music is so different from that of Chopin (whose music shared the program), or indeed from *Petrushka*, that it is still difficult for many listeners to feel comfortable with Stravinsky's angular and irregular rhythms, his static and nontonal harmonies, his fabrication of larger forms from the rearrangement of small musical patterns in a patchwork of repetition. Nonetheless, this music has fascinated listeners from Walt Disney to Pierre Boulez and has been appreciated, puzzled over, written about, and analyzed perhaps more than any other piece of twentieth-century orchestral music.

But *Le sacre* was not, despite Stravinsky's protestations after the fact, a piece of music: it was a ballet. There are places in the music that are best explained as moments of stage action: the procession of the Sage, which begins in an undertone and gradually overwhelms the other music in a crescendo of tubas as the procession arrives on stage; the mystical chord played on string harmonics for the moment of the ritual kiss itself; the hesitations and interruptions that mark the process of choosing the sacrificial victim.

Le sacre was a collaboration of dancers, scene designers, and choreographers, an entertainment to be seen as well as heard. Along with the unconventional theme and music, the oddness of the dancing and the scandal surrounding the Diaghilev company gave the premiere a cachet of modernity. And for this we must consider the context of Paris in 1913.

Paris of that period was, as always, a focus of culture, style, and elegance. The beau monde who leafed through their programs on May 29, 1913, saw advertisements for motor cars by Benz, Hispano-Suiza, Rolls-Royce, and other makes now forgotten; they saw publicity photographs of leading ladies of the stage posing in long, elaborately draped gowns by the foremost couturiers of the day. Most of the men arrived in evening dress with stiff top hats or bowlers: the bohemians, the artistic crowd, could be identified by their soft hats and caps.

Nearly three million people lived in the twenty arrondissements, with many more arriving every day from the suburbs and beyond. Traffic was intense; carriages, automobiles, bicycles, electric streetcars, and buses, all competed with pedestrians for space. The underground *métro* had been in service since the beginning of the century, and the vast railway stations connected Paris with the world in all directions. Recent additions to the landscape included the Tower of Three Hundred Meters, constructed by the engineer Gustave Eiffel for the exposition of 1889, and the Grand Palais and the Petit Palais, for the exposition of 1900.

Technology was the darling of the time; it had not yet caused the death of millions in war. The Salon de l'Automobile, an annual show of the latest in motor-car fashion, was an attraction as important then as now. The year 1913 is a great one in French aeronautics; French aviators set speed records (126 miles per hour), flew the Mediterranean to Algeria nonstop, attained altitudes of twenty thousand feet, and performed the first loop. Electronic media, in their infancy, were still a novelty. The *théâtrophone* allowed subscribers to hear live operas and concerts on an amplified telephone, sparing them the necessity of going out (Proust listened this way several times to Debussy's opera *Pelléas et Mélisande* in 1911). Some owned their own phonographs; those who did not could listen to recorded music in a number of *salons des phonographes.*

In 1913 Marcel Proust shaved his beard for the last time, leaving the moustache for which he is best known. He also finished the first part of *A la recherche du temps perdu,* and spent much of the year attempting to find a publisher. He had failed with Fasquelle, despite the intercession of Gaston Calmette, editor of *Le Figaro* (who would be shot dead by Madame Caillaux in February 1914), as well as with the *Nouvelle Revue Française* (André Gide had rejected it outright). The young publisher Bernard Grasset finally took the book, attracted by Proust's offer to pay publication costs, and published *Du côté de chez Swann* without reading it.

Proust, despite self-imprisonment in his cork-lined bedroom, had been a devotee of the Ballets Russes since its founding by Sergey Diaghilev in 1911, and his close friend Reynaldo Hahn had composed *Le dieu bleu,* to a scenario by Jean Cocteau, for the first season. Proust dined with friends at Larue's restaurant on a May evening in 1913 after the Russian Ballet—perhaps it was *Le sacre du printemps* they saw.

Along the tree-lined *grands boulevards,* which stretched five miles from the church of the Madeleine to the Place de la Bastille, theaters, music halls, restaurants, cafés, shops, and a variety of sidewalk entertainments beckoned. The electric advertisements themselves, in the form of colored neon lights, attracted many visitors. The venerable Edmond Rostand could have seen his own *Cyrano de Bergerac* presented for the umpteenth time at the Théâtre de la Porte Saint-Martin in March. The fashionable people gathered at the Grand Café on the Boulevard des Capucines, near the Opéra, and at other, equally famous watering spots.

The Folies Bergère (where the best seat cost ten francs) and the Moulin Rouge (nine francs) were the leading music halls. Singers such as the great Yvette Guilbert could command a thousand francs a night at the Olympia, a sum equivalent to half a year's salary for a government clerk. In these music halls one act followed another without pause—a juggler, a singer, and always music. As the novelist Colette complained in

1913, "Between two tangos, between a slow waltz and a ragtime dance there is no longer even the normal interval . . . the moment of silence and moral darkness during which the brain and the stomach can collect themselves again." (The tango was wildly in vogue in 1913; Stravinsky was not to write one until 1918, in *Histoire du soldat*.)

The new cinema, until recently merely a novelty to be seen in a music hall or a fair, was coming into its own as a form of entertainment. Even the eminent Camille Saint-Saëns had composed music for film, though the cinema remained a treat mostly for the working classes. In 1913 receipts from the two-hundred-odd movie houses in Paris reached about nine million francs. Many former palaces of live entertainment had been converted to movie houses: the Cirque d'Hiver, the Hippodrome, the Parisiana music hall, and many more such establishments would meet the same fate.

Other divertissements included horse racing at Longchamps and elsewhere, sixteen cycling tracks, several ice skating arenas, and four wax museums. Circuses remained a favorite attraction, presenting single-ring events that centered on equestrian acts, though some, such as the Nouveau Cirque on the rue St. Honoré, had such novelties as aquatic acts.

The musical establishment in Paris ranged from such luminaries as Camille Saint-Saëns, who received the Grand Cross of the Legion of Honor in 1913, to Claude Debussy, the avant-garde composer whose *Pelléas et Mélisande* had created such partisan rivalries.

Musical institutions, many of them familiar from Berlioz's day, were well entrenched. The Opéra, in the magnificent 1875 Palais Garnier, continued in the tradition of Grand Opéra, gradually got around to Wagner, and was the venue of the greatest elegance, if not the greatest musical adventurousness. In 1913 everybody was celebrating the Wagner centenary. Richard Wagner had been born almost exactly a century before the premiere of *Le sacre,* but Paris needed the full hundred years to show him the recognition he achieved elsewhere much earlier. Wagner's late operas had appeared in Paris only recently: *Parsifal* was first performed in Paris in 1911, so his music was almost a novelty. In 1913 his *Tétralogie* was presented in its entirety at the Opéra. The cycle opened on May 25 with *L'or du rhin; La walkyrie* followed on the 27th; on the 29th concertgoers had to choose between the premiere of *Le sacre* and the Opéra's *Siegfried; Le crépuscule des dieux* was given on June 1. There were forty-eight performances of eight Wagner operas during 1913 at the Opéra: far more than all French or Italian operas together.

In recent years, the Opéra-Comique had been the scene of the most interesting premieres, including *Carmen* (in 1875), *Les contes d'Hoffmann* (1881), and *Lakmé* (1883). Since moving into the refurbished Salle Favart in 1889, the Opéra-Comique had given first performances of, among others, Lalo's *Le roi d'Ys* (1889), Charpentier's *Louise* (1900), Debussy's *Pelléas* (1902), Dukas's *Ariane et Barbe-Bleu* (1907), and Ravel's *L'heure espagnole* (1910).

Le Figaro, May 29, 1913:

Le sacre du printemps, which the Russian ballet will perform for the first time
tonight at the theatre of the Champs-Elysées, is the most surprising realization that
the admirable troupe of M. Serge de Diaghilew has ever attempted. It is the
evocation of the first gestures of pagan Russia evoked by the triple vision of Strawinsky, poet and musician, of Nicolas Roerich, poet and painter, and of Nijinsky, poet
and choreographer.

One will find there the strongly stylized characteristic attitudes of the Slavic
race with an awareness of the beauty of the prehistoric period.

The prodigious Russian dancers were the only ones capable of expressing
these stammerings of a semi-savage humanity, of composing these frenetic human
clusters wrenched incessantly by the most astonishing polyrhythm ever to come
from the mind of a musician. There is truly a new thrill which will surely raise
passionate discussions, but which will leave all true artists with an unforgettable
impression.

The Conservatory orchestra was still presenting an important season, but it
was no longer the height of concert life that it had been in Berlioz's time; now several
Sunday afternoon concert series, including the Concerts Pasdeloup, Colonne, and
Lamoureux, all competed with other entertainments for the attention of the musically
inclined.

Debussy had up to now been the radical of music. His *Pelléas et Mélisande* of
1902 had become first a cause célèbre at the Opéra-Comique and then a cult favorite.
The 1912 premiere of Nijinsky's choreography to Debussy's *Prelude à l'après-midi d'un
faune* had caused a scandal, owing mostly to Nijinsky's famous sexual gesture. And on
May 15, just two weeks before *Le sacre,* Diaghilev premiered Debussy's *Jeux,* again
with choreography by Nijinsky and again raising objections in the press.

Gabriel Fauré's opera *Pénélope* opened in May 1913, in alternation with the
Ballets Russes, at the Théâtre des Champs-Elysées. Gustave Charpentier's new opera
Julien, a sequel to his popular *Louise,* was in final rehearsals when *Le sacre* was first
performed.

In late April, when the musical season ended, theaters were vacant, and a variety of entrepreneurs and impresarios presented what was commercially called the "Grande Saison de Paris," an attempt to keep visitors entertained, to keep Parisians in town and in the theaters, and to sell tickets. This was the time of year that Diaghilev and his Ballets Russes created their famous Parisian seasons.

The Ballets Russes of Sergey Diaghilev was not only an attraction in Paris of the belle époque but a bright moment in all of Western culture. The Russian impresario and his company managed in a few years to present some of the most imaginative, energetic, and influential works of music and dance of all time. Diaghilev brought together artists, designers, choreographers, dancers, composers, and performers, in a sort of Gallo-Russian *Gesamtkunstwerk*.

Among the artists who provided set designs for the Russian Ballet were Picasso, Matisse, Juan Gris, Braque, Henri Laurens, Coco Chanel, Maurice Utrillo, André Derain, Max Ernst, Joan Miró, and many others. Choreographers included Léonide Massine, Vaslav Nijinsky, and George Balanchine. Among the performers were the two most famous ballet dancers of all time: Nijinsky and Pavlova.

Diaghilev commissioned scores from composers known and unknown that in many cases have become classics, among them *Daphnis et Chloë* (Ravel, 1912); *Jeux* (Debussy, 1912); *Josephslegende* (Strauss, 1914); *Le tricorne* (De Falla, 1915); *Les biches* (Poulenc, 1924); and *Le train bleu* (Milhaud, 1924). The ballet *Parade* (1917), a collaboration among Satie, Picasso, Cocteau, and Massine, is one of the truly great moments in theater history. In the late twenties, Prokofiev contributed *Le pas d'acier* (1927) and *L'enfant prodigue* (1929).

And we haven't even mentioned Stravinsky. Diaghilev commissioned from the young Stravinsky not only the three famous early ballets—*Firebird* (1910), *Petrushka* (1911), and *Le sacre* (1913)—but a whole series of brilliant scores that mark more than a composer's artistic progress: they identify Stravinsky as an adopted Frenchman, as a man born to the theater. Stravinsky's later scores for Diaghilev—*Le rossignol* (1914), *Pulcinella* (1920), *Mavra* (1922), *Renard* (1922), *Les noces* (1923), *Oedipus Rex* (1927), and *Apollon musagète* (1928)—are a catalogue that makes Stravinsky's contribution to the dance, and Diaghilev's contribution to twentieth-century music, incalculable.

As a young man in St. Petersburg, Sergey Diaghilev had been an all-around connoisseur. He studied composition at the conservatory; played the piano and sang a fine baritone, appearing in concert at least once (performing arias from *Parsifal* and *Lohengrin*); painted a bit; edited a journal (*World of Art*) and led a group of young esthetes, including Alexandre Benois, Léon Bakst, and Nicholas Roerich; and later attracted to his circle Michel Fokine, who was to dance for him and become his choreographer.

By 1907 Diaghilev the esthete had become the impresario. At the Paris Opéra he organized a series of seven concerts featuring Russian music, including works by

Lydia Sokolova remembered the arrival of the opera performers in 1913 (Diaghilev was to present *Boris Godunov* and *Khovantchina*):

A day or two after we [the dancers] arrived in Paris, trainloads of singers began to arrive from Russia. Most of these people had never before been in Western Europe, and quite a number of the men wore their national costume—Russian shirts and baggy trousers tucked into their boots. As some of them had beards as well, they appeared to have stepped straight off the stage. When they walked down the street people thought they were an advertisement for the Russian Opera and Ballet, and Diaghilev very soon gave orders that they were to wear ordinary suits.

Rimsky-Korsakov; the second piano concerto of Rachmaninov, played by the composer; and scenes from Borodin's *Prince Igor*, sung by the great Russian bass Fyodor Ivanovich Chaliapin. The next season he was back, this time with opera, including Chaliapin in *Boris Godunov*. In 1909 Diaghilev launched the Ballets Russes, presenting at the Théâtre du Châtelet a season entirely choreographed by Fokine, with spectacular costumes by Léon Bakst, and featuring a dazzling company of dancers led by Pavlova, Nijinsky, and Tamara Karsavina. Favorite items included the Polovtsian Dances from *Prince Igor* and Rimsky-Korsakov's *Schéhérazade*. The company consisted of fifty-five Russian dancers, on leave from the imperial theaters of Moscow and St. Petersburg. The business matters were managed by Gabriel Astruc.

By 1912 the Ballets Russes had become a focal point of the season, having captivated *le tout Paris* with its skill, the beauty of its presentations, and in particular the novelty of its Russian themes and folk imagery. Adolphe Boschot spoke for many: "So we have to admire the Ballets Russes. In fact, for several years we acclaimed their *splendide barbarie*. There were new elements, a vehement glitter, an irresistible movement." Marcel Proust's reaction was similar: "This charming invasion, against whose seductions only the most vulgar critics protested, brought on Paris, as we know, a fever of curiosity less acute, more purely aesthetic, but perhaps just as intense as that aroused by the Dreyfus case."

Diaghilev had an energetic momentum that left a large wake, and a strong, magnetic personality. The dance historian Cyril Beaumont described Diaghilev, whom he knew for years:

You had only to meet him to realize at once that you were in the presence of a personality, for he radiated authority and determination. He was of medium height, broad-shouldered, and heavily built. . . .

His head was broad-browed, square, and massive, and firmly set on a short and thick neck. His glossy black hair, parted at the side, had a highlight in the form of a white lock which early earned him the nickname of Chinchilla. He had a heavy jaw, full cheeks, thick and sensual lips, and eyebrows arched in a supercilious stare. His features were pale and clean-shaven, except for a clipped moustache in the form of an inverted "v". The back of his head was curiously flat, and anyone sitting behind him and aware of this fact, could easily single him out. His well kept, unusually small hands were plump, white, and warm. He walked slowly and deliberately as though his body were heavy to bear, often with a stick which had something of the character of a third leg.

He carried a monocle suspended from the neck by a narrow black ribbon which, on occasion, he manipulated like the quizzing glass of an eighteenth-century exquisite; and when, following a discussion, he allowed the monocle to fall from his eye, it produced a sense of finality. . . .

Diaghilev had the charming manners of the born aristocrat. As a general rule, he had a suave address, not unlike the bedside manner of a fashionable physician. His voice had a soft caressing tone, infinitely seductive. His *"mon cher ami"*, accompanied by an affectionate touch of his hand on your wrist or forearm, was irresistible. On the other hand, when cross, he could be brutally curt and arrogant, and no one could snub with more biting sarcasm. He always dressed his hair with a brilliantine perfumed with almond blossom . . . and if the fragrance of almonds were perceptible in a passage or room you might be sure that Diaghilev had passed by only a short while before.

Diaghilev's homosexuality was recognized by all, but it is not always mentioned in reports of the day. In 1913 he was insanely fond of the handsome Vaslav Nijinsky, an affection that was often overshadowed by jealousy and protectiveness. Diaghilev's decision to make Nijinsky the exclusive choreographer of his company was seen by many as a serious mistake in judgment, although it may also have been intended to retain Nijinsky's interest in the company—and its director.

When Enrico Cecchetti said of *Le sacre* that "the whole thing was done by four idiots," he was right about the collaborative aspect, but the idiocy of the partners has been judged differently by others. Any ballet is a collaboration: scenario, music, cho-

Sergey Diaghilev (right) and Igor Stravinsky, Beausoleil, 1911

Diaghilev's Ballets Russes had been the talk of Paris since 1909. Stravinsky
had already collaborated with Diaghilev by providing orchestrations of
Chopin and composing his two famous early ballets, *The Firebird* and
Petrushka. The ballet critic Cyril Beaumont described Diaghilev's striking
appearance: "His head was broad-browed, square, and massive, and firmly set
on a short and thick neck. His glossy black hair, parted at the side, had a
highlight in the form of a white lock which early earned him the nickname of
Chinchilla." Pictured with them is General Bezobrazov, of St. Petersburg.

reography, sets, costumes, dancing, all must come together at once. But for this particular ballet, each of the collaborators was a fascinating personality in his own right; and
together, they formed a new constellation in the artistic heavens.

Henri Postel du Mas, in a piece designed to arouse interest in *Le sacre,* described Stravinsky thus: "Monsieur Stravinsky is short and he seems tall because he
carries his head in the air and his look dominates his interlocutor; he speaks from on
high, and his eyes wander over objects and persons with a divergence and a mobility
that surround them like a sudden rainshower" (document 31). Stravinsky was also a
natty dresser and kept himself fit. In the many paintings and sketches done of him during this period, he always appears neat, stylish, and perhaps a bit aloof. The success of

The Firebird, and the unique position of Paris as the hub of the Western artistic world and the center for Diaghilev's ballet seasons, made Stravinsky realize that his future lay not so much in Russia as in being a Russian composer in the West.

Stravinsky in 1913 was not yet the most famous composer in the world, but he was at least an *enfant terrible* and well on his way to lasting fame. The enormous success of *Firebird* and *Petrushka* catapulted Stravinsky to fame in Paris, and the two pieces have held the stage—or at least the concert platform—ever since.

The three early ballets for Diaghilev were something of a "Russian group"; *Firebird,* really a continuation of Stravinsky's apprenticeship to his teacher, Rimsky-Korsakov, perhaps spawned the other two: the idea of a ritual pagan sacrifice—what would become *Le sacre*—came to Stravinsky, as he tells it, while he was finishing the orchestration of *Firebird.* But that idea was interrupted by another one, a piece for piano and orchestra about a puppet; this latter idea, with Diaghilev's encouragement, became *Petrushka.* Only after *Petrushka* was performed did Stravinsky return to *Le sacre.*

These ballets are often grouped together, and with good reason. They were composed in close succession; all are ballet scores for Diaghilev; all are for large orchestra; all are on Russian themes. And yet they are strikingly different: *Firebird* is a late Romantic score; *Petrushka* reflects the awakening of Stravinsky's personal language; and *Le sacre* is so revolutionary in sound that its kinship with its siblings is almost lost in the polemical noise.

Just before the first performance of *Le sacre du printemps,* Stravinsky had two musical experiences that must have deeply influenced him. In the summer of 1912 he went with Diaghilev to hear a performance of Wagner's *Parsifal* at Bayreuth. Many people made the trip to the German city as a sort of artistic pilgrimage, to worship at the shrine of the master of the Total Work of Art. (This trek had been fashionable since the late nineteenth century; Albert Lavignac, in *Le voyage artistique à Bayreuth* (7th ed., 1897), told French-speaking pilgrims not only what to listen for but who was who, listing the names of distinguished visitors to the Wagner Festspielhaus.) In the winter, in the course of the Ballets Russes tour, he visited Berlin, met Arnold Schoenberg, and heard a performance of *Pierrot lunaire.* He reports that he was deeply impressed.

But if Stravinsky was impressed with Wagner and Schoenberg, it was not to have an immediate and direct effect on his music. The grandeur and emotionalism of Wagner, with its strong tonal organization and its continuous motion, is as far from Stravinsky's score for *Le sacre* as is the atonal, contrapuntal music of Schoenberg. In fact, Wagner's overwrought style may have affected Stravinsky negatively, though he surely admired the composer's magnificent orchestration. Schoenberg's strong influence was to be felt only many years later. In 1913, Stravinsky's music for *Le sacre* was based on ritual, on myth, on folklore, and on a kind of static pulsation of rhythms and harmonies.

Nicholas Roerich, *Seven Figures in Costume*, ca. 1912

Roerich was the originator of the scenario of *Le sacre* and the designer of the
sets and costumes. He was considered an anthropological authority on ancient
Slavic culture, which contributed to the "primitive" qualities that critics saw in
Le sacre. This sketch, which may be related to Roerich's planning for the
ballet, shows his attention to detail and his concern for authenticity.

Of the three chief collaborators in the creation of *Le sacre*, Nicholas Roerich is
less well remembered in performing circles than his famous colleagues, and yet he had
perhaps the most varied and fascinating career. As one of the first members of Diaghilev's
group in St. Petersburg, Roerich's paintings had been shown in exhibitions as early as
1899 and been reproduced in Diaghilev's *World of Art*. Roerich studied art in Paris in
1900 and was one of the painters represented in an exhibition of Russian art mounted
by Diaghilev at the Salon d'Automne in 1906. Roerich had also worked in the theater; in
1908 he designed *The Snow Maiden* for the Moscow Arts Theater, and in 1909 he was
commissioned by Diaghilev to design sets and costumes for *Prince Igor* (they would be
seen again in the performance that accompanied the premiere of *Le sacre*).

Roerich had a reputation as an expert on matters of Slavic folklore and history,
having studied ancient Slavic architecture under the sponsorship of the Russian Ar-
chaeological Society. The bears that often appear in his paintings (and the bearskins
worn as part of the costumes in *Le sacre*) reflect the ancient Slavic belief that the bear
was the human's ancestor.

In a letter to Diaghilev, Roerich explained his conception of the work:

In the ballet of the *Sacre du Printemps* conceived by myself and
Stravinsky, my object was to present a number of pictures of earthly

joy and celestial triumph, as understood by the Slavs. I don't propose to set down a list of all the items in the ballet; such a list hardly matters when we are dealing with sets and groupings. My intention, therefore, stated simply, is that the first set should transport us to the foot of a sacred hill, in a lush plain, where Slavonic tribes are gathered together to celebrate the spring rites. In this scene there is an old witch, who predicts the future, a marriage by capture, round dances. Then comes the most solemn moment. The wisest ancient is brought from the village to imprint his sacred kiss on the new-flowering earth. During this rite the crowd is seized with a mystic terror, and this our excellent Nijinsky has stylized for us admirably well.

After this uprush of terrestrial joy, the second scene sets a celestial mystery before us. Young virgins dance in circles on the sacred hill, amid enchanted rocks, then they choose the victim they intend to honor. In a moment she will dance her last dance, before the ancient old men, wrapped in bearskins, to show that the bear was man's ancestor. Then the graybeards dedicate the victim to the god Yarilo. I love antiquity for its sublime happiness and its deep thoughts.

Roerich was later strongly influenced by the Theosophical movement; he traveled to India, where he studied art and religion and concerned himself with the unity of human creative experience. A large exhibition of his paintings in New York in 1920, which traveled to twenty other cities, preceded the foundation of his Master Institute of United Arts in New York in 1921 (its credo began "Art will unify all of humanity . . ."). Roerich founded the Banner of Peace Movement, which ultimately led to the so-called Roerich Pact, an international agreement for the protection of artistic heritage, signed by many nations in 1935.

Viewed by some as a money-hungry charlatan, Roerich used his paintings as collateral to finance personal travel. When the United States Internal Revenue Service accused him of tax fraud in 1935, his museum and institute were closed and his paintings sold. Two decades later, in 1958, a new Roerich museum and institute were established in New York.

From the beginning Nicolas Roerich worked closely with Stravinsky on the development of the scenario for *Le sacre*. He designed the backdrops for the two acts as well as the colorful costumes, which seemed to Stravinsky, and to others, to be historically accurate. Roerich was considered an expert archaeologist and folklorist, and his assertions as to what was prehistoric and Russian were generally believed (though modern anthropologists might have serious doubts).

The twenty-five-year-old Vaslav Nijinsky was a legendary dancer, the acknowledged star of the Ballets Russes. His lightness, his athletic prowess, and above all his

Vaslav Nijinsky, Photographed by Stravinsky, Monte Carlo, 1911

The handsome Nijinsky, with his vaguely Asiatic look, fascinated observers
onstage and off. Amazingly strong, he was known not only for his fabulous
leaps but for the catlike smoothness and agility of his dancing.

uncanny elastic ability to leap as if floating attracted all eyes in the world of dance. Critics repeatedly described his motions as catlike; he moved like a tiger, a panther. The
famous roles he created are still associated with him: Petrushka, the Faun, Daphnis.
And he appeared in virtually every program presented by Diaghilev through 1913.

Although he was constantly in the company of Diaghilev, Nijinsky was in fact
surrounded by his family. His sister, Bronislava, was a member of the company, as was
her husband, Sasha; his mother, Eleonora, was constantly on tour with them.

Nijinsky was Diaghilev's lover for a time, and it may have been Diaghilev's fascination with Nijinsky, and his desire to keep him close to the company and to himself, that led the impresario to replace Fokine with Nijinsky. In 1912, Nijinsky had choreographed *L'après-midi d'un faune,* and by 1913 Fokine was out and Nijinsky was in. The next year, Nijinsky married, a decision that enraged Diaghilev, who excluded Nijinsky from his company. Nijinsky apparently could not understand Diaghilev's reasons for doing so. He continued to dance for a few years, but by 1919 his growing mental instability had become obvious. He spent the rest of his life in various mental institutions and died in 1950.

Although there were doubts about his abilities as a choreographer, Nijinsky's main contributions to dance as a choreographer were innovative and far-reaching. He had sought the flat look of a Grecian frieze for *L'après-midi d'un faune,* with feet and profile turned sideways and the body facing forward. In *Jeux,* the ballet set to Debussy's music that premiered just two weeks before *Le sacre,* he had used modern costume, three-quarter rather than full pointe to suggest a tennis service, and sexually suggestive groupings. Sexual overtones, the unusual use of the body, and the rejection of classical ballet poses and of narration and mime pointed the way for many new directions in dance.

On Nijinsky's musicality, Stravinsky is not at pains to disguise his disdain, at least twenty years after *Le sacre:* "His ignorance of the most elementary notions of

Pierre Monteux

Monteux, Diaghilev's regular conductor, had a keen ear and an enormous talent for detail. At the age of eighty-eight, on the fiftieth anniversary of its premiere, he conducted *Le sacre* in London.

music was flagrant. The poor boy knew nothing of music. He could neither read it nor play any instrument. . . . My apprehensions can be readily understood, but I had no choice in the matter." Nijinsky's sister insisted, though, that he could play several instruments (the balalaika, clarinet, and piano) but had little patience with scores.

Whatever Stravinsky remembered later, he liked Nijinsky's work at the time; and the choreography and the dancing, like the other elements of the ballet, were integral to the conception of the piece.

Pierre Monteux, conductor of the orchestra for *Le sacre*, was thirty-eight years old; he had taken a Premier Prix at the Conservatoire in 1898 and began his career as a violist: he was the principal viola at the Opéra-Comique for the premiere of Debussy's *Pelléas et Mélisande* in 1902. In the late spring every year from 1911 to 1914 he conducted the ballet orchestra for Diaghilev and was thus the first conductor of *Petrushka, Le sacre, Le rossignol, Daphnis et Chloë, Jeux,* and many other works. Monteux later went to the Metropolitan Opera and then conducted the Boston Symphony Orchestra. He returned to Europe to work at the Concertgebouw under Willem Mengelberg; at the same time he organized and conducted an orchestra in Paris. He was conductor of the San Francisco Symphony Orchestra from 1936 to 1952, the year he also became an American citizen. In 1961, at the age of eighty-six, he signed a twenty-five-year contract as principal conductor of the London Symphony Orchestra. At the age of eighty-eight, on the fiftieth anniversary of its premiere, he conducted *Le sacre* in London. He died in Hancock, Maine, in 1964 at the age of eighty-nine.

Monteux was a careful, thorough worker. He had a faultless ear, though he was not ostentatious about this gift, and he enjoyed the full respect of his musicians. Henri Girard, a bass player who performed in the *Sacre* orchestra, remembered that "he was also indefatigable. I heard him say after rehearsing three hours, 'I could take another orchestra and rehearse another three hours.'"

For all his superb musicianship, Monteux may not have found *Le sacre* completely to his liking. "My one desire," he reported on hearing Stravinsky play a preliminary version of *Le sacre* on the piano in Monte Carlo in 1912, "was to flee that room and find a quiet corner in which to rest my aching head. Then my Director [Diaghilev] turned to me with a smile and said, 'This is a masterpiece, Monteux, which will completely revolutionize music and make you famous, because you are going to conduct it.' And of course, I did."

Although Monteux conducted *Le sacre* for years, he apparently never came to love it. At the Eastman School in the 1950s he was asked about his first reaction to the piece: "I detested it"; and how does he like it now? "I still detest it."

The Théâtre des Champs-Elyséâées

The Avenue Montaigne was and is as elegant an address as fashionable Paris can offer. Its new theater, called the Théâtre des Champs-Elysées, opened on April 2, 1913, with the intention of being a magnet for persons of style.

The program for the Diaghilev ballets carried a blurb, used throughout the season, which explained the importance, and extolled the perfections, of the brand-new theater: "The incessant surge of Paris towards the West and the daily more luxurious conditions of worldly life had inevitably to make the quarter of the Champs-Elysées the center of the elegance of the city, and thus to give it new needs; in the front rank of these latter is the need for a theatre corresponding to the tastes and the artistic instincts of modern life." The formula according to which it was designed might seem unusual today: it was to be "a union of the French taste for comfort with Anglo-Saxon technology."

It was Gabriel Astruc, a manager and impresario with vision and imagination, who conceived and constructed the Théâtre des Champs-Elysées. Astruc brought to Paris a series of artists of the first rank: Wanda Landowska, Artur Rubinstein, Enrico Caruso, and Arturo Toscanini together with the Metropolitan Opera orchestra. Astruc also loved the circus—not so strange, perhaps, given his love of entertainment. He had met Diaghilev in 1906 and managed his concerts and ballet appearances in Paris for six years, beginning with the season of Russian operas in 1907.

Astruc originally wanted his theater to be located on the Champs-Elysées itself, but the opposition he encountered finally forced him to move down the Avenue Montaigne, although he kept the name of the first site. Astruc was Jewish, and it is easy to imagine that a part of the hostility was based on an anti-Semitism still heard, if more discreetly voiced, in a France that had recently experienced such prejudice overtly in the Dreyfus affair.

Antagonistic relations continued for years between Astruc and the public, which associated him with the exotic and the recondite, the outlandish and the ugly.

Exterior of the Théâtre des Champs-Elysées

The Théâtre des Champs-Elysées, built at the expense of the impresario
Gabriel Astruc, was brand-new in 1913. It was the first theater made of
reinforced concrete; the façade is clad in marble and incorporates sculptured
reliefs by Emile Bourdelle.

There was too much foreign influence in the design of the theater, too much support of German music and Russian ballet, and so on.

In view of the Wagner craze enveloping the Opéra, it is hard to take some of this criticism at face value, and indeed Astruc did his best to represent French music. The concert he organized for the opening of the theater was a showcase of Gallic grandeur; the program included the most famous French composers of the day conducting their own works: Saint-Saëns, Debussy, d'Indy, Fauré, Dukas. In 1913, the first year of the theater, he produced Berlioz's *Benvenuto Cellini,* which had not been performed since 1838; Felix Weingartner (who knew Frau Grebner, who had sung for Beethoven) conducted. In addition to *Cellini,* there were productions of Donizetti's *Lucia di Lammermoor,* Rossini's *Barber of Seville,* and Fauré's *Pénélope.* Most concerts were under the direction of the resident conductor, D. E. Englebrecht, but Weingartner also conducted Beethoven, and Mengelberg the Concertgebouw orchestra. Pavlova starred in several ballet evenings; Nellie Melba and Jan Kubelik gave concerts. The first spring season concluded with the "saison russe" of opera and ballet, alternating with

Interior of the Théâtre des Champs-Elysées

Decorated in gold and red velvet, the interior is relatively simple. The
balconies are free-floating, and waist-high partitions separate the boxes. For
the premiere Stravinsky was seated in the fourth or fifth row on the right.

the first production of Gabriel Fauré's opera *Pénélope*. (For May performances, see
document 1.)

For the 1913 season Astruc paid Diaghilev twenty-five thousand francs per performance (in earlier years he had paid twelve thousand at the Opéra and the Châtelet).
This largesse showed how highly Diaghilev was valued, and it permitted the development of *Le sacre,* with its enormous orchestra and endless rehearsals, but ruined Astruc within a year.

The Théâtre des Champs-Elysées was, and remains, modern, comfortable,
and elegant. Designed by a collaboration of architects, including Auguste Perret and
Henry Van de Velde, it was the first theater made of reinforced concrete; the structure,

of skeletal beams filled in with nonbearing walls, is seen clearly in the façade, which is clad in marble and incorporates sculptured reliefs by Emile Bourdelle.

Inside, the walls are sheathed in marble; appointments include bronze grilles and moldings, a gold proscenium framing a silver curtain, and a sunburst overhead providing both natural and artificial light and illuminating a circle of friezes and panels by the painter Maurice Denis, including scenes from modern operas (*Louise, Fervaal, Ariane et Barbe-Bleu, Pelléas*). The look, for that time, was modern, and compared with the houses the public was used to—like Garnier's Opéra of 1875—it was simple and sparely decorated.

Because of the concrete construction, no pillars were needed to support the balconies, and the acoustics were more resonant than was usual in Parisian theaters. Waist-high partitions separated the boxes; though the panels had no function structurally, they created the sense of privacy that only a box can provide. The hall emphasizes a separation between audience and stage—not a feature of traditional theaters, in which the boxes overlook the stage from the sides. Here the proscenium curtain was set within an open box, which concealed a fifty-two-stop organ; the box, whose floor is the apron of the stage and the opening of the pit, is a unique space that clearly separates performers from spectators. The stage itself was ample: about 100 feet wide, 65 deep, and 135 high.

Naturally the theater was criticized: it was too foreign ("Cosmopolis may feel at home with this façade, but it is not to Paris's taste"); too German ("the Zeppelin of the Avenue Montaigne"); too modern ("dryly solemn, deliberately poor, and thus far from all French tradition"), and so on. The critic for *Art et Décoration*, however, thought it showed "what might be accomplished in our country when the Republic tires at last of Renaissance town halls and neo-Grecian post offices."

The Parisian press took sides, of course. The daily entertainment journal, *Comoedia*, with its beautiful bimonthly illustrated supplement, championed Astruc, the theater, Diaghilev, and the Russian Ballet. Its rival, *La Gazette des Théâtres et des Grands Concerts*, never mentioned the Russian Ballet and spoke of the Théâtre des Champs-Elysées only to cite its orchestral concerts.

When Stravinsky joined the Diaghilev company in 1912 at Monte Carlo, he had already completed most of the music of *Le sacre*. He performed a piano version for Diaghilev and Monteux there ("Before he got very far I was convinced he was raving mad," said Monteux) and later for Debussy and Louis Laloy (editor of *La Grande Revue*) in Paris.

For the dance, Nijinsky's working style involved playing each section, then each phrase, over and over. Nijinsky choreographed the sacrificial dance first, in two rehearsals, for his sister, Nijinska. When she later became pregnant, the role of the sacrificial victim was taken by Maria Piltz, a fine dancer who was as yet little known to the Parisian public. As in *Jeux*, the choreography aimed at doing away with mime, anecdote, and narrative, instead presenting movement in a context of simplicity.

But Stravinsky already had his own detailed plan of movement. He had intended that the dance rhythms correspond little to his musical rhythms ("The dance is almost always in counterpoint to the music," he says in his notes to the transcription of the choreographic notes). Nijinsky was of a different mind; the choreography is full of the same insistent reiterations as the music. The repetition of gesture and action, according to Cocteau, is what caused laughter in the audience; he notes in the movements a "lack of *play,* of counterpoint." It seems clear from reports, however, that the audience began to hoot *before* the curtain went up, so they could hardly have been mocking the gesture and positions of the dancers. Is Cocteau perhaps reporting a later point of view by Stravinsky?

Serge Lifar claimed that Diaghilev had practically invented the choreography himself and used the poor Nijinsky as his mouthpiece, as he had in the previous "Nijinsky" choreographies for *L'après-midi* and *Jeux.* There is no doubt that Diaghilev influenced every aspect of every production, but according to the dancers in *Le sacre* the creation and rehearsal of the choreography were the work of Nijinsky.

There was no skimping on rehearsals for this very difficult ballet, either for the musicians or for the dancers. "Nijinsky began," says Stravinsky, "by demanding such a fantastic number of rehearsals that it was physically impossible to give them to him." More than a hundred rehearsals were held, to the piano accompaniment of Maurice Steinman, nicknamed "Kolossal."

"The dancers had been rehearsing for months," said Stravinsky (document 36). "They knew what they were doing, even though what they were doing often had nothing to do with the music. 'I will count to forty while you play,' Nijinsky would say to me, 'and we will see where we come out.' He could not understand that though we might at some point come out together, this did not necessarily mean we had been together on the way. The dancers followed Nijinsky's beat, too, rather than the musical beat; Nijinsky counted in Russian, of course, and as Russian numbers above ten are polysyllabic—eighteen, for example, is *vosemnádsat*—in fast-tempo movements neither he nor they could keep pace with the music."

The dance was not easy to learn. Hilda Munnings (a dancer who disguised her non-Russian origin by performing as Lydia Sokolova) remembers being added to the show after rehearsals were already in progress: "We had to run about more or less *ad lib,* and stamp to various rhythms [here she is speaking of the Dance of the Earth that closes part one]. We were really allotted no definite place on the stage, and the curtain came down on a stampede of humanity. . . . Some of the girls used to be running around with little bits of paper in their hands, in a panic, quarrelling with each other about whose count was right and whose wrong."

Nijinsky's demands for an un-balletic, characteristic look for the ballet, combined with his tireless energy, took their toll on the dancers. Unhappy both with the difficulty and strangeness of the choreography and with the dismissal of Fokine, they

Anatole Bourman remembers rehearsing the dance:

Nijinsky rehearsed like an inexhaustible demon until he nearly dropped in his tracks. Jumps were no longer completed on toes with slightly flexed knees, but flat-footed and straight-legged in a fashion to preclude the possibility of lightness, and to convey an impression of antediluvian festivity that nearly killed us. With every leap we landed heavily enough to jar every organ in us. Our heads throbbed with pain, leaving us continually with nerves jangled and bodies that ached. Nijinsky had to rehearse with every single group, and danced hour after hour, pounding his feet onto the stage with mighty thumps that must have cost him untold agony, for he had been used to dancing with the lightness and freedom of a feather tossed by the wind.

were in no hurry to cooperate with Nijinsky. Diaghilev engaged Marie Ramberg (later Rambert), from Emile Jaques-Dalcroze's school of eurhythmics, near Dresden, to help the company learn Nijinsky's choreography and to act as an interpreter of his wishes. Given the physical and mental difficulties involved, Ramberg's job of helping to mediate between Nijinsky and the company could not have been easy. Nicknamed "Rhythmitchka," she helped Nijinsky to plan, and the company to learn, the choreography that assigned a movement to almost every musical event.

Stravinky's orchestra ended up being very large. He had originally intended it to be smaller, but encouraged by Diaghilev (who was no doubt feeling expansive because of the enormous sums Astruc was paying for the 1913 season), he increased its size. It included quintuple winds—that is, five of each wind instrument, though the five musicians were often required to double by switching from one instrument to another. Thus, in the course of the ballet there are two piccolos, three flutes, and a bass flute in G (but five players); four oboes and two English horns (five players); E-flat clarinet, piccolo clarinet in D, three clarinets in A and B, and two bass clarinets (five players); four bassoons and two contrabassoons (five players); eight(!) horns, with eight players, two of whom also play tenor tuba for the procession of the Elders; a piccolo trumpet, four trumpets in C, a bass trumpet in E-flat (five players); three trombones and two tubas (sometimes joined by the two tenor tubas played by two of the horn players); and a sizable array of percussion: piccolo timpani, four timpani, bass drum, triangle, antique cymbals, tam-tam, rapc (gucro), tambourine, cymbals (in the hands of five players).

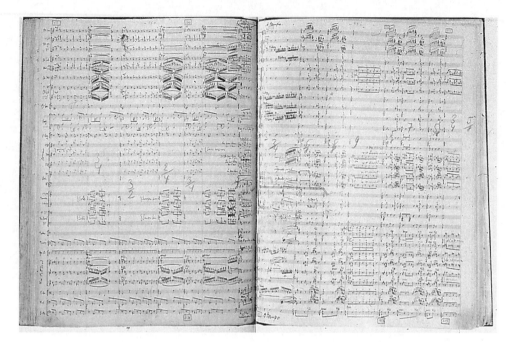

Stravinsky's Score of *Le sacre*

These pages from Stravinsky's autograph score show a passage from the
"Glorification of the Chosen Victim." Stravinsky had an extraordinarily
careful hand, which proved advantageous in such a complex composition.
Large numbers indicating changes in time signature show that this score
was used for conducting.

And of course there were strings: eight desks of first violins (all eight desks are
needed on p. 20 of the score); seven desks of second violins (all needed on p. 77); six
desks of violas (all needed on p. 84); at least seven cellos (five soloists plus "the others" on p. 75); and a famous passage that calls for six solo double basses (p. 7).

This may well be an enormous orchestra, but in a sense it is also chamber
music, in that practically each player, even in the strings, has a unique part. The regular ballet orchestra of eighty-two freelance musicians, drawn mostly from the orchestra of the Concerts Colonne, was supplemented for *Le sacre* by seventeen players engaged especially for that piece, making a total of ninety-nine players.

The orchestra pit, though ample, was small for the enormous orchestra of *Le
sacre*. Stravinsky wanted to expand the seating area by changing the layout of the
theater. To remove the front seats in the auditorium, however, would have required taking welding torches to the brand-new theater, in addition to resulting in a loss of revenue. Ultimately the orchestra succeeded in fitting into the pit, though the seating was
not ideal.

Seventeen orchestral rehearsals were called—far fewer than the dancers had

had but an enormous number nevertheless (*Firebird* had needed nine). They took place in the large, unfinished studio of the Théâtre des Champs-Elysées, which later became a small theater itself (the Comédie des Champs-Elysées). The thorough and businesslike Monteux, writing many years later (document 15), remembered the procedure: "We rehearsed the strings first, then woodwinds and brass, each section of the orchestra alone, except for the percussion instruments which were there all the time. The musicians thought it absolutely crazy, but as they were well paid, their discipline was not too bad! When at last I put the whole thing together, it seemed chaotic but Stravinsky was behind me pointing out little phrases he wished heard. We rehearsed over and over the small difficult parts, and at last we were ready for the ballet."

"When we saw the parts for the first time we couldn't believe they could be played," remembered Louis Speyer, first oboe for *Le sacre* and later a player in the Boston Symphony Orchestra. "We were pleased to know our solfeggio with so many changes of meter, for we never had seen anything so complicated."

Henri Girard, a member of the double-bass section (who joined the Boston Symphony Orchestra in 1920 and remained there until 1966), prepared his reminiscences for Truman Bullard in 1970:

> It is hard to describe the astonishment of the orchestra when we started the first rehearsal. Except for Monteux, who had studied the score with Stravinsky, everybody was confused by the complicated rhythms, atrocious dissonances, and strange sounds to which our ears were not accustomed. Musicians started to stop Monteux, asking if the parts were correctly printed, wanting to know, for example, if "my B-natural is correct as my neighbor is playing B-flat." This went on for a certain time until Monteux said angrily, "Do not stop me asking if you have a mistake. If you have one, I will let you know."

Girard was impressed, as were many other members of the orchestra, by the acuity of Monteux's ear: even now, when *Le sacre* is essentially standard repertory, an out-of-place note is not always noticed. Speyer, too, was impressed with Monteux: "Monteux didn't seem afraid, he kept his admirable calm all the way, asking Stravinsky questions who would bang his cane on the floor, giving the rhythm."

Monteux may have remained calm, but orchestral discipline was not always perfect. "We came to a place," says Girard, "where all the brass instruments, in a gigantic fortissimo, produced such an offending conglomeration that the whole orchestra broke down in a spontaneous nervous laugh and stopped playing. But Stravinsky jumped out of his seat, furious, running to the piano and saying, 'Gentlemen, you do not have to laugh. I know what I wrote,' and he started to play the awful passage, reestablishing order."

Five full rehearsals, including the *répétition générale,* the dress rehearsal, were needed to combine and coordinate the orchestra and the dance. "When the first performance approached," remembers Louis Speyer, "everyone was nervous, more difficulties [arose] between the stage and the music, also Nijinsky, the great dancer, was not as great as a ballet master. The musicians kept their eyes glued to the baton, and the big orchestra filled the pit, but we were far away from one another and it made it more difficult, yet, little by little, we started to learn our parts. Already *Le Sacre* was the talk of the town, so many telling stories making it even bigger and more impossible."

Many of the critics attended the répétition générale, held on May 28, rather than the premiere; this dress rehearsal was meant to be a private event for a privileged few, but it also allowed the critics to publish their reviews in timely fashion and kept prime seats available for sale on opening night. But of course it also means that some of the press reports we have do not describe the first performance itself. Stravinsky was surprised, as he says in his autobiography, that the premiere caused such a furor: "Oddly enough, at the dress rehearsal, to which we had, as usual, invited a number of actors, painters, musicians, writers, and the most cultured representatives of society, everything had gone off peacefully, and I was very far from expecting such an outburst."

May 29, 1913, was the anniversary of the first performance of *L'après-midi d'un faune,* a date Diaghilev had chosen for luck. On that morning an announcement was printed in several papers (including *Le Figaro*), no doubt planted by Diaghilev, which assured readers that a remarkable event was to take place that evening (document 2). *Montjoie!,* an avant-garde review, published an article by "Stravinsky" entitled "What I Wanted to Express in the *Sacre du printemps.*" It was well timed for keeping interest high, and although Stravinsky later denied authorship, it tells much about attitudes toward the ballet and its reception (document 32).

Adolphe Boschot, who had attended the dress rehearsal, wondered how the audience would react: "The public . . . is beginning to realize that it is being made fun of, and it is protesting. . . . Will the public, the supreme judge, have noticed? will they have understood they have the right to laugh? will they be enraged? or will they have found this marvelously admirable?"

The cost of seats was just about double those of normal ballet evenings, standard practice for events including a first performance. Prices ranged from a high of forty francs, for the loges and the *fauteuils de corbeille* (the armchairs at the front of the balcony), down to two francs for seating at the top of the theater. The entire house had been sold, almost all through subscription to the Russian season. May 29 was unseasonably hot (eighty-five degrees Fahrenheit) and humid for Paris; even the evening remained sultry. The performance began at 8:45 sharp.

By virtue of their subscriptions, the audience for the premiere of *Le sacre* had seen *Jeux* and *Boris,* and there is every evidence that some were prepared for, and expecting, a scandal. Most of the fashionable members of the audience, however, showed up to see Karsavina and Nijinsky dance, to see beautiful costumes by Bakst, and to hear

Russian Romantic music (there was none of this in *Le sacre*). They were upper-class Parisians, tourists, and members of the artistic élite. Cocteau described them (document 23) with a literary sweep: "To a practiced eye, all the material needed for a scandal is assembled there; a fashionable audience, low-cut dresses, tricked out in pearls, egret and ostrich feathers; and side by side with tails and tulle, the sack suits, headbands, showy rags of that race of esthetes who acclaim, right or wrong, anything that is new because of their hatred of the boxes (whose incompetent acclamations are more intolerable than the sincere hisses of the former). And in addition to fevered musicians, a few sheep of Panurge caught between fashionable opinion and the credit owed to the *Ballet Russe*."

A great many of the opening-night crowd wrote about their experience: they include Astruc, Ravel, Frederick Delius, Romola Nijinsky, Misia Sert, Marie Rambert, Bronislava Nijinska, Cocteau, Carl Van Vechten, and Valentine Gross-Hugo. Others, like Gertrude Stein, have implied that they were present, when in fact they attended a different performance—much like the critics who reviewed the dress rehearsal as though they had been at the opening.

Valentine Gross-Hugo, who attended all four Paris performances, and whose memory might be cumulative, remembers the reactions of many in the audience: the composer Maurice Delage, "garnet-red with indignation"; Ravel "aggressive as a small fighting cock"; the poet Léon-Paul Fargue, "roaring vengeful epithets towards the hissing boxes." The report that Saint-Saëns walked out, says Stravinsky, is impossible because he wasn't there.

Debussy's *Jeux*, which had premiered two weeks earlier, had set the tone for the audience. It involved a sensual trio of Nijinsky with two women. Nijinsky leaps onto the stage in pursuit of a bouncing tennis ball, followed by the two female dancers, all with tennis racquets. The ballet—perhaps the first in modern dress—ends with a suggestive triple embrace. This elicited hissing and laughter. Critics said Diaghilev and Nijinsky were being purposefully scandalous. They were probably right.

It may be that Paris was beginning to tire of the novelty of the Diaghilev Ballet. Before the season, the critic Emile Vuillermoz wrote, "Once again the Northern Barbarians come to show us Latins their superior instinct over our culture, and to humiliate the Occident with all the subtle splendor of Oriental wisdom. We are docilely going to take our annual lessons in painting, decorative art, choreography, staging and orchestration."

Some in the audience may have been dismayed, too, at the dismissal of Fokine and chose *Sacre* as the moment to voice their protest. Adolphe Jullien, for one, wrote in the *Journal des Débats:* "Never was more forcefully demonstrated the influences which a choreographer, rich or poor in ideas, can exercise upon a composer with whom he collaborates."

The audience, in short, was prepared for excitement.

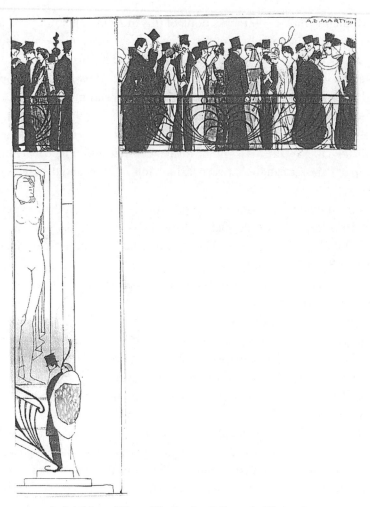

André-Edouard Marty, *The Russian Ballet at the Théâtre des Champs-Elysées,* 1913

A fashionable Parisian audience assembles in the newest and most fashionable theater to see the fashionable Ballets Russes; they are depicted in the *Gazette du Bon Ton,* a new magazine of the period.

The Rite Performed

Le sacre was preceded and followed by proven crowd-pleasers of the Diaghilev Ballet. The program provided something for everybody, but of course Diaghilev, the born showman, also put *Le sacre* in its most outré context.

The program began with *Les sylphides,* the company's 1909 "rêverie romantique," with music by Chopin and decors by Alexandre Benois and choreography by

Fokine; in this Nijinsky performed a waltz with Karsavina and other solos. He then put on his frock coat so that he could appear for a curtain call as choreographer of the next ballet, *Le sacre.* The intermission following *Le sacre,* which has two acts, gave Nijinsky time to change again. Next he danced, again with Karsavina, in *Le spectre de la rose,* which contains the famous solo in which he floats through a window and enchants a sleeping maiden. The evening concluded with the Polovtsian dances from Borodin's *Prince Igor,* another Diaghilev chestnut, featuring Adolphe Bolm, the entire corps, and the chorus of the Imperial Opera of St. Petersburg.

There are many descriptions of the events that took place before, during, or after this particular performance, but nothing evokes the general character of Diaghilev's performances like Cyril Beaumont's description of the company backstage:

> The visitor who passes behind the stage some time before the performance is due to begin will find the opening scene set, but all is dark save for a tiny pilot lamp which sheds an eerie glow. Everything is as depressing and as cold as though you had stepped at night into an empty warehouse. Nothing seems more incredible than that a performance would ever take place. . . .
>
> As the zero hour approaches there are signs of activity. Stagehands assemble under the direction of the carpenter. The electrician switches on a few lamps, while some of his men drag out portable "floods" with their lengths of heavy cable which writhe over the boards like so many snakes. There is a tinkle of metal as the lids of

The Program for the Evening, Pages 1 and 2

These two pages of the four-page insert provide details of the first
performance of *Le sacre du printemps*. The program began with the classic
Les sylphides, set to music of Chopin. Note that Nijinsky performed a
mazurka. (See document 5.)

small square traps in the stage are jerked open and the cables plugged
in.

The tall spare silhouette of the company's *régisseur*, Grigoriev,
appears near the prompt corner. He strolls on to the stage and in-
spects the setting of the scenery. If there are properties to be used, he
checks them over. The electrician gives his men their orders and now
some lamps are dimmed, and others brought up, until the requirements of the lighting plot are fulfilled. Grigoriev glances at his wrist-
watch, peeps unseen into the auditorium, and, finding the majority of
the spectators seated and expectant, gives the signal . . . then flashes
another warning to the conductor at his desk in the orchestra-pit,
whereupon the overture begins.

Meanwhile, the dancers begin to arrive in ones and twos and little
groups, some chatting, some laughing, some with a serious look of
concentration on their faces. Some smooth the folds of their dresses,
some pull up their tights, some indulge in a few *échappées* and *change-*

ments to work in a new pair of shoes. Most of them take the opportunity to "warm up", that is to say, to execute some of the traditional exercises to make the muscles supple and elastic, holding on to a vertical batten, a piece of scenery, or a fixed ladder for support. To attempt to dance without such preliminaries might induce muscular cramp or strain a tendon. Some dancers prefer to "warm up" in their dressing-rooms, others choose the stage.

In odd corners you may come across a dancer rehearsing a phrase of steps. Suddenly a pair of soloists bound on to the stage to put the final touches to their *pas de deux,* which is rehearsed with an astounding sense of detachment, as though they had a whole month before them.

As the overture draws to its climax, the dancers take up their positions on the stage or in the wings, as the case may be, ready to dance their respective roles. It might be thought that at the first note of the overture every dancer was keyed up, waiting for the curtain to rise. Far from it, they are often strolling about the stage, chatting or comparing notes, as if they were taking a walk in a park. . . . Only at the very last moment, when it seems that nothing can prevent their discovery by the audience, do they swiftly vacate the stage and take up their positions for their entrance.

The company danced *Les sylphides* in classic style, to Chopin's beautiful music: this was surely intended to set Nijinsky's choreography for *Le sacre* into strong relief. The same magnificent Russian dancers who performed in *Les sylphides* came on again for *Le sacre.* They had rehearsed at great length and were virtuosi; nobody ever doubted that they performed well the task they were set by Nijinsky.

Nijinsky was actively involved in pushing beyond tradition in dance and had already made a name for himself—though perhaps not a very good one—as a choreographer. Now he presented the primitive and the nonrefined, seeking to negate the basic elements of classical ballet. Among the many distinctive postures called for in this ballet, the dancers are required to turn their toes not out but in, keeping the knees together, to jump on straight legs, and to repeat many of the same motions over and over, all trademarks that immediately identify *Le sacre*—and are easily mocked. The recent reconstruction by Millicent Hodson for the Joffrey Ballet has done much to give us an idea of how the dancing must have appeared.

Adolphe Boschot (document 7) described the dancing in unflattering terms:

Imagine people tricked out in the most garish colors, pointed bonnets and bathrobes, animal skins or purple tunics, gesticulating like people possessed, who repeat the same gesture a hundred times: they stamp in place, they stamp, they stamp, they stamp, and they stamp. . . . Suddenly: they break in two and salute. And they stamp, they stamp, they stamp. . . . Suddenly: a little old woman falls down headfirst and shows us her underskirts. . . . And they stamp, they stamp. . . .

And then there are groups that develop close-order drill. The dancers are up against each other, packed like sardines, and all their charming heads fall onto their right shoulders, all congealed in this contorted pose by a unanimous crick in the neck. . . .

In the second act, here is a delicious dancer, Mademoiselle Piltz. The choreographer destroys her at will: he deforms her legs by making her stand still with her toes turned in as far as possible. It's hideous. . . . And later, when she does move, she must hold her head in both hands, and glue it to her shoulder, as if to show that she suffers from a terrible toothache combined with that same crick in the neck which is the signature of the "poet-choreographer."

Obviously, all this can be justified: what that is is prehistoric dance. The uglier and more deformed it is, the more prehistoric.

Prehistoric, perhaps: most observers assumed this to be authenticated by Roerich's participation ("Un ballet sociologique," said Jacques Rivière). Not everybody was convinced, however. Pierre Lalo (son of the composer Edouard), wrote in *Le Temps:* "As to prehistoric times, I really have no objection; I just marvel that the spectators at the Théâtre des Champs-Elysées have such a familiarity with those times that they recognize its image instantly, and can affirm unhesitatingly that things were that way, and not this; and I'd like to ask them what a certain grande dame of the eighteenth century asked her husband, on a different subject: 'How does it happen, Monsieur, that you are so sure about these things?'"

Paintings by Roerich served as backdrops for the two tableaux; a third painting was lowered between the two parts. Representing day and night, grove and glade, they set a brightly colored scene far different from the Romantic ruined castle seen at a distance in *Les sylphides*. Cyril Beaumont remembered the settings and costumes as he saw them in London: "The settings were suited to the required mood—dreary, half savage, half mystical landscapes, in the painting of which Roehrich is unequalled. The colours of the costumes, if I remember correctly, were flaxen and bright scarlet. The women wore simple smocks decorated at the hem with bands of simple designs in colour; their legs were wrapped in strips of cloth, cross-gartered, and on their feet they wore bast shoes. Their hair was twisted into long, straggling pigtails; their cheeks were crudely daubed with red. The men wore a shorter smock, similar leg-coverings, and, I think, a pointed cap of some animal's skin."

Diaghilev expected trouble, of course, and to some extent he wanted it. He had asked Monteux and the dancers to persevere to the end, regardless of what happened.

Six Women Dancers in *Le sacre*, from *The Sketch*, 1913

This studio photograph of members of the original cast was superimposed on
a new background for publication in England. It shows not only the
"primitive" costumes and makeup but the characteristic poses adopted by the
dancers. The second dancer from the left is Marie Rambert, who helped
Nijinsky teach the choreography.

"He entreated the dancers," says Grigoriev, "to keep calm and carry on, and asked
Monteux on no account to let the orchestra cease playing. 'Whatever happens,' he said,
'the ballet must be performed to the end.'"

In the darkened theater, with everyone primed for scandal, the curtain is down
and the prelude begins with a single instrument. Louis Speyer: "Already the introduction was a surprise, a bassoon in that register, we all looked and even some composers
present asked if it was a saxophone. Abdon Laus, who later became the first bassoon of
the Boston Symphony Orchestra, under Monteux, was the first to attack this difficult
solo; he had to find fingerings, which was a terrible experience. Today any good player
knows this solo."

The curtain rose shortly before the famous repeated chords that mark the start
of the dancing. But by then trouble had started. The noise began halfway through the
prelude, say Monteux and Casella. Apparently there were rival camps: not only opposition, but a group of supporters. Two writers record that some spectators had brought
whistles with them: they were expecting to need them.

Stravinsky himself twice described the first performance and his feelings. Both
reports were written considerably after the fact; both must be a mixture of accurate rec-

ollection, literary skill, and the possibly changed attitudes and intentions of a world-famous composer.

In his autobiography, published at twenty years' distance, he remembers the premiere this way (document 33):

> As for the actual performance, I am not in a position to judge, as I left the auditorium at the first bars of the prelude, which had at once evoked derisive laughter. I was disgusted. These demonstrations, at first isolated, soon became general, provoking counter-demonstrations and very quickly developing into a terrific uproar. During the whole performance I was at Nijinsky's side in the wings. He was standing on a chair, screaming "sixteen, seventeen, eighteen"—they had their own method of counting to keep time. Naturally the poor dancers could hear nothing by reason of the row in the auditorium and the sound of their own dance steps. I had to hold Nijinsky by his clothes, for he was furious, and ready to dash on to the stage at any moment and create a scandal. Diaghileff kept ordering the electricians to turn the lights on or off, hoping in that way to put a stop to the noise. That is all I can re-member about that first performance.

Stravinsky's commentary of 1962 provides essentially the same recollections, in a more literary style (document 36):

> Mild protests against the music could be heard from the very begin-ning of the performance. Then, when the curtain opened on the group of knock-kneed and long-braided Lolitas jumping up and down (Danse des adolescentes), the storm broke. Cries of "Ta gueule" came from behind me. I heard Florent Schmitt shout "Taisez-vous garces du seizième"; the "garces" of the sixteenth arrondisse-ment were, of course, the most elegant ladies in Paris. The uproar continued, however, and a few minutes later I left the hall in a rage; I was sitting on the right near the orchestra, and I remember slamming the door. I have never again been that angry. The music was so famil-iar to me; I loved it, and I could not understand why people who had not yet heard it wanted to protest in advance. I arrived in a fury back-stage, where I saw Diaghilev flicking the house lights in a last effort to quiet the hall. For the rest of the performance I stood in the wings be-hind Nijinsky holding the tails of his *frac,* while he stood on a chair shouting numbers to the dancers, like a coxswain.

It is possible, of course, perhaps even likely, that Nijinsky would have shouted numbers regardless of the noise; the choreography was difficult, and so was the music,

Drawing of Marie Piltz in the Sacrificial Dance, by Valentine Gross-Hugo, from *Montjoie!* 1913

Published in June 1913, Valentine Gross-Hugo's sketches attempt to match Marie Piltz's motions with specific moments in the score. André Levinson recalled that Marie Piltz "fac[ed] calmly a hooting audience whose violence completely drowned out the orchestra. She seemed to dream, her knees turned inward, the heels pointing out—inert. A sudden spasm shook her body out of its corpse-like rigor. At the fierce onward thrust of the rhythm she trembled in ecstatic, irregular jerks."

and his cues would surely have helped the dancers remember their moves and keep together.

Jean Cocteau, too, notes that "the audience played the role it had to play; it immediately rebelled. It laughed, scoffed, whistled, cat-called, and perhaps might have got tired in the long run if the mob of the esthetes and a few musicians in their excessive zeal had not insulted and even jostled the people in the boxes. The uproar degenerated into a free-for-all."

Monteux noted that "the audience remained quiet for the first two minutes. Then came boos and cat-calls from the gallery, soon after from the lower floors. Neighbors began to hit each other over the head with fists, canes or whatever came to hand. Soon this anger was concentrated against the dancers, and then, more particularly, against the orchestra, the direct perpetrator of the musical crime. Everything available was tossed in our direction, but we continued to play on. The end of the performance was greeted by the arrival of gendarmes. Strawinsky had disappeared through a window backstage, to wander disconsolately along the streets of Paris."

Everybody agrees, however, that the performance did not stop, though the noise was at times deafening. Monteux kept going: "I decided to keep the orchestra together, at any cost, in case of a lull in the hubbub. I did, and we played it to the end absolutely as we had rehearsed it in the peace of an empty theater." Diaghilev ("I beg you, let the show finish!") and Astruc ("Listen first: you can whistle later!") are both reported to have shouted for quiet: whether they did so during the prelude is not clear.

Diaghilev or Astruc (reports vary) ordered the house lights turned on, perhaps between scenes. Grigoriev says this was so the police could arrest or eject troublemakers. Carl Van Vechten says that "some forty of the protestants were forced out of the theatre, but that did not quell the disturbance"; was it the police that did the ejecting, or the crowd? Grigoriev, of course, was normally backstage, so the presence of the police in the house must have been a rumor (or a wish!). Also uncorroborated is Girard's report that Astruc appeared before the curtain after part one to offer a refund.

The second part did take place, and apparently there was reasonable quiet for the *danse sacrale* (though Carl Van Vechten remembers differently). Perhaps everybody recognized that Marie Piltz's sacrificial dance, essentially the only solo in the entire score, would be worth watching.

Between the time that Marie Piltz is chosen for sacrifice and the moment that she begins her dance, she stands in one pose, trembling while the ceremonies go on around her. Mary Clarke tells one version of an often repeated story: "She stood on the stage, her chin leaning on her folded hands, and just trembling for some nineteen bars of music. Someone called 'Un docteur!' another, 'Un dentiste!' Then, 'Deux dentistes!' It seemed that pandemonium would prevail, but the power of the dance which Nijinsky had composed for Piltz communicated itself to the spectators; they became silent and shared for a little while the torment and the ecstasy of the girl singled out for sacrifice."

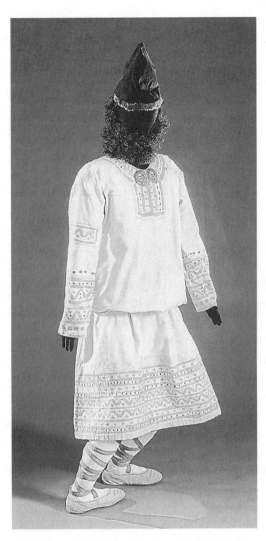

Nicholas Roerich's Costume for One of the Elders

This original costume, which has been preserved in the Wadsworth Atheneum, features painted bands of orange and gold at the neck, sleeves, and hem. Long purple ribbons are wrapped around the legs.

It was a remarkable dance. André Levinson described it later: "Then in this magic circle, the victim until that moment motionless, wan under her white fillet, begins the death dance. And I recall Marie Piltz facing calmly a hooting audience whose violence completely drowned out the orchestra. She seemed to dream, her knees turned inward, the heels pointing out—inert. A sudden spasm shook her body out of its corpse-like rigor. At the fierce onward thrust of the rhythm she trembled in ecstatic, irregular jerks."

Many tales have been told about the premiere, some so good that they may have been embroidered a bit. The curtain in the second act goes up on the circle of "knock-kneed and long-braided Lolitas," their cheeks painted and their hands clasped as in prayer and held against sides of their faces. Florent Schmitt shouted, "Down with the whores of the 16th arondissement" (a reference to the painted cheeks); and someone else, "They are ripe for colonization!" (what hopeless primitives compared with the modern imperialist French). The venerable if overly made-up countess Marie de Pourtalès is reported to have said, "This is the first time in sixty years that anyone has dared to make fun of me!" (more painted cheeks). Romola Nijinsky claims that a duel was fought the next morning; a society lady is said to have spat in a fellow spectator's face. And so on.

At the close of the thirty-four-minute ballet, applause as well as shouting broke out. Indeed, there were four or five curtain calls—including a well-deserved one for Monteux and his band—before the evening continued.

There were five further performances of *Le sacre*, the last on June 13. Among those attending the second performance were Stéphane Mallarmé, Gertrude Stein and Alice Toklas, and the composer Giacomo Puccini. The company then traveled to England, where *Le sacre* was given a few additional performances. After that, the score was almost immediately revived as a concert piece, again under Monteux, and in 1920 Diaghilev revived the ballet, this time with choreography by Massine. But the Nijinsky choreography, so striking, so outrageous, so frail as to its preservation, disappeared without a trace until the attempts at reconstruction by the Joffrey Ballet in 1987.

Although some reviews were written before the premiere, even those reviewers who attended the opening and published on May 31 had little time for reflection. Henri Quittard, in *Le Figaro* of May 31 (document 8), wrote as though he had been there: "Here is a strange spectacle," he begins, "of a laborious and puerile barbarity, which the audience of the Champs-Elysées did not respect." Quittard goes on to describe the dance and the music in terms familiar to those who write and read negative criticism, giving the impression that Stravinsky was influenced by Nijinsky's ideas for the choreography. He ends, "*Le Sacre du Printemps* was received rather badly yesterday, and the audience could not restrain its laughter. It would have been in good taste, then, for those who thought differently—and they were not many—to spare the authors a curtain call whose comic impertinence was obvious to all." But he does not describe the noise that drowned out the orchestra, so perhaps he was not present.

Comoedia, perhaps the leading theatrical journal, published a long evaluation by three authors (document 9) but had little to say about the performance. Gustave de Pawlowski, like many, believed he was seeing something authentically "primitive," but he argued that a work of art cannot be based on ugliness (this is still a familiar phrase) and wished that Nijinsky had danced. And Louis Vuillemin describes what happens when an audience arrives with its opinions already formed: "The curtain goes up—no, even before it goes up—there are murmurs, cries of 'Oh!', they sing, they whisper, they whistle. They applaud, they yell 'Bravo!' they yelp, they cheer. They revile it, they exalt it. And voilà, the first performance of *Le sacre du printemps.*"

The noise was certainly noticed by Emile Raulin, writing in the magazine *Les Marges:* "These are the superficial remarks that I can report from a single performance of this work, which I could barely hear, on account of the tumult of an overexcited audience. Couldn't we ask M. Astruc, next year, to set aside one performance for well-intentioned spectators? It would obviously be difficult to eliminate from a public theatre everybody who is ill-bred. We could at least propose to evict the female element."

Those who praised and those who disapproved have a few elements in common. Everybody seems to have understood that they were watching something primitive, something Russian, which could be expected to differ from what a fashionable audience was used to ("Evidently all this is defensible; it is prehistoric dance. The more ugly and deformed it is the more prehistoric"). The question really was whether such representations of the activities of another culture could reasonably be regarded as art.

Pierre Lalo, writing in *Le Temps*:

I remember that, on the evening of the first performance, finding myself in the balcony of the Théâtre des Champs-Elysées, I was placed under a loge full of elegant and charming persons, whose joking remarks, joyous prattling, the remarks shouted with loud high voices, and finally high convulsive laughter, made a racket similar to that that deafens one on going into a bird-house; the men who accompanied them did their best to second them by massive vociferations, to which they suddenly added, when their indignation grew too strong, the strident noise one gets by blowing through a key. But I had at my left a group of esthetes in whose soul the *Sacre du Printemps* aroused a frenetic enthusiasm, a sort of ejaculatory delirium, and who riposted incessantly to the occupants of the loge with admiring interjections, by furious "Brââvo!," and with the rolling fire of their clapping hands; one of them, furnished with a voice like that of a horse, whinnied from time to time, but without addressing anyone in particular, "Away with you!," whose rending vibrations were prolonged throughout the hall. Who was better, Lord, the defenders of *Le Sacre du Printemps* or its adversaries? Surely neither the ones nor the others; and only the horse-voiced esthete was right: all those people should have been ejected, and he first of all.

Exaggerated elements were criticized: in the choreography, the odd postures and the repetitive motions; in the music, the same repetitions, the melodies played in parallel dissonant intervals, and the strange orchestration emphasizing the winds and percussion. But even the music was seen as a part of the cultural conception. As Florent Schmitt put it (document 10):

> M. Igor Strawinsky's music, by its frenetic agitation; by the senseless whirl of its hallucinating rhythms; by its aggregations of harmonies beyond any convention or analysis, of an aggressive hardness that no one—not even M. Richard Strauss—had dared until now; by the obsessive insistence of its themes, their savor and their strangeness; by seeking the most paradoxical sonorities, daring combinations of tim-

bres, systematic use of extreme instrumental ranges; by its tropical orchestration, iridescent and of an unbelievable sumptuosity; in sum, by
an excess, an unheard-of luxuriance of refinement and preciosity, the
music of M. Igor Strawinsky achieves this unexpected—but intentional—result, that it gives us the impression of the darkest barbarity.

Critics writing about the audience generally mentioned shouts and catcalls,
but they also noted that the audience laughed at the performance. Laughter is a curious
reaction, because there was nothing whatever funny about the *intention* of the performance; there were no jokes on stage. If the audience laughed at what was intended
seriously, it did so out of a sense of inappropriateness, from a lack of understanding,
from a sense, as several critics suggested, that it was being mocked. Many writers reacted by counterattacking the audience, accusing them of being snobbish, ill-bred,
badly informed socialites who were happy only with more of what they were used to.

The critics regretted that the combination of deadlines and the uproar in the
hall made it difficult for them to do what after all was their job: to report on the work
and its performance. Everybody acknowledged that the dancers and the musicians did
their parts superbly. Many felt that what they had heard and seen was far different from
what they would have predicted from Nijinsky and Stravinsky; and many were careful
to leave room for the possibility that the event might mark the beginnings of something
new and influential.

Le sacre as Collaboration

Le sacre is such an important piece of music, with such a long critical history,
that it is often easy to forget that what became a classic piece of concert music was originally a theater piece. Stravinsky had decades in which to contemplate his composition,
and his successive statements reflect changing times and attitudes to the piece. Over
time, two essential points seem to have changed; both involve the relation of music to
the other arts.

In the first place, the question of whether the music was created independent
of the scheme for the ballet has been answered differently at different times. Stravinsky's
original conception arose in the context of the theater and in collaboration with
Roerich, though later Stravinsky overlooked this. "Sooner or later we will have to tell
him [Diaghilev] about the 'Great Sacrifice,'" wrote Stravinsky to Roerich in June 1910.
In a letter to a Russian editor in December 1912, and in his 1936 autobiography, Stravinsky says he had a dream of pagan rites in which "sage elders, seated in a circle, watched
a young girl dance herself to death." He interrupted work on *Sacre* to write a *Konzertstück*: *Petrushka*. It was only during a second stage, he says, that he needed the help of
Roerich in designing a scenario for *Le sacre;* the two developed a sequence of the

The Sage

At the climactic moment of the first act, the oldest and wisest of the tribe kisses the earth. It is a mime role, requiring little in the way of dancing. This 1913 photograph may show the original Sage, listed in the program as "M. Voronizow"; he is apparently not a dancer, since this name appears nowhere else in the program.

scenes, and then Stravinsky began to compose. The story therefore came before the music, according to this version; the music was conceived to accompany the scenario.

But in a 1920 interview, Stravinsky says that the music came before the ballet, and not from the idea. "But be aware that this idea comes from the music and not the music from the idea. I wrote a work that was architectonic, not anecdotal."

Richard Taruskin has marshaled a great deal of evidence, consisting of correspondence between Stravinsky and Roerich and of analogies between the scenario and actual accounts of Slavic and other rituals, indicating clearly that the scenario is essentially Roerich's and that Stravinsky followed it in composing the music.

Stravinsky also changed his mind about Nijinsky's choreography. At first he was delighted with Nijinsky and his choreography, and with the success (and the scandal) of the *Sacre*. During the rehearsals (in December 1912) he wrote to a Russian editor: "Nijinsky directs it with passionate zeal and with complete self-effacement." He is reported in 1916 to have commented, on seeing the first rehearsals, that "the dance that had been evolved was the most perfectly beautiful" that he had ever seen. And in the article in *Montjoie!* (whose authorship Stravinsky later denied; document 32), he says. "I am glad to have found in M. Nijinsky the ideal collaborator for movement." In an interview given perhaps the day after the premiere (document 31), Stravinsky said, "They have criticized M. Nijinsky's staging and said that it seemed foreign to the music. They were wrong. Nijinsky is an admirable artist. He is capable of renewing the art of ballet. We never for a second failed to be in absolute communion of thought. Later you will see what he will do. He is not just a marvelous dancer, he is capable of creating, of innovating, and his part in the collaboration on *The Rite of Spring* was fruitful."

Soon afterward, however, Stravinsky dissociated himself from Nijinsky's choreography. This may simply have involved a change of mind, on longer reflection, but it may also have been related to the success that *Le sacre* soon achieved as a concert piece in its own right. As a symphonic piece, it would be best if viewed as a work independent of a constellation of other arts for its life. As early as the 1936 autobiography, Stravinsky wrote: "What the choreography expressed was a very labored and barren effort rather than a plastic realization flowing simply and naturally from what the music demanded. How far it all was from what I had desired! . . . Nijinsky was incapable of giving intelligible form to its essence, and complicated it either by clumsiness or lack of understanding."

Curiously inconsistent with his later published views of Nijinsky's choreography is Stravinsky's 1967 remark to Yuri Grigorovich, as reported by Nijinska: "Of all the interpretations of *Sacre* that I have seen, I consider Nijinsky's the best." But this remark, of course, makes *Le sacre* a creation of Stravinsky, which other artists (such as the original collaborators, Roerich, Nijinsky, and Diaghilev) "interpreted" in a second and derivative stage of creativity.

But in 1913 Stravinsky was aware that he was taking part in an artistic collaboration. Diaghilev's enterprise allowed for the creation of a performance to which Stravinsky, Roerich, and Nijinsky all added artistic elements. Although these were viewed by the thirty-odd reviewers in the press with a variety of opinions, and although some of the reviewers spoke individually of the music, the sets, and the choreography, it seems to have been generally understood that this was a theater piece, an event, a performance, in which all the elements worked together. Jacques Rivière of the influential *Nouvelle Revue Française* acknowledged this unity in his long essay published in August 1913: "Who is the author of *Le sacre du printemps?* Who did that? Nijinsky, Stravinsky, or Roerich? That preliminary question which we cannot evade makes no sense except for occidentals like ourselves. For us everything is individual; a strong characteristic work always bears the mark of a single mind. It is not so with the Russians."

After the performance Stravinsky, Nijinsky, and Diaghilev dined together in a restaurant, one of the many in Paris that stayed open late; perhaps it was Larue's—and perhaps it was the night Proust was there.

Cocteau remembered the rest of the evening (document 23): "At two o'clock in the morning, Stravinsky, Nijinsky, Diaghilev and myself piled into a cab and were driven to the Bois de Boulogne. We kept silent; the night was cool and clear. The odor of the acacias told us we had reached the first trees. Coming to the lakes, Diaghilev, bundled up in opossum, began mumbling in Russian. I could feel Stravinsky and Nijinsky listening attentively and as the coachman lighted his lantern I saw tears on the impresario's face. . . . You can't imagine the gentleness and the nostalgia of these men, and no matter what Diaghilev may have done later, I shall never forget, in that cab, his great tear-stained face as he recited Pushkin in the Bois de Boulogne."

Drawing of Stravinsky Playing *Le sacre du printemps,* by Jean Cocteau, 1913

A dazzling literary and cultural figure, Cocteau was to be an important
collaborator of Diaghilev and Stravinsky and had a lot to say about the
premiere of *Le sacre* (see document 23). He wrote that *Le sacre* was
"impregnated with savage pathos, with earth in the throes of birth, noises of
farm and camp, little melodies that come from the depths of the centuries, the
panting of cattle, deep convulsions, prehistoric georgics."

Stravinsky never forgot it either, because he never remembered it: according to
him, the evening did not go at all like that. "After the 'performance' we were excited,
angry, disgusted, and . . . happy. I went with Diaghilev and Nijinsky to a restaurant. So
far from weeping and reciting Pushkin in the Bois de Boulogne as the legend is, Diaghilev's only comment was, 'Exactly what I wanted.' He certainly looked contented."
It was the next day that Stravinsky ate the oysters that disagreed with him so seriously.
The June 29 issue of *Le Cri de Paris* reported: "Stravinsky, the henceforth famous composer of *Le sacre du printemps* has been struck with an attack of typhoid fever. The reception given to his score by Parisians can only have worsened his condition. In those
moments of lucidity which the fever allows him, he whispers, 'They hissed Wagner at
forty-five years of age. I am only thirty-five. I too shall witness my triumph before I die.'"

Documents: Stravinsky, *Le sacre du printemps*

Background and Personalities

1. Performances at the Théâtre des Champs-Elysées, May 15–29, 1913 (asterisks indicate ballets in which Nijinsky performed):

Thursday, May 15, Ballets Russes, Premières représentations
    Stravinsky: *L'oiseau de feu*
    Debussy: *Jeux* (première)*
    Rimsky-Korsakov: *Shéhérezade**

Friday, May 16, Théâtre des Champs-Elysées, Opéra et Ballet
    Fauré: *Pénélope* 8 h.
    Debussy: *Nocturnes* 11 h.

Saturday, May 17, Ballets Russes
    Stravinsky: *L'oiseau de feu*
    Debussy: *L'après-midi d'un faune**
    Weber: *Le spectre de la rose**
    Borodin: Danses de *Prince Igor*

Sunday, May 18, Théâtre des Champs-Elysées, Opéra et Ballet
    Fauré: *Pénélope* 8 h.
    Debussy: *Nocturnes* 11 h.

Monday, May 19, Ballets Russes
    Stravinsky: *L'oiseau de feu*
    Debussy: *Jeux**
    Chopin: *Les sylphides**
    Borodin: Danses de *Prince Igor*

Tuesday, May 20, RELACHE (répétition générale de *Boris Godounov*)

Wednesday, May 21, Théâtre des Champs-Elysées, Opéra et Ballet
    Fauré: *Pénélope* 8 h.
    Debussy: *Nocturnes* 11 h.

Thursday, May 22, Première représentation
    Moussorgsky: *Boris Godounov*

Friday, May 23, Ballets Russes
    Stravinsky: *L'oiseau de feu*
    Debussy: *L'après-midi d'un faune**
    Rimsky-Korsakov: *Shéhérezade*
    Weber: *Le spectre de la rose** [added by popular demand]

Saturday, May 24, Moussorgsky: *Boris Godounov*

Sunday, May 25, Théâtre des Champs-Elysées, Opéra et Ballet
    Fauré: *Pénélope* 8 h.
    Debussy: *Nocturnes* 11 h.

Monday, May 26, Ballets Russes
    Rimsky-Korsakov: *Shéhérezade**

Debussy: *Jeux* *
Weber: *Le spectre de la rose* *
Borodin: Danses de *Prince Igor*
Tuesday, May 27, Moussorgsky, *Boris Godounov*
Wednesday, May 28, RELACHE (répétition générale du *Sacre du printemps*)
Thursday, May 29, Ballets Russes
Chopin: *Les sylphides* *
Stravinsky: *Le sacre du printemps* (première)
Weber: *Le spectre de la rose* *
Borodin: Danses de *Prince Igor*
[Adapted from Truman Bullard, "The First Performance of Igor Stravinsky's 'Sacre du Printemps,'" 3 vols. (Ph.D. diss., Eastman School of Music, University of Rochester, 1971), 1:124–25]

2. The announcement, a sort of press release, that was printed in several newspapers on the morning of the performance:

Le sacre du printemps, which the Russian Ballet will perform for the first time tonight at the theatre of the Champs-Elysées, is the most surprising realization that the admirable troupe of M. Serge de Diaghilew has ever attempted. It is the evocation of the first gestures of pagan Russia evoked by the triple vision of Strawinsky, poet and musician, of Nicolas Roerich, poet and painter, and of Nijinsky, poet and choreographer.

One will find there the strongly stylized characteristic attitudes of the Slavic race with an awareness of the beauty of the prehistoric period.

The prodigious Russian dancers were the only ones capable of expressing these stammerings of a semi-savage humanity, of composing these frenetic human clusters wrenched incessantly by the most astonishing polyrhythm ever to come from the mind of a musician. There is truly a new thrill which will surely raise passionate discussions, but which will leave all true artists with an unforgettable impression.

["Le sacre du printemps," *Le Figaro,* May 29, 1913]

3. Sergei Grigoriev and the Ballet Russes:

There is another name which can be found on every programme of the Diaghilev Company during its twenty years of existence, that of his *régisseur,* Grigoriev. . . .

[Sergei Leonidovich Grigoriev] was Diaghilev's right hand and, from what I have seen of him, I should say that no man was better served. His responsibilities were so vast and so all-embracing as to be almost illimitable. . . .

He watched all the rehearsals and knew at once when a movement had been omitted or badly executed. He inspected the materials of which the costumes were made. He saw the lighting rehearsals, and, if the company appeared at a theatre where the lighting equipment was indifferent, he had to devise means to obtain the best results possible. He knew the music cues for the curtain to rise and fall, and those for the various dancers to make their entrance, and the *tempo* at which each number should be played. He knew how each costume had to be worn and the type of make-up required. He knew how each scene had to be set. . . .

He was always on the stage well in advance of the performance, ready to consider any of the innumerable requests that might arise—a plea to be excused on a certain rehearsal, a request for an advance of salary, and so on. . . .

A few moments before the performance was due to begin he was at his post in the prompt corner, his cold gaze directed on every phase of the performance. If he thought the ballet were well rehearsed he would cross the stage behind the back-cloth, slip through the pass door, and watch the ballet from the auditorium, noting the lighting and any omission on the part of the dancers. A little while before the curtain was due to fall, he would be back at his post to regulate the number of curtain calls to be given, and when the principals should make their final triumphant appearance before the now lowered curtain, the central fold of which would be drawn back for the dancers to pass through.

[Cyril W. Beaumont, *Bookseller at the Ballet* (London: C. W. Beaumont, 1975), 323–25]

4. Vaslav Nijinsky's journals:

[In a period of mental instability in the winter of 1918–19, Nijinsky wrote regularly in a journal. Its contents are mostly about his pen, his food, his mystical thoughts, and occasionally it includes reminiscences like the following.]

I liked girls. Diaghilev thought I was bored, but I was not bored. I did my dance exercises, and I composed my ballet all alone. Diaghilev did not love me, because I composed my ballet all alone. He didn't want me to do things that did not suit him all alone. I could not agree with him in his ideas about art. I told him one thing and he told me another. I often argued with him. I locked myself in, because our rooms were side by side. I let nobody in. I was afraid of him, because I knew that my whole practical life was in his hands. I did not come out of my room. Diaghilev too remained alone. Diaghilev was annoyed, because everybody noticed our dispute. It was disagreeable for Diaghilev for people to ask him what was going on with Nijinsky. Diaghilev liked to show that Nijinsky was his pupil in everything. I did not want to show that I was in agreement with him, that's why I often argued with him in front of everybody. Diaghilev asked Stravinsky for help, it was in a hotel in London. Stravinsky supported Diaghilev, since he knew that Diaghilev would abandon me. And so I felt hatred for Stravinsky, because I saw that he was supporting a lie, and I pretended to be defeated. I was not a savage man. Stravinsky thought I was a savage boy. I was not older than twenty-one. I was young, that's why I made mistakes [141–42].

I was in luck, because I liked him at once. I trembled like a leaf with trembling. I detested him, but I pretended, because I knew that my mother and I would die of hunger. I understood Diaghilev from the first minute, that's why I pretended to agree with all his ideas. I understood that one needs to live, that's why the sacrifice didn't matter. I practiced dance a lot, that's why I always felt tired. But I pretended not to be tired and to be happy so that Diaghilev wouldn't be bored. I know Diaghilev felt it, but Diaghilev liked boys, that's why it was hard for him to understand me. I don't want people to think that Diaghilev is a criminal and that he should be put in prison. I would weep if harm came to him. I don't love him, but he is a human being. [142–43]

Diaghilev is also an impresario, since he leads a company. Diaghilev learned to deceive from other impresarios. He understands what that means, "impresario." All impresarios pass for robbers. Diaghilev does not want to be a robber, that's why he wants to be called a patron. Diaghilev wants to be a part of history. Diaghilev deceives people thinking that nobody knows his purpose. Diaghilev dyes his hair so as not to seem old. Diaghilev's hair is white. Diaghilev buys black pomades and rubs them into his hair. I've seen this pomade on Diaghilev's pillows, their pillowcases were black. I don't like dirty pillowcases, that's why seeing them disgusted me. Diaghilev has two false teeth in front. I noticed it, because when he gets angry he touches them with his tongue. They move, and I see them. [149]

I'm now twenty-nine years old. I know that I was nineteen when I met Diaghilev. I loved him sincerely, and when he told me that the love of women was a horrible thing, I believed it. If I hadn't believed him, I would not have done what I did. Massine does not know life, because his parents were rich. They lacked nothing. We had no bread. My mother did not know what to give us to live. My mother went to the Cinizelli circus, to earn a little money. My mother was ashamed of such work, because she was a well-known artist in Russia. Being a child I understood everything. I wept in my soul. My mother wept also. [151]

[*Nijinsky: Cahiers,* trans. from the Russian by Christian Dumais-Lvowski and Galina Pogojeva. Librairie de la Danse ([Arles]: Actes Sud, 1995); trans. from the French by the author]

5. *Text appearing in the program of the Ballet Russes, May 29, 1913:*

[This is a paraphrase of a scenario by Roerich; see Richard Taruskin, *Stravinsky and the Russian Traditions: A Biography of the Works through Mavra,* 2 vols. (Berkeley: University of California Press, 1996), 1:876.]

Le sacre du printemps (Argument)
FIRST ACT
The Adoration of the Earth

Spring. The Earth is covered with flowers. The Earth is covered with grass.

A great joy reigns on the Earth. Mankind delivers itself up to the dance and seeks to know the future by following the rites. The eldest of all the Sages himself takes part in the Glorification of Spring. He is led forward to unite himself with the abundant and superb Earth. Everyone stamps the Earth ecstatically.

SECOND ACT
The Sacrifice

After the day: After midnight.

On the hills are the consecrated stones. The adolescents play the mystic games and seek the Great Way. They glorify, they acclaim Her who has been designated to be delivered to the God. The ancestors are invoked, venerated witnesses. And the wise Ancestors of Mankind contemplate the sacrifice.

This is the way to sacrifice to Iarilo the magnificent, the flamboyant [flaming].

Reviews

6. *Gustave Linor, "At the Théâtre des Champs-Elysées:* Le sacre du printemps," Comoedia, *May 30, 1913:*

It was a hot evening, in every sense, last night at the Théâtre des Champs-Elysées. Vuillemin, who has the delicate but interesting duty of reporting to you on the new choreographic poem of Monsieur I. Strawinsky—who has as his collaborator in the scenic adaptation M. Nicolas Roerich, not having been able to be present at the private rehearsal on Wednesday evening, will entertain you tomorrow. [See document 9.]

Certainly the new work which Messieurs Astruc and Diaghilew presented to the public yesterday evening is well calculated to surprise in some places, and it contains, from the musical point of view, and still more from the choreographic, certain excesses. Nevertheless, it deserved, like any effort in the world of art worthy of attention and interest, to be listened to in silence.

When, like this one, a work needs perhaps an effort in order to be grasped, at least in its intentions, attention and silence are even more necessary. We were sadly lacking in this point yesterday evening. One part of the audience disturbed the performance with laughter, protests, and even "chut!" ["Shhhh!"] when somebody else replied in the opposite sense with an equally loud vigor and in equally inappropriate terms. This performance almost degenerated into a rowdy debate. It is deplorable from every point of view!

Let us discuss the performance. It was superb, that is to say, *all* the participating artists of the corps of the Russian Ballet expressed exactly, by their movements, their gestures, the successive fresco poses so quickly changing, and often so perfectly harmonious, that which was conceived by M. Nijinsky, who guided the choreography of *Le sacre du printemps*. This was a further step forward on the path that this dancer-creator has chosen. Here again, there are exaggerations, and perhaps intentions that cannot be grasped at first sight; I sincerely believe so, for I admit that I neither understood nor approved everything. But even if the principle is criticized at the same time that it arouses interest, the realization is absolutely perfect. We will speak of it again on another occasion.

So let us praise Mlle Piltz as she deserves, who demonstrated remarkable qualities of style and a great security of performance. Mme Gaulouk, M. Varontzow and their many partners, who are all astonishing artists.

Never was a more delicate and arduous task given to an orchestra and to a conductor; M. Monteux—who was given a personal ovation at the end—and his instrumentalists surpassed themselves last night; they deserve the sincerest praise.

Never, either, has the hall been so full, or so resplendent; the stairways and the corridors were crowded with spectators eager to see and to hear. Four or five times the curtain went up again after the second tableau; M. Stravinsky, his collaborator M. Nijinsky, and the corps de ballet had to come on stage to greet the public to the applause of one part of the audience, and, it must be impartially noted, the protests of the other.

Then came *Le spectre de la rose.* The reaction which should have happened did happen. Karsavina, Nijinsky, and that good Weber, who is good for some things, were madly and unanimously applauded.

Also on the program were the expressive dances from *Prince Igor,* in which M. A. Bolm and the highly-disciplined Russian choirs triumphed, and *Les sylphides,* of which we will also speak again.

We will soon be given the occasion.

The receipts yeaterday at the Théâtre des Champs-Elysées amounted to 38,000 francs. We will not cite any names; one should simply repeat the brilliant list of political, artistic, and social personalities which we published a week ago, but expanded even more.

7. Adolphe Boschot, "Le 'Sacre du printemps': Ballet de MM. Roerich, Stravinsky et Nijinsky," Echo de Paris, *May 30, 1913:*

I would have liked to report on how the audience received this new Russian ballet. But the critics were invited only to a rehearsal; I saw the work; I do not know how the spectators reacted to this double shower of vitriol.

The public is sometimes so strange, so foreign (so foreign to any sort of culture), so desirous of seeming intelligent and up-to-date, so eager to be ranked among the *Incroyables* or the *Précieuses ridicules! . . .* For mankind does not change, and under the fashions of 1913 can easily be discovered the sheep-like quality of humanity. A crowd is always the flock of Panurge: they follow the leaders who think themselves an élite.

And so, we must admire the Ballets Russes. And indeed, for several years we have acclaimed their splendid barbarity. They had new elements, a vehement glow, an irresistible seething—and sometimes the music had a delicious fantasy.

For the last two years, we have noticed that the Russian Ballet is incapable of renewal. When they try to adapt to other subjects their qualities touch us less, their faults are exaggerated and they annoy us. One only has to remember two obvious failures: *The Afternoon of a Faun* and *Jeux.* So that even the public, despite the most foreign esthetes, begins to notice that it is being made fun of, and it protests. It protested loudly at *Jeux.*—Did it protest at *Le sacre du printemps?*

To judge from the rehearsal, there were nine chances in ten that the ballet would be *shouted down*—and shouted down by an irresistible force: hysterical laughter.

* * *

They want to show us the dances of prehistoric Russia: so they present us, to *make primitive,* dances of savages, of the Caribees and the Kanaks. . . . So be it, but it's impossible not to laugh.

Imagine people decked out in the most garish colors, pointed bonnets and bathrobes, animal skins or purple tunics, gesturing like the possessed, who repeat the same gesture a hundred times: they stamp in place, they stamp, they stamp, they stamp, and they stamp. . . . Suddenly: they break in two and salute. And they stamp, they stamp, they stamp. . . . Suddenly: a little old woman falls down headfirst and shows her underskirts. . . . And they stamp, they stamp. . . .

And then there are groups that develop close-order drill. The dancers are up against each other, packed like sardines, and all their charming heads fall onto their right shoulders, all congealed in this contorted pose by a unanimous crick in the neck.

We could continue the analysis of this choreography and this mime: there would always be something to laugh at. Should we be angry over failed pirouettes?

In the second act, here is a delicious dancer, Mademoiselle Piltz. The choreographer destroys her at will: he deforms her legs by making her stand still with her toes turned in as far as possible. It is hideous. . . . And later, when she does move, she must hold her head in both hands, and glue it to her shoulder, as if to show that she suffers from a toothache combined with that same crick in the neck which is the signature of the "poet-choreographer."

Obviously, all that can be justified: what that is is prehistoric dance. The uglier and more deformed it is, the more prehistoric.—That's one conception. I would prefer another, which would lead to beauty and not ugliness. And perhaps it would contain as much truth.— One of the deformations that M. Nijinsky delights in is to contort his dancers as on the most ancient bas-reliefs. But the shortcomings in drawing of primitive artists do not prove that people were deformed, any more than the paintings of the Cubists prove that our amiable contemporaries are conglomerations of tetrahedra. . . .

* * *

Stravinsky's music is disconcerting and disagreeable. No doubt it wanted to resemble the barbarescent choreography. One regrets that the composer of *The Firebird* allowed himself to make such mistakes.

Certainly one finds, in the *Sacre du printemps,* an undoubted virtuosity of orchestration, a certain rhythmic force, a facile invention of melodic fragments or of sound-patterns, designed to accompany, or to situate, or to characterize the scenic movements. This is a musician who is auspiciously talented, ingenious, subtle, capable of force and of emotion, as he has already proved.

But in the apparent desire to *make primitive,* prehistoric, he has worked to *make his music like noise*. For that, he set to work to destroy any impression of tonality. I would have liked to follow in the score (which I have not received) this eminently *a-musical* endeavor. You can get an idea of it which corresponds to my impression: play on two pianos, or four-hands, transposing one part by a tone but not the other: thus, for example, when you have C, E, G in one part, you have D, F, A in the other, *and at the same time*. What is more, if you prefer to untune by a semitone, feel free. It's simply a matter of almost never having one of those ignoble chords which used to be called consonant.

And this savage music, for a half an hour, accompanied by the dances of the Caribees.

The public, that supreme judge, did they notice? Did they understand that they had the right to laugh? Will they be angry? . . . Or will they have found this extraordinarily admirable?

On this little experiment concerning the psychology of a contemporary crowd, one would like to know the judgement of impartial and independent critics.

Adolphe Boschot

8. Henri Quittard, *"Théâtre des Champs-Elysées:* Le Sacre du printemps: *scenes of pagan Russia, in two acts, music by M. Igor Strawinsky: choreography by M. Nijinsky: sets and costumes by M. Roerich,"* Le Figaro, *May 31, 1913:*

Here is a strange spectacle, of a laborious and puerile barbarity, which the audience of the Théâtre des Champs-Elysées received without respect. And we are sorry to see an artist such as Mr. Strawinsky involve himself in this disconcerting adventure, from whom Music, after *The Firebird* or *Petrushka,* could have expected further beautiful works.

Because it is not necessary, I think, to say anything about the choreography of M. Nijinsky, and of the inventions with which this exasperated schoolboy affirms the genius which he felt come upon him one fine day. If we suspected his good faith even for a moment there would perhaps be reason to be angry. After having made fun of the public once, the repetition of this joke with such heavy insistence would not be in very good taste. Unfortunately for him, M. Nijinsky's sincerity is only too evident. He will continue, no doubt about it. And if his creations seem a little more ridiculous every day, it is too clear that it is not his fault.

But the case of M. Strawinsky is quite different.

How can a musician like him let himself be overcome by the contagion and transpose this dancer's esthetic into his art? M. Nijinsky may think that by taking the counter-movement of everything that has been done before him and applying himself with a detestable and laughable ingenuity to deforming the human body he will realize beauties unknown to the masses. But can M. Strawinsky imagine that a melody, because it is doubled a second higher or lower for fifty measures—or both at once—will gain a decisive and eloquent intensity? It seems so since it is so, and since the novelties contained in the score of the *Sacre du Printemps* are normally of this order. And since no one has the right to suspect the sincerity of an artist—especially when he has already proven that he is—what is left to do? Give up trying to understand it, and deplore such a strange aberration.

I know perfectly well that in taking this attitude one risks seeming to be a retrograde spirit closed to any new efforts. It's a risk one needs to know how to run. Certainly the history of music is full of anecdotes where the ignorance of critics shines forth when they were unable to recognize creative genius when it appeared. Is the future saving up a triumphant revenge for new music as M. Strawinsky seems to understand it today? That is its own secret.

But to tell the truth, I doubt that our disgrace is very near. Though the music of *Le Sacre du Printemps* is complex in appearance, though it tries to be far outside the received forms and conventions, it is easy to decipher its outlines, freed of the tinsely barbarism and the noisy discord which the composer saw fit to provide it. After all this analytical work, it seems that it contains no prodigious innovations from which a rejuvenation of the art might one day spring. Its underpinnings are quite regular, more than might be expected from a revolutionary. And if there is rhythmic sense with a nice vigor and often gripping variety, the melodic invention is seen to be extremely weak. The harmonic sense also seems to be quite ordinary; the presentation and development of ideas never presents anything outstanding.

In sum, the basis of this art is rather slender and of an entirely primitive simplicity. It sorely needs, to relieve its insipid flavor, these external artifices violently spiced, which the composer—thank God!—did not spare. But *The Firebird* and *Petrushka* had an interior life cooked up in an entirely different way. Both of them seem young and seductive works, despite some arguable eccentricities. Works with a future, above all. But this one? . . .

This art, such as it is, has its admirers. Doesn't M. Nijinsky have his?—and the pity, for the composer, is that they are the same. We could wish, though, that in certain cases they showed their enthusiasm more discreetly. *Le Sacre du Printemps* was received rather badly yesterday, and the audience could not restrain its laughter. It would have been in good taste, then, for those who thought differently—and they were not many—to spare the authors a curtain call whose comic impertinence was obvious to all.

9. Gustave de Pawlowski, Louis Vuillemin, Louis Schneider, "At the Théâtre des Champs-Elysées: 'Le Sacre du Printemps', ballet in two acts, by M. Igor Stravinsky," Comoedia, May 31, 1913:

—Where were those slobs brought up?

That was the most accommodating thing that was said, among many others, in the course of this elegant and memorable evening.

It describes in itself the astonishment one feels at the stupid intentional viciousness of what we are used to calling the Parisian élite, when presented with any really new and bold initiative. This same audience which for years never protested against the flattest vaudevilles or against the leftovers of operetta served with English sauce which are offered every day, this audience, above all, which every day sees the ugliest that the plastic arts have to offer, and which hears the stupidest things, because they buy mirrors and receive visitors, this same audience affects an intolerable pain when an artist smitten with strangeness tries to make them glimpse a new concept, by trying to amuse them with formerly unknown lines and movements.

True snobism, ever since Thackeray, despite what one may think, is made of reaction, not of boldness. It allows only old boldness, tried a hundred times and approved by a caste. True audacity belongs only to artists. Thus we admired the *Dances from Prince Igor* for the hundredth time with respect and attention, since their primitive naiveties are photographed in manuals of history and geography, but it was with horror that we received *Le Sacre du printemps,* since it enacted even older customs, earlier than society's history manuals. It is true that most of the audience must not have understood the title. The men must have thought it had to do with insults, and the women that it was new fashions promoted by a department store.

So it was only by listening in the midst of an indescribable uproar that we could get an approximate idea of the new work, prevented from hearing both by its defenders and its detractors. We fully respect the rights of the defense in any court of law; but artists who have made their proof do not have the same rights in the theatre. It makes you want to become an outlaw.

None of this means, I hasten to say, that this new work is protected from any criticism. Far from it. The artists and the performers have created an unparalleled *tour de force* in putting on the stage, for two acts, primitive unconscious puerile gestures, frenetic primitive decimations, awakings to the mysteries of life; but a work of art—I was just saying it again recently—cannot be based solely on the gross or the ugly. Whatever, for example, our ethnographic curiosity in France may be for druidic monuments, we would not normally adopt their decorative style in our private lives. Only the Munich style of furniture can conceive such errors. If the ugly is used in art, it can only be for purposes of comparison. There is no reason, for example, that we could not have been shown in *Le Sacre du printemps* the inferior gestures of primitive peoples, provided that they be brief, secondary, and not fill up two acts.

That is the mistake of all artists who discover something new, not to be able to synthesize enough at first. Their little discovery, brilliant though it is, is always shown with too much satisfaction. The great advantage of time-honored ideas is that they are expressed with elegance and brevity. A few gestures, amusing, new, apt, are enough to suggest barbaric peoples; useless to repeat them at length.

An artist must, I repeat, a bit like the Romantics, always offer beauty as well as ugliness. A personal appearance by Nijinsky would have been enough, perhaps, to put *Le Sacre du printemps* right; perhaps also a physical evocation of nature, which was as beautiful then as now, perhaps finally some hint of style in the invention of the creator. When a writer like J. H. Rosny describes the life of primitive peoples with a gripping realism, he does not write his novel in the style of the period, he does not give us a series of bizarre and crude onomatopoeia: he writes in beautiful French. But the evocation is no less surprising.

The authors of *Le Sacre du printemps* have not just employed onomatopoeias. Their personal style is not clearly enough affirmed. In a certain sense, and in a domain where we are not used to such genres, it is a slice of life carved out of a fossil aurochs. From an artistic point of view, the effort remains highly interesting: it gives us something new at a moment when the artistic world seems incapable of it.

Furthermore, even if the general idea of this work seems a little weak, nevertheless, by the care with which it is ordered, by the matching of gesture to music, a sort of curious new stylization arises, a style which I might call the style of reflex movements, or if you like, of automaticity.

You have probably had occasion to be struck, at a fair, by the vertigo that arises from orchestral cacophony and from the absurdity of contradictory gestures that can be seen at any fair-booth. The song played by the carousel-organ is not the same as that of the roller-coaster, the siren of the steam calliope shouts without caring about the victorious fanfares from the shooting-gallery, the magnesium flare of the photographer explodes for its purposes without concern for the rifle-shots or the bells of the Aunt Sally stand. A sugar Russian general perched on an organ beats a triangle with little jerky motions; further on other automata jiggle frenetically; it is an intense uproar which nevertheless creates a strange general impression of harmony. It is this same impression that we get from these jerky motions of prehistoric automata, from the spontaneous and irrational attitudes that *Le Sacre du printemps* offers us, and the whole, despite the dissonances, gives an impression of animal automaticity, of convulsive reflexes in a very precise style, of a clearly-defined genre. And is it not precisely this animal impression, these instinctive reflexes, that the authors wanted to give us?

However that may be, never was an attempt so completely misunderstood. It was not the *Sacre,* but the *Massacre du printemps,* and the fact might seem scandalous at the least.

That an audience that spends, not evenings, but a lifetime doing nothing and learning nothing useful lacks the patience to try to understand a new idea for half an hour beggars the imagination and gives a discouraging idea of the theatre. Truly, painters and writers are better served. Stéphane Mallarmé passed for a semi-god, and nobody ever dreamed of saying that Goya was making fun of the public when he engraved his *proverbs* or his *caprices*.

Making fun of the public! That is what one hears in such circumstances, and I hardly know of anything so painfully stupid. Where, I ask you, is the artist worthy of the name, or even the vilest art-monger who would ever dream of making fun of the public? What a contradiction, what a defiance of good sense! On the contrary, does anyone imagine the anguishes, the apprehensions, the courage needed by the artist who wants to break with traditions and try to display a new vision? It's a bit as if one said that Molière intended to make fun of the public when he wrote comedies instead of tragedies.

Without even speaking of the respect that an artist's effort merits, what admiration must we not have for attractive and able performers who do not hesitate to dress up as grotesques, to give painful study to rude gestures and to primitive movements which are not at all theirs and whose perfection, whose stylization costs them infinitely more work, care and trouble than the staging of a routine banality!

Such an effort in other circumstances would deserve more than admiration: it would deserve gratitude. The audience thinks it is showing collective spirit and good taste by its uproar. It is no mere snobism, it is vicious hatred of art.

But we must console ourselves by thinking that everyone shows gratitude as he can: the toad by slobbering when the sun warms him a bit too much, women of the world by agitating their birds' feathers, their companions by giving dangerous signs of congestion, the crowd by giving plain animal cries.

And that, for a long-sighted artist, is the prettiest concert of praise he can hope for. For everyone expresses himself as he can, and the performers still have the advantage, even when the author puts savages on the stage.

G[ustave]. de Pawlowski

[The same article continues, with a new author: Louis Vuillemin.]

It could well be awkward to formulate, on the day after a single hearing, a judgement on the new work of M. Igor Stravinsky. Because it is extraordinarily audacious, revolutionary, bewildering? Not so much, I assure you. Except for a couple of dozen shocks, which were perhaps not indispensable, *Le Sacre du Printemps,* where generous qualities abound, brings I think hardly any new elements to music. Only the audience created the trouble. And here is how and why.

Some people, summoned by chance to a few final rehearsals, went about in Paris wildly, convinced that they needed to do so. They were of two kinds, equally wild and convinced. "Marvelous, magnificent, dazzling, definitive!" cried one group to whomever would listen for a moment. "Abominable! odious! ridiculous, impertinent!" shouted the others, even to those who did not have a moment to listen. I leave you to discern the damage of such a passion. It invades suddenly, and thirty-six hours before the curtain goes up, invades the whole audience. "Attention!," said the convinced, "we are going to be present at the great musical revolution. It is tonight that the symphony of the future is defined." "Be careful," warned the skeptics, "they are just going to make fun of our ears! They take us for fools. We must defend ourselves!" Result: the curtain goes up—no, even before it goes up—there is murmuring, cries of "Oh!," they sing, they hiss, they whistle. They applaud, they yell "Bravo!" They yelp, they cheer. They revile it, they exalt it. And voilà, the first performance of *Le Sacre du Printemps*. You can see how much it allowed the dozen spectators who were not fanatics to form a clear, logical and reasoned opinion.

At this point, then, I will tell you, not the opinion I shall have in a few days, but only the impression that was mine yesterday. This latter does not promise anything about the former. It could be, in fact, that they will not be contradictory. First, an observation. After the prelude, it was judged better to stop listening to the music so as to make more fun of the choreography. So, is it really so amusing? No: it succeeds at certain points, and is even sometimes attractive or interesting. At other times it seems a total failure, and thus becomes ugly or mediocre. It is pretty two or three times, interesting occasionally, and mediocre for a long while. It sometimes becomes ugly. Always, though, it corresponds to the desires of the music.

The audience should have been informed of what this choreography wanted to signify, and of what it did in fact signify when it worked. It concerns rites which in prehistoric Russia accompanied the cult of Jarilo, the god of light. This explains the barbaric strangeness of many of these frolics, representing the interrogation of the stars, the veneration of ancestors, and other episodes besides. The audience would thereby have understood better. In its ignorance, which could have been predicted, it saw only bizarre gestures which it considered all equally grotesque. But they are not all so, though some are. And it is entirely natural. M. Nijinsky, wanting to be new, could hardly keep himself from exaggeration, as desirable as that would have been. He has multiplied the process—that's always the way with these things. The characters represented, having some intelligence and some dignity, had precisely the mission of selecting, of transmitting, happiness and sadness, of reasoning and of coming to conclusions. At the end, I would have thought howls were in order. Not that I find them indispensable in such cases, much less justified, but because everyone has the right to demonstrate. But nobody has the right, though everyone seems to think so, to disturb a performance from one end to the other, to sabotage a work that an author has worked on for two years, to believe, as a snob or a dilettante, that one is free from any misunderstanding or error. One ridiculous minute—or one that seems ridiculous—is not enough to condemn a performance that lasts an hour. Those who laughed the most at *Tannhäuser,* at *Tristan and Ysolde,* at *Pelléas,* are the most laughable today. I am not saying that half the spectators at the Théâtre des Champs-Elysées will be equally laughable tomorrow. But what does seem to me very evident is the lack of courtesy, the senselessness, and the prejudice of an audience as ever hostile to any effort and prompt to find it laughable. Furthermore, it matters little. Let us get to know the works and to judge them sanely. Let us be content to disdain people.

People have never prevented works. Art stands outside of stupidity, of superficiality, of ill will. These are as prosperous as ever, but art is no less well off. . . . If I despised—and I will avoid this ridicule—the collaboration of Messieurs Nijinsky and Stravinsky, if I thought them stupid, I would still have far greater respect for them than I do for their adversaries of yesterday. We must always distinguish between those who make occasional mistakes in trying to do something and those who have never tried do do anything and yet make mistakes all the time.

Monsieur Nijinsky's mistakes seem to me to be more numerous than those of M. Stravinsky. I have told you what they are. A frequent exaggeration causes them. They weaken the effect of expressive and unconventional gestures, of new and significant poses, of different and truly eloquent groupings. But it matters little. M. Nijinsky's choreography is not durable. It will not outlast him. It is secondary to the work; the work alone is susceptible of lasting. M. Stravinsky's work, will that last? I have absolutely no idea. But it has been printed; it is fixed. It can be played when M. Stravinsky is not there; it thus has for us a greater importance than the dance. And then, as a creator, M. Stravinsky shows more breadth than his choreographic collaborator, who is above all a gifted dancer.

What has M. Stravinsky done? The same thing, perhaps, as M. Nijinsky: exaggerated. Carried away by his earlier boldnesses—which everyone justly admired—has he added new ones? No. Perhaps he has only accumulated them. They do not bother me. I set them aside, I ignore them. Fifteen harsh sonorities have only a small importance in three hundred pages of orchestral score. They seem preponderant only to those who care nothing for the rest. You ask what is the rest? An admirable force of rhythm and life, of movement. A violence that delights in magnificent frenzy. A virtuosity in instrumentation which verges on the prodigious. Generosity, imagination, enormous talent. The laughers happily trampled on all of that. Heavens! How could they get an impression of it? The genius of Ibsen, manifested in words, formerly at the Oeuvre [theater], made the audience split their sides laughing! As for *Ubu Roi,* you know what they remembered: one word. . . . Dissonance: their observation stops there. That suited them fine, naturally. Is it any surprise, then, that the talent of M. Stravinsky totally escaped them?

For it may be, despite his fiercest admirers, that M. Stravinsky has until now only showed talent. Neither in *The Firebird,* nor in *Petrushka,* nor in *Le Sacre du Printemps*—perhaps—has M. Stravinsky given evidence of anything other than a considerable talent not as original as one thinks. He owes an enormous debt to his ancestors, the Russian musicians. He owes a great deal to a few French musicians. This does not in any way diminish, in my thinking, M. Igor Stravinsky. Time will tell. It will complete this composer to the extent that this composer is capable of completion. It will calm or excite enthusiasms again. It will certainly kill absolute negations.

We will speak of all that again. Let me summarize: M. Stravinsky's score has value, much value. I do not think it a work of genius. If, in a few days, it should seem to me on the contrary that it is, I shall hasten to admit it. That is everything, in good conscience, that I can tell you. Please forgive me for being, yesterday, the least intelligent man in the theatre. . . .

Louis Vuillemin

[Louis Schneider continues the same article.]

Staging and sets

The two sets of the *Sacre du Printemps* are perhaps the only elements of the performance on which a critic can give an opinion without hesitation. They are in the tradition of Russian sets, but they renew it; they are surprising in tonality but they do not overthrow it; they are robust, vigorous in composition, barbarian, to be colorful, but there is nothing in them that is not profoundly evocative. They are both green; the first lighter, the second darker; this latter, with its neutral sky, its verdant hills, its handsome red costumes which sing joyfully on the greening landscape is the very image one might have of an original spring; the other, where the green of the sky has tragic overtones, with its sacrificial stones, its terrible funerary monuments, creates by itself the atmosphere for sacrifice, for astral dance, for the gestures of a frenetic and not fully organized cult. The red costumes of the flower-pickers in the first tableau are of a ravishing red tonality, the stiffly contorted braids frame the faces admirably; the red makeup on the cheeks, though a little crude, still has an ardent savor not without charm. The other costumes are distinctly out of the usual; the clothes, the hair of the five young men, of the old man, of the three-hundred-year-old woman, all full of character, would still surprise us, if they were not, like the sets, by Nicolas Roerich, one of Russia's greatest painters and one of the most knowledgeable persons in the matter of Russian prehistory.

The staging is mingled with the choreography in *Le Sacre du Printemps;* and you know what Nijinsky's choreographic principles are. However surprised one may be by its new realization, however irritating it may be at times, one cannot deny that it produces an impression of vigor, of intentional heaviness, of tenacity, which borders sometimes on greatness. Origin of a new art—not yet master of its form, or error of a too-curious mind, too preoccupied with research—the choreography of the *Sacre du Printemps* is in any case *a work*. That opinionated stylization of all the gestures, that symbolizing in attitudes the least thoughts coming from barbarian brains, that schematizing of man's first conquest of form, rendered with an unmatched frenzy, gave a bit of surprise to an audience placed brutally before a particularly unusual art. But perhaps we should speak with some prudence. How many productions despised in the past are now received as masterpieces!

Louis Schneider

10. *Florent Schmitt,* "Les Sacres du Printemps, *de M. Igor Strawinsky, au Théâtre des Champs-Elysées,*" La France, *June 4, 1913:*

In showing us *Les Sacres du Printemps,* the Théâtre des Champs-Elysées could not have a more impressive way of demonstrating its reason for existence: a free theatre, it prides itself on being a home to the freest art there is: the music of M. Igor Strawinsky, aggravated by the choreography of M. Waslaw Nijinsky and the settings of M. Nicolas Roerich. With *Les Sacres du Printemps,* a suite of tableaux of pagan Russia, we come to the high point, not only of the Russian season, but of Russian art—perhaps even of art itself. In fact, no musician, no director, no decorator, treating ancient traditions so scornfully, has ever ventured so far in the realm of sound, movement, and color, or expressed the inexpressible in such brilliant discoveries.

The task was correspondingly more difficult as it dealt with translating the atmosphere of a profoundly rudimentary epoch, the prehistoric epoch of a stammering and savage humanity. M. Igor Strawinsky's music, by its frenetic agitation; by the senseless whirl of its hallucinating rhythms; by its aggregations of harmonies beyond any convention or analysis, of an aggressive hardness that no one—not even M. Richard Strauss—had dared until now; by the obsessive insistence of its themes, their savor and their strangeness; by seeking the most paradoxical sonorities, daring combinations of timbres, systematic use of extreme instrumental ranges; by its tropical orchestration, iridescent and of an unbelievable sumptuosity; in sum, by an excess, an unheard-of luxuriance of refinement and preciosity, the music of M. Igor Strawinsky achieves this unexpected—but intentional—result, that it gives us the impression of the darkest barbarity. We must actually see in *Les Sacres du Printemps* the arrival of a new music, already felt in *Petrushka,* and yet so distant from *Petrushka.* This latter work, like *The Firebird,* already made a great impression by its novelty and its strangeness. But this is surpassed in *Les Sacres*. The force and the speed of M. Strawinsky's evolution are disconcerting. The author, at thirty-one, of three such different masterpieces, not to speak of the admirable *Scherzo fantastique*, of *Feux d'artifice* and of his highly evocative Japanese melodies, Igor Strawinsky is, I believe, the Messiah we have waited for since Wagner and for whom Mussorgsky and Claude Debussy, as well as Richard Strauss and Arnold Schoenberg, prepared the way.

Igor Strawinsky's genius could not receive a more striking confirmation than the incomprehension of the crowd and its vicious hostility. This group of what is called "worldly people"—the world of Doctor Moreau—unable to see, hear, and feel for themselves, these overgrown children who are overcome with gravity at the beastly and academic clownings of low boulevard theatre, could find nothing but brutal infantile laughter at these splendors, so immeasurably distant from their weak understanding. In this disturbing and sublime music they saw only cacophony, in these primitive geometric gestures, so moving in their gaucherie, they saw puppet farces. Bringing everything down to their mediocre vain level, they will not admit, they cannot tolerate, that an artist should create without being concerned for them, any more than the princess of Paul Claudel worried about the rats and snakes that lived in the walls of her palace. These people of the *Sacres* proved themselves worthy of their elders of *Tannhäuser,* of *Briséis,* of *Pelléas et Mélisande*. With an implacable and infallible logic, human stupidity never loses its rights.

It may be of some interest to give you the "argument"—horrible word!—of this work, so elevated and so human. Here it is, reduced to its simplest expression. This is simply a transcription: [here Schmitt transcribes the argument of the program; document 5, above].

It is the poem of all of humanity, a poem more beautiful for the impressions it suggests than by the actions themselves. The direction of M. Nijinsky, which aroused so much disapproval, seems to me so adequate to the music that this time I will not weaken my enthusiasm by any of the qualification I allowed myself with regard to M. Debussy's *Jeux*. Mlle Piltz, whom we had already noticed in *The Firebird,* realized the Sacrificial Dance with a sad and tragic passion, and the studied grotesqueries of her movements did not disguise her grace, which is infinite. One must admire the coolness, the extraordinary courage, of this young woman who, appearing not to notice a hysterical audience, brings this marvelous precision to the interpretation of such complicated rhythms. That is a commendation that should also be given to M. Pierre Monteux, the able and tireless conductor of the Russian performances. Completely at ease amid these unheard-of difficulties, he can pride himself henceforth on having realized the most difficult score there is, and that is a glory, it seems to me, equal to that of those illustrious names ending in *-er* or *-isch,* so proud to conduct pastorales by heart.

If not M. Strawinsky's music, if not M. Nijinsky's direction, at least the sets of M. Nicolas Roerich should receive mercy before the abject intransigence of the crowd. We recognize the beauty of the first tableau: it is the ardent realism of colors, the symphony of spring greens, in sober lines, close to the bare earth still without trees. It is a stylized chaos gradually clothing itself with moss and greenery. Perhaps I find the dancers' costumes a bit too striking, too rich. Wouldn't it have been appropriate to dress them in primitive fabrics with neutral shades, or better, in mammoth or diplodocus hides, or still more simply in magnificent hair, flowing beards and handsome limbs? The set for the second tableau, in its macabre impressionism, reminds me—wrongly?—of the last chapters of *The Time Machine:* dying humanity, stuttering out all the actions of past life? Or perhaps, humanity being born from chaos and beginning the rhythm of all actions? This second set moves me more.

Florent Schmitt

11. Anonymous, *"The Premiere of* Le Sacre du Printemps *by the Russian Ballet at the Théâtre des Champs-Elysées,"* Comoedia Illustré, *June 5, 1913:*

One can observe that it was rather tormented. There were, as in the Chambre [the lower house of the legislature], interruptions, violent interjections, between the audience, conservative of choreographic and musical traditions, and the young modern school of composers. Certain words deserve to be recorded for history. One of them was offered by a well-known French musician.

Faced with the murmurs and sneers of the well-to-do audience assembled in this gala hall and representing 35,000 francs' worth of tickets, the indignant composer cried out: "They are ripe for colonization!" The violence and the surprise of his challenge had the effect of calming the protests for a moment. From the balcony a voice said: "The artists can no longer hear the music!" That was the unflappable Serge de Diaghilew, who with an Olympian calm watched the dancers through the brouhaha of shouts, worrying only about their work. He thought, perhaps, that great works of art were consecrated by the same storms.

12. Lise Léon Blum, *"Le goût au Théâtre," from* Gazette du Bon Ton *(a fashion magazine), June 1913, 246–47:*

[After discussing Fauré's opera *Pénélope,* Blum goes on to discuss the Russian Ballet.]

Then the Russians returned faithfully, with their vivid costumes, their scintillating settings, their ardent, voluptuous dancing. There was more to come: the admirable *Boris Godounow,* the *Firebird,* the *Spectre de la Rose,* the white-winged *Sylphides* and the impetuous black of *Shéhérazade,* all found the favorable welcome to which we have accustomed them.

But the great novelty, the unexpected and disconcerting spectacle which gave rise to polemics and quarrels was the *Sacre du Printemps* whose decors, by M. Roerich, choreography by Nijinsky, and music by Stravinsky, are equally sensational and bizarre. Is it absurd and insignificant? Is it an effort, a step forward, a new stage in our taste? I don't dare decide: I saw men of sincere feeling applauding, true artists; I saw a hall divided by two contrary currents; and this disagreement shows at least that we are approaching a dangerous moment in our esthetic culture.

It may well be that Messieurs Roerich and Nijinsky have truly rediscovered the appearance and the movement of one age of humanity. It may also be that the emotions of certain spectators arose from contact with this primitive sensibility, expressed and re-created before their eyes. Humanity certainly needs, at certain moments, to recover the sensations of its childhood. That moment may perhaps be coming for us, since the most refined of our contemporaries, the subtlest, the most cultivated, are agitated at the *Sacre du Printemps.*

13. *Léon Vallas*, "Le sacre du printemps," La Revue Française de Musique, *June–July 1913, 601–3:*

Right from the first day, this new work that the Russian ballet troupe has just presented in Paris was baptized the *Massacre du Printemps.*

Massacre, first because one could hear only a little bit of it, because the protests that accompanied M. Igor Strawinsky's ballet were so loud. The Parisians gave on this occasion a striking proof of their stupidity and their reactionary spirit. It is true that the so-called Parisian audience is at least half composed of persons as foreign to France as they are to art, and more than a quarter of society people incapable of being moved by a bold artistic effort. Let us try to believe that the audience who normally go to opera houses and concerts had little to do with the inappropriate uproar that lasted throughout the performances of the *Sacre du Printemps.* Moreover, even if we must attribute this spiteful welcome to actual Parisian spectators, we should not conclude that the French are destined to periodic renewal of the scandal of *Tannhäuser,* because, as Dumas *fils* affirmed, God created the Parisians so that foreigners would never know what to make of the French.

A Massacre, too, because to more than one amateur it seemed monstrous to celebrate spring with the epileptic convulsions guided by M. Nijinsky and by a painfully discordant music. Here we must mark the difference between the dance and the music. The dance is ridiculous: to prolong a marionette choreography for more than an hour and a half might seem to be a bad joke if we did not know from repeated experience the sincerity and the conviction of M. Nijinsky, the acrobat with incomparable leaps, but a ballet-master incredibly deprived of general ideas and of simple good sense. And yet the essential stupidity of a dance reduced to mindless gestures did not deserve the unleashing of noisy protests that served as its accompaniment and commentary. M. Nijinsky, wanting to represent the frenetic and almost bestial joy of our distant ancestors, can certainly be excused for having dared this shocking realization of barbaric and outlandish rites. Furthermore, there is less of gross stupidity and of animal doltishness in the rhythmic and prehistoric crises imagined by the Russian dancer than in the braying and slavering indignation of a refined twentieth-century audience faced with a new spectacle.

If we can unhesitatingly condemn—with extenuating circumstances—the choreography of M. Nijinsky, we must confess to much less certainty about the extraordinary music of M. Stravinsky. Assuredly it seemed far beyond the normal limits of dissonance; it shows an evident preference for continuous exaggeration. It is sometimes very ugly: I mean that to those of us in 1913 it seems ugly. We have difficulty understanding the need to juxtapose with itself a melodic motive taking care to transform a banal unison into an obstinate parallelism at the interval of the minor second, or to hear a melody in *C* with an accompaniment in *B,* or to write all the instrumental parts in a very long score in impossible tessituras. We understand it even less when, in the middle of a continuous and intentional grating sound remarkable melodic qualities show themselves, an infectious rhythmic life vibrates, and harmonic bouquets, so to speak, blossom in the most iridescent color. M. Strawinsky's entire score, of a startling richness and a rare originality, seems to be the result of a wager. Carried away in the ardor of his youth, no doubt with complete sincerity, the composer with an impetuous energy has leaped forward, burned his bridges and offered us this year the music that we should hear around 1940. Heard thirty years later, his music would not have provoked in the well-intentioned amateur this resistance which, while recognizing the innovator's genius, they could not resist. So the score of *Le Sacre du Printemps* is a premature specimen of the music of the future? Yes, if the current trend continues towards a growing complexity at once rhythmic, polyphonic, and instrumental. But since in the heart of every musician, even the most progressive, there is a conservative asleep, we can imagine that the taste for excessive complexity will be followed by a desire for simplicity. Remember the rapid triumph of simple accompanied melody in the seventeenth century over the extreme polyphony which had pleased the Byzantinism of the musicians of the previous age. And we long for it even more since, only a few days after the brutal revelation of this very irritating but still seductive music of M. Strawinsky, the same theatre of the Champs Elysées offered to our surprised admiration the very simple score of *Pénélope*, which seems to open a new path in the enchanted forest of music, to show through the thickets an overgrown path where nobody had gone.

Memoirs of People Associated with the Ballets Russes

14. Sergei Leonidovitch Grigoriev:

[Grigoriev was the *régisseur*—a sort of stage manager—of the Diaghilev company; his view is of course from behind the scenes.]

[Diaghilev] clearly had misgivings about the reception of Stravinsky's music and warned us that there might be a demonstration against it. He entreated the dancers, if so, to keep calm and carry on, and asked Monteux on no account to let the orchestra cease playing. "Whatever happens," he said, "the ballet must be performed to the end."

His fears were well founded. We began with *Les Sylphides*. Then, after the first interval the curtain rose on *Le Sacre*, and not many minutes passed before a section of the audience began shouting its indignation, on which the rest retaliated with loud appeals for order. The hubbub soon became deafening; but the dancers went on, and so did the orchestra, though scarcely a note of the music could be heard. The shouting continued even during the change of scene, for which music was provided; and now actual fighting broke out among some of the spectators; yet even this did not deter Monteux from persisting with the performance. Diaghilev, who was with us on the stage, was extremely agitated; and so was Stravinsky. The dancers, on the other hand, were quite unmoved and even amused by this unprecedented commotion. As for Nijinsky, he stood silent in the wings. Although he realized that the demonstration was directed rather against the music than against his choreography, it upset him that for the second time a work of his should be so rowdily received. Diaghilev tried every device he could think of to calm the audience, keeping the lights up in the auditorium as long as possible so that the police, who had been called in, could pick out and eject some of the worst offenders. But no sooner were the lights lowered again for the second scene than pandemonium burst out afresh, and then continued till the ballet came to an end.

The dancers, rather naturally, were reluctant to take their curtain calls; and I purposely prolonged the next interval so as to give the excitement the more time to subside. When the curtain next rose, on *Le Spectre,* quiet was in fact restored, and this ever-delightful ballet evoked the usual enthusiastic response.

* * *

As for the execution of *Le Sacre* by the dancers, it was beyond praise. The countless rehearsals had in fact borne fruit; and the company had triumphantly overcome all the difficulties of the score. Maria Piltz, who danced the one solo part, of the sacrificial victim, was truly excellent, and her performance was much admired by everyone, including Diaghilev.

[S. L. Grigoriev, *The Diaghilev Ballet, 1909–1929,* trans. Vera Bowen (London: Constable, 1953), 83–84]

15. Pierre Monteux:

[Monteux, the conductor of the first performances, reminisced many years later, in the book written by his wife.]

In the summer of 1912 Diaghilev came to me one day, as I was working in the theatre, and in a rather secretive manner whispered, "Stravinsky has written an extraordinary new work that I want you to hear with me this afternoon."

I was elated all through luncheon thinking, Stravinsky no doubt has reverted to the lovely melodies of *L'Oiseau de Feu* or perhaps even farther. Of course this "reverting" did not come until years later, in the *Pulcinella Suite, Apollon Musagète* and other lovely works. So you see, *chérie,* I was little prepared for the music I was to hear that afternoon.

The room was small and the music was large, the sound of it completely dwarfing the poor piano on which the composer was pounding, completely dwarfing Diaghilev and his poor conductor listening in utter amazement, completely dwarfing Monte Carlo, I might say. The old upright piano quivered and shook as Stravinsky tried to give us an idea of his new work for ballet.

I remember vividly his dynamism and his sort of ruthless impetuosity as he attacked the score. By the time he had reached the second tableau, his face was so completely covered with sweat that I thought, "He will surely burst, or have a syncope." My own head ached badly, and I decided then and there that the symphonies of Beethoven and Brahms were the only music for me, not the music of this crazy Russian! I must admit I did not understand one note of *Le Sacre du Printemps.* My one desire was to flee that room and find a quiet corner in which to rest my aching head. Then my Director turned to me and with a smile said, "This is a masterpiece, Monteux, which will completely revolutionize music and make you famous, because you are going to conduct it." And of course, I did.

Day after day I studied the score with Stravinsky at the piano. I studied all that winter. In the spring we brought it to the orchestra engaged for the Paris season. We rehearsed the strings first, then woodwinds and brass, each section of the orchestra alone, except for the percussion instruments which were there all the time. The musicians thought it absolutely crazy, but as they were well paid, their discipline was not too bad! When at last I put the whole thing together, it seemed chaotic but Stravinsky was behind me pointing out little phrases he wished heard. We rehearsed over and over the small difficult parts, and at last we were ready for the ballet. We had in all, seventeen rehearsals. . . .

You may think this strange, *chérie,* but I have never seen the ballet. The night of the première, I kept my eyes on the score, playing the exact tempo Igor had given me and which, I must say, I have never forgotten. As you know, the public reacted in a scandalous manner. They filled the new Champs Elysées Theatre to overflowing, manifested their disapprobation of the ballet in a most violent manner. The elegant Parisians in the stalls and boxes shouted outrageous insults to the enthusiastic crowd in the balconies. They in turn responded by screaming imprecations both salty and provocative, due to their infinitely richer vocabulary. "*A bas les grues du 16ème!*" (the 16th was the chic quarter of Paris) and similar insults were hooted in unison over and over, causing many a countess to gnash her teeth over these intolerable affronts. One of my bass players who from his stand at the end of the pit had a partial view of the stalls, told me that many a gentleman's shiny top hat or soft fedora was ignominiously pulled by an opponent down over his eyes and ears, and canes were brandished like menacing implements of combat all over the theatre.

The gendarmes arrived at last. Well, on hearing this near riot behind me I decided to keep the orchestra together at any cost, in case of a lull in the hubbub. I did, and we played it to the end absolutely as we had rehearsed it in the peace of an empty theater.

[Doris Monteux, *It's All in the Music: The Life and Work of Pierre Monteux* (London: William Kimber, 1965), 90–92]

16. Romola Pulsky:

[Pulsky was a dancer who married Vaslav Nijinsky in 1913.]

On the 29th of May, 1913, at the Champs Elysées Theatre, the *Sacre du Printemps* was performed for the first time, on the very anniversary of the *première* of *Faune,* for Diaghileff was superstitious. I wondered what the reaction of the brilliant, excited audience would be. I knew the music of *Sacre,* and had seen bits of the dancing from back stage during the last rehearsals, where I hid behind Karsavina and Schollar, and had been escorted by Dmitri Gunsburg, and Grigorieff threw furious looks at me, but I just looked through him as if he were of air. With Gunsburg beside me he could do nothing. I thought the public might fidget, but none of us in the company expected what followed. The first bars of the overture were listened to amid murmurs, and very soon the audience began to behave itself, not as the dignified audience of Paris, but as a bunch of naughty, ill-mannered children. . . .

Yes, indeed, the excitement, the shouting, was extreme. People whistled, insulted the performers and the composer, shouted, laughed. Monteux threw desperate glances towards Diaghileff, who sat in Astruc's box and made signs to him to keep on playing. Astruc in this indescribable noise ordered the lights turned on, and the fights and controversy did not remain in the domain of sound, but actually culminated in bodily conflict. One beautifully dressed lady in an orchestra box stood up and slapped the face of a young man who was hissing in the next box. Her escort rose, and cards were exchanged between the men. A duel followed next day. Another Society lady spat in the face of one of the demonstrators. La Princesse de P. [Pourtalès] left her box, saying "I am sixty years old, but this is the first time anyone has dared to make a fool of me." At this moment Diaghileff, who was standing livid in his box, shouted, "*Je vous en prie, laissez achever le spectacle*" [I beg you, let the show finish]. And a temporary quieting-down followed, but only temporary. As soon as the first tableau was finished the fight was resumed. I was deafened by this indescribable noise, and rushed back stage as fast as I could. There it was as bad as in the auditorium. The dancers were trembling, almost crying; they did not even return to their dressing-rooms.

The second tableau began, but it was still impossible to hear the music. I could not return to my stall, and as the excitement was so great among the artists watching in the wings I could not reach the stage door. I was pushed more and more forward in the left wing. Grigorieff, Kremeneff, were powerless to clear this part of the stage. Opposite me there was a similar mob in the back of the scenery, and Vassily had to fight a way through for Nijinsky. He was in his practice costume. His face was as white as his *crêpe de Chine* dancing shirt. He was beating the rhythm with both fists shouting, "*Ras, dwa, tri*" to the artists. The music could not be heard even on the stage, and the only thing which guided the dancers was Nijinsky's conducting from the wings. His face was quivering with emotion. I felt sorry for him, for he knew that this ballet was a great creation. The only moment of relaxation came when the dance of the Chosen Maiden began. It was of such indescribable force, had such beauty, that in its conviction of sacrifice it disarmed even the chaotic audience. They forgot to fight. This dance, which is perhaps the most strenuous one in the whole literature of choreography, was superbly executed by Mlle Piltz.

[Romola Nijinska, *Nijinsky* (London: Gollancz, 1933), 199–200.]

17. Bronislava Nijinska:

[Nijinska was Vaslav Nijinsky's sister, originally intended to dance the Sacrificial Dance in the *Rite of Spring*.]

The dress rehearsal went smoothly, irreproachably, an ideal execution, with perfect harmony between stage and orchestra. All of us and particularly Vaslav were confident about the performance. There were, of course, the usual background grumblings, mainly among the men, who were unhappy about the makeup, the bears, the heavy hats, and who knows what else.

The historic day arrived: May 29, 1913, the first performance of *Le Sacre du Printemps:* A tableau of pagan Russia in two acts, music by Igor Stravinsky, book by Igor Stravinsky and Nicholas Roerich, sets and costumes by Nicholas Roerich, choreography by Vaslav Nijinsky.

The Théâtre des Champs-Elysées was filled and Mother had a seat in the front row. I remained back in the wings, more to be near Vaslav than to watch the action on the stage.

The orchestra sounded, the curtain opened, and suddenly from the audience came a cry of outrage. Vaslav turned pale. The noise from the public was drowning the orchestra, making it difficult for the artists to hear the music. I could see that Vaslav was in a state of extreme anxiety lest the artists miss their execution. He appeared on the point of rushing onstage to restore some kind of order in case the artists went to pieces. I wanted to grab Vaslav to prevent him from running out, but fortunately this was not necessary. From somewhere Diaghilev yelled out to the audience, "Let them finish the performance!" Standing in the wings I had felt weak and my legs had failed me. My heart was tight, not so much for the fate of the ballet as for Vaslav.

The noise and tumult continued, and it was not until near the end of the ballet, when Maria Piltz began to dance her solo, that the public quieted down.

[*Bronislava Nijinska: Early Memoirs,* trans. and ed. Irina Nijinska and Jean Rawlinson (New York: Holt, Rinehart and Winston, 1981), 469–70]

IV. Memoirs of Members of the Audience

18. Pierre Lalo, "Le 'Sacre du Printemps' au concert," Feuilleton du Temps, April 21, 1914:

[Lalo, son of the composer Edouard Lalo, remembers the first performance in the course of his review of a concert performance.]

I remember that, on the evening of the first performance, finding myself in the balcony of the Théâtre des Champs-Elysées, I was placed under a loge full of elegant and charming persons, whose joking remarks, joyous prattling, the remarks shouted with loud high voices, and finally high convulsive laughter, made a racket similar to that that deafens one on going into a bird-house; the men who accompanied them did their best to second them by massive vociferations, to which they suddenly added, when their indignation grew too strong, the strident noise one gets by blowing through a key. But I had at my left a group of esthetes in whose soul the *Sacre du Printemps* aroused a frenetic enthusiasm, a sort of ejaculatory delirium, and who riposted incessantly to the occupants of the loge with admiring interjections, by furious "Brâàvo!," and with the rolling fire of their clapping hands; one of them, furnished with a voice like that of a horse, whinnied from time to time, but without addressing anyone in particular, "Away with you!," whose rending vibrations were prolonged throughout the hall. Who was better, Lord, the defenders of *Le Sacre du Printemps* or its adversaries? Surely neither the ones nor the others; and only the horse-voiced esthete was right: all those people should have been ejected, and he first of all.

19. John Gould Fletcher, 1914:

[Fletcher, a wealthy American poet and balletomane, writes to Cyril Beaumont just after the first performance.]

Friday 31 [May 1913]

Dear Beaumont,

Have seen the Sacre du Printemps. Scenery and costumes by Roerich, time the Stone Age, music by Stravinsky—gestures by Nijinsky on the model of Petrouchka and Après-Midi.

Result half the audience were yelling bravo all the time the ballet was being played (I was one of them) the other half were hooting. There was nearly a fight, and I was afraid that they would call in the gendarmes and ring down the curtain in the middle, but they went on to the end, when the demonstration was terrific. . . .

Nijinsky is greater than Fokine. Sacre du Printemps is the most savage, the most original, the most gorgeous thing the Russian Ballet has ever done.

There is no story. Merely savage folk dances done at the beginning of spring, and the priests lead in an old man who embraces the earth (first act). In the second act it is night of the same day and a young girl (done marvellously by Piltz) is dedicated to the Gods. The ghosts of the ancestors come out of their graves and get her. Weird barbaric!!!!!!!! And the music is the most amazing music ever written—perfectly futurist music—knocks Debussy into a cocked hat.

[Cyril Beaumont, *Bookseller at the Ballet* (London: C. W. Beaumont, 1975), 141]

20. *Valentine Gross-Hugo:*

[Valentine Gross-Hugo, known for her sketches of dancers in action, attended all four Paris performances; some of her sketches of *Le sacre* are reproduced in this volume.]

At that time, there existed in this new theatre a kind of promenade between the *loges de corbeille* and the large boxes. There were as yet no bracket-seats. All the painters, poets, journalists, musicians, friends of Serge de Diaghilev, who represented the new and young aspirations of this truly marvellous epoch gathered together here. . . .

All descriptions of the battle of *Le Sacre du printemps* remain inferior to the truth. It was as if the auditorium had been shaken by an earthquake and seemed to quiver in the tumult. Shrieks, abuse, howls, sustained whistles drowned the music and then came slaps and even blows. Words are too mild to recall such an evening. Calm was slightly restored when the auditorium was suddenly lighted. I was very much amazed at seeing certain people in the boxes who were vindictive and noisy in the darkness but who immediately calmed down in the light. I will not hide the fact that our calm river had become a tumultuous torrent. Among others were Maurice Delage, garnet-red with indignation; Maurice Ravel aggressive as a small fighting cock. Fargue, roaring vengeful epithets towards the hissing boxes. I am amazed that this work, so difficult for 1913, could be played and danced to the very end in such an uproar. Everything has been said on the subject; the dancers who could no longer hear the music, Nijinsky, very pale, calling out the beats from the wings. Diaghilev thundering orders from his box, and the blows given and received. . . .

As for me, I lost nothing of the performance which was as much in the auditorium as on the stage. I stood between the central boxes, feeling very much at ease in the midst of the storm and applauded with my friends. I felt a tremendous admiration and respect for the great efforts by which a supernatural cohesion was maintained between the musicians who could not be heard, the dancers who could not hear and the invisible choreographer.

The performance was of surprising beauty. The movements appeared to be in perfect accord with the rhythms, and later views of the ballet made me increasingly appreciate the perfect ensemble.

[1951 radio interview, in Françoise Reiss, *Nijinsky,* trans. Helen Haskell and Stephen Haskell (London: Adam and Charles Black, 1960), 122–23]

21. Carl Van Vechten, 1916:

[Van Vechten had been music and dance critic for the *New York Times;* in 1913 he was drama critic for the *New York Press.*]

Cat-calls and hisses succeeded the playing of the first few bars, and then ensued a battery of screams, countered by a foil of applause. We warred over art (some of us thought it was and some thought it wasn't). . . . Some forty of the protestants were forced out of the theater but that did not quell the disturbance. The lights in the auditorium were fully turned on but the noise continued and I remember Mlle. Piltz executing her strange dance of religious hysteria on a stage dimmed by the blazing light in the auditorium, seemingly to the accompaniment of the disjointed ravings of a mob of angry men and women.

[Carl Van Vechten, *Music and Bad Manners* (New York, 1916), 470]

22. Carl Van Vechten, 1915:

[Compare this with the passage above: perhaps here he is confusing the first with a subsequent performance? Cf. Gertrude Stein, below.]

I attended the first performance in Paris of his anarchistic (against the canons of academic art) ballet "The Sacrifice of Spring" [Van Vechten's translation], in which melody and harmony, as even so late a composer as Richard Strauss understands them, do not enter. A certain part of the audience, thrilled by what it considered a blasphemous attempt to destroy music as an art, and swept away with wrath, began very soon after the rise of the curtain to whistle, to make cat-calls, and to offer audible suggestions as to how the performance should proceed. Others of us, who liked the music and felt that the principles of free speech were at stake, bellowed defiance. It was war over art for the rest of the evening and the orchestra played on unheard, except occasionally when a slight lull occurred. The figures on stage danced in time to the music they had to imagine they heard and beautifully out of rhythm with the uproar in the auditorium. I was sitting in a box in which I had rented one seat. Three ladies sat in front of me and a young man occupied the place behind me. He stood up during the course of the ballet to enable himself to see more clearly. The intense excitement under which he was laboring, thanks to the potent force of the music, betrayed itself presently when he began to beat rhythmically on the top of my head with his fists. My emotion was so great that I did not feel the blows for some time. They were perfectly synchronized with the beat of the music. When I did, I turned around. His apology was sincere. We both had been carried beyond ourselves.

[Carl Van Vechten, *Music after the Great War* (New York: Schirmer, 1915), 87–88]

23. *Jean Cocteau:*

[Cocteau, author, scenarist, filmmaker and critic—and collaborator with Diaghilev, Picasso, and Satie on the ballet *Parade*—writes in 1918 about his impressions of the ballet and the performance.]

Le sacre du printemps was performed in May 1913, in a new hall, without patina, too comfortable and too cold for an audience used to elbow-to-elbow emotions, in a swelter of red velvet and gold. I do not think that *Le sacre* would have had a better reception on a less pretentious stage, but this luxurious hall symbolized at first glance the mistake of pitting a work of youth and force against a decadent audience. A drained audience, lying in Louis XVI garlands, in Venetian gondolas, soft couches and cushions of an orientalism for which we have the Russian Ballet to blame.

On this diet you digest in a hammock, you snooze; you wave away the truly new like a fly: it's bothering you.

* * *

Perhaps its would be interesting to look, in the totality of the work, for the part played by each of the collaborators: Stravinsky the musician, Roerich the painter, Nijinsky the choreographer.

Musically, we were in the middle of Impressionism.

And suddenly, in the middle of these charming ruins, grew the tree of Stravinsky.

All things considered, *Le sacre* is still a "fauve" work [the word means "wild beast," but it also refers to the school of painters known as "les fauves"], but an *organized* "fauve" work. Gauguin and Matisse bow before it. But if the fact that music lags behind painting necessarily prevents *Le sacre* from coinciding with other anxieties, it still brought an indispensable dynamite. Furthermore, let us not forget that the tenacious collaboration of Stravinsky with the Diaghilev enterprise, and the care which he takes of his wife, in Switzerland, kept him away from the center of things. His audacity was thus accidental.

Finally, whatever else there is, the work was and remains a masterpiece; a symphony impregnated with savage pathos, with earth in the throes of birth, noises of farm and camp, little melodies that come from the depths of the centuries, the panting of cattle, deep convulsions, prehistoric georgics.

Stravinsky had certainly looked at the canvases of Gauguin, but by transposition the weak decorative register had become a colossus. At that time I was not up to date on each little wrinkle of the Left, and thanks to my ignorance I could completely enjoy *Le sacre* sheltered from the petty schisms and narrow formulas that condemn unfettered value and too often mask a lack of spontaneity.

Roerich is a mediocre painter. In one sense he costumed and decorated *Le sacre* in a way that was not foreign to the work, but in another, he attenuated it by the slackness of his accents.

There remains Vaslav Nijinsky. At home, that is to say, in the Palace Hotels where he camps, this Ariel scowls, looks through picture-books, and overturns the syntax of gesture. Ill-informed, his modern models are not the best; he uses the *Salon d'automne* [an annual art show]. He rejects grace, having known too well its triumph. He systematically seeks the opposite of that which earned him his glory; in order to escape old formulas, he locks himself into new formulas. But Nijinsky is a *mujik,* a Rasputin: he has the magic that charms crowds and he despises the public (though he does not refuse to please it). Like Stravinsky, he turns the weakness that makes him fertile into a strength; by all these atavisms, this lack of culture, this cowardice, this humanity, he escapes the German danger, the system that dries up a Reinhard.

I heard *Le sacre* again without the dances; I want to see them again. In my memory of them, impulse and method were balanced, as in the orchestra. The defect was in the parallelism of the music and the movement, in their lack of *play,* of counterpoint. We were given proof that the same chord often repeated is less tiring to the ear than is the frequent repetition of a single gesture to the eye. The laughter came more from a monotony of automata than from the violation of posture, and more from the violation of posture than from polyphony.

It is appropriate to distinguish two parts in the work of the choreographer:

A dead part (example: the direction of the immobile feet, a simple desire to contradict the dancer's traditional pose with the toes turned out), and a living part (example: the Storm [dance of the earth?], and that dance of the chosen one, a naive and mad dance, an insect-dance, of a doe fascinated by a boa, of a factory blowing up, in fact the most overpowering spectacle in the theatre that I can remember.

These different elements thus formed an ensemble both homogeneous and heterogeneous, and whatever might have been defective in the details was evaporated, uprooted by irresistible temperaments.

Thus we got to know this historic work, in the middle of such an uproar that the dancers could no longer hear the orchestra, they had to follow the rhythm that Nijinsky, stamping and shouting, marked for them in the wings.

After this sketch of what was to happen on stage, let us take the small metal doorway and move into the hall. It is crowded. To a practiced eye, all the material needed for a scandal is assembled there; a fashionable audience, low-cut dresses, tricked out in pearls, egret and ostrich feathers; and side by side with tails and tulle, the suits, headbands, showy rags of that race of esthetes who acclaim, right or wrong, anything that is new because of their hatred of the boxes (whose incompetent acclamations are more intolerable than the sincere hisses of the former). And in addition to fevered musicians, a few sheep of Panurge caught between fashionable opinion and the credit owed to the Russian Ballet. And if I don't go into detail, it is only that I would have to point out a thousand details of snobbism, super-snobbism, anti-snobbism, that would need a chapter to themselves.

I should note here a particularity of our hall: the absence, with two or three exceptions, of young painters and their teachers. An absence motivated, I later found out, for the former by their ignorance of these ceremonies to which Diaghilev did not invite them, and for the others by social prejudice. This censure of luxury, which Picasso professes as a cult, has its good and bad sides. I attack this cult as well as its antidote, but perhaps it narrows the horizons of certain artists who avoid contact with luxury more from jealous hatred than from worship. However that may be, it is true that Monparnasse [the artists' quarter] knew nothing of *Le sacre du printemps;* that *Le sacre du printemps* played by the orchestra of the Concerts Monteux suffered, from the Left, from the bad press of the Russian Ballet; and that Picasso first heard Stravinsky in Rome with me in 1917.

* * *

Let us return to the hall in the avenue Montaigne, waiting for the conductor to tap his music stand with his baton and for the curtain to be raised on one of the most noble events in the annals of art.

The audience played the role it had to play; it immediately rebelled. It laughed, scoffed, whistled, cat-called, and perhaps might have got tired in the long run if the mob of the esthetes and a few musicians in their excessive zeal had not insulted and even jostled the people in the boxes. The uproar degenerated into a free-for-all.

Standing in her box, her tiara askew, the old comtesse de Pourtalès brandished her fan and cried red-faced: "This is the first time in sixty years that anyone has dared make fun of me!" The worthy lady was sincere; she thought it was a hoax.

* * *

At two o'clock in the morning, Stravinsky, Nijinsky, Diaghilev and myself piled into a cab and were driven to the Bois de Boulogne. We kept silent; the night was cool and clear. The odor of the acacias told us we had reached the first trees. Coming to the lakes, Diaghilev, bundled up in opossum, began mumbling in Russian. I could feel Stravinsky and Nijinsky listening attentively and as the coachman lighted his lantern I saw tears on the impresario's face. . . . You can't imagine the gentleness and the nostalgia of these men, and no matter what Diaghilev may have done later, I shall never forget, in that cab, his great tear-stained face as he recited Pushkin in the Bois de Boulogne.

[Jean Cocteau, *Le coq et l'arlequin* (Paris: Editions de la sirène, 1918; rpt., Paris: Stock, 1979), 87–96]

24. Misia Sert:

[Misia Sert at the time was a patron of Diaghilev and Stravinsky.]

It was from Diaghilev's box that I witnessed the real battle which took place at the first night [the French text has "*répétition générale,* the dress rehearsal, but this description sounds like the public performance] of this work. The howls of enthusiasm, interrupted by whistles and catcalls, created such an uproar that Astruc had to address the audience to re-establish some semblance of order. It was such a striking novelty that it was, of course, impossible to hope that a first-night audience would assimilate it immediately. But Diaghilev was so certain that he had a masterpiece on his hands that he did not bother about the success of the first impact. As for me, I had attended all the orchestral rehearsals, and had been seized with such a passion for *Sacre* that I had no doubt at all that the public would very soon be forced to recognise its magnificence.

. . . And precisely at the moment when I was marvelling at the possibility of the co-existence of three such violent loves [*Boris Godunov, Pelléas et Mélisande,* and *Le Sacre*] in one heart, due to the miracle of the unconscious, secret affiliation, my glance fell on Debussy sitting next to me in the box. A terrible sadness was reflected on his anxious face. He bent over me and whispered:

"It is horrible—I can hear nothing."

[*Misia* (Paris: Gallimard, 1952), 182–183; as translated in Moura Budberg, *Two or Three Muses: The Memoirs of Misia Sert* (London: Museum Press, 1953), 132.]

25. Gertrude Stein:

[Gertrude Stein implies that she was present at the first performance when in fact she was not.]

We could hear nothing. . . . One literally could not, throughout the whole performance, hear the sound of music. [Maybe not, but there are parts of the score that would be hard to drown out entirely.]

[Nigel Gosling, *Paris, 1900–1914* (London: Weidenfeld and Nicolson, 1978), 217; also cited in John Malcolm Brinnin, *The Third Rose: Gertrude Stein and Her World* (Boston: Little, Brown, 1959), 190–91]

26. Giacomo Puccini:

[The famous composer of operas writes to Tito Ricordi; letter is undated.]

I went to hear the *Sacre de Printemps:* the choreography is ridiculous, the music sheer cacophony. There is some originality, however, and a certain amount of talent. But taken together, it might be the work of a madman. The public hissed, laughed, and . . . applauded.

[Giacomo Puccini, *Letters,* ed. Giuseppe Adami, trans. Ena Makin; new ed., rev. and introduced by Mosco Carner (London: Harrap, 1974), p. 251, letter 159]

27. Gian Francesco Malipiero:

[The influential Italian composer attended the premiere on a visit to Paris.]

Huge audience, enormous uproar. Claude Debussy, Gabriele d'Annunzio from a box were applauding and also cursing the dominant barbarity. The exuberant Florent Schmitt was insulting his compatriots.

We could hear the music of the *Sacre du printemps* at the second performance when the opposition was in the minority, and from the third onward their behavior gradually became almost normal. . . . Among the listeners who were composed, though not at all "enraptured," was Ildebrando Pizzetti [the Italian composer, conductor, and critic].

[Gian Francesco Malipiero, *Strawinsky* (Venice: Cavallino, 1945), 9–10]

28. Alfredo Casella:

[The Italian composer attended *Le sacre* with Malipiero, above.]

Those who, like this writer, had the good luck to be there, can testify about the formidable, one could almost say "historic," scandal of that evening. From the middle of the prelude there arose from that hall, crowded with the usual heterogeneous and elegant audience, an uproar through which one could hear nothing of the work. A scandal that was repeated at the other four performances, but which—according to the memories of those who were present on that memorable evening, was more on account of the clumsy and heavy mediocrity of Nijinsky's spectacle than the terrifying violence of the music.

[Alfredo Casella, *Strawinski* (Brescia: La Scuola, 1947), 57]

29. Michel Dmitri Calvocoressi:

[The critic Calvocoressi wrote extensively on Russian music and served as an adviser to Diaghilev in the early stages of Diaghilev's career in Paris.]

I must say that although far more noisy than at [the 1902 premiere of Debussy's] *Pelléas*—and indeed so noisy at times that you could not hear the music—the disturbances at the *Rite* were far less loathsome. People were really roused, not merely bewildered and scandalized. They protested angrily, not prudishly and in shocked "Oh-Oh-Oh's!" Nor was there in their demonstrations anything of the note of personal hostility to the composer which was so definitely discernible in 1902. No: the *Rite* was simply too much for part of the audience. . . .

It was obvious that the dancing had caused as much irritation as the music. The evolutions of the dancers had been made as constrained, gawky, and heavy as possible, in order to evoke the primitive, apprehensive mentality of the men and women of the stone age, struggling against the awesome forces of nature arrayed against them. The idea was excellent, but not successfully carried out. Nijinsky's choreography stopped half-way, taking into account all the rhythmic suggestions of the music separately, but not coordinating them into a whole. . . .

And yet how beautiful most of the *Rite* was! Nobody who witnessed the 1913 production will ever forget the wonderfully impressive entry of the warriors clad in eland skins and wearing eland skulls on their heads, nor the strangely inhuman, hysterical dance of the maiden before the sacrifice.

[Michel Dmitri Calvocoressi, *Music and Ballet* (London: Faber & Faber, 1934), 244–45]

30. Emile Henriot:

I remember the première, at the Champs-Elysées: the secretly spreading laughter, the resistance of a disconcerted audience, their anger, the outcries and disorder which ensued in the hall. I admit retrospectively that I felt some uneasiness the first day. That was all so new: those dissonances, that frenetic barbarism on stage, that unknown liturgy, all that escaped us. I remember, however, under my uncertainty, the deep and reassuring impression that this work caused me, and the feeling of a great force, as yet confused, but real.

[Emile Henriot, "Les Ballets Russes," *La Revue Musicale* 11 (December 1930; a special number on the Russian Ballet): 398–99]

V. What Stravinsky Did or Did Not Say at the Time

31. Henri Postel du Mas interviews Stravinsky, 1913:

Igor Strawinsky is not satisfied. The audience of the Russian Ballet welcomed his new work with cries, discordant noises and laughter which covered the applause of a few initiates. However, I speak the truth when I say that the author of the *Sacre du printemps* showed only a little melancholy, and was not too violently vituperative with his detractors while we spoke together yesterday about these incidents. Monsieur Stravinsky is short and he seems tall because he carries his head in the air and his look dominates his interlocutor; he speaks from on high, and his eyes wander over objects and persons with a divergence and a mobility that surround them like a sudden rainshower. Thus we spoke:

"That not everything was understood immediately, I certainly admit," he told me in the wings of the Théatre des Champs-Elysées, "but what seems unjustifiable to me is the lack of willingness of this audience before whom I confidently presented myself. It seems that one should wait for the end of the ballet to show displeasure; that would have been polite, that would have been honest. I have done something new, I expected to disconcert a little those who applauded *Petrouchka* and *The Firebird,* and I expected the same sympathy. I acted in all conscience and I do not think I was mistaken; the works I have already had performed and which have been well received, should be tokens of my sincerity and should show that I had no wish to make an uncomprehending public laugh.

The other night, when the ruckus kept the artists from hearing the music, I assure you that we, they and I, were very sad, not only because of our vanity, but also because we were afraid we would not be able to continue. There is the result of a hundred and thirty rehearsals and a year of work.

They have criticized M. Nijinsky's staging and said that it seemed foreign to the music.

They were wrong. Nijinsky is an admirable artist. He is capable of renewing the art of ballet. We never for a second failed to be in absolute communion of thought. Later you will see what he will do. He is not just a marvelous dancer, he is capable of creating, of innovating, and his part in the collaboration on *The Rite of Spring* was fruitful. The public only needs an education in order to recognize success in this order of things. But I am at ease, I will be understood one day, before long no doubt. An unexpected novelty upsets Paris, but Paris knows how to pull herself together and forget her bad mood. . . .

Paris, which admires M. Nijinsky as a dancer, does not admire him as a director at all. It is a great shame, but it is so. Remember *The Afternoon of a Faun* and *Jeux* where M. Debussy must have spent—silent, philosophical, prudent—some bad quarter-hours. That Nijinsky should dance, even to Weber, so be it: he dances like a young god. But let him, at least for us poor French souls, renounce directing others, renounce combining the texts of poets and renounce making of the *sacre* a *massacre du printemps.*

[Henri Postel du Mas, "Un entretien avec M. Stravinsky," *Gil Blas* 25 (June 4, 1913): 1]

32. *Remarks attributed to Stravinsky, published in* Montjoie!:

[*Montjoie!* a journal founded in February 1913, described itself as "the organ of French artistic imperialism."]

The Paris public had been kind enough to grant a kind reception, for several years now, to my *Firebird* and to *Pétrouchka*. My friends noticed the evolution of the animating idea, which moves from the fantastic fable in the one work to the fully human generalization in the other. I fear that *Le sacre du printemps,* where I appeal neither to the spirit of fairy tales nor to human sadness and joy, but where I seek for a somewhat wider generalization, will disturb those whose sympathy had until now been precious to me.

With *Le sacre du printemps* I have tried to express the sublime rise of nature renewing herself; the total rise, *panique,* of the universal sap.

In the Prélude, before the curtain goes up, I have entrusted to my orchestra that great fear that weighs on every sensitive spirit before powerful things, the "thing in itself," which *can* grow, can develop indefinitely. The frail sound of a flute can contain this value of power, enlarging itself throughout the orchestra. It is the obscure and immense sensation that everything has at the moment when Nature renews her forms; and it is the vague and profound unease of universal puberty. I have tried to evoke it with my orchestration, and with my melodic play.

The whole Prélude is based on an always-equal "mezzo-forte." Melody is developed along a horizontal line, which only the mass of the instruments—the intense dynamism of the orchestra and not the melodic line itself—increases or diminishes.

As a consequence, I have excluded from this melody the *strings,* too evocative and representative of the human voice, with their crescendo and diminuendo—and placed the *winds* in the foreground, drier, clearer, less rich in facile expressions, and thereby more moving to my taste.

In short, I wanted to express in the Prélude nature's terrible fear for the beauty which is rising, a sacred terror in the noonday sun, a sort of cry of Pan. The musical material itself inflates, grows, spreads. Each instrument is like a shoot which grows on the trunk of an ancient tree; it is part of a formidable whole.

And the whole orchestra, this whole ensemble, should have the significance of the birth of Spring.

In the First Tableau, we see adolescents with an old woman, a very old woman, whose age, whose century, are unknown, who knows the secrets of nature and teaches her sons to tell the future. She runs, curved over the earth, half-woman, half-beast. The adolescents beside her are the Portents of Spring, who mark with their steps, in place, the rhythm of Spring, the pulsebeats of Spring.

Meanwhile, the young women come to the stream. They make a circle which is united with that of the boys. These are not already-formed beings: their sex is unique and double, like that of trees. They mix together; but in their rhythms can be sensed the cataclysm of groups being formed. Indeed, they divide right and left. Form is being realized, the synthesis of rhythms; and the thing formed produced a new rhythm.

The groups separate and begin to dispute; messengers go from one to the other, and quarrel. It is the definition of force by contest, that is, by games.

But then the arrival of a procession is heard. It is the Holy Man arriving, the Sage, the Pontifex, the oldest of the clan. A great terror overcomes everyone. And the Sage gives his benediction to the Earth, stretched out and prostrate, his arms and legs spread, himself becoming a single thing with the Earth. His blessing is like a signal for rhythmic bursting forth. Everyone covers his or her head and runs in spirals, rushing without stopping and in great numbers, like the new energies of the Earth. This is the Dance of the Earth.

The Second Tableau begins with the obscure games of the adolescents. At the beginning, a musical Prélude is based on the mysterious chant which accompanies the dances of young girls. They mark with their round the signs where at the end the Chosen One will be enclosed, who will not be able to get out again. The Chosen One is she whom the Spring must consecrate, who must give back to Nature the power which her youth took from Her.

The maidens dance around the Chosen One, who is immobile, a sort of glorification. Then there is the purification of the ground and the evocation of the Ancestors. And the Ancestors gather around the Chosen One, who begins to dance the Sacrificial Dance.

As she is about to fall senseless, the Ancestors take note, slide to her like rapacious monsters, so that she should not touch the ground when she falls; and they take her and lift her towards the sky.

The annual cycle of forces which are reborn and which fall in the cycle of nature is accomplished, in its essential rhythms.

And I am glad to have found in M. Nijinsky the ideal collaborator for movement, and in M. Roerich the ideal creator of pictorial atmosphere, for this work of faith.

["Igor Stravinsky," "Glories and Miseries of the Current Theatre: What I Wanted to Express in *Le sacre du printemps*," *Montjoie!* May 29, 1913, 1]

Note: In his autobiography, Stravinsky remarked on the article cited above: "Among the most assiduous onlookers at the rehearsals had been a certain Ricciotto Canuedo, a charming man, devoted to everything advanced and up to date. He was as that time publishing a review called *Montjoie*. When he asked me for an interview, I very willingly granted it. Unfortunately, it appeared in the form of a pronouncement on the *Sacre,* at once grandiloquent and naive, and, to my great astonishment, signed with my name. I could not recognize myself, and was much disturbed by this distortion of my language and even of my ideas, especially as the pronouncement was generally regarded as authentic, and the scandal over the *Sacre* had noticeably increased the sale of the review."

[Igor Stravinsky, *Chroniques de ma vie,* written with Walter Nouvel, (Paris, 1935); translated under the title *Igor Stravinsky: An Autobiography* (London: Victor Gollancz, New York: Simon and Schuster, 1936; rpt., New York: Norton, 1962)]

VI. What Stravinsky Said Later

33. Igor Stravinsky on Le sacre, *from his autobiography of 1935:*

One day, when I was finishing the last pages of *L'Oiseau de Feu* in St. Petersburg, I had a fleeting vision which came to me as a complete surprise, my mind at the moment being full of other things. I saw in imagination a solemn pagan rite: sage elders, seated in a circle, watched a young girl dance herself to death. They were sacrificing her to propitiate the god of spring. Such was the theme of the *Sacre du Printemps*. I must confess that this vision made a deep impression on me, and I at once described it to my friend, Nicholas Roerich, he being a painter who had specialized in pagan subjects. He welcomed my inspiration with enthusiasm, and became my collaborator in this creation. In Paris I told Diaghileff about it, and he was at once carried away by the idea, though its realization was delayed [p. 31].

The complexity of my score had demanded a great number of rehearsals, which Monteux had conducted with his usual skill and attention. As for the actual performance, I am not in a position to judge, as I left the auditorium at the first bars of the prelude, which had at once evoked derisive laughter. I was disgusted. These demonstrations, at first isolated, soon became general, provoking counter-demonstrations and very quickly developing into a terrific uproar. During the whole performance I was at Nijinsky's side in the wings. He was standing on a chair, screaming "sixteen, seventeen, eighteen"—they had their own method of counting to keep time. Naturally the poor dancers could hear nothing by reason of the row in the auditorium and the sound of their own dance steps. I had to hold Nijinsky by his clothes, for he was furious, and ready to dash on the the stage at any moment and create a scandal. Diaghileff kept ordering the electricians to turn the lights on or off, hoping in that way to put a stop to the noise. That is all I can remember about that first performance. Oddly enough, at the dress rehearsal, to which we had, as usual, invited a number of actors, painters, musicians, writers, and the most cultured representatives of society, everything had gone off peacefully, and I was very far from expecting such an outburst [pp. 46–47].

[Stravinsky, *Chroniques de ma vie*; *Igor Stravinsky: An Autobiography*]

34. Stravinsky on the premiere, 1959:

I was sitting in the the fourth or fifth row on the right and the image of Monteux's back is more vivid in my mind today than the picture of the stage. He stood there apparently impervious and as nerveless as a crocodile. It is still almost incredible to me that he actually brought the orchestra through to the end. I left my seat when the heavy noises began—light noise had started from the very beginning—and went backstage behind Nijinsky in the right wing. Nijinsky stood on a chair, just out of view of the audience, shouting numbers to the dancers. I wondered what on earth these numbers had to do with the music, for there are no "thirteens" and "seventeens" in the metrical scheme of the score.

From what I heard of the musical performance it was not bad. Sixteen full rehearsals had given the orchestra at least some security. After the "performance" we were excited, angry, disgusted, and . . . happy. I went with Diaghilev and Nijinsky to a restaurant. So far from weeping and reciting Pushkin in the Bois de Boulogne as the legend [i.e., Cocteau's story] is, Diaghilev's only comment was, "Exactly what I wanted."

[Igor Stravinsky and Robert Craft, *Conversations with Igor Stravinsky* (New York: Doubleday, 1959), 47–48]

35. Stravinsky on Nijinsky, 1960:

My own disappointment with Nijinsky was due to the fact that he did not know the musical alphabet. He never understood musical metres and he had no very certain sense of tempo. You may imagine from this the rhythmic chaos that was *Le Sacre du Printemps,* and especially the chaos of the last dance where poor Mlle Piltz, the sacrificial maiden, was not even aware of the changing bars. Nor did Nijinsky make any attempt to understand my own choreographic ideas for *Le Sacre.* In the *Danses des Adolescentes,* for example, I had imagined a row of almost motionless dancers. Nijinsky made of this piece a big jumping match.

I do not say that Nijinsky's creative imagination lacked abundance; on the contrary, it was almost too rich. The point is simply that he did not know music, and therefore his notion of the relation of dance to it was primitive. To some extent this might have been remedied by education, for of course he was musical. But at the time he was made chief choreographer of the Ballet he was hopelessly incompetent in musical technique. He believed that the choreography should re-emphasize the musical beat and pattern through constant co-ordination. In effect, this restricted the dance to rhythmic duplication of the music and made of it an imitation. Choreography, as I conceive it, must realize its own form, one independent of the musical form though measured to the musical unit. Its construction will be based on whatever correspondences the choreographer may invent, but it must not seek merely to duplicate the line and beat of the music. I do not see how one can be a choreographer unless, like Balanchine, one is a musician first.

If Nijinsky was the least capable musically of my choreographic collaborators, his talent was elsewhere—and one talent such as he had is never enough. To call him a dancer is not enough, however, for he was an even greater dramatic actor. His beautiful, but certainly not handsome, face could become the most powerful actor's mask I have ever seen and, as Petroushka, he was the most exciting human being I have ever seen on a stage.

[Igor Stravinsky and Robert Craft, *Memories and Commentaries* (London: Faber & Faber, 1960), 37–38]

36. Stravinsky on the conception, rehearsal, and performance of Le sacre, 1962:

The idea of *Le sacre du printemps* came to me while I was still composing *The Firebird.* I had dreamed a scene of pagan ritual in which a chosen sacrificial virgin danced herself to death. This vision was not accompanied by concrete musical ideas, however, and as I was soon impregnated with another and purely musical conception that began quickly to develop into, as I thought, a *Konzertstück* for piano and orchestra, the latter piece was the one I started to compose. I had already told Diaghilev about *Le sacre* before he came to see me in Lausanne, at the end of September 1910, but he did not know about *Petroushka,* which is what I called the *Konzertstück....*

That the first performance of *Le sacre du printemps* was attended by a scandal must be known to everybody. Strange as it may seem, however, I was unprepared for the explosion myself. The reactions of the musicians who came to the orchestra rehearsals were without intimation of it, and the stage spectacle did not appear likely to precipitate a riot. The dancers had been rehearsing for months and they knew what they were doing, even though what they were doing often had nothing to do with the music. "I will count to forty while you play," Nijinsky would say to me, "and we will see where we come out." He could not understand that though we might at some point come out together, this did not necessarily mean we had been together on the way. The dancers followed Nijinsky's beat, too, rather than the musical beat. Nijinsky counted in Russian, of course, and as Russian numbers above ten are polysyllabic—eighteen, for example, is *vosemnádsat*—in fast-tempo movements, neither he nor they could keep pace with the music.

Mild protests against the music could be heard from the very beginning of the performance. Then, when the curtain opened on the group of knock-kneed and long-braided Lolitas jumping up and down (Danse des adolescentes), the storm broke. Cries of "Ta gueule" came from behind me. I heard Florent Schmitt shout "Taisez-vous garces du seizième"; the "garces" of the sixteenth arrondissement were, of course, the most elegant ladies in Paris. The uproar continued, however, and a few minutes later I left the hall in a rage; I was sitting on the right near the orchestra, and I remember slamming the door. I have never again been that angry. The music was so familiar to me; I loved it, and I could not understand why people who had not yet heard it wanted to protest in advance. I arrived in a fury backstage, where I saw Diaghilev flicking the house lights in a last effort to quiet the hall. For the rest of the performance I stood in the wings behind Nijinsky holding the tails of his *frac,* while he stood on a chair shouting numbers to the dancers, like a coxswain.

[Igor Stravinsky and Robert Craft, *Expositions and Developments* (London: Faber & Faber, 1962), 140–43]

Conclusion

In these pages we have been acting more as investigators than as art lovers. We have had a close look at five moments when a work of art came into being through performance in search of answers to specific questions: Who listened? Who performed? How much did they rehearse? What did the building look like and how did it sound? Was it a good performance? How was the music played at the premiere different from what we know today? These are interesting questions, and the answers, when they are available, have much to say about the place of music in different societies, about the significance of musical performance, and about varied attitudes toward works of art. Perhaps we should step back for a moment and consider where we've been.

Music is music, some might say. That is one possible approach: to assume a common esthetic ground for music—indeed perhaps for all the arts. In such a system all parts of the musical canon are timeless works of art and deserve equal and consistent consideration. It is a matter of setting a uniformly high standard that performances attempt to approximate.

Such an attitude would be familiar to Monteverdi's listeners or Handel's. The difference is that they generally listened to music from one time and place—their own; whereas we can, if we wish, hear a vast range of music, which we sometimes try to put together in a single musical category. When we do so, however, we run the risk of missing nuances and the richness of shades and contrasts. If we want to hear music from many times and places, we can hear it best if we are aware of its many possibilities of style and effect.

One of the central points of this book has been that each moment of music is, at least at its origin, a moment of a particular culture, the expression of a society of individuals. A performance is accomplished through many agents: the composer, performers, and audience as well as the surrounding society that provides a physical space, pay for the musicians, income for the concertgoers, and a shared backlog of experience for hearers. The music's particular sound results from the organization of that society; the music reinforces and renews (and sometimes shocks) that society's expectations and contributes to a social fabric of which it is both a description and an element. The details of cultural context presented here have helped us sense what Vienna experienced in 1824 when it heard Beethoven's new symphony, and to see that Paris in 1830—only a short time later, yet so distant culturally!—viewed Berlioz and what he represented in an entirely different way.

What are the elements about Mantua's performance of *Orfeo* in 1607 that are most strikingly different from our current approach to music, and to *Orfeo?* Would we not be a little surprised to have the beautiful Euridice acted by a little priest singing soprano? Monteverdi's audience apparently wasn't.

The Dublin performances of *Messiah* were different from many given today. What does it say that a concert was held on Tuesday at noon? This was a society in which many concertgoers did not have regular jobs or schedules. Note the number of lawyers in the audience. How many lawyers today go to performances of oratorios at that time of the day? Then there are the distinctions in contemporary performance, for *Messiah* as for all these pieces: men singing alto; a small chorus compared to the gigantic ones often heard today; a comparatively small orchestra; choirboys singing soprano in the chorus; soloists merging back into the chorus.

One's appreciation of the beauty and importance of the Ninth Symphony is unaffected by the knowledge that Beethoven was wearing his green coat because his black one was being repaired; but the fact that Beethoven's chorus stood in front of the orchestra and that a pianist was used in the performance will make us wonder about the sound of the Ninth Symphony in Vienna in 1824. Then no one noticed anything odd; things have changed.

Today the *Rite of Spring* may be part of a program that includes a Mozart concerto and a Dvořák serenade — the connection is that all are pieces for symphony orchestra. Beethoven's audience, on the other hand, would think it perfectly normal to hear songs, solo piano music, chamber music, opera excerpts, and symphonies on the same occasion but would have thought it extraordinary, and probably undesirable, to hear music from three centuries and three countries in the same concert. With a few antiquarian exceptions, audiences before the twentieth century have expected to hear music from their own time, in a style entirely familiar, even though the music itself might be a new expression of that style. Concert audiences of our own day also usually want familiar music — but they rarely mean new music of our time. Musical taste, or at least musical experience, used to be narrower but more focused. Whereas we have an enormous range of styles, concertgoers of the past had a far greater range of experience within their own style.

Certain historical themes recur in thinking about these five pieces in context. Each could be the subject of another book, but it is worth pointing out some of them here, since our exploration has shown that important questions are resolved differently in different times and places.

From Monteverdi to Stravinsky we see an enormous change in attitude toward the composer, from musician-as-servant to musician-as-entertainer to musician-as-prophet. Monteverdi may have been a great composer, and the duke may have been proud of him, but Monteverdi was not, as his librettist was, a member of the Academy.

How could he be? He was a servant. Handel was a great deal more independent, but he still relied on the nobility to support his operatic efforts, to invite him to Ireland, and to provide continuing patronage. Beethoven's daily involvement in the practical and commercial aspects of giving a concert seems at odds with the view of him as a Jupiter hurling artistic thunderbolts from some musical Olympus. And yet Beethoven was both those things, for in order to be independent and to compose whatever music he chose he had to see to it that his income was not contingent on the whim of an individual—he had to create a career for himself, and that involved a great deal of work. Although he started as a court musician and became a renowned piano virtuoso, by the end of his life Beethoven was viewed as an artist and a poet. It was in this climate that Berlioz started out. His world even had institutions that encouraged and supported composers and other artists, institutions that paid them salaries and sent them to Roman villas so that they might develop their creative talents. That world, which later bought tickets to the exotic Russian Ballet, is essentially the world of today: a world in which art is valued as an indispensable part of what makes society run and what makes life better.

We have seen the variety of ways in which music interacts with religion. Was *Orfeo* an expression of a humanism opposed in some respects to religion? Or could it be a Christian allegory? Handel was strongly criticized for putting sacred words into a theater. And for reasons of religious censorship Beethoven had to rename his *Missa Solemnis* "Hymns." Berlioz uses the ecclesiastical *Dies irae* and then makes it grotesque —adding the serpent to the orchestra to show that this is church music. Even Stravinsky is writing music for ritual—but now the ritual is that of an unknown pagan religion.

From a purely musical point of view we have seen the rise of ever larger and more controlled structures for compositions, from Monteverdi's elegant but simple counterpoint to Handel's fugues to Beethoven's even more complex double fugue, to say nothing of the increasing concern with large-scale tonal regions and structures. Then these structures seem to provide the platform for their own destruction, as Berlioz and Stravinsky experiment with irrationality, disorder, and primitivism.

We have seen striking differences in how music is financed, from the private music paid for by a single purse to the public concert supported by all its listeners. *Orfeo* is very expensive to produce nowadays because of the elaborate sets and costumes required and the vast array of instrumentalists and singers needed. It is no longer possible to "borrow" singers from the grand duke of Tuscany. Few private individuals own their own theaters or have a staff of instrumentalists and singers (though this might be an interesting concept for certain wealthy patrons). Handel's arrangements in Dublin depended to some extent on the support of influential persons and powerful institutions: his use of the Music Hall, musicians of the State Music of Ireland, and members of the cathedral choirs make it clear that Handel was not merely a professional musician passing through and trying to make some money. And yet his concerts were, in principle, open to the public, even though that public was the highly restricted one of the upper reaches of Dublin society.

The growth of musical institutions—conservatories, concert societies, orchestras—is an important step in a society's cultivation of music. Although Beethoven did have the assistance of some institutions (especially the Gesellschaft der Musikfreunde), he was essentially on his own in producing his concert. There was no regular concert orchestra to play his symphony, no concert hall in which to perform it, no subscription audience. We think of Beethoven as a composer, but at that moment he was essentially operating as a producer. Berlioz's situation was similar, though his task was made easier by the existence of a concert hall and a regularly constituted symphony orchestra: all he needed was the money. Stravinsky was blessed with having everything organized for him. He was asked for the music, he was handsomely paid for it, and all the rehearsals and performances were arranged by others; indeed, he was urged to use an orchestra larger than he had planned in order to make a splendid impression. In principle the public was to pay for all these expenses through the cost of tickets. (As we know, it did not work out that way, and Gabriel Astruc was ruined in his first season.)

A paying audience seldom covers the cost of a musical event. Some blend of individual patronage, institutional support, government advocacy, and individual ticket sales seems to be necessary to finance musical performance, or indeed any aspect of the arts. These ingredients have been combined in a great array of recipes in the past, and it remains to be seen whether they will continue to nourish music in the future.

Our Attitude toward Art

What do these premieres, and their listeners, show us about how we view a work of art, about what we think art is? Why is attending a premiere thought to be more important than attending any other performance? How have our views about art changed over the centuries?

In many of the performances we have explored, the music was more in the making than in the finished product. Our composers took performance seriously. That is, they suited their piece to their circumstances. Monteverdi expressed his willingness to alter the music for the tardy castrato; Handel made changes in *Messiah* to accommodate the singers of the moment; even Beethoven ultimately relented and allowed a singer to change notes. What mattered was that it worked in performance. If Berlioz made many subsequent changes in the *Symphonie fantastique,* it was surely owing in large measure to the effects the composition possessed—and the effects it lacked—in its 1830 performance. And even Stravinsky, the most finicky of composers, made music for performance as part of a collaboration of music, dance, and spectacle that came to life only when performed. Only afterward did Stravinsky manage to extract his score from the theater and place it on the concert platform.

These performances seem to have been livelier, more animated, and less a sort of ritual than most concerts today. Animation during a performance might seem strange to us, but it does represent an active engagement with the music. The constant interruption between movements; the repetition of movements, if favorably received; the police commissioner shouting for silence at Beethoven's concert; the uproar at *Le sacre:* how often are we so demonstrative or enthusiastic or engaged at a concert?

Recommended Recordings
Jen-yen Chen

The following list of recommended recordings of the five works includes a brief commentary on any special aspects of the given performance (e.g., version of the work, scoring, performance venue) and an evaluation of its artistic merits. In general there is a preference for performances on historical instruments, which do a great deal to recapture the first-night experience of these works. Recommendations for performances on modern instruments are also provided, however, partly for the purposes of comparison and partly in recognition of the fact that performance on period instruments does not by itself guarantee a greater closeness to the experience of the premiere. This discography is not intended as an exhaustive selection of good recordings, and a wider exploration of the many interpretations of these great classics is encouraged.

Recordings of *Orfeo*

Nigel Rogers/Charles Medlam, Chiaroscuro/London Baroque Soloists. EMI 764947 2 (1984)

John Eliot Gardiner, English Baroque Soloists. Deutsche Grammophon Archiv 419 250–2 (1987)

Philip Pickett, New London Consort. Oiseau-Lyre 433 545–2 (1992)

Gwendolyn Toth, ARTEK. Lyrichord 9002 (1995)

Nigel Rogers and Charles Medlam take a small-scale approach to *L'Orfeo*, which results in a performance notable for its intimate and personal character. Rogers's interpretation of the title role is distinguished by its finely accented spoken quality and delicate inflections; the singers and instrumentalists as a whole adopt a light, transparent manner that is well suited to an opera originally composed for a private, aristocratic occasion and set in the rarefied world of gods and godlike heroes.

John Eliot Gardiner's recording is a more intense, muscular account that emphasizes the emotional power of Monteverdi's music. In the program notes to the recording, Gardiner writes, "To participate, as performer or listener, in either work [*L'Orfeo* or the *Vespro della Beata Vergine*] is, potentially, to be exposed to music's power in one of its rawest, most concentrated forms." The seriousness with which he takes this notion is evident throughout this performance, most stunningly in the heart-wrenching rendition of the messenger scene by Anne Sofie von Otter. Taking the title role is Anthony Rolfe Johnson, who executes the virtuoso difficulties of the part with such ease and beauty that one readily imagines Orfeo's music to be capable of swaying the gods. Johnson is a most satisfying Orfeo, and his performance is completely persuasive in its gentle portrayal of Orfeo's sorrow and anguished desire for the restoration of Euridice.

The carefully researched approach that characterizes some performances of early music is illustrated by Philip Pickett's recording of *L'Orfeo*. Pickett attempts to justify through historical evidence virtually every aspect of his performance, including placement of performers, instrumentation, and use of accidentals. For the interested listener, he explains each of his decisions in program notes, which run to forty pages. Its heavily researched nature aside, Pickett's performance is a fresh and lively account of Monteverdi's opera. This is due in large part to the general excellence of his performers, including John Mark Ainsley in the title role. Ainsley proves to be a fine Orfeo, less passionate but more robust and energetic than Anthony Rolfe Johnson.

Gwendolyn Toth's recording typifies a different tendency in the performance of early music from that found in Pickett's. In contrast to Pickett's detailed historical research, Toth approaches Monteverdi's opera with great flexibility, basing her decisions principally on what sounded attractive to her ear. This results in a notably idiosyncratic performance whose features include a resonant church acoustic and great liberty in phrasing by the singers. Such a flexible approach is of course no less historically authentic than one based upon detailed research, for the musical practice of earlier centuries was characterized above all by interpretive freedom and spontaneity. If the goal of historical performance practice is not the retrieval of single "authentic" versions of musical works, but rather a greater understanding of the aesthetic spirit underlying these works, then Toth's vital and engaging performance succeeds admirably. Of course, opinions are likely to vary significantly in the case of so idiosyncratic a reading of Monteverdi's opera, and it remains for the listener to judge the degree of success achieved by Toth's interpretation.

Recordings of *Messiah*

George Solti, Chicago Symphony Orchestra. London 414 396–2 (1985)

Trevor Pinnock, English Concert. Deutsche Grammophon Archiv 423 630–2 (1988)

Nicholas McGegan, Philharmonia Baroque Orchestra. Harmonia Mundi 907051.52 (1991)

William Christie, Les Arts Florissants. Harmonia Mundi 901498.99 (1994)

Messiah is a work whose performance history includes grandiose renditions that employ large forces in an attempt to convey the full splendor of Handel's music.

Unfortunately such renditions frequently obscure the many subtle details of Handel's oratorio, including the wonderful touches of word painting and the intricate counterpoint. George Solti's recording preserves the grandeur of Handel's music but happily does not suffer from muddiness of texture. Solti's ability to produce a transparent sound with large numbers of performers is especially evident in the chorus "For unto us a child is born," which is rendered with an extraordinary lightness throughout. Elsewhere, Solti unleashes his large orchestra and chorus in the display of the more familiar grandiose side of the oratorio. On the whole he achieves a highly satisfactory balance between the expansive and lyrical tendencies of Handel's masterpiece.

If ever evidence was needed that historical instruments are as capable as modern instruments of conveying a sense of gravity and weightiness, then it is provided by Trevor Pinnock's unforgettable account of *Messiah*. Throughout this moving performance, a tone of deep reverence befitting a work on the most sacred of subjects prevails. Pinnock takes tempos that are slower than those typical of *Messiah* performances on historical instruments and thereby lends his performance a feeling of great concentration and intensity. His carefully paced approach allows every number to unfold and build gradually, and never is a detail glossed over or denied its full expressive weight. The result is a passionate and compelling performance that leaves one wondering how Charles Jennens could have felt that Handel had failed to produce music worthy of the oratorio's sacred text.

Nicholas McGegan's recording has the great virtue of making available all surviving material from the many different versions of *Messiah* and allowing the listener to select a desired version by programming his or her CD player. Handel revised his oratorio on numerous occasions between 1741 and 1759, and as a result any prospective recording of *Messiah* must either choose a particular version of the oratorio or do what McGegan has done. Most existing recordings, including the other three recommended here, opt for the first course and usually select a later version of the oratorio. In McGegan's recording, all versions can be heard, including the one presented at the Dublin premiere on April 16, 1742. In purely musical terms, McGegan's interpretation is somewhat disappointing in comparison to Pinnock's enthralling account, though it may be fairer to say that McGegan's interpretative priorities are rather different from Pinnock's. He treats Handel's oratorio in a witty rather than a reverential manner, and the result is a lighthearted performance characterized by some rather mannered phrasing and ornamentation. This is not a *Messiah* for everyone's taste, but it is one that offers an interesting new perspective on a familiar masterpiece.

William Christie's account of *Messiah* is more intimate than Pinnock's and more heartfelt than McGegan's. Christie generally adopts quick tempos, producing a transparent, luminous reading that is remarkable for its beauty and lyricism. The choruses become somewhat less the center of attention with such an approach, and more weight falls upon the solo vocal numbers. This is a rather different kind of emphasis from that found in most recordings of *Messiah,* yet it is rewarding to see someone give central recognition to the lyrical element of the work and furthermore to see this recognition in a performance by musicians as masterful and accomplished as those of Les Arts Florissants.

Recordings of Beethoven's Ninth Symphony

Herbert van Karajan, Berlin Philharmonic Orchestra. Deutsche Grammophon 435 095–2, with Coriolan Overture (1963, Coriolan Overture 1966). Also Deutsche Grammophon Originals 447 401–2, with Coriolan Overture (1963, Coriolan Overture 1966)

Roger Norrington, London Classical Players. Virgin Veritas 61378 (original EMI recording 1987; Virgin reissue 1997)

Christopher Hogwood, Academy of Ancient Music. Oiseau-Lyre 425 517–2 (1989)

John Eliot Gardiner, Orchestre Révolutionnaire et Romantique. Deutsche Grammophon Archiv 447 074–2 (1994)

Herbert van Karajan's 1963 recording of Beethoven's Ninth Symphony remains a spellbinding and powerful account of this work. Karajan successfully combines fast tempos and a pointed rhythmic attack with a beautiful aural sheen to produce a performance that is at once urgent and spacious. Climactic passages are achieved with a ferocious intensity, while lyrical sections have a memorable breadth and sweep. An inspired level of playing is maintained throughout the first three movements, but the musicians give the finest account of themselves in a transcendent reading of the finale, which does full justice to Beethoven's sublime vision of a perfect society.

In his recording of the Ninth Symphony, Roger Norrington attempts to settle once and for all the controversial issue of Beethoven's metronome markings. Norrington argues in the program notes to the recording that these markings make perfect sense when the symphony is performed on period instruments and thus sticks rigorously to the markings in the actual performance. The resulting lightness may come as a shock to listeners used to the more conventionally weighty interpretations of this work. However, such lightness allows Norrington to concentrate upon an aspect of the symphony that is somewhat underemphasized in most interpretations but that may have been central to Beethoven's original conception. In this performance one especially hears the witty and mercurial side of Beethoven's personality, thanks to Norrington's careful highlighting of accent and his fluent phrasing. This manner is preserved throughout and is heard even in the slow movement, in which the usual weightiness is replaced with an almost dancelike quality. Playing an essential role in realizing Norrington's playful vision are his instrumentalists and singers, who demonstrate great technical skill and finesse in executing this uncompromisingly difficult work.

Christopher Hogwood follows in Norrington's footsteps by precisely following Beethoven's metronome markings but tries to achieve the conventional weighty interpretation within the context of the fast tempos. The weightier sound heard on this recording is in part accomplished through a slightly heavier instrumentation, consisting of a doubling of wind parts that may correspond with Beethoven's own practice. This performance as a whole is admirable in its intensity, but it lacks the technical fluency and precision of Norrington's interpretation and has a rather rough, coarse sound. It is as if the musicians were straining too hard to give a tough account of symphony, with the result that the performance has an unrelenting, undifferentiated quality that is less than wholly rewarding to experience.

John Eliot Gardiner also adopts a tough, muscular approach but produces a more distinguished account of the symphony than Hogwood's. Gardiner shows a greater willingness than Hogwood to relax in lyrical passages, and as a result his performance has greater variety and contrast. Of the three recordings on historical instruments that are recommended here, this one achieves the best overall balance between the weightier and lighter aspects of the symphony. Once again Beethoven's metronome markings are followed, although Gardiner argues that the 84 marking for the finale's Turkish march applies to a dotted half note and not to a dotted quarter note, which he believes to represent a notational error in the sources. His tempo for the march and also for the succeeding fugato and choral reprise of the Ode to Joy theme, to which the 84 indication also applies, is therefore twice as fast as in the Norrington and Hogwood recordings. This faster tempo is preferable by far, for although a deliberate pacing of the march is plausible enough, a precipitously fast tempo for the fugato and the reprise of the main theme seems the only adequate way to achieve the ferocious energy and dynamism that are such essential aspects of Beethoven's style and that surely apply here in these two sections.

Recordings of Berlioz's *Symphonie fantastique*

Colin Davis, Vienna Philharmonic Orchestra. Philips 432 151–2 (1991)
Roger Norrington, London Classical Players. EMI 7495 41 (1989)
John Eliot Gardiner, Orchestre Révolutionnaire et Romantique. Philips 434402–2 (1993)

Colin Davis is often regarded as the premier modern interpreter of Berlioz's music, and his recording of the *Symphonie fantastique* with the Vienna Philharmonic does nothing to contradict this reputation. Davis demonstrates a complete mastery of every detail and nuance of this complex score, and his performance is marked by the self-assured, unforced expressiveness of an artist in full command of his interpretive faculties. The collaboration of Davis with the Vienna Philharmonic is a most success-ful one, and Davis draws from the orchestra a rich and supple sound that he shapes to suit the varied moods of the symphony. In this performance one can therefore experi-ence the many diverse emotions of this most Romantic of musical masterpieces, all of them richly expressed by an interpreter with an incomparable understanding of Berlioz's unique style and personality.

Roger Norrington's recording of the *Symphonie fantastique* uses not only his-torical instruments but also the seating arrangement of the first performance. This arrangement consists of groups of instruments placed on raised tiers ranged away from the conductor, so that each group has maximum projective power. Norrington also uses instruments that were part of the premiere but that Berlioz substituted with related, more accessible instruments for the symphony's publication. The value of such a his-torical reconstruction is immediately apparent in this recording, in which the details of Berlioz's score emerge with unaccustomed vividness. Norrington, displaying his usual smoothness and finesse, produces a lively and elegant interpretation that nicely cap-tures the emotional arc traversed by Berlioz's narrative of a failed love interest.

John Eliot Gardiner also adopts the instrumentation and seating of the pre-miere and brings his performance still one step closer to the original performance by recording in the original venue, the old hall of the Paris Conservatoire. According to Gardiner, this hall is characterized by a dry acoustic that permits the diverse colors of Berlioz's orchestra to emerge with great clarity. This claim is substantiated in the actual performance, which is fiercer and more incisive than Norrington's, if lacking some of the latter's lyricism. True to his orchestra's name, Gardiner emphasizes the revolution-ary and Romantic aspects of the symphony. His charged and emotional performance gives a clear idea of why the symphony was so shocking in its day, nowhere more so than in the fierce and unforgettable account of the concluding Witches' Sabbath. Here, Gardiner outdoes even Davis and achieves what must be one of his greatest triumphs, a fearless performance that shows no inhibitions in its presentation of some of Berlioz's most terrifying, twisted, and brilliant music.

Recordings of Stravinsky's *Le sacre du printemps*

Pierre Monteux, Boston Symphony Orchestra. RCA Victor 09026–61898–2, with *Petrushka* (1951, *Petrushka* 1959; digital reissue 1994)

Igor Stravinsky, Columbia Symphony Orchestra. CBS MK 42433, with *Petrushka* (1962; digital reissue 1988)

Pierre Boulez, Cleveland Orchestra. Sony SMK 64 109, with *Petrushka*, performed by the New York Philharmonic (1969, *Petrushka* 1972; digital reissue 1994)

Of the five works presented in this book, *Le sacre du printemps* is the only one for which the matter of historical instruments has little significance, for the instruments of 1913 were substantially the same as those of today. However, there remain other important ways of recapturing the first-night experience of such a work, and two such ways are illustrated by the first two recordings recommended here. Stravinsky was of course the creator of this music, and Pierre Monteux its first interpreter. Although Monteux's recording was made nearly forty years after the premiere of *Le sacre*, it may still give some idea of what it was like to experience Stravinsky's music on the evening of May 29, 1913. Monteux takes an overtly aggressive approach that shows little restraint in emphasizing the savage and primitivist qualities of the score. He generally adopts broad tempos and allows for a maximum of textural activity within these tempos, bringing out the jarring accents of the music with great force and imparting to the ubiquitous repetition of short melodic cells a headlong, driving quality. If this dynamic performance is similar to the one at the premiere, then it is little wonder that the audience was scandalized to the point of starting a riot.

Stravinsky made several recordings of *Le sacre du printemps* during his lifetime. The one recommended here is from 1962, and although some of the other recordings were made closer to the ballet's premiere, this one has been selected because of its ready availability. Stravinsky's interpretation is markedly different from Monteux's and has a lighter, more fluid character. His tempos are considerably quicker, and his orchestral musicians generally play with less force and weight. As a result, his interpretation has much more of a transparent, coloristic quality that may indicate his link with earlier "coloristic" composers, such as his teacher Rimsky-Korsakov. The lightness of the interpretation also lends it a dancelike character, which is only fitting for music originally composed to be danced to. Although this performance does not ignore the primitivism of the score and gives plenty of its own emphasis to this fundamental aspect of the music, it is interesting to note how the creator of the music balances its contrasting tendencies in a rather different manner from other well-known interpreters of this work.

Boulez's celebrated 1969 recording with the Cleveland Orchestra takes tempos more akin to Monteux's, but the savage qualities of the music are less overt and seethe more under the surface. Boulez is more analytical, but the result is a more rather than less compelling performance. Boulez's precision is highly effective in evoking the barbaric tone of the music, because of its complete lack of sentimentality. The impression throughout this performance is of a barely contained explosiveness, one that leaves the listener constantly anxious and on edge. A performance such as this leaves little doubt about music's extraordinary power to affect the listener.

Further Reading

Chapter 1: Monteverdi, *Orfeo*

A useful source of further information about *Orfeo* is a volume edited by John Whenham in the Cambridge Opera Handbook series (*Claudio Monteverdi: Orfeo* [Cambridge: Cambridge University Press, 1986]). In addition to much else of interest, Iain Fenlon's article "The Mantuan Orfeo" provides in one place references to most of the primary sources of information about the first performance; relevant portions of the series of letters between Francesco Gonzaga and his brother, Ferdinando, are accompanied by an English translation by Steven Botterill.

Recent volumes on Monteverdi include Paolo Fabbri, *Monteverdi*, trans. Tim Carter (Cambridge: Cambridge University Press, 1994); Silke Leopold, *Monteverdi: Music in Transition*, trans. Anne Smith (Oxford: Clarendon, 1991). On the historical and humanistic background to the creation of early opera, including *Orfeo*, with a broad selection of citations from contemporaneous theorists, see Barbara Russo Hanning, *Of Poetry and Music's Power: Humanism and the Creation of Opera* (Ann Arbor: UMI Research Press, 1980).

References to Monteverdi's letters are taken from *The Letters of Claudio Monteverdi*, trans. and with an introduction by Denis Stevens (London: Faber and Faber, 1980).

A facsimile of Monteverdi's 1609 score and of the 1607 libretto is *L'Orfeo: Favola in musica* . . . Archivum Musicum. Musica Drammatica, 1 (Florence: Studio per Edizioni Scelte, 1993). Jacopo Peri's *Euridice* is also available in facsimile: *Le Musiche sopra l'Euridice*, Monuments of Music and Music Literature in Facsimile, 1st ser., Music, 28 (New York: Broude Brothers, 1973).

Some specific studies related to musical and other questions in *Orfeo* include Janet E. Beat, "Monteverdi and the Opera Orchestra of His Time," in *The Monteverdi Companion*, ed. Denis Arnold and Nigel Fortune (New York: Norton, 1968), 277–301; Thomas Forrest Kelly, "Orfeo da Camera: Estimating Performing Forces in Early Opera," *Historical Performance* 1 (1988): 3–9: David D. Boyden, "Monteverdi's *violini piccoli alla francese* and *viole da brazzo*," *Annales Musicologiques* 6 (1958–1963): 387–401; Jack A. Westrup, "The Continuo in Monteverdi," in *Claudio Monteverdi e il suo tempo*, ed. Raffaello Monterosso (Verona: Stamperia Valdonega, 1969), 497–502; Joseph Kerman, *Opera as Drama* (New York: Knopf, 1956; new and rev. ed., Berkeley: University of California Press, 1988).

Nino Pirrotta, *Music and Culture in Italy from the Middle Ages to the Baroque: A Collection of Essays* (Cambridge: Harvard University Press, 1984), contains three particularly relevant contributions: "The Orchestra and Stage in Renaissance *Intermedi* and Early Opera," 210–16; "Theater, Sets, and Music in Monteverdi's Operas," 254–70; and "Monteverdi and the Problems of Opera," 235–53.

Nino Pirrotta and Elena Povoledo, *Music and Theatre from Poliziano to Monteverdi,* trans. Karen Eales (Cambridge: Cambridge University Press, 1982), contains material on *Orfeo* and a valuable section on the physical aspects of Renaissance theater.

On the theatrical relationship of Mantua with Ferrara, see A. Cavicchi, "Teatro monteverdiano e tradizione teatrale ferrarese," in *Claudio Monteverdi e il suo tempo,* ed. Raffaello Monterosso, 139–56, including useful illustrations.

On Mantua, the ducal palace, and the life of the court, see Susan Parisi, "Ducal Patronage of Music in Mantua 1587–1627: An Archival Study" (Ph.D. diss., 2 vols., University of Illinois at Urbana-Champaign, 1989); Renato Berzaghi, *The Palazzo Ducale in Mantua,* trans. David Stanton (Milan: Electa, 1992; this is the English translation of the excellent illustrated short guide to the palace, its history, and its decoration by a leading Mantuan scholar); *Splendours of the Gonzaga: Exhibition, 4 November 1981–31 January 1982,* ed. David Chambers and Jane Martineau (London: Victoria & Albert Museum, 1981).

Details of the financing and staffing of the court of Mantua can be found in Aldo da Maddalena, *Le finanze del ducato di Mantova all'epoca di Guglielmo Gonzaga* (Milan: Istituto Editoriale Cisalpino, 1961; the most detailed information comes from 1577; later archival information is much less complete); *Pittura a Mantova dal Romanico al Settecento,* ed. Mina Gregori (Mantua: Cassa di Risparmio delle Provincie Lombarde, 1989), which contains reproductions of many works of art now and formerly in Mantua; Ercolano Mariani and Chiara Perina, *Mantova: Le arti,* pt. 3, in 2 vols. (Mantua: Istituto Carlo d'Arco per la Storia di Mantova, 1965); and Iain Fenlon, *Music and Patronage in Sixteenth-Century Mantua* (Cambridge: Cambridge University Press, 1980).

The site of the first performance is difficult to determine. Many scholars have suggested it was the room now called the *galleria degli specchi,* but this was evidently an open loggia at the beginning of the seventeenth century, and the recent discovery of the name of the painter of its frescoes (Carlo Santner) and a date (1618) seem to make clear that the room was not *yet* in use in 1607 (see Gregori, *Pittura a Mantova,* 252); Carlo Magno's letter (document 12) indicates that the performance is in a room of the apartment that the former duchess of Ferrara had the use of. This apartment is identified, in a letter of January 4, 1580, written by the Florentine ambassador Urbani, as being the "camere lunghe" on the ground floor of the portion of the palace called *corte vecchia* (see Alfonso Lazzari, *Le ultime tre duchesse di Ferrara* [Florence, 1913], 215). For the identification of this space, see Renato Berzaghi, "Ferdinando Gonzaga e il Palazzo Ducale," in *Domenica Fetti, 1588/89–1623,* ed. Eduard A. Safarik (Milan: Electa, 1996), 37. For orientation to the present layout of the palace, I am grateful to Professor Berzaghi and to Paolo Carpeggiani, Rodolfo Signorini, and Roberto Soggia.

A Note on the Ending

Does Apollo in fact come down in his cloud? There is a particular difficulty with the ending of *Orfeo:* the printed libretto contains one version of the story, and the published score another. In the libretto, Orfeo finishes his beautiful act 5 monologue and notices the approach of "an enemy troop of women friends of the drunken Deity" (that is, of Bacchus). He withdraws, and the stage is taken by a group of Bacchantes singing a choral refrain and many verses in praise of Bacchus; a first reference to Orfeo ("he shall not escape punishment") is enough to put him out of their minds, and they continue their frenzied merrymaking to conclude the drama.

In the score, at the same point after Orfeo's monologue, Apollo appears from heaven and invites Orfeo to join Euridice among the stars, where his unruly passions will no more trouble him. A chorus of praise to Orfeo and Apollo, and a final dance, conclude the drama.

The problem is this: Which version was performed in February 1607? It can be argued either way. For example, why would Alessandro Striggio compose, and Francesco Gonzaga print, a libretto that was not going to be sung? Some say that the poetry of the Apollo ending is inferior and surely not the work of Striggio and that the Bacchante ending must have been composed and performed first. The surviving happy ending may result from the alteration of the original score. So goes that argument.

An appropriate time for the Apollo revision wold have been the further performance of *Orfeo* planned for the spring of 1607 during a visit by Duke Carlo Emanuele of Savoy, the prospective father-in-law of the ducal heir Francesco. A happy ending, and one that revives and reconciles the lovers, would be most appropriate for such a visit: Iain Fenlon thus suggests that the Apollo ending might have been composed for this event, the Bacchante ending, as in the libretto, being the original. As it happened, the visit never took place, and neither did the performance, although preparations for it might well have included a revised ending.

Barbara Russano Hanning, in *Of Poetry and Music's Power*, suggests that Monteverdi may have substituted the Apollo ending for the original Bacchantes in the printed score of 1609 after the 1608 success of the *Ballo delle ingrate* and of his opera *Arianna* (which also featured the miraculous appearances of gods), using poetry composed by Ottavio Rinuccini.

On the other hand, Nino Pirrotta has argued that Apollo's descent must have figured in the original version and that the Bacchantes are a poetic addition, perhaps a last-minute accommodation in the first performance of the fact that, in a narrow room, it is not possible to manage the machinery needed to fly Apollo in on a cloud. Apollo was always intended, the argument goes, but had to be altered at the last moment: thus the libretto *does* reproduce the performance ("so that everyone in the audience can have a copy to follow while the performance is in progress," as Francesco Gonzaga says), and the score restores the original Apollo ending, which, though it may not have been performed, is surely the proper end for the opera.

Anthony Pryer has recently argued ("Monteverdi, Two Sonnets and a Letter," *Early Music* 25 [1997]: 357–71) that Monteverdi's interest in Emilio de' Cavalieri's music, mentioned in 1607, and his composition of the madrigal "Zefiro torna" in that year, are related to the final chorus and the moresca of *Orfeo*. This could be true only if the Apollo ending had been composed by, and presumably performed in, 1607.

For me, Apollo is so central to the structure of the opera that it is inconceivable that the sun god would not have made his appearance at the end. One reason for thinking so is perhaps trivial but worth noting. The cast list printed in the score concludes with the "chorus of shepherds who danced the moresca at the end." This does not imply, as a modern edition might, a "chorus of Shepherds who should dance the moresca when this present score is performed"; it says that they *did* dance it: and if they did, it was surely not in the Bacchante ending (which has no men onstage at the end, and certainly no shepherds), but the one we have in the score.

But even more important is the centrality of Apollo to the concept of the work as a whole. We cannot do without him at the end. Internally, Apollo is central to the plot of the opera and in a way even more central to the music. Apollo is himself the god of music as well as of the sun, the father of Orfeo, and the worker of miracles. And these miracles are worked partly in music. Orfeo's first words in the opera are addressed to his father, in his guise as the sun: "Rosa del ciel," rose of the heaven, life of the world.

Apollo is also central musically. The little sinfonia before Orfeo sings his plea (I think it is his invocation of Apollo) returns after Caronte refuses him passage, and there it is Apollo sending Caronte to sleep. The same music returns later in a way that makes clear what was only suggested earlier. When Orfeo finishes his act 5 monologue, the sinfonia is heard again, and for those who were uncertain about its meaning before, Apollo appears in person (descending in a cloud, says the score) and again rescues Orfeo, this time from his excesses of self-pity, and carries him up to heaven.

These three brilliant uses of the same music signify something only gradually revealed but central to the opera—both in its plot and in its theme of human passionate excess contrasted with Apollonian balance. They are essential to the completeness of the work. If the Bacchante ending were the original, the third sinfonia would not be heard, Apollo would not appear, and the magic of the first two sinfonias would lose almost all of their ultimately revealed significance. At least from Monteverdi's point of view, it is impossible to separate the Apollo ending from the opera as an integrated whole.

Chapter 2: Handel, *Messiah*

Recent biographies of Handel include Paul Henry Lang, *George Frideric Handel* (New York: Norton, 1966); Christopher Hogwood, *Handel* (London: Thames and Hudson, 1984), with good illustrations; Jonathan Keates, *Handel: The Man and His Music* (New York: St. Martin's Press, 1985). Much illustrative material about Handel and his environs is found in *Handel: A Celebration of His Life and Times, 1685–1759,* ed. Jacob Simon (London: National Portrait Gallery, 1985), and in H. C. Robbins Landon, *Handel and His World* (London: Weidenfeld and Nicolson, 1984).

Several books are devoted specifically to *Messiah*. They include Watkins Shaw, *A Textual and Historical Companion to Handel's* Messiah (London: Novello, 1965); John Tobin, *Handel's 'Messiah': A Critical Account of the Manuscript Sources and Printed Editions* (London: Cassell, 1969); Jens Peter Larsen, *Handel's Messiah: Origins, Composition, Sources,* 2d ed. (New York: Norton, 1972); Donald Burrows, *Handel, Messiah,* Cambridge Music Handbooks (Cambridge: Cambridge University Press, 1991); Richard Luckett, *Handel's Messiah: A Celebration* (New York: Harcourt Brace, 1992).

Most documentary information about Handel and his surroundings is gathered in Otto Erich Deutsch, *Handel: A Documentary Biography* (New York: Norton, 1955). Of particular interest is Charles Burney, *An Account of the Musical Performances in Westminster-Abbey* (London, 1785; rpt., with an introduction by Peter Kivy, New York: Da Capo, 1979).

On the history of Dublin, see John T. Gilbert, *A History of the City of Dublin,* 3 vols. (Dublin: J. McGlashan, 1854–59; rpt., with introduction by F. E. Dixon, index by Diarmuid Breathnach, Shannon: Irish University Press, 1972); Maurice Craig, *Dublin, 1660–1860* (Dublin: Hodges, Figgis, 1952; rpt., London: Penguin, 1992); La Tourette Stockwell, *Dublin Theatres and Theatre Customs (1637–1820)* (Kingsport, Tenn.: Kingsport Press, 1938).

Chapter 3: Beethoven, Ninth Symphony

Recent books in English on Beethoven include William Kinderman, *Beethoven* (Berkeley: University of California Press, 1995), and Maynard Solomon, *Beethoven* (New York: Schirmer, 1977).

An important source of valuable information not recorded elsewhere is *Thayer's Life of Beethoven,* ed. Eliot Forbes (Princeton: Princeton University Press, 1967); this is a careful revision of Henry Edward Krehbiel's translation (New York, 1921) of Alexander Wheelock Thayer, *Ludwig van Beethovens Leben* (Leipzig: Breitkopf and Härtel, 1901–19).

The letters of Beethoven are edited and translated in Emily Anderson, *Letters of Beethoven* (New York: St. Martin's Press, 1961); for his thoughts on this concert, see letters 1272–89. The standard edition in German is Ludwig van Beethoven, *Briefwechsel Gesamtausgabe,* ed. S. Brandenburg, 8 vols. (of which 6 have appeared) (Munich: G. Henle Verlag, 1996–). The other side of Beethoven's correspondence is reported in *Letters to Beethoven and Other Correspondence,* trans. and ed. Theodore Albrecht, 3 vols. (Lincoln: University of Nebraska Press, 1996); volume 3 covers the years 1824–28.

Many of the quotations having to do with preparations for this performance come from Beethoven's conversation books, in which Schindler, Schuppanzigh, and many others involved in the concert wrote their comments and questions to Beethoven; Beethoven spoke his replies, so we have only half of the conversations, but they are enormously valuable. Beethoven's conversation books have been edited by Karl-Heinz Köhler and Grita Herre, with the collaboration of Peter Pötschner, as *Ludwig van Beethovens Konversationshefte,* 10 vols. (Leipzig: Deutscher Verlag für Musik, 1972–88); conversations relative to this performance are found in volumes 5 and 6 (1970, 1974).

Anton Felix Schindler, *Beethoven as I Knew Him,* ed. Donald W. MacArdle, trans. Constance S. Jolly (Chapel Hill: University of North Carolina Press, 1966; rpt., New York: Norton, 1972) is a translation of the 3d ed. (Münster: Aschendorff, 1860) of Schindler's *Biographie von Ludwig van Beethoven,* first published in 1840. Schindler's account of the preparations and performance are found on pp. 272–84. Schindler is notorious among historiographers for his liberty in reporting facts; he was present during the preparations for this performance, but any report from Schindler is worth checking against other sources.

Highly valuable here is David Benjamin Levy, "Early Performances of Beethoven's Ninth Symphony: A Documentary Study of Five Cities" (Ph.D. diss., Eastman School of Music, University of Rochester, 1979); in addition to his commentaries, Levy has assembled in one place, and translated, all the known press reports of the concert. Levy's recently published *Beethoven: The Ninth Symphony* (New York: Schirmer, 1994) includes a chapter on the first performance. Another study of the performance of the Ninth Symphony is Andreas Eichhorn, *Beethovens Neunte Symphonie: Die Geschichte ihrer Aufführung und Rezeption* (Kassel: Barenreiter, 1993). On the symphony, see also Nicholas Cook, *Beethoven Symphony no. 9,* Cambridge Music Handbooks (Cambridge: Cambridge University Press, 1993).

Two volumes edited by H. C. Robbins Landon contain much illustrative and documentary material: *Beethoven: His Life, Work and World* (London: Thames and Hudson, 1992), and *Beethoven: A Documentary Study* (New York: Macmillan, 1970).

An articulate visitor's account of Vienna is Henry F. Chorley, *Modern German Music,* 2 vols. (London: Smith, Elder, 1854; rpt., with introduction and index by Hans

Lenneberg, New York: Da Capo, 1973). Another important source of information from a contemporaneous Englishman is reported in *Leaves from the Journals of Sir George Smart,* ed. H. Bertram Cox and C. L. E. Cox (London: Longmans, Green, 1907). A variety of accounts of Vienna and its inhabitants is found in John Lehmann and Richard Bassett, *Vienna: A Travellers' Companion* (New York: Atheneum, 1988).

Two books giving extensive background on life and music in Vienna are Mary Sue Morrow, *Concert Life in Haydn's Vienna: Aspects of a Developing Musical and Social Institution,* Sociology of Music 7 (Stuyvesant, N.Y.: Pendragon Press, 1989), and Alice M. Hanson, *Musical Life in Biedermeier Vienna* (Cambridge: Cambridge University Press, 1985). Important articles on the subject include Otto Biba, "Concert Life in Beethoven's Vienna," in *Beethoven, Performers, and Critics: The International Beethoven Congress, Detroit, 1977,* ed. Robert Winter and Bruce Carr (Detroit: Wayne State University Press, 1980), 77–93; and Clive Brown, "The Orchestra in Beethoven's Vienna," *Early Music* 16 (1988): 4–20. Carl F. Pohl, *Die Gesellschaft der Musikfreunde des österreichischen Kaiserstadts und ihr Conservatorium* (Vienna: K.K. Akademie für Musik und Darstellende Kunst, 1912), gives a history of this important institution.

On more technical aspects of musical performance, see Robin Stowell, *Violin Technique and Performance Practice in the Late Eighteenth and Early Nineteenth Centuries* (Cambridge: Cambridge University Press, 1985).

Chapter 4: Berlioz, *Symphonie fantastique*

Recent biographies of Berlioz in English include D. Kern Holoman, *Berlioz* (Cambridge: Harvard University Press, 1989); David Cairns, *Berlioz, 1803–1832: The Making of an Artist* (London: André Deutsch, 1989); Jacques Barzun, *Berlioz and the Romantic Century,* 3d ed., 2 vols. (New York: Columbia University Press, 1969).

Berlioz's memoirs have been translated into English as *Memoirs of Hector Berlioz, Member of the French Institute, Including His Travels in Italy, Germany, Russia, and England, 1803–1865,* trans. and ed. David Cairns (New York: Knopf, 1969; rpt., New York: Norton, 1975).

The authoritative edition of Berlioz's correspondence is Hector Berlioz, *Correspondance générale* (6 vols. to date), edited under the direction of Pierre Citron, vol. 1, 1803–32 (Paris: Flammarion, 1972–).

Two recent editions of the symphony have improved our understanding of its text and provided much important information. Edward T. Cone's edition for the Norton Critical Scores (*Fantastic Symphony: An Authoritative Score; Historical Background; Analysis; Views and Comments* [New York: Norton, 1971]) includes an edition, a thorough introduction, interesting textual notes, an analysis, and translations of the program and of other historical documents to which I am much indebted. Nicholas

Temperley's edition in the new Berlioz edition (*Hector Berlioz: New Edition of the Complete Works,* vol. 16, *Symphonie fantastique* [1972], issued by the Berlioz Centenary Committee, London, in association with the Calouste Gulbenkian Foundation, Lisbon [Kassel: Barenreiter, 1967–]) has a number of important appendices.

D. Kern Holoman has done substantial work on deciphering Berlioz's autograph manuscript; see *The Creative Process in the Autograph Musical Documents of Hector Berlioz, c. 1818–1840,* Studies in Musicology, no. 7 (Ann Arbor: UMI Research Press, 1980), 262–82.

The following volume contains many significant contributions to the understanding of the musical life of Paris in 1830: *Music in Paris in the Eighteen-thirties / La musique à Paris dans les années mil huit cent trente,* ed. Peter Bloom (Stuyvesant, N.Y.: Pendragon Press, 1987). Particularly useful articles include Jacques Barzun, "Paris in 1830" (1–22); David Cairns, "Reflections on the *Symphonie fantastique* of 1830" (81–96); D. Kern Holoman, "The Emergence of the Orchestral Conductor in Paris in the 1830s" (387–430); Jean-Michel Nectoux, "Trois orchestres parisiens en 1830" (471–505; English summary, 506–7); Nicole Wild, "La musique dans les mélodrames des théâtres parisiens" (589–609; English summary, 571–73).

The editor of the above volume has himself contributed much to our understanding of Berlioz, Paris in 1830, and this concert in particular. Peter Bloom, "'Politics' and the Musical Press in 1830," *Periodica Musica* 5 (1987): 9–16, gives a list (14) of journals that reviewed the performance and suggests (15*n*17) that the author of the anonymous review in *Le Temps* may have been Berlioz's friend Ernest Legouvé. Bloom's "Episodes in the Livelihood of an Artist: Berlioz's Contacts and Contracts with Publishers," *Journal of Musicological Research* 15 (1995): 219–73, gives an idea of the economics of music. See also his "Berlioz in the Year of the *Symphonie fantastique,*" *Journal of Musicological Research* 9 (1989): 67–88. Difficult to find but worth reading is Bloom's "*Sardanapale* and the *Symphonie fantastique*: A Programme, a Letter, a Coincidence," *Berlioz Society Bulletin* 128 (Summer 1986): 1–10, with facsimile facing p. 1.

A highly readable account of the literary and dramatic activities in Paris in these years is Linda Kelly, *The Young Romantics: Paris, 1827–37* (London: Bodley Head, 1976).

Much of the information here on theaters and their repertories and orchestras is from *Almanach des spectacles pour 1830. Neuvième année* (Paris: Barba, 1830); and from *Agenda musical ou indicateur des amateurs, artistes, et commerçans en musique. Pour 1836. Par Planque, musicien et accordeur de pianos* (Paris, 1836; rpt., Geneva: Minkoff, 1981, together with *Agenda musica . . . 1837*). Fascinating details of Parisian musical life can be found in *La musique à Paris en 1830–1831,* ed. François Lesure et al. (Paris: Bibliothèque Nationale, 1983). Historical information on Parisian theaters in the nineteenth century, with interesting plans, can be found in Nicole Wild, *Diction-*

naire des théâtres parisiens au XIXe siècle, Domaine Musicologique, 4 (Paris: Aux Amateurs de Livres, 1989).

On the history of the Conservatoire in this period and on Habeneck's concerts, see A. Dandelot, *La Société des Concerts du Conservatoire de 1828 à 1897,* 3d ed. (Paris: Havard, 1898); Antoine Elwart, *Histoire de la Société des Concerts du Conservatoire impérial de musique* (Paris: S. Castel, 1860); Henri de Curzon, *L'histoire et la gloire de l'ancienne salle du Conservatoire de Paris (1811–1911)* (Paris: Senart, 1917).

On Berlioz and the orchestra, see Adam Carse, *The Orchestra from Beethoven to Berlioz* (Cambridge, Eng.: Heffer, 1948; New York: Broude, 1949). Berlioz's treatise on orchestration, full of his opinions and experience, has been translated and revised many times.

Chapter 5: Stravinsky, *Le sacre du printemps*

There is an enormous amount of material available about *Le sacre du printemps.* Most of the works listed here concern the first performance and its background.

The best book on Stravinsky is the recent two-volume work by Richard Taruskin, *Stravinsky and the Russian Traditions: A Biography of the Works through Mavra* (Berkeley: University of California Press, 1996).

Stravinsky himself wrote and spoke often about *Le sacre.* The following publications are particularly relevant: *Igor Stravinsky: An Autobiography* (New York: Simon and Schuster, 1936; rpt., New York: Norton, 1962); Igor Stravinsky and Robert Craft, *Conversations with Igor Stravinsky* (New York: Doubleday, 1959), 47–48; Igor Stravinsky and Robert Craft, *Expositions and Development* (London: Faber and Faber, 1962), 140–43; and Igor Stravinsky and Robert Craft, *Memories and Commentaries* (London: Faber and Faber, 1960), 35–40, 42–53.

Stravinsky's 1913 score was published by Editions Russes de Musique, Paris, and copyright problems have generated many reprints (and perhaps some of Stravinsky's later revisions). Stravinsky's sketches for the ballet have been published in a beautiful facsimile; the publication contains much other useful material: Igor Stravinsky, *The Rite of Spring: Sketches, 1911–1913. Facsimile Reproductions from the Autographs* (London: Boosey and Hawkes, 1969), with a preface by François Lesure and "Genesis of a Masterpiece," by Robert Craft (in English, French, and German), vii–xlvii. An appendix (47 pp.) includes "Commentary to the Sketches," by Robert Craft; Stravinsky's letters to N. C. Roerich and N. F. Findeizen ; "The Stravinsky-Nijinsky Choreography," by Igor Stravinsky; and "The Performance of the Rite of Spring," by Robert Craft. See also Robert Craft, "*The Rite of Spring:* Genesis of a Masterpiece," *Perspectives of New Music* 5 (Fall–Winter 1966): 20–36.

A dissertation by Truman Bullard, in addition to providing a fascinating analysis of the performance and its background, transcribes and translates into English almost all the journalistic materials published in connection with the first performance of *Le sacre.* I am naturally much indebted to his work; the documents included here are those most closely related to the performance itself and are newly translated. See Truman Bullard, "The First Performance of Igor Stravinsky's 'Sacre du Printemps,'" 3 vols. (Ph.D. diss., Eastman School of Music, University of Rochester, 1971; Ann Arbor: University Microfilms).

Facsimiles or semifacsimiles of many of the newspaper and magazine reviews are found in *Igor Stravinsky, Le sacre du printemps: Dossier de presse: press-book,* ed. François Lesure, with Gertraut Haberkamp, Malcolm Turner, and Emilia Zanetti (Geneva: Minkoff, 1980).

An enormous amount of research on the Nijinsky choreography has been carried out by Millicent Hodson, whose progress has been reported in a series of publications, and whose reconstruction of the original choreography was first performed by the Joffrey Ballet in Los Angeles on September 30, 1987, and televised on January 12, 1990, in "The Search for Nijinsky's *Rite of Spring*" (Thirteen/WNET and Danmarks Radio). See Millicent Hodson, *Nijinsky's Crime against Nature: Reconstruction Score of the Original Choreography for Le Sacre du Printemps,* Dance and Music Series, 8 (Stuyvesant, N.Y.: Pendragon Press, 1996).

On the theater, see *Théâtres des Champs-Elysées, 1913–1963: Cinquante années de créations artistiques,* ed. Michel Brunet (Paris: Olivier Perrin, 1963).

On Nicholas Roerich, see Jacqueline Decter, with the Nicholas Roerich Museum, *Nicholas Roerich: The Life and Art of a Russian Master* (Rochester, Vt.: Park Street Press, 1989).

Memoirs of persons connected with the first performance include Lydia Sokolova, *Dancing for Diaghilev,* ed. Richard Buckle (London: John Murray, 1960); Anatole Bourman and D. Lyman, *The Tragedy of Nijinsky* (New York: McGraw-Hill, 1936); *Bronislava Nijinska: Early Memoirs,* trans. and ed. Irina Nijinska and Jean Rawlinson, with an introduction by and in consultation with Anna Kisselgoff (New York: Holt, Rinehart and Winston, 1981); Doris G. Monteux, *It's All in the Music* (New York: Farrar, Straus, and Giroux, 1965); Gabriel Astruc, *Le pavillon des fantômes* (Paris: Grasset, 1929).

Books on the Diaghilev Ballet and Nijinsky include Cyril W. Beaumont, *Bookseller at the Ballet* (London: C. W. Beaumont, 1975); Cyril W. Beaumont, *Vaslav Nijinsky* (London: C. W. Beaumont, 1933; rpt., 1942); Romola Nijinska, *Nijinsky* (London: Victor Gollancz, 1933); Richard Buckle, *Diaghilev* (New York: Atheneum, 1979); Sergei Leonidovitch Grigoriev, *The Diaghilev Ballet, 1909–1929,* trans. Vera Bowen (London: Constable, 1953); Richard Buckle, *Nijinsky* (London: C. W. Beaumont, 1933; rpt., 1943); Nathalie Gontcharova, Michel Larionov, and Pierre Vorms, *Les Ballets Russes: Serge de Diaghilew et la décoration théâtrale* (Belvès, France: Vorms, 1955).

Nijinsky's journal of 1918–19 is edited as *Nijinsky: Cahiers*, trans. from the Russian by Christian Dumais-Lvowski and Galina Pogojeva, Librairie de la Danse (Arles: Actes Sud, 1995).

For wider information on Parisian life in 1913, see Glenn Watkins, *Pyramids at the Louvre: Music, Culture, and Collage from Stravinsky to the Postmodernists* (Cambridge: Belknap Press of Harvard University Press, 1994); Modris Eksteins, *Rites of Spring: The Great War and the Birth of the Modern Age* (Boston: Houghton Mifflin, 1989; rpt., New York: Doubleday, 1990).

Popular entertainment and diversion in Paris before the First World War is the subject of Charles Rearick, *Pleasures of the Belle Epoque: Entertainment and Festivity in Turn-of-the-Century France* (New Haven: Yale University Press, 1985).

Two further, and very different, works are Liliane Brion-Guerry, ed., *L'annee 1913: Les formes ésthetiques de l'oeuvre d'art* (Paris: Klincksieck, 1971; rpt., 1990), and *Pleasure Guide to Paris for Bachelors* (London: Nilsson, n.d. [ca. 1903]).

Notes

Chapter 1: Monteverdi, *Orfeo*
Boxes

9 The Venetian ambassador describes Mantua: *Relazioni degli ambasciatori veneti al senato,* ed. Arnaldo Segarizzi, 4 vols. (Bari: G. Laterza, 1912–16; rpt., ed. Angelo Ventura, Rome: G. Laterza, 1976), 1:78–82; rpt. in Paolo Fabbri, *Monteverdi,* trans. Tim Carter (Cambridge: Cambridge University Press, 1994), 25–26.

12 The Venetian ambassador describes Duke Vincenzo: *Relazioni degli ambasciatori,* ed. Segarizzi, 78–82, adapted from the translation in Fabbri, *Monteverdi,* 25–26.

15 Francesco Morosini in 1608 reports back to Venice: "Relazione di Francesco Morosini, ritornato ambasciatore di Mantova, presentata e letta nell'Eccellentissimo Senato [of Venice] à 21 zugno 1608," in *Relazioni degli ambasciatori,* ed. Segarizzi, 1:88.

17 "Every Friday night": *The Letters of Claudio Monteverdi,* ed., trans., and with an introduction by Denis Stevens (London: Faber and Faber, 1980), 85.

19 Vincenzo Giustiniani: *Hercole Bottrigari: Il desiderio . . . , Vincenzo Giustiniani: Discorso sopra la musica,* trans. Carol MacClintock, Musicological Studies and Documents, no. 9 (n.p.: American Institute of Musicology, 1962), 69.

23 Giovanni Battista Doni, *Trattato della musica,* ca. 1630, as cited in Silke Leopold, *Monteverdi: Music in Transition,* trans. Anne Smith (Oxford: Clarendon, 1991), 85.

24 Marsilio Ficino: quoted in D. P. Walker, "Ficino's *Spiritus and Music,*" *Annales musicologiques* 1 (1953): 139.

30 Dedicatory letter from the first edition (1609) of the score of *Orfeo.*

35 Cast list: Author.

36 Giustiniani on the double harp: *Hercole Bottrigari, Vincenzo Giustiniani,* 78.

Text

3 Epigraph: "For this century": *The Portable Renaissance Reader,* ed. and trans. James Bruce Ross and Mary Martin McLaughlin (New York: Viking, 1953), 9.

4 "The fortune I have known in Mantua": translation adapted from *Letters of Claudio Monteverdi,* 58.

4 "Because of his responsibility for both church and chamber music": The preface to the *Scherzi musicali* of 1607 is translated in Oliver Strunk, *Source Readings in Music History* (New York: Norton, 1965); this passage is on p. 406.

16 "I am not satisfied with our Courtier": Baldassare Castiglione, *Il cortegiano* (1528), trans. by Charles S. Singleton as *The Book of the Courtier* (Garden City, N.Y.: Doubleday, 1959), 74.

24 "Keeping in mind those modes and accents": Strunk, *Source Readings,* 374.

28 "This is to introduce Giovanni Gualberto": John Whenham, ed., *Claudio Monteverdi, Orfeo* (Cambridge: Cambridge University Press, 1986), 169; see document 6.

29 "I had expected that the castrato would have arrived by now": Whenham, *Orfeo,* 169; see document 7.

29 "He knows only the Prologue": Whenham, *Orfeo*, 170; see document 8.

29 "The musical play is to be performed in our Academy tomorrow": Whenham, *Orfeo*, 170–71; see document 9.

29 "Tomorrow evening the Most Serene Lord the Prince": Whenham, *Claudio Monteverdi*, 170; see document 12.

31 "I have nothing else to tell your lordship about *Orfeo*": *Letters of Claudio Monteverdi*, 64.

33 "That signor Francesco Rasio": Eugenio Cagnani, *Raccolta d'alcune rime di scrittori mantovani* (Mantua, 1612), 9, quoted from Warren Kirkendale, "Zur Biographie des ersten Orfeo, Francesco Rasi," in *Claudio Monteverdi: Festschrift Reinhold Hammerstein zum 70. Geburtstag*, ed. Ludwig Finscher, 304–6; see document 14.

33 "Sang, whether bass or tenor": *Hercole Bottrigari . . . Vincenzo Giustiniani*, 1.

33 "A handsome man, jovial and with a strong and sweet voice": Severo Bonini, *Discorsi e regoli*, ed. and trans. Mary Ann Bonino (Provo: Brigham Young University, 1979), 149–50.

34 "That little priest—*pretino*—who played Euridice": mentioned by the Mantuan agent Gabriele Bertazzuolo in 1608; see Angelo Solerti, *Musica, ballo, et drammatica alla corte medicea dal 1600 al 1637* (Florence: Bemporad, 1905; rpt., Bologna: Forni, 1969), 55; see also Iain Fenlon, "The Mantuan Orfeo," in Whenham, *Orfeo*, 4.

34 Report of 1608 that the duke did not allow female singers in public: from the report of Federico Follini on the 1608 festivities in Mantua, in Angelo Solerti, *Gli albori del melodramma*, 3 vols. (Milan: R. Sandron, 1904), 3:208.

36 "That group of cornet and trombone players"; "play all the wind instruments": *Letters of Claudio Monteverdi*, 64.

36 Monteverdi has one more candidate for Prince Francesco's wind band: *The Letters of Claudio Monteverdi*, 81.

38 "When the candelabra were lit inside the theatre": Federico Follino's description of the festivities in Mantua in 1608 and the opening of "L'idropica," in *Compendio delle sontuose faste . . .*; translation adapted from "Theater, Sets, and Music in Monteverdi's Operas," in Nino Pirrotta, *Music and Culture in Italy from the Middle Ages to the Baroque: A Collection of Essays* (Cambridge: Harvard University Press, 1984), 256.

49 "The play was performed to the great satisfaction": Whenham, *Orfeo*, 171; see document 10.

51 "Ariadne moved us because she was a woman": *Letters of Claudio Monteverdi*, 117.

51 "[Monteverdi] has shown me the words": Whenham, *Orfeo*, 167; see document 13.

Chapter 2: Handel, *Messiah*
Boxes

68 Burney's account of Handel in Chester: Charles Burney, *An Account of the Musical Performances in Westminster-Abbey* (London, 1785); rpt., with an introduction by Peter Kivy (New York: Da Capo, 1979), 26 n.

73 Jennens on Messiah: see document 13; *Autograph Letters of George Frideric Handel and Charles Jennens: Property of Earl Howe, C. B. E.*, illustrated catalogue (sold by Christie, Manson and Woods, July 4, 1973), 23; cited in Otto Erich Deutsch, *Handel: A Documentary Biography* (New York: Norton, 1955), 622.

82 Signora Avolio's concert: Deutsch, *Handel*, 543.

84 Jonathan Swift to the subdean: see document 6; Deutsch, *Handel*, 537.

85 Dubourg's ornaments: Burney, *Musical Performances*, 27 n.

87 The Foundling Hospital parts: John Tobin, *Handel's Messiah* (London: Cassel, 1969), 4.

99 The *Universal Spectator:* Deutsch, *Handel,* 564–65.

100 Handel's leave-taking: Deutsch, *Handel,* 757.

Text

61 Epigraph: "Han't you been at the Oratorio?": from a pamphlet entitled *See and Seem Blind: Or a Critical Dissertation on the Publick Dversions* [*sic*] (1732); Deutsch, *Handel,* 301.

67 "It has fed the hungry": Burney, *Musical Performances,* 27.

68 "Other considerations suggested to him": see document 4; Sir John Hawkins, *A General History of the Science and Practice of Music,* 5 vols. (London, 1776); rpt., 3 vols. (New York: J. L. Peters, 1875); latter rpt. in 2 vols., with a new introduction by Charles Cudworth (New York: Dover, 1963), 2:889.

73 "His Messiah has disappointed me": see document 13; *Letters of Handel and Jennens,* 23; cited in H. C. Robbins Landon, *Handel and His World* (London: Weidenfeld and Nicolson, 1984), 172.

73 "As to the Messiah, 'tis still in his power": see document 13; *Letters of Handel and Jennens,* 23; cited in Landon, *Handel and His World,* 172.

76 "The only Kingdom I ever heard or read of": Jonathan Swift, *Gulliver's Travels and Selected Writings in Prose and Verse,* ed. John Hayward (London: Nonesuch, 1990), 507.

78 "Order'd [by the Governors of Mercer's Hospital]": see document 5; Deutsch, *Handel,* 534.

80 "Then tragedy expired with her": Richard Luckett, *Handel's Messiah: A Celebration* (New York: Harcourt Brace, 1992), 130.

81 "Very fond of Mrs Cibber": Burney, *Musical Performances,* 34.

81 "Native sweetness and power of expression": Charles Burney, *A General History of Music,* first published 1776–89; new edition, ed. Frank Mercer (New York: Harcourt Brace, 1935); rpt., 2 vols. (New York: Dover, 1957), 2:1003.

81 "A mere thread, and knowledge of Music, inconsiderable": Burney, *Musical Performances,* 26–27.

82 "Woman, for this be all thy sins forgiven thee!": Luckett, *Handel's Messiah,* 128.

83 "I presume he is qualified for that which he desires": *The Correspondence of Jonathan Swift,* ed. Harold Williams, 5 vols. (Oxford: Clarendon, 1963–65), 5:126.

83 "Has one good quality": *Correspondence of Jonathan Swift,* 5:124–25.

83 "I recommend one Mr Mason": *Correspondence of Jonathan Swift,* 3:332.

83 "I have form'd an other Tenor Voice": see document 3; Deutsch, *Handel,* 530–31.

84 "The Basses and Counter Tenors are very good": see document 3; Deutsch, *Handel,* 530–31.

84 "Dubourg was first fiddle": Deutsch, *Handel,* 218.

85 "Obliged to put off his Day": Deutsch, *Handel,* 540.

88 "Mr. Charles the Hungarian, Master of the French Horn": Deutsch, *Handel,* 542.

88 "Gentlemen and Ladies are desired to order their Coaches": Deutsch, *Handel,* 534–35.

89 "As it will greatly encrease the Charity": Deutsch, *Handel,* 545. This notice concerns the hoops. A notice about the swords appeared three days later.

89 "The audience being composed": see document 3; Deutsch, *Handel,* 530–31.

91 "Handel wore an enormous white wig": Burney, *Musical Performances,* 36.

91 "Indeed, his hand was then so fat": Burney, *Musical Performances,* 35.

92 "Yesterday Mr. Handell's new Grand Sacred Oratorio": see document 10; *Dublin Journal,* April 10; Deutsch, *Handel,* 545.

93 "Yesterday Morning, at the Musick Hall": see document 9; *Dublin News-Letter,* April 10; Deutsch, *Handel,* 544–45.

94 "On Tuesday last": see document 11; *Dublin Journal,* April 10; the same report, minus the last sentence, appeared in the *Dublin Gazette* and the *Dublin News-Letter;* Deutsch, *Handel,* 546.

94 "The *Messiah* was performed in Dublin": Burney, *General History of Music,* 2:1006–7.

95 "As Mr. Handel in his oratorio's": see document 12; *Letters of Handel and Jennens;* quoted in Christopher Hogwood, *Handel* (London: Thames and Hudson, 1984), 179, in a shortened version. The text here is from Richard Luckett, *Handel's Messiah,* 129–30.

95 "Without Vanity the Performance was received": see document 3; Deutsch, *Handel,* 530–31.

95 "HANDEL's general look": Burney, *Musical Performances,* 37.

98 "I have with great difficulty made him correct": see document 13; Deutsch, *Handel,* 622.

98 "They seem'd indeed throughly engag'd": see document 12; *Letters of Handel and Jennens;* quoted in Hogwood, *Handel,* 179, in a shortened version. The text here is from Luckett, *Handel's Messiah,* 129–30.

99 "It seems to be a Species of Musick": see document 12; *Letters of Handel and Jennens;* quoted in Hogwood, *Handel,* 179, in a shortened version. The text here is from Luckett, *Handel's Messiah,* 129–30.

99 "It was agreed by all the judges present": *Dublin Journal,* May 22, 1742, referring to the rehearsal; Deutsch, *Handel,* 549.

100 "In order to keep the Room as cool as possible": *Dublin Journal,* May 29, 1742; Deutsch, *Handel,* 550.

Chapter 3: Beethoven, Ninth Symphony

Beethoven's conversation books have been edited by Karl-Heinz Köhler and Grita Herre, with the collaboration of Peter Pötschner, as *Ludwig van Beethovens Konversationshefte,* 9 vols. (Leipzig: Deutscher Verlag für Musik, 1972–88); conversations relative to this performance are found in vols. 5 and 6 (1970, 1974); citations below are to volume and page; translations by the author. Beethoven's letters are cited by number from *Letters of Beethoven,* ed. and trans. Emily Anderson (New York: St. Martin's, 1961).

Boxes

111 To Count Moritz Dietrichstein: see document 3; letter 1273. Memorandum in the Imperial Royal High Steward's office, *Letters to Beethoven and Other Correspondence,* trans. and ed. Theodore Albrecht, 3 vols. (Lincoln: University of Nebraska Press, 1996), 3:16.

112 Carl Czerny on Beethoven's concert: see document 25; Albrecht, *Letters to Beethoven,* 3:37.

118 The English physician Richard Bright on Vienna: *Travels in Vienna . . . in the Year 1814,* cited in John Lehmann and Richard Bassett, *Vienna: A Travellers' Companion* (New York: Atheneum, 1988), 55–56.

123 J. F. Reichardt on the Viennese theater: J. F. Reichardt, *Briefe geschrieben auf einer Reise nach Wien* (1810), trans. Oliver Strunk, *Source Readings in Music History* (New York: Norton, 1950), 728–30.

126 A concert in Vienna: Reichardt, *Briefe,* trans. Strunk, *Source Readings,* 736.

130 Anton Schindler's official request for the Kärntnertor Theater: see document 6; Albrecht, *Letters to Beethoven,* 28–29.

131 Beethoven letter to a copyist: see document 5; letter 1275.

137 Translation of poster, p. 136.

140 A description of Henriette Sontag: Alphonse de Pontmartin, *Souvenirs d'un vieux mélomane* (Paris: Calman Levy, 1879), 5–6.

144 The singer Franz Wild: trans. in Elliot Forbes, ed., *Thayer's Life of Beethoven* (Princeton: Princeton University Press, 1967), 570.

146 Johannn Friedrich Reichardt on Schuppanzigh: Reichardt, *Briefe,* trans. Strunk, *Source Readings,* 733–34.

147 Henry Chorley on Mayseder: Henry F. Chorley, *Modern German Music,* 2 vols. (London: Smith, Elder, 1854), 2:137–39.

156 Beethoven to Henriette Sontag: see document 21; letter 1289.

Text

109 Epigraph: "After talks and discussions": see document 12; letter 1281.

110 "He was an artist, and who shall arise to stand beside him?": quoted from the translation of Grillparzer's oration in O. G. Sonneck, *Beethoven: Impressions of Contemporaries* (New York: Schirmer, 1926); rpt. as *Beethoven: Impressions by His Contemporaries* (New York: Dover, 1967), 230.

112 "The concert opened with a Haydn symphony": *Allgemeine musikalische Zeitung,* May 29, 1805, trans. in Mary Sue Morrow, *Concert Life in Haydn's Vienna* (Stuyvesant, N.Y.: Pendragon, 1989), 143.

112 "First a quartet or a symphony": *Allgemeine musikalische Zeitung,* October 22, 1800, trans. in Morrow, *Concert Life,* 143.

113 "I was very attentive": Friedrich Nicolai, *Beschreibung einer Reise durch Deutschland und die Schweiz, im Jahre 1781,* 12 vols. (Berlin: Stetlin, 1783–96), trans. in Morrow, *Concert Life,* 144.

122 "Vienna is swarming with teachers": letter 90.

122 Czerny gave eleven or twelve lessons a day: Carl Czerny, "Recollections from My Life," *Musical Quarterly* 42 (1956): 313.

124 "Small and dirty": George Smart, 1838, quoted in H. Bertram Cox and C. L. E. Cox, *Leaves from the Journal of Sir George Smart* (London: Longmans, Green, 1907), 99.

124 "Dingy, ugly, and inconvenient in form": Frances Trollope, *Vienna and the Austrians* (London: Richard Bentley, 1838), 319.

129 There should be arias or duets ("which are so pleasing to the public"): Köhler and Herre, *Beethovens Konversationshefte,* 5:185.

133 "12 on each [violin] part": Köhler and Herre, *Beethovens Konversationshefte,* 5:106.

134 "Twenty to twenty-four for each part are already on hand": Köhler and Herre, *Beethovens Konversationshefte,* 5:235.

135 "Oh, all right!": Anton Felix Schindler, *Beethoven as I Knew Him,* ed. Donald W. MacArdle, trans. Constance S. Jolly (Chapel Hill: University of North Carolina Press, 1966; rpt., New York: Norton, 1972), 283.

139 "Not very full" … "many boxes empty"; see document 26; from the autograph in the Handschriftensammlung of the Österreichisches Nationalbibliothek, as trans. in H. C. Robbins Landon, *Beethoven: A Documentary Study* (New York: Macmillan, 1970), 355.

141 "I still see that simple room": letter to Ludwig Nohl, printed in Ludwig Nohl, *Mosaik für Musikalisch-Gebildete* (Leipzig: Gebruder Senf, 1882), 282, trans. in Landon, *Beethoven*, 363.

141 Haizinger's voice was described as "very beautiful": Julian Marshall and John Warrack, "Haizinger, Anton," in *The New Grove Dictionary of Music and Musicians*, ed. Stanley Sadie, 20 vols. (London: Macmillan, 1980), 9:38.

143 "In singing the Italians have always been the model": *Caecilia* 1 (1824), cols. 195–96; trans. in David Benjamin Levy, "Early Performances of Beethoven's Ninth Symphony: A Documentary Study of Five Cities," Ph.D. diss., University of Rochester, 1979, 29–30.

143 "The opera was capitally prepared": Forbes, *Thayer's Life of Beethoven*, 583.

151 "Black dress coat, white neckerchief": Forbes, *Thayer's Life of Beethoven*, 909.

152 "Schuppanzigh praises the master who cut your hair": Köhler and Herre, *Beethovens Konversationshefte*, 6:170.

154 "The winds did very bravely": Köhler and Herre, *Beethovens Konversationshefte*, 6:161.

154 "The *harmonie* of the theater is going to the devil": Köhler and Herre, *Beethovens Konversationshefte*, 6:116, 117.

154 "How many contrabasses should play the recitative?": *Beethovens Konversationshefte*, 6:249.

154 "But what about Preisinger?": Köhler and Herre, *Beethovens Konversationshefte*, 6:129.

155 "I attended all (or most) of the orchestral rehearsals": *Allgemeine musikalische Zeitung*, n.s. 2 (1864): 245–46; trans. in Landon, *Beethoven*, 355–56.

155 "For all the large forces, little effect": from the autograph in the Handschriftensammlung of the Österreichisches Nationalbibliothek, trans. in Landon, *Beethoven*, 355.

155 "The obvious thing happened": Forbes, *Thayer's Life of Beethoven*, 907.

155 The people burst out four times: Köhler and Herre, *Beethovens Konversationshefte*, 6:167.

156 Schindler remarked that even Sontag and Unger received little of the applause they normally enjoyed: Köhler and Herre, *Beethovens Konversationshefte*, 6:167.

157 "He was very particular about expression": in an appendix of reminiscences in Ignaz Ritter von Seyfried, *Ludwig van Beethoven's Studien im Generalbasse, Contrapuncte und in der Compositions-Lehre* (Vienna: Haslinger, 1832); trans. by Henry H. Pierson as *Beethoven: Studies in Thorough-bass, Counterpoint and the Art of Scientific Composition* (Leipzig: Schuberth, 1853); Seyfried's reminiscences are partially translated in Sonneck, *Beethoven*, 41.

157 "Abstain from all superfluous appoggiaturas": Louis Spohr, *Violinschule* (Vienna: Haslinger, 1832), trans. Clive Brown, "The Orchestra in Beethoven's Vienna," *Early Music* 16 (1988): 18.

Chapter 4: Berlioz, *Symphonie fantastique*
Boxes

192 Berlioz describes Paris: *The Memoirs of Hector Berlioz*, edited by David Cairns (New York: Alfred A. Knopf, 1969; rpt. Norton, 1975), 342.

196 Some Parisian orchestras, circa 1830: adapted from material presented by Jean-Michel Nectoux and Nicole Wild in their articles in *Music in Paris in the Eighteen-thirties / La musique à Paris dans les années mil huit cent trente*, ed. Peter Bloom (Stuyvesant, N.Y.: Pendragon Press, 1987); Jean-Michel Nectoux, "Trois Orchestres parisiens en 1830" (471–505, English summary, 506–7); Nicole Wild, "La Musique dans les mélodrames des théâtres parisiens" (589–609; English summary, 571–73).

199 Saint-Saëns on Habeneck: trans. from Jean Michel Nectoux, "Trois Orchestres parisiens en 1830," in Bloom, *Music in Paris in the Eighteen-thirties*, 487, who quotes from Camille Saint-Saëns, *Ecole buissonière* (Paris: Lafitte, 1913), 35.

201 Seats and prices: Antoine Elwart, *Histoire de la Société des Concerts du Conservatoire impérial de musique* (Paris: S. Castel, 1860), 115–17.

213 Fétis's announcement: see document 6; *Le Revue Musicale*, November 27, 1830.

217 Berlioz's opinion of the serpent: Hector Berlioz, *Grand traité d'instrumentation et d'orchestration modernes* (Paris: Schonenberger, 1843), 230.

220 Felix Mendelssohn describes the Conservatoire orchestra: *Felix Mendelssohn Bartholdy Briefe*, ed. Rudolf Elvers (Frankfurt: Fischer, 1984), 154; English trans. from *Felix Mendelssohn: A Life in Letters*, ed. Rudolf Elvers, trans. Craig Tomlinson (New York: Fromm, 1986), 176–77.

Text

181 Epigraph: "Here is a young man": see document 11; from the review in *Le Temps*, December 26, 1830, col. 5637.

185 "What immense resources we possess in this maelstrom that is Paris": *Memoirs of Hector Berlioz*, 263.

187 "A young musician": see document 17, the program of the symphony.

188 "This Estelle, however, was a girl of eighteen": *Memoirs of Hector Berlioz*, 37.

189 "The impression made on my heart and mind": *Memoirs of Hector Berlioz*, 95.

189 "By the third act, hardly able to breathe": *Memoirs of Hector Berlioz*, 97.

190 "The marvellous book fascinated me from the first": *Memoirs of Hector Berlioz*, 125.

191 "The composer's purpose has been to develop": see document 17, the program of the symphony.

195 "Genre eminently French . . . where the end of every scene brings on a well-known tune": *Reisebriefe von Felix Mendelssohn Bartholdy, aus den Jahren 1830 bis 1832*, ed. Paul Mendelssohn Bartholdy (Leipzig: Hermann Mendelssohn, 1862; rpt., Bonn: H. C. Schaak, 1947), 315–16.

195 "Two lions, one Bengal tiger, the hyena of Asia and the llama of Peru": *Almanach des spectacles pour 1830* (Paris: Barba, 1830), 250.

199 "Habeneck had the bad habit of letting the audience in on the secret": Charles de Boigne, *Petits mémoires de l'Opéra* (Paris: Librairie Nouvelle, 1857), 298.

200 "'Gentlemen,' he said to the exhausted players": Antoine Elwart, *Histoire de la Société des Concerts du Conservatoire impérial de musique* (Paris: S. Castel, 1860), 62.

201 "You think you're hearing four gigantic instruments": *Correspondance de Frédéric Chopin*, ed. Bronislas Edouard Sydow, with Suzanne and Denise Chainaye, 3 vols. (Paris: Richard Masse, 1953–60), 2:69.

202 "The Théâtre des Nouveautés had for some time been performing opéras-comiques": see document 3; *Memoirs of Hector Berlioz*, 126–27.

205 "The Permanent Secretary, holding in one hand": see document 4; *Memoirs of Hector Berlioz*, 136–37.

217 "In all of Paris you can hear no Sunday Mass": *Reisebriefe von Felix Mendelssohn Bartholdy*, 309.

221 "Zé n'ai pas besoin": *Memoirs of Hector Berlioz*, 141.

223 "I organized a concert at the Conservatoire": see document 9; *Memoirs of Hector Berlioz*, 139–40.

224 "At precisely two o'clock": see document 12, review in *Le Temps,* December 26, 1830, col. 5637.

224 "That terrible fracas which is still punishing the vaults": see document 12, *La Revue de Paris,* vol. 21 (1830).

224 "This music arouses astonishment rather than pleasure": see document 14; *La Revue Musicale,* December 11, 1830, 151.

225 "The most bizarre monstrosity": see document 10; *Figaro,* December 7, 1830, 3–4.

225 "A great concert which will be a milestone": see document 14, *Le National,* December 6, 1830, 3.

225 "At last came the day when M. Berlioz gave us a concert": François-Joseph Fétis, *La Revue Musicale,* February 1, 1835; translation adapted from Edward T. Cone, *Fantastic Symphony: An Authoritative Score; Historical Background; Analysis; Views and Comments,* Norton Critical Scores (New York: Norton, 1971), 217.

226 "The audience at that one was small": François-Joseph Fétis, *La Revue Musicale,* February 1, 1835; translation adapted from Cone, *Fantastic symphony,* 217.

226 "The audience thought it was having a nightmare": François-Joseph Fétis, *La Revue Musicale,* February 1,1835; translation adapted from Cone, *Fantastic symphony,* 217.

226 "The most bizarre monstrosity": see document 10; *Figaro,* December 7, 1830, 3–4.

226 "We have religious music, and plenty of it": see document 5, *Figaro,* December 4, 1830, 3.

227 "The adagio (the Scene in the Country)": *Memoirs of Hector Berlioz,* 126.

229 "Next I took the score of the Ball Scene": *Memoirs of Hector Berlioz,* 153.

229 "The Scene in the Country made no impression at all": see document 9; *Memoirs of Hector Berlioz,* 140.

232 "The programme consisted of my Fantastic Symphony": see document 17; *Memoirs of Hector Berlioz,* 214–17.

Chapter 5: Stravinsky, *Le sacre du printemps*
Boxes

263 An announcement of the performance of *Le sacre:* see document 2; *Le Figaro,* May 29, 1913.

265 Lydia Sokolova remembered the arrival of the opera performers in 1913: Lydia Sokolova (Hilda Munnings, pseud.), *Dancing for Diaghilev,* ed. Richard Buckle (London: J. Murray, 1960), 44.

272 From Nijinsky's journals: see document 4; *Nijinsky: Cahiers,* trans. from the Russian by Christian Dumais-Lvowski and Galina Pogojeva, Librairie de la Danse (Arles: Actes Sud, 1995), 141, 149.

279 Anatole Bourman remembers rehearsing the dance: Anatole Bourman, with D. Lyman, *The Tragedy of Nijinsky* (New York: McGraw-Hill, 1936), 216.

285 The critic Louis Vuillemin describes the audience's prejudices: see document 9; G. de Palowsky, Louis Vuillemin, and Louis Schneider, "Au Théâtre des Champs-Elysées: 'Le Sacre du Printemps,' ballet en deux actes, par M. Igor Stravinsky," *Comoedia,* May 31, 1913, 2.

295 Pierre Lalo, writing in *Le Temps* a year later, remembers: see document 18; Pierre Lalo, "Le 'Sacre du Printemps' au concert," *Feuilleton du Temps,* April 21, 1914, rpt. in *Igor Stravinsky: Le sacre du printemps: dossier de presse: press-book,* ed. François Lesure, with Gertraut Haberkamp, Malcolm Turner, and Emilia Zanetti (Geneva: Minkoff, 1980), 48–49.

Text

257 Epigraph: "I think the whole thing has been done by four idiots": Arnold Haskell, *Balletomania* (London: Victor Gollancz, 1934), 75.

257 "The choreography is ridiculous": see document 26; Giacomo Puccini, *Letters*, ed. Giuseppe Adami, trans. Ena Makin, new ed., rev. and introduced by Mosco Carner (London: Harrap, 1974), 251, letter 159.

258 "The work was and remains a masterpiece": see document 23; Jean Cocteau, *Le coq et l'arlequin* (Paris: Editions de la Sirène, 1918; rpt., Paris: Stock, 1979), 89.

258 "Has offered us this year the music that we should really hear around 1940": see document 13; *La Revue Française de Musique*, June–July 1913, 603.

262 "Between two tangos, between a slow waltz and a ragtime dance": Colette, *The Thousand and One Mornings* (New York: Bobbs-Merrill, 1973); originally published in *Le Matin* of November 13, 1913.

265 "So we have to admire the Ballets Russes": *L'Echo de Paris*, May 30, 1913.

265 "This charming invasion": Marcel Proust, *A la recherche du temps perdu*, vol. 3, *La prisonnière* (Paris: Bibliothèque de la Pléiade, 1954), 236–37.

266 "You had only to meet him to realize at once": Cyril W. Beaumont, *Bookseller at the Ballet* (London: C. W. Beaumont, 1975), 319–20.

267 "Monsieur Stravinsky is short and he seems tall": see document 31; Henri Postel du Mas, "Un entretien avec M. Stravinsky," *Gil Blas* 25 (June 4, 1913): 1.

269 "In the ballet of the *Sacre du Printemps* conceived by myself and Stravinsky": Serge Lifar, *Diaghilev: His Life, His Work, His Legend* (London: Putnam, 1940), 278.

273 "He was also indefatigable. I heard him say after rehearsing three hours, 'I could take another orchestra and rehearse another three hours'": remarks prepared by Henri Girard for Truman Bullard, presented in Bullard, "The First Performance of Igor Stravinsky's 'Sacre du Printemps,'" 3 vols. (Ph.D. diss., Eastman School of Music, University of Rochester, 1971; Ann Arbor: University Microfilms), 1:97.

274 "My one desire was to flee that room": see document 15; Doris Monteux, *It's All in the Music: The Life and Work of Pierre Monteux* (London: William Kimber, 1965), 89.

274 "I detested it": Charles Warren Fox, cited in Bullard, "The First Performance," 1:12.

277 "Cosmopolis may feel at home with this façade": Raymond Escholier in *Le Nouveau Paris*, 1913, cited in Jean Louis Cohen, "Le théâtre de l'ossature," in Frédérique de Gravelaine, *Le théâtre des Champs Elysées* (Paris: Groupe Expansion, n.d.; a booklet reproducing, along with additional material, articles originally appearing in *Architecture d'Aujourd'hui*, vol. 271), 4.

277 "The Zeppelin of the Avenue Montaigne": Jean-Louis Forain in *L'Illustration*, April 1913, cited in Cohen, "Le théâtre de l'ossature," 4.

277 "Dryly solemn, deliberately poor, and thus far from all French tradition": Jean-Louis Forain in *L'Illustration*, April 1913, cited in Cohen, "Le théâtre de l'ossature," 4.

277 "What might be accomplished in our country": anonymous writer in *Art et Décoration*, 1913, cited in Cohen, "Le théâtre de l'ossature," 4.

277 "Before he got very far I was convinced he was raving mad": Pierre Monteux, "Early Years," *Dance Index* 6, nos. 10–12 (1947): 242; cited in Bullard, "The First Performance," 1:12.

278 "The dance is almost always in counterpoint to the music": Igor Stravinsky, *The Rite of Spring: Sketches, 1911–1913* (London: Boosey & Hawkes, 1969), appen., 35.

278 "Lack of *play*, of counterpoint": see document 23; Cocteau, *Le coq et l'arlequin*, 91.

278 "Nijinsky began by demanding such a fantastic number of rehearsals": see document 33;

Igor Stravinsky: An Autobiography (New York: Simon and Schuster, 1936; rpt., New York: Norton, 1962), 41.

278 "The dancers had been rehearsing for months": see document 36; Igor Stravinsky and Robert Craft, *Expositions and Development* (London: Faber and Faber, 1962), 142–43.

278 "We had to run about more or less *ad lib*": Sokolova, *Dancing for Diaghilev*, 42.

281 "We rehearsed the strings first": see document 15; Monteux, *It's All in the Music*, 89.

281 "When we saw the parts for the first time": Louis Speyer, cited in Bullard, "The First Performance," 1:98–99.

281 "It is hard to describe the astonishment": Henri Girard, cited in Bullard, "The First Performance," 1:97.

281 "Monteux didn't seem afraid": Louis Speyer, cited in Bullard, "The First Performance," 1:98.

281 "We came to a place": Louis Speyer, cited in Bullard, "The First Performance," 1:98.

282 "When the first performance approached": Louis Speyer, cited in Bullard, "The First Performance," 1:99.

282 "Oddly enough, at the dress rehearsal": see document 33; *Stravinsky: An Autobiography*, 47.

282 "The public . . . is beginning to realize that it is being ridiculed": see document 7; Adolphe Boschot, "Le 'Sacre du printemps': Ballet de MM. Roerich, Stravinsky et Nijinsky," *L'Echo de Paris*, May 30, 1913.

283 "To a practiced eye, all the material needed for a scandal": see document 23; Cocteau, *Le coq et l'arlequin*, 93.

283 "Garnet-red with indignation": Ravel "aggressive as a small fighting cock" "roaring vengeful epithets towards the hissing boxes": see document 20; trans. from a 1951 radio interview with Valentine Gross-Hugo in Françoise Reiss, *Nijinsky*, trans. Helen Haskell and Stephen Haskell (London: Adam and Charles Black, 1960), 122.

283 "Once again the Northern Barbarians come": Emile Vuillermoz, "Igor Stravinsky," *S.I.M.*, May 15, 1912, 15.

283 "Never was more forcefully demonstrated": Adolphe Jullien in *Journal des Débats* (June 8, 1913), 1; rpt. in Bullard, "The First Performance," 3:118.

285 "The visitor who passes behind the stage": Beaumont, *Bookseller at the Ballet*, 235–36.

287 "Imagine people tricked out in the most garish colors": see document 7; Boschot, "Le 'Sacre du printemps.'"

288 "Un ballet sociologique": Jacques Rivière, "*Le sacre du printemps*," *La Nouvelle Revue Française* 7 (November 1913): 706–30; rpt. in Bullard, "The First Performance," 3:237–75.

288 "As to prehistoric times, I really have no objection": Pierre Lalo, "Considérations sur le 'Sacre du printemps,'" *Feuilleton du Temps*, August 5, 1913; rpt. in *Igor Stravinsky*, ed. Lesure, 32–33.

289 "The settings were suited to the required mood": Beaumont, *Bookseller at the Ballet*, 136.

289 "He entreated the dancers to keep calm": see document 14; Sergei Leonidovitch Grigoriev, *The Diaghilev Ballet, 1909–1929*, trans. Vera Bowen (London: Constable, 1953), 83.

289 "Already the introduction was a surprise": Louis Speyer, cited in Bullard, "The First Performance," 1:99.

290 "As for the actual performance, I am not in a position to judge": see document 33; *Igor Stravinsky*, 47.

290 "Mild protests against the music": see document 36; Stravinsky and Craft, *Expositions and Development*, 143.

292 "The audience played the role it had to play": see document 23; Cocteau, *Le coq et l'arlequin,* 94–95.

292 "The audience remained quiet for the first two minutes": John. N. Burk, "Le Sacre du Printemps," *Boston Symphony Orchestra Programmes* (1950–51), 664, citing Pierre Monteux in *Dance Index* 6, nos. 10–12 (1947): 242.

292 "I decided to keep the orchestra together": see document 15; Monteux, *It's All in the Music,* 90.

292 "I beg you, let the show finish!": Romola Nijinska, *Nijinsky* (London: Gollancz, 1933), 200; also Nathalie Gontcharova, Michel Larionov, and Pierre Vorms, *Les Ballets Russes: Serge Diaghilew et la décoration théâtrale* (Belvès: Vorms, 1955), 17.

292 "Listen first: you can whistle later!": Gabriel Astruc, *Le pavillon des fantômes* (Paris: Grasset, 1929), 286.

292 "Some forty of the protestants were forced out of the theatre": see document 21; Carl Van Vechten, *Music and Bad Manners* (New York: Knopf, 1916), 470.

292 "She stood on the stage, her chin leaning": Mary Clarke, *Dancers of Mercury: The Story of the Ballet Rambert* (London: A. and C. Black, 1962), 27. The doctor-dentist story is repeated in Romola Nijinsky, *Nijinsky,* 200, and elsewhere.

293 "Then in this magic circle, the victim until that moment motionless": André Levinson, "Stravinsky and the Dance," *Theater Arts Monthly* 8 (1924): 741–54; rpt. in Bullard, "The First Performance," 1:152.

293 "Knock-kneed and long-braided Lolitas": see document 36; Stravinsky and Craft, *Expositions and Developments,* 143.

293 "Down with the whores of the 16th arrondissement": see document 15; Monteux, *It's All in the Music,* 90.

293 "They are ripe for colonization!": see document 11; "The Premiere of *Le Sacre du Printemps* by the Russian Ballet at the Théâtre des Champs-Elysées," *Comoedia Illustré,* June 5, 1913.

293 "This is the first time in sixty years that anyone has dared to make fun of me!": see document 23; Cocteau, *Le coq et l'arlequin,* 95.

294 "Here is a strange spectacle": see document 8; Henri Quittard, "Théâtre des Champs-Elysées: *Le sacre du printemps,*" *Le Figaro,* May 31, 1913, 5.

294 "The curtain goes up—no, even before the curtain goes up": see document 9; Pawlowsky, Vuillemin, and Schneider, "Au Théâtre des Champs-Elysées."

294 "These are the superficial remarks that I can report": Emile Raulin, "*Le sacre du printemps,*" *Les Marges* (Summer 1913): 105–7; transcribed in Bullard, "The First Performance," 3:182–83.

294 "Evidently all this is defensible": see document 7; Boschot, "Le 'Sacre du printemps.'"

295 "M. Igor Strawinsky's music, by its frenetic agitation": Florent Schmitt, "*Les Sacres du Printemps,* de M. Igor Strawinsky, au Théâtre des Champs-Elysées," *La France,* June 4, 1913, 2.

296 "Sooner or later we will have to tell him [Diaghilev] about the 'Great Sacrifice'": Stravinsky to Roerich, letter of June 1910; Stravinsky, *Rite of Spring: Sketches,* appen., 27.

296 "Sage elders, seated in a circle, watched a young girl dance herself to death": see document 32; *Stravinsky: An Autobiography,* 31; the letter is in Stravinsky, *Rite of Spring: Sketches,* appen., 32–33.

297 "But be aware that this idea comes from the music": Michel Georges-Michel, "Les deux *Sacre du printemps,*" *Comoedia* (December 11, 1920); rpt. in his *Ballets Russes: Histoire anecdotique* (Paris: Edition du Monde Nouveau, 1923), 48.

297 "Nijinsky directs it with passionate zeal and with complete self-effacement": see document 33; *Stravinsky: An Autobiography,* 31; the letter is in Stravinsky, *Rite of Spring: Sketches,* appen., 33.

297 "The dance that had been evolved was the most perfectly beautiful": C. Stanley Wise, "Impressions of Igor Stravinsky," *Musical Quarterly* 2 (1916): 251.

297 "I am glad to have found in M. Nijinsky": see document 32; "Igor Stravinsky," "Gloires et misères du théâtre actuel: Ce que j'ai voulu exprimer dans 'Le sacre du printemps,'" *Montjoie!* May 29, 1913. Some of these same words are reported in Edmond Stoullig, *Les annales du théâtre et de la danse,* no. 39 (January 1914): 327.

297 "They have criticized M. Nijinsky's staging": see document 31; Postel du Mas, "Un entretien avec M. Stravinsky." On the date of the interview, see Bullard, "The First Performance," 1:30–31 n. 45.

298 "What the choreography expressed": see document 33; *Stravinsky: An Autobiography,* 74.

298 "Of all the interpretations of *Sacre* that I have seen, I consider Nijinsky's the best": *Bronislava Nijinska: Early Memoirs,* trans. and ed. Irina Nijinska and Jean Rawlinson (New York: Holt, Rinehart and Winston, 1981), 471.

298 "Who is the author of *Le sacre du printemps?*": Jacques Rivière, "*Le sacre du printemps,*" *La Nouvelle Revue Française* (August 1, 1913): 109.

298 "At two o'clock in the morning": see document 23; Cocteau, *Le coq et l'arlequin,* 95–96.

299 "After the 'performance' we were excited": see document 34; Stravinsky and Craft, *Conversations with Igor Stravinsky,* 48

299 "Stravinsky, the henceforth famous composer": "Comme Wagner!" *Le Cri de Paris,* June 29, 1913, 12; cited in Bullard, "The First Performance," 1:163.

Photo Credits

Illustrations are listed by page number.

America's Shrine to Music Museum, University of South Dakota: 38
Archivio di Stato, Mantua: 8
Beinecke Rare Book and Manuscript Library, Yale University: 5, 77, 79
Bibliothèque Nationale de France: 139, 212, 228
British Library: 70, 90
Conservatoire National Supérieur d'Art Dramatique, Paris: 209, 210
Galleria degli Uffizi, Florence: 49
George C. Izenour Archive, Pennsylvania State University: 21
George Eastman House, Rochester, N.Y.: 230
Gerald Coke Handel Collection: 93 (photo: courtesy National Portrait Gallery, London)
Gesellschaft der Musikfreunde, Vienna: 158
Handel House Collections Trust, London: 64
Harvard University Libraries: 93
Historisches Museum der Stadt Wien: 116, 125, 127, 135, 142, 145
Library of Congress, Washington, D.C.: 75
Musée de la Musique, Paris: 32 (photo: Dominique Santrot)
Musée d'Orsay, Paris: 259 (photo: RMN, Jean Schormans)
Musée du Louvre, Paris: 6 (photo: Giraudon)
Museo del Palazzo Ducale, Mantua: 10, 14, 39, 42
Nationalmuseum, Stockholm: 28
Osterreichisches Nationalbibliothek: 136, 138, 141
Paul Sacher Stiftung, Basel: 267, 271, 280
Peter Schweitzer: 50
Staats- und Universitätsbibliothek Hamburg Carl von Ossietzky: 63
Wadsworth Atheneum, Hartford: 269, 293
Yale Center for British Art, Paul Mellon Collection: 81
Yale Collection of Musical Instruments, Belle Skinner Collection: 89 (photo: Joseph Szaszfai/Carl Kaufman)
Yale Music Library: 110, 183, 189, 198, 222
Yale University Libraries: 150

Index